GRACE COOLIDGE AND HER ERA

GRACE COOLIDGE
AND HER ERA

THE STORY OF A PRESIDENT'S WIFE

BY

ISHBEL ROSS

ILLUSTRATED

DODD, MEAD & COMPANY

NEW YORK, 1962

Acknowledgment is gratefully made to the following publishers for permission to use excerpts from books on their lists and to individuals who now hold copyrights:

Cosmopolitan Book Corporation: *The Autobiography of Calvin Coolidge*, 1929. Copyright 1960 by John Coolidge.

Harper & Brothers: *It Costs to be President* by Henry L. Stoddard, 1938, and *Capital Kaleidoscope* by Frances Parkinson Keyes, 1937.

Hearst Corporation: *The Open Door*, Good Housekeeping, 1929, and *The Quest*, Good Housekeeping, 1930, poems by Mrs. Calvin Coolidge. Copyright by the Hearst Corporation, publishers of Good Housekeeping. Reprinted by permission of John Coolidge.

Houghton, Mifflin Company: *Forty-Two Years in the White House* by Irwin H. (Ike) Hoover, 1934. *Have Faith in Massachusetts* by Calvin Coolidge, 1919. Copyright by John Coolidge.

Little, Brown & Company: *Calvin Coolidge* by Claude M. Fuess, 1940. Copyright by Claude M. Fuess.

Charles Scribner's Sons: *Across the Busy Years* by Dr. Nicholas Murray Butler, 1939.

Simon and Schuster, Inc.: *Starling of the White House* by Edmund W. Starling, as told to Thomas Sugrue. Copyright 1946 by Simon and Schuster, Inc. Reprinted by permission of the publishers.

ACKNOWLEDGMENTS

In preparing this biography of Mrs. Calvin Coolidge I am indebted to scores of individuals whose paths crossed hers at one time or another, and who were good enough to give me the benefit of their recollections, as well as letters, photographs and memorabilia in a number of instances.

I am particularly grateful to John Coolidge, only surviving son of President and Mrs. Coolidge, and to his wife, Florence Trumbull Coolidge, for their cooperation and hospitality, both at their home in Farmington, Connecticut, and at their summer place in Plymouth, Vermont, where Calvin Coolidge was born. They generously gave me access to family letters and pictures, in addition to sharing with me many personal recollections of Mrs. Coolidge.

Few persons knew Mrs. Coolidge better than Mrs. Reuben B. Hills, of Haydenville, Massachusetts, and Mrs. Florence B. Adams, of Princeton, New Jersey. Mrs. Hills was her close friend from their early married days. She stayed with her for long periods in the White House and was near at hand during the last years of her life. Mrs. Adams shared houses with Mrs. Coolidge after the President's death, accompanied her on her one trip to Europe and saw her constantly

v

in the last twenty-five years of her life. These two friends were generous in giving me glimpses of Grace Coolidge that no one else could supply. I am indebted to them for letters and photographs as well as reminiscences.

I am deeply grateful to Dr. Claude M. Fuess, outstanding authority on Calvin Coolidge, for his counsel, recollections and the documents he gave me relating to Mrs. Coolidge. While he was writing *Calvin Coolidge,* her husband's definitive biography, he saw her on many occasions and had full access to the family papers. Among other authorities who gave me the benefit of their recollections and impressions of Mrs. Coolidge were Admiral Joel Boone, family physician when she was in the White House and a trusted friend; Bruce Barton, who had frequent opportunities to observe her at close range; and Dr. Clarence S. Brigham, president of the American Antiquarian Society in Worcester, Massachusetts. Mrs. Aubrey N. Morgan (formerly Miss Constance Morrow), Mrs. Charles A. Lindbergh and Dwight W. Morrow, Jr., kindly gave me permission to use Mrs. Coolidge's letters to Mrs. Dwight W. Morrow, now in the Sophia Smith Collection, Smith College. Mrs. Morrow and Mrs. Coolidge, like their husbands, were close friends and Anne Morrow was one of Calvin Coolidge's favorite small friends.

Miss Ivah Gale, of Northampton, and Mrs. Charles C. Guptil, of Hamden, Connecticut, were generous in supplying me with fresh facts about Grace Goodhue's college days and the courtship of Calvin Coolidge. Both were her classmates in college and Mrs. Guptil, then Ethel M. Stevens, was her sole bridesmaid. Miss Gale, whom she regarded as a sister, lived at Road Forks in Northampton with Mrs. Coolidge during the last years of her life and knew her perhaps as well as anyone could. I am particularly grateful to Miss Gale, to Mrs. Guptil and to her daughter, Miss Constance Guptil, for all their assistance.

Among others in Burlington and Shelburne, Vermont, who were helpful in giving me specific information on various aspects of Mrs. Coolidge's life were Mrs. R. Rea Reed, who now lives in the house on Maple Street where the Coolidges were married; George Marks, who was one of her playmates when she was a growing girl; Mrs.

Fred Ruble, Mrs. D. Williams, Mrs. L. M. Valyeau, Miss H. Barbara Hunt, and the Rev. D. H. Sears. Mrs. Sophie Kerr Underwood, author and editor, who knew Grace Goodhue at the University of Vermont, was kind enough to revive for me some memories of that period.

Mrs. Coolidge's work for the deaf was one of the major interests of her life and I am most grateful to Dr. Archibald V. Galbraith, president, and Dr. George T. Pratt, principal of the Clarke School for the Deaf in Northampton, for their enlightening recollections, and for the letters, reports, documents and pictures they gave me bearing on this most interesting phase of her life. Scores of persons still living in Northampton helped me to reconstruct the picture of her life there, and among those to whom I owe special thanks are Mrs. Ralph W. Hemenway, widow of the President's law partner and a lifelong friend; Walter L. Stevens, legal associate of Calvin Coolidge, who died in 1960; Mrs. S. A. Bailey, who bought The Beeches from Mrs. Coolidge and was an old family friend; Karl S. Putnam, the architect who designed Road Forks, and Mrs. Putnam; Miss Blanche Cole, Miss Edith N. Hill, Mrs. Helen Woods, Mrs. Robert Huxley, Mrs. C. W. Hodges, Mrs. Harold P. Kingsbury, Mrs. Merrill Torrey, Mrs. Evelina Flibotte, Miss Lillian Carver and John Bukosky.

During World War II Mrs. Coolidge let the Waves, training at Smith College under the command of Captain Herbert W. Underwood, use her house and I am indebted to him and to his wife, Mrs. H. Whitwell Underwood, of Glenburn, California, for the information they gave me on her associations with the Waves. Others across the country who have supplied me with pertinent information and anecdotes include Miss Ellen A. Riley of Boston, housekeeper and custodian of White House property during the Coolidge administration; Mrs. Carl Medinus of Chicago; Lucius Beebe of Virginia City, Nevada, an old Bostonian; Miss Mary Benjamin of New York; and Clarence Noyes, of Ludlow, Vermont, an early suitor of Grace Goodhue. Joseph McInerney, a member of the small group present when Calvin Coolidge was sworn in as President by his father at the family homestead in Plymouth, was good enough to give me his eyewitness impressions of this historic event. Mrs. Herman Pelkey,

Joseph Moor and Mr. and Mrs. Lewis O. Chamberlain all were helpful to me on my visits to the birthplace of Calvin Coolidge.

While Mrs. Coolidge was at the University of Vermont the Vermont Beta Chapter of Pi Beta Phi was organized in her home and
she became a lifelong member of this fraternity. She attended conventions, was a national officer, received them as a group at the
White House, and from 1915 up to 1957, the year of her death, engaged in a round robin correspondence with some of the members.
Pi Beta Phi members in Massachusetts who have gone to great effort
to assemble reminiscences, round robin letters and official documents
for me include Mrs. Francis A. Rugg, of Newton Highlands; Mrs.
David D. Nickerson of Malden; Mrs. Howard D. Corkum of Marshfield; Miss E. Louise Richardson of Watertown; Mrs. Carl Rhoades
of Weston; Mrs. Harry McWade of Duxbury; Miss Olive Gilchrist
of Boston, and Miss Sophie P. Woodman of Greenfield. The book
jacket was designed from personal copies of the Howard Chandler
Christy painting owned by Mrs. Nickerson and Miss Richardson.
Mrs. Oliver Simmons, of Kansas City, national historian of the fraternity, has been most helpful in supplying me with old records, and
Dr. May L. Keller, former dean of Westhampton College, University
of Richmond, and president emeritus of Pi Beta Phi, was good
enough to share with me some memories of Mrs. Coolidge.

Among many persons in Washington who supplied me with anecdotes and comment bearing on Mrs. Coolidge I should like to thank
Miss Stella Stewart, who trained with her at the Clarke School for
the Deaf and often saw her in her White House days; Miss Nellie E.
Dalrymple, daughter of the late Clarence L. Dalrymple, captain of
the White House Police; Mrs. Rena Ridenour; Mrs. Elizabeth A.
Bonsteel, chief clerk of White House files; and Harry Waters, who
for a time was kennel master and took care of Mrs. Coolidge's famous white collies.

Much of the documentary material for this biography was drawn
from the Coolidge papers in the Manuscript Division of the Library
of Congress and from the fine resources of the Coolidge Memorial
Room in the Forbes Library at Northampton. I should like to ac-
knowledge the assistance given me by David C. Mearns, chief of

the Manuscript Division; Russell M. Smith, assistant head of Presidential Papers; Dr. C. P. Powell, Dr. Elizabeth G. McPherson, Miss Kate M. Stewart, Stewart Dickson, and Miss Virginia Daiker and Carl Stange of the Prints and Photographs Division. I am especially indebted to Lawrence Wikander for his able assistance at the Forbes Library, and to Mrs. Agnes Macgregor Collis, Mrs. Kathleen Doland and other members of his staff.

I have used the resources of a number of libraries and historical societies and am grateful to Edward Connery Lathem, assistant librarian, Dartmouth College, and editor of *Meet Calvin Coolidge;* Newton F. McKeon, Converse Library, Amherst College; T. D. Seymour Bassett, Wilbur Library, University of Vermont; Zoltan Haraszti, Boston Public Library; Miss Helen Tedford, Massachusetts State Library; Malcolm Freiberg, Massachusetts Historical Society; Mrs. Margaret S. Grierson and Miss Elizabeth Duvall of the Sophia Smith Collection, Smith College; Miss Sylvia Hilton, Miss Helen Ruskell and other staff members of the New York Society Library.

For period background I have used the newspapers and periodicals ranging from 1900 to 1957 and have drawn freely from my own recollections of the 1920s and the early 1930s when I covered for the New York *Herald Tribune* many of the stories to which I allude. I had an opportunity to observe Mrs. Coolidge at the inauguration of President Harding and President Coolidge and on many other occasions.

I.R.

CONTENTS

ILLUSTRATIONS

Following page 146

CHAPTER I

SPRINGTIME IN VERMONT

THE WIND BLEW BRISKLY across Lake Champlain on a May day in 1898, scattering apple blossoms in a pinkish mist close to its shores. Grace Anna Goodhue leaned against the railing of the *Vermont II* studying the jagged purple line of the Adirondacks in the west and the gentler wooded slopes of the Green Mountains rising transversely against the sky in the east. One day she would cruise down the Potomac on the *Mayflower* as wife of the President of the United States but now she was preparing for college. She was nineteen and in love, although not with Calvin Coolidge, whom she had yet to meet.

Behind her lay her native city, Burlington, picturesquely terraced above the chill cobalt blue of the lake. The spire of the University of Vermont and its Old Mill Tower reminded her that when autumn came she would be part of the student life on the hill. The residential section, thick with elms, fanned out on a lower level. A third terrace encompassed the business streets, winding ribbonwise down the hill to tangle at the waterfront with warehouses and docks. Here her father had his office. Captain Andrew I. Goodhue, a mechanical engineer, was appointed steamboat inspector for the Champlain

1

Transportation Company by Grover Cleveland in 1886 and trips around the lake were the special treats of Grace's childhood and adolescence.

There was cause for rejoicing on this occasion and flags flew from the paddle steamer. George Dewey, a native Vermonter, had just destroyed the Spanish fleet in Manila Bay without the loss of a ship or a man on the American side. Bulletin boards were mobbed. Newsboys shouted extras in New York and San Francisco. The name Dewey had flashed into fame overnight. It was a good hour for Vermont, and its quiet people celebrated in their own restrained way.

The news of the day was reflected in the group of passengers surrounding Grace. No young men were in sight, but the decks were lively with girls in long gored skirts and high-necked blouses, clutching at sailor hats as the wind blew off the lake. Their elders clustered on the circular Victorian settee in the lobby, studying their own reflections in the gilded mirror at the head of the stairs, or leaned back in orderly rows of velour-covered chairs and discussed the war. A gong sent them hastening into the dining saloon for the hearty fare provided by the steamship company but Grace and her friends had brought picnic lunches. She took pride in the lake boats and was well versed in their construction, from their Fletcher boilers to their butternut and cherry panels; from their pink marble basins, traceable to the quarries of Vermont, to their Bavarian carvings and gold leaf adornments.

Grace had grown up on tales of these boats and was familiar with their romantic history, as well as with the machinery that her father inspected. They had a tradition nearly as old as the showboats of the Mississippi River and matched them in luxury and the carefree spirit. The company was chartered in 1826, three years after the opening of the Champlain Canal connecting the lake with the Hudson River. President Van Buren sailed on the steamer *Burlington* in 1840. General Grant and General Sheridan cruised on the *Vermont II* after the Civil War. Now a new war was being fought, and American soldiers were dying on distant soil.

Dewey's victory was followed quickly by Captain Charles E. Clark's trip from San Francisco round Cape Horn in the *Oregon* to share in the annihilation of the Spanish fleet in Santiago Harbor. Clark was a Vermonter, too, like Redfield Proctor, the owner of large marble quarries close to Proctor, a Senator who had helped to push the United States into the Spanish-American War with his startling report that year on conditions in Cuba. The First Vermont Regiment had now set up camp in nearby Rutland. The men drilled daily and all the talk was of war. There had not been so much excitement since the Civil War, when 34,328 Vermonters joined the Union Army and a Confederate raid was staged in the state.

The nineteenth century was fading in a blaze of gunfire and the American front-page headlines reflected the prevailing unrest. Britain was sympathetic to the American cause but Russia and Germany leaned to Spain. Political titans were falling. New idols were coming into view. Gladstone was dying in England. Theodore Roosevelt was retiring as Secretary of the Navy to organize the Rough Riders. There were bread riots in Italy and Germany, and American missionaries were killed in an uprising on the Gold Coast. Echoes of the larger world ruffled the calm of Burlington through the summer of 1898 and Captain Goodhue talked knowingly about the naval engagements. All matters involving ships and the sea were of major interest in his home.

The Captain, who came originally from Hancock, New Hampshire, was a jovial man of medium height, shiningly bald, with a heavy brush mustache and ruddy complexion. With brass-buttoned uniform and nautical cap he seemed a sturdy figure striding along the waterfront. Grace, his only child, was believed to have inherited her warm and friendly spirit from her father. As deacon of the College Street Congregational Church, he stood at the door greeting all comers. He was of Puritan stock, a descendant of Ebenezer Knight who moved from New Ipswich in 1797 to the historic David Hubbard House in Hancock, New Hampshire.

His wife, Lemira Barrett Goodhue, was quite unlike the Captain and Grace in temperament and was naturally reserved to the point of being dour. She came from an old New England family and was the daughter of Thomas Barrett, of Nashua, New Hampshire. Her childhood was passed in Merrimac and she moved to Burlington in

1870. Mrs. Goodhue was of medium height and rather stocky build. She had bright blue eyes and dark hair. Her pride and independence sometimes stiffened her manner to strangers and she was a woman of deep convictions.

Grace's outlook broadened when she entered college that autumn. Her life had been simple and uneventful from her earliest days in the house on Maple Street in which she was born on January 3, 1879. There had been trouble with her spine as a child but vigorous exercises had strengthened her. One of her earliest recollections was a severe accident her father had had on one of the boats, and the long months he had passed at home convalescing. Beyond that she had little but happy memories of her childhood. At the age of five she first went to a small brick schoolhouse near her home where she was taught by Miss Cornelia C. Underwood. After her graduation from Burlington High School in 1897 she stayed at home for a year because of her health.

At nineteen, when she entered college, she was five feet four and not at all enamored of her looks. She considered herself much too plump and when beaux loomed on her horizon she starved herself at a time when the buxom girl commanded attention. She had masses of lustrous dark hair but her eyes were her most remarkable feature. Gray-green, they seemed hazel in certain lights. They were wide-set and grave, even when her face was alight with laughter. It was her habit to focus them with close attention on anyone she was addressing. Her generous mouth gave character to her face, which was strong rather than symmetrical. At this age she gave visible promise of the handsome woman she would later become, but she did not yet have the grace of bearing that was characteristic of Mrs. Calvin Coolidge.

Her friends knew her as a lively extrovert, with an unquenchable taste for good times, an infectious laugh and the knack of endearing herself to others. She became a strong force in her class but was never a zealous student. She was vice-president in her sophomore year, sang contralto in the Glee Club, took part in college plays and was one of the founders of the Vermont chapter of the Pi Beta Phi Fraternity, so named because sororities were still unknown when the first of the Greek letter women's societies came into being. The organizers of the Vermont group stayed at the Goodhue home and held their first meeting in the parlor where Grace and Calvin Coolidge later were married.

When she entered college Captain Goodhue built a new house for his family, higher up on the hill, at 312 Maple Street. It was only a few doors away from the smaller house in which she was born. Pale yellow, with green shutters, its porch overlooked the shady street, with a maple and fir tree planted nearby. Today it belongs to the family of Mrs. R. Rea Reed and is much the same as it was when Calvin Coolidge and his bride walked down the front steps to enter a carriage on their wedding day. The Captain finished off the attic of the new three-story dwelling for the use of Grace's fraternity. They met there on Saturday nights to discuss college matters, exchange notes on books and beaux, sing the popular songs of the day and eat their hostess's fudge. As time went on Grace papered the walls with hundreds of pictures of celebrities clipped from magazines.

Sophie Kerr Underwood, author and editor in later years, arrived from Maryland at the turn of the century to do graduate work at the University of Vermont. She knew Grace Goodhue as a cheerful girl, with a blooming complexion, whose laughter rang out as she crossed the campus. She favored bright colors and often wore a flowing silk tie loosely knotted at the neck of her crisp shirtwaists, in the fashion of the day. Sophie sang soprano and Grace contralto at an entertainment given by the coeds, and laughed at themselves when cast as the two high and mighty sisters of Cinderella. Everyone who knew Grace in her college days remembered that she was always ready to sing, or play the piano, or join in a skit.

It was 28 degrees below zero in Burlington that winter and the students skated, tobogganed and drove to dances in jingling sleighs. Grace startled her mother by joining in the sleighing and skating parties organized by the college youths. She had skated well from the age of eight. In summer the young people sailed on the lake, picnicked and went buggy riding. Under pressure the Goodhues permitted Grace to take dancing lessons but they balked at letting her attend the formal dances. Church sociables were more in the family tradition. She turned out poetry in odd moments and toward the end of her college years wrote the history of her fraternity in verse and sang it to the tune of *Nellie Gray*.

In 1900 Ivah Gale, a shy girl from a farm on the shores of Lake Memphremagog, moved in with the Goodhues. Grace had observed how lonely and lost she seemed on the college campus. They became lifelong friends and Ivah was the first to pass judgment on Calvin Coolidge as a suitor for Miss Goodhue. She was Grace's confidante in all her romances as they studied together in Grace's room on the second floor. But Ivah observed that she was always ready to abandon textbooks for the latest novel, for her embroidery, or for some outdoor diversion, such as coasting after dark. "She was always jolly and would warm up the scene," Ivah recalled. They had swift runs down the hill in icy starlight, and when Captain Goodhue, coming home late one night, found them engaged in this childish pursuit, he laughed and thought it fine that the girls should be having such fun.

The Goodhues were Methodists as well as Democrats, but when she entered college Grace persuaded them to join the College Street Congregational Church, which was popular with the students and was attended by many of her friends. It was quite a compromise for the older Goodhues to make but their daughter's will prevailed, and she became active in the church, frequently singing in the choir. On Sundays Grace and Ivah stayed for Bible class after the morning service and they attended Christian Endeavor meetings on Sunday nights. Clarence Noyes, one of her earliest beaux, was usually on hand to escort Grace home from these affairs. Eventually he became principal of the high school in Franklin, Vermont, married and had two children. Years afterward, first as the wife and then as the widow of Calvin Coolidge, Grace would visit the general store in Ludlow, Vermont, that he still maintained in 1960, and greet him cheerfully. "It was a pleasant memory all round," Clarence liked to tell his friends after her death.

But Grace was more in earnest about Frank Joyner. It was while he was courting her that she began to worry about her weight. Her family disapproved of him as a suitor for their daughter. When he left town she continued to correspond with him and had to break things off when Calvin Coolidge came into her life. It was half understood that she and Frank were engaged.

Although not an outstanding student Miss Goodhue was graduated in 1902 with an honorable working record behind her and a host of friends. Professor E. Tupper, English instructor at the University, remembered her coming up the hill to class, "an amiable student who fell into her class work and associations very easily." Dean George H. Perkins thought her a "quiet, sensible girl who was always up in her studies." Charlotte Hale, a fraternity member, considered her the most spontaneously generous girl she had ever known, "charming, unassuming."

Grace was more interested in contemporary events while in college than in her textbooks. When she prepared a paper on the theme "Life" it was returned to her with the comment: "I suggest that you refrain from writing upon this subject until you have had more experience." But the turn of the century was rich in excitement for the two young girls in Burlington. The Spanish-American War was over, but the Boxer Rebellion held the headlines. The Boer War was being fought in South Africa and Queen Victoria was within a few months of her death. John Hay was pushing the Open Door policy. William Jennings Bryan had just suffered his second defeat as a Presidential candidate. The United States had won the Olympics of 1900. Eight thousand motor cars were jolting along the nation's roadways at an erratic tempo, "bubbles" that were fair game for the cartoonists. Phonographs and pianolas were the parlor accompaniment to stereopticon slides. Carry Nation was wielding her hatchet on Kansas saloons. Jane Addams was steadily building up a new social pattern at Hull House in Chicago. H. G. Wells was probing into the future with a prescience later confirmed, and George Bernard Shaw was searing past and present with his acid wit.

The assassination of President McKinley in 1901 shocked the country. Theodore Roosevelt, holidaying at Isle La Motte, close to Burlington, rushed back to take office in much the same way as Calvin Coolidge was summoned from Plymouth when Warren G. Harding died in San Francisco. In the following year, on her graduation, Grace Goodhue took the step that fixed her destiny and brought her into touch with the man who would be her husband and the thirtieth President of the United States.

For years she had been hearing about the work done at the Clarke Institute for the Deaf in Northampton. Along the street from the Goodhues lived John Lyman Yale, whose sister, Miss Caroline A. Yale, headed the school. She and her niece, June Yale, who was training there, often discussed with Grace the need for help in this neglected field. With college behind her she came to the conclusion that she would rather teach the handicapped than the healthy child. Mrs. Goodhue was reluctant to see her leave Burlington but Grace enrolled at the Institute training school in the autumn of 1902. There she learned lip reading and all the techniques she would need to teach deaf children. Her sympathies were deeply aroused as she worked with them. She taught first in the primary, and then in the intermediate school, devoting three years to this work and developing a lifelong interest in the deaf. It became one of her major causes and she did much in her later years to raise funds for the school and extend the scope of work for the deaf in general. Her most noted predecessor as a teacher at the school was Dr. Alexander Graham Bell, whose wife was deaf.

Grace was in her second year of teaching when Calvin Coolidge came into her life, in a surprising and humorous way. The school was situated on Round Hill, the verdant region made famous by Jenny Lind, who spent her honeymoon in the Round Hill Hotel, called the region paradise, and so gave its name to Paradise Pond. Coolidge, a rising young lawyer and politician, boarded nearby in the home of Robert N. Weir, the school steward.

One day as Grace was watering the flowers outside Baker Hall, where she lived with the other middle school teachers, she chanced to look up at the Weir house and saw a strange spectacle. A man stood at the window, shaving. Grace stared, for undeniably he wore a hat, and also apparently his union suit. She burst out laughing, then turned away and continued sprinkling the flowers. The man was Calvin Coolidge and he had heard the hearty laughter that was to become a familiar part of his future life.

In later years Grace liked to tell her intimates this story of their first encounter. She developed an affectionate way of telling jokes on Calvin without wounding his sensibilities. Unquestionably that spontaneous laugh focused his attention on Miss Goodhue. Who was she? He inquired around and learned from Weir that she taught in the school. After that he watched her with interest as she swung past in her neat Eton suit and magenta bow tie. But she did not look up again. Weir, a friendly and loquacious fellow, soon arranged matters so that they met at a friend's house. His bon mot on the subject has been widely quoted—that having taught the deaf to hear, Miss Goodhue might perhaps cause the mute to speak. Even Grace made use of it in time.

Calvin went right to the heart of the matter when they were introduced. He told her solemnly that he had heard her laughter. Then, in a voice of curiously nasal timbre, he carefully explained that he had an unruly lock of hair that always got in the way when he shaved. He had finally resorted to plastering it down with a comb and anchoring it firmly with his hat while he washed his face and lathered up.

Grace had been unaware of the young lawyer but now she studied his sandy-red hair and white, intense face with interest. The unflinching gaze of his blue eyes was disconcerting but once having made his explanation he had little more to say. Soon her friends were amazed to see her often in the company of quiet Calvin Coolidge. They had one thing in common—he came from her own state. She quickly learned that he was born in Plymouth, had attended Black River Academy in Ludlow and was a graduate of Amherst. He was admitted to the Massachusetts bar in 1897, after studying law in the Northampton firm of Hammond and Field. Since 1898 he had conducted his own law office on Main Street and had served as City Solicitor, Clerk of the Courts and chairman of the Republican City Committee. He was respected in the community and was inconspicuous in all his ways.

Miss Goodhue quickly observed that he lived a lonely and frugal life, aside from his political interests. He had most of his meals at Rahar's Inn. She knew that he read history in the evenings and rarely made social engagements, but reserve and taciturnity were native qualities familiar to a Vermonter. He dressed with neatness and circumspection and was inclined to philosophize in his conversation. His political career was beginning to flower and he was thinking seriously of settling down in marriage. "I suppose I began to want a home of my own," he recalled in his autobiography. By then he was thirty-two years old. But three years earlier he had written to his father: "You are fortunate that you are not still having me to support. If I ever get a woman some one will have to support her, but I see no need of a wife so long as I have my health."

However, his views changed radically and when Miss Goodhue came into his life he was recovering from an infatuation for a red-haired Northampton girl who had refused to marry him. After he became world-famous she sometimes wondered why she had been so indifferent to Calvin Coolidge. As an aging spinster she watched his progress, step by step, to the White House, with a radiant wife beside him. But after meeting Grace he had no thought of anyone else. He fell in love and wooed her with fewer words than the eloquent Miss Goodhue would have believed possible. As she came to know him better, however, she found that he could be quite discursive on subjects that interested him, and if no strangers were around. In later years he confessed that he had been in public office for years before he had mastered his dread of meeting people. This fear had its roots in his misery as a child when he was called into the kitchen of his home in Plymouth to greet strangers. "I'm all right with old friends," he revealed, "but every time I meet a stranger, I've got to go through the old kitchen door, back home, and it's not easy."

Miss Goodhue seemed to know instinctively from the start that behind his impassive manner was the shrinking of a shy and sensitive nature. She gave him great reassurance. Here was the kind of wife he needed—a fellow Vermonter, intelligent, educated, good to look at, a respected teacher in the New England tradition and a warm human being. He took her for streetcar and buggy rides, to church sociables, to meetings, to picnics. They went for long walks in the lovely woods surrounding Northampton. Grace was observant of the flowers and trees and Calvin listened to her attentively. They went up Mount Tom and he bought her a porcelain plaque as a souvenir. They were a familiar sight walking down the street together from Round Hill, past the new Forbes Library of granite and brownstone with its great semicircular portal and cavernous arch, a building designed by William C. Brocklesby of Hartford.

Except for Ivah, who was well primed on Calvin's latest comments, Grace's friends gave no serious thought to their comings and goings. He was seven years her senior and was as grave as she was merry. They knew him for a man of substance but he did not dance or skate, make bright conversation or show any of the social graces. Nor did he spread warmth to others. He made a great effort to mellow his ways and please Miss Goodhue but his incommunicability was deep-rooted. He bought a pair of skates and joined the youthful crowd on the Connecticut River one night. Cheeks glowing, a long Phoenix scarf and tam she had knitted finishing off her costume, Grace made an animated figure as she dragged Calvin over the ice. To Alfred Pearce Dennis, one of his friends who taught at Smith College, she seemed a "creature of spirit, fire, and dew."

It was no use. Finally her suitor took off his skates, slung them over his shoulder and took her home through the crunching snow. The flowing grace of the young skaters, sweeping through the icy air in the Dutchman's roll, had been too much for him. The dance floor was no better. He had taken some lessons at Amherst but after a brief try Grace decided that he lacked the necessary sense of rhythm. However, he seemed more in step when he took her to meetings and public functions. He was in his element at a reception given by the D.A.R. at City Hall to celebrate the 250th anniversary of the founding of Northampton. They strolled about until they were tired and then unwittingly they took the seats reserved for Governor John L. Bates and his wife. An usher promptly told them to move. In 1918, when he was elected Governor of Massachusetts, Mr. Coolidge remarked to his wife: "The Daughters of the American Revolution cannot put us out of the Governor's chair now." In time Mrs. Coolidge became an honored member of this organization.

They made an uncommon pair—the girl with the wide smile, fine eyes and friendly manner, and the spare, tight-lipped lawyer. Actually Calvin Coolidge was a good-looking man in full maturity, with breadth of forehead, a jutting nose both delicate and pointed, a keenly chiseled profile and cleft chin. His mouth was his most forbidding feature—a thin slash sweeping down at the corners with a suggestion of perpetual gloom. He seemed aloof because of his remote and frosty manner and his declarative chopped-off statements, as sharp as exclamation points. But Miss Goodhue, after all, was a Vermonter. She was used to the unemotional approach and had grown up with people spare of speech, undemonstrative by nature. If she did not gauge Calvin's unique qualities at first she came to treasure them later on, and to accept the fact that in some respects he would always baffle her.

Her suitor's lack of outward ardor was more than made up for by his persistence. At first each took friendly counsel about the other. Grace turned to Ivah and Calvin discussed the matter with his philosopher-friend, James Lucey, the Irish shoemaker on Gothic Street with whom he had many discussions on public affairs. Although a Democrat, Lucey admired Coolidge so much that he herded his friends into the Republican fold to vote for him.

The story runs that when Lucey asked him if he were having luck up on the hill, he expressed doubt that he was making any headway at all. Lucey counseled him to sharpen his approach and compliment his girl on her looks and dress. This was not in the nature of Calvin Coolidge but it is an undeniable fact that all through their married life he was profoundly interested in Grace's looks and attire, whether or not he commented on the final effect. Practicing the utmost frugality in all other areas of their life together he encouraged her to buy expensive and beautiful clothes and to refrain from appearing twice in the same gown at public functions. From time to time he selected things for her himself, particularly hats. It was the one Coolidge extravagance and it was wholly out of character, but he seemed to derive great satisfaction from his wife's appearance.

During his courtship Calvin found an unexpected ally in Ivah Gale. Grace often told her that she thought they had traits in common. Each fought shy of strangers. At one point Grace sent them off on a long buggy ride alone together as something of a test for Calvin. She wanted to know what Ivah really thought of her new suitor.

The drive lasted for three hours. Grace had warned her what it would be like. On their return she asked:

"Well, Ivah, did he talk any?"

"Yes," said Ivah comfortingly. "I liked him."

Years later Miss Gale recalled that he had not uttered a single word in three hours, but she was on his side and she wished to be reassuring. Next Grace showed Ivah the first love letter she ever received from him. It was five lines long, a businesslike note, with no mention of the magic word. "It wouldn't have seemed a love letter to me if I hadn't been told," Ivah confessed.

But thirty years later, one month before his sudden death, Calvin Coolidge sent his wife another five-line love letter, the last he ever wrote her. Summing up in one sentence the depth of his feeling for his wife it was classic in its simplicity and implication. It was written at the Vanderbilt Hotel in New York on December 8, 1932. He had been in New York attending a meeting and was about to return home. He signed his name in full, as he always did, even in his most intimate correspondence. The public called him "Cal" but his wife never took the liberty. He wrote:

> My dear Grace:
> Tomorrow I shall go home. Unless you have not heard send the car to Springfield at 8.40 Friday. I have thought of you all the time since I left home.
> With much love,
>
>   Calvin Coolidge

"I think he wanted her right off," Ivah recalled in her aging years. "He worked his way with her." And in time he proved that his way was remarkably successful in getting what he wanted out of life. In one of his own speeches he gave his views on persistence, the quality which was most marked in his courtship of Miss Goodhue: "Nothing in the world will take the place of persistence . . . Persistence and determination alone are omnipotent. The slogan 'Press On' has solved and always will solve the problems of the human race."

In any event, by the summer of 1905 things had come to a head, with combined family visits to Plymouth and Burlington. Calvin had not yet proposed but marriage was in the air and Grace was weakening. He had begun to talk to her about the future and had cannily given her a glimpse into his more intimate past. She learned much about Calvin Coolidge from her first visit to Plymouth, the hamlet in the Green Mountains where he was born in a farmhouse on July 4, 1872. She warmed to the unpretentious ways and sincere manners of his family. They were quiet, hardy people, proud in spirit. Her own upbringing had been more urban but Grace felt at home in the company of Calvin's relatives. She was particularly drawn to his father, Colonel John C. Coolidge, a fine old gentleman of sturdy build and Spartan outlook.

There was a strong family resemblance between father and son—the same reddish hair, the same penetrating eyes, the same incisive way of making a point, but the Colonel was more rugged in contour, toughened by the outdoor life he led. Calvin seemed fragile by comparison. His father served three terms in the Vermont state legislature, and was road commissioner, constable, deputy sheriff, postmaster, farmer, local merchant and notary at different periods of his life. It was clear to Grace that Calvin's taste and capacity for politics came from his father. He was named after the Colonel but dropped the John when he took up the practice of law.

She studied with great interest the picture on the farmhouse wall of Calvin's mother, Victoria Josephine (Moor) Coolidge, who died when he was twelve and she was thirty-nine. In his autobiography he recalled this event as a turning point in his life: "The greatest grief that can come to a boy came to me. Life was never to seem the same again." Victoria's intense, delicately modeled face suggested her invalid state. Her son always believed that she died of tuberculosis. She was of Scotch, Welsh and English stock. Her complexion was fair, her forehead wide and calm, and her brown hair had glints of gold. She was mystical in her outlook and observant of the moods of nature, of the mountain sides "struck with crimson and gold." She liked to work in her garden, to read poetry and novels and, in her son's words, "to watch the purple sunsets and the evening stars."

Although bedridden toward the end she lavished great affection on Calvin and his lively, red-haired sister Abigail, who died in 1890 at the age of fifteen, with Calvin at her bedside. Grace was always understanding of her husband's intense devotion to the memory of his mother. After his death his son John found tucked away in his dinner suit the thin silver case in which he carried her picture for a lifetime. It had been with him on his last public appearance in New York.

The Colonel liked Miss Goodhue on this first meeting and to the day of his death. He thought her the right wife for Calvin. And so did Carrie A. Brown, the Plymouth school teacher he had married six years after Victoria's death. Grace already knew that Calvin was devoted to his stepmother. "For thirty years she watched over me and loved me," he wrote of her. Thus he had two mothers—one who lived chiefly in his dreams; the other who was a living, helpful presence. Carrie, who liked books and music, had found him a studious boy, who would tap his foot to the music of the Virginia Reel and the Lancers but never attempt to dance them. He did not skate or hunt or swim but she watched him poring by the hour over Cicero's Orations, the life and state papers of Lincoln, the history of the Indian Wars, and other treasured books on his little reading shelf.

Matters of discipline were left largely to Calvin's grandmother, the hearty Sarah Almeda Brewer, who spun, knitted, made herbs for the sick, and was known to everyone as "Aunt Mede." She observed Miss Goodhue with shrewd attention.

"That's a likely looking girl, Calvin," she observed. "Why don't you marry her?"

"Maybe I will, Grandma," said the young lawyer, whose decision had already been made.

Thus the family dowager, who had brought a distant strain of Indian blood into the Coolidge family when she married Calvin Galusha Coolidge, had given Grace the final accolade. The young teacher of the deaf was to spend both sad and happy days at Plymouth, where she would watch her husband being sworn in as President in the farm parlor, where she would see both him and her younger son buried in the hilly little cemetery down the road. But at twenty-six, with the best part of her life still ahead, she took frank delight in roaming over the countryside with Calvin by horse and buggy. She walked with him through tall ferns and spotted familiar trees—red spruce and ash, cherry, elm and oak, and everywhere the stout maples that gave Vermont its endless flow of sap. It was wilder country than any she had known, with its narrow valleys and rugged hillsides, its streams flowing over rocks, its deer and its trout, and the rambling farmhouse in a little cluster of white dwellings, all without gas, running water or coal fires.

But Grace was much more warmly received in Plymouth than Calvin was in Burlington when he appeared suddenly after she had gone home for her summer vacation. He sat as stiff as a stick in the parlor while the genial Captain Goodhue fumbled around for an opening:

"Up here on some law business, Mr. Coolidge?" he asked.

"No. Up here to ask your permission to marry Grace."

"Does she know it?" said the startled Captain.

"No, but she soon will."

Later, discussing the matter with Grace, her father asked her what she saw in this young lawyer. Before long he was to reverse his opinion of Calvin Coolidge and to honor him highly—long before his son-in-law had reached the White House. Grace was greatly influenced by her father, then and later, and she listened attentively to what he had to say about her suitor. She received no comfort from her mother, who was cold and resistant to Calvin from the start and did not hide her feelings. She was already upset over Grace's earlier romance, and was surprised when she swung to someone so different from herself.

"I had heard Grace speak of him many times," Mrs. Goodhue remarked. "In fact, he had been to Burlington before but he had not called at our house. The first time I met him was in the parlor where they later were married, and I asked him if he was from the country."

She thought him awkward and fumbling when he tried to enlist her aid with Grace and she let him know that he need not expect any help from her. He would have to fight his own battle. Mrs. Goodhue never became genuinely fond of him although they had courteous relations and he was kind to her at all times. His success in life made no dent in her armor. When reminded that Calvin Coolidge had installed her daughter in the White House she was apt to retort that he got where he did because of Grace. She was in no doubt as to which had the better disposition. It was a matter of deep regret to Mrs. Coolidge that her mother felt about him as she did.

The air was electric on Maple Street that summer while Grace went about her native city with Calvin Coolidge. Her mother was morose but the lake lay blue and beautiful, the mountains loomed on the horizon, the air was fresh and golden and the young pair were in love. They drove into the country and picked raspberries and blueberries along the way. They strolled through the University campus, past the statue of Lafayette, then a familiar landmark; past Grassmount, the fine Georgian building acquired in 1895 as a woman's dormitory. Grace told Calvin tales of her childhood days—of sliding down Maple Street with George Marks, the boy who lived in the big house down the street. She showed him the route of the great toboggan slide that started high on the hill and finished with a swift run out on the lake. She recalled the thrill it was to whisk down this slide in a big bobsled with a score of college boys and girls. Earlier in life, before she could skate, she had amused herself sliding on ice near the back-yard pump and over the glazed cellar door. In spite of her passion for dolls she had been a bit of a tomboy at that age. She could whistle and throw a ball as straight as a boy.

After the combined visits and the varying emotions stirred up, Calvin Coolidge decided that the time had come to speak officially to Grace. Before the summer of 1905 was over he proposed to her in his own original way. It was more of a declaration than a proposal. "I am going to be married to you," he told her abruptly. Later he wrote of her: *The woman whom I chose to be my wife.*

Grace could scarcely register surprise after all that had occurred. She was cheerfully acquiescent for, in Calvin's own words: "From our being together we seemed naturally to come to care for each other." Even more significant was another of his comments: "We thought we were made for each other." But Mrs. Goodhue did not think so. She urged her daughter to leave Clarke Institute and spend a year at home before getting married. She hoped that a period of separation from Calvin might modify Grace's viewpoint or even change her mind. One of her delaying arguments was that Grace must first learn to bake bread before she could get married. But Calvin smartly told her that he could buy bread but he wanted his girl. He had been dead for a decade before she finally learned to bake bread, during World War II. "I have always turned pale at the mere mention of a cake of yeast," she wrote to the Robins, but she pronounced breadmaking her favorite accomplishment when she saw how much her grandchildren enjoyed her baking.

Mrs. Coolidge admitted in *Good Housekeeping* of March, 1935, that inevitably there was a bitter argument between her mother and her suitor over the date of the wedding. Both were accustomed to having their own way. One pair of cold blue eyes stared into another pair of the same icy hue as they debated the matter back and forth. "Mr. Coolidge took the position that we were both old enough to know our own minds, that he was able to support a wife, and that there was no reason to delay," Grace commented. "In the course of the debate the wedding date was advanced until Mother held out for November and Calvin October. Eventually he won in the draw."

Neither one felt it necessary to consult Grace about her wishes in the matter and she held her peace. Although pliant in her relations with others she was neither weak nor gullible. She had dignity and independence but she never tried to impose her will on others. Her own final impression was that her mother never forgave Calvin "but he proved himself so considerate and dependable that she had to admit that it might have been worse." In one of her merry quips Mrs. Coolidge remarked that her husband did not readily forget that Mother Goodhue showed a "neutrality toward his annexation to her dynasty which would have thrilled even Woodrow Wilson." The matriarch limited her White House visits to ten days during the five years and seven months that her daughter was First Lady. She surprised them all by traveling to Washington for the inaugural ceremonies of 1925 and she visited them briefly at Paul Smith's, a resort in the Adirondacks, but stayed in her own cabin and would not meet their guests.

Mrs. Goodhue's half-sister, Mary Barrett, who later became Mrs. John Hazel and lived in West Roxbury, Massachusetts, was a stout champion of Calvin's and backed his suit. When she ran an upstairs millinery shop on Tremont Street in Boston she was always glad to welcome him and would talk politics to the rising young lawyer. The feeling prevailed, even in Northampton where Coolidge had sound political rating, that he was the lucky one. Right up to the day of their wedding Miss Goodhue did her best to get her friends to warm up to her fiancé. Two months before their marriage she urged him to drive her to the home of Ethel M. Stevens, a college friend who lived at Williston, eight miles out in the country. The horse and buggy were hired from a local livery stable and Calvin appeared nattily dressed, with the widest pair of silk shoelaces that she had ever seen. His suit was of dark blue serge and a black derby rested squarely on his red hair. At the last minute he slipped a whisk broom into the back of the carriage, since he could not endure a scrap of lint on his clothing or a crease in the wrong place.

Every move he made was so slow and deliberate that Grace felt as if she were watching a small boy reluctantly performing a hated task under pressure. He hitched up the horse in the back yard, applied the whisk broom to his suit and went indoors to meet her friend. There he sat on the edge of the parlor sofa and, as Grace later described the scene: "Not one word did he utter and when, at last, he could bear it no longer, he arose and said simply, with one of his best smiles, 'We'll be going now.' "

While he was getting into the buggy her friend whispered to her: "My land, Grace, I'd be afraid of him!"

For once she was annoyed with him. She had wanted desperately to have him show his best side, and she burst out: "Now, why did you act like that? She thinks that you are a perfect stick and said she'd be afraid of you."

"She'll find I'm human," said Calvin gravely.

Later Grace conceded that she understood his attitude, although it distressed her at the time. He realized that she was putting him on display and "he made every possible preparation to present an appearance which would do me honor," she noted. "Beyond that his natural shyness would not permit him to go, and he would not make a pretense of enjoying the position in which I had placed him."

But although she understood that it was hard for him to break through this infrangible quality in his nature, her companions were less perceptive and took him at face value. However, laughter often saved the day and the Clarke School teachers watched Grace with interest when she made neat packages of sandwiches and lowered them with string tò her suitor from her dormitory window. She quickly learned that Calvin had no taste for picnics, nor did he ever change in this respect. He disliked the general messiness, the spontaneous touch and the ants and mosquitoes that haunted these festivities. But for Grace's sake he went to one picnic after another while he was wooing her, and brought his own contribution to each. At one picnic for four he supplied two chicken sandwiches, a strawberry shortcake and a dozen macaroons. When it was over he counted the macaroons and asked how many each had eaten. One half macaroon was missing, and he made them all laugh when in his own wry fashion he insisted on finding out what had become of it.

But in spite of their different natures, or perhaps because of the attraction of opposites, their romance flourished and Grace and Calvin Coolidge were married in Burlington on October 4, 1905. Their nuptials were of the simplest while that same week, a few miles away at Shelburne, Fredericka Webb was married to Ralph Pulitzer at the four-thousand-acre estate of her father, W. Seward Webb. New York's most prominent social figures flocked up to Vermont for this wedding and the overflow of guests stayed on the *Vermont III*, which lay at anchor on Lake Champlain. By contrast a group of fifteen intimates gathered in the plainly furnished parlor of the Goodhue house on Maple Street. Rain beat on the roof. Autumn leaves drifted down at the front door and settled in the gutter. The bride stood close to the bay window, gowned in gray, with her one bridesmaid, Miss Stevens, who later became Mrs. Charles C. Guptil, in attendance. Ethel's gown was gray with a faint check and green velvet trimming. Both girls had combs on their high pompadours and velvet bows. Grace clasped a bouquet of autumn flowers from the Goodhue garden. Calvin stood gravely at her side. He had arrived from Northampton the day before with his best man, Dr. A. H. McCormick, whom Grace had laughingly described as the bridegroom's "general manager." But the doctor had forgotten to send a carriage for the Rev. Edward A. Hungerford, who was to officiate. Years later the bride recalled: "A bare minute before the hour set for the ceremony he drove up to the house in much elegance behind his own spanking pair of horses."

Colonel and Mrs. Coolidge had come from Plymouth for the wedding and Calvin's aunt, Mrs. Don C. Pollard of Proctorsville, was a lively onlooker. Aunt Mede had said as they all left that it looked as if Calvin might have a wet day for his wedding. When this was repeated to him he is quoted as having said: "I don't care anything about the rain so long as I get the girl." But local interest in the wedding centered chiefly on popular Grace Goodhue. None suspected that the quiet, red-haired man who stood, white-faced and tense beside her, was destined to be President of the United States. Nothing could have seemed more unlikely in the year 1905. Her mother stood by with mental reservations about her daughter's future. Her father had come to the conclusion that Calvin must have sound values if Grace cared enough for him to marry him. The Plymouth group knew the bridegroom's history and heritage and put their own sympathetic valuation on his character and abilities. Although his political career was gathering momentum he was greatly underestimated at this time—a case of the silent man who shed no visible light.

The house was decorated with autumn flowers and leaves and they drove off in a shower of rice. Grace had tucked into her small trunk their most prized wedding gift, a counterpane knitted by Calvin's mother. They went to Montreal for their wedding trip and planned to stay two weeks, but were back at the end of one. Calvin had business on his mind as well as romance. They had soon seen all the sights and had been to the theater several times. Then and later Grace had keen interest in the theater, as she did in music, but her husband was cool to both. As far back as 1894 he had written to his stepmother that he had gone to see Julia Marlowe but in the same week had found Ingersoll, lecturing on Lincoln, much more to his taste.

Grace could see that her bridegroom was anxious to get back to

Northampton. He was low in funds after the expenses of the wedding, and she readily agreed to cut short their wedding trip. Later she jestingly pointed out that "he made the amusing explanation that he was in a hurry to get back to Northampton in order to show off his prize." But she knew better. "It was his first political campaign which drew him. Perhaps it was a judgment on him that he lost the election." He was running for the School Board against John J. Kennedy, an insurance agent, and it was one out of two defeats for office that he experienced in a long and remarkable career. When a Republican friend told him that he had voted for his opponent because he felt that the school committeemen should have children in the public schools, Coolidge replied: "Might give me time."

Northampton was a blaze of autumn glory on their return. The wide streets and the distant woods were a miracle of merging tints. Smoke curled from leaves burning on the lawns and autumn flowers still bloomed. The distant hills were shadowed in violet mist. The Connecticut River ran like a silver thread past tawny banks and clusters of trees. Paradise Pond lay deep green and still in its sylvan surroundings. The city had a population of more than twenty thousand and life was brisk around Smith College campus, with an ever increasing number of emancipated girls seeking degrees. Northampton already seemed like home to Mrs. Coolidge and would remain so for the rest of her life.

They settled down at the close of a year conspicuous for its peace and prosperity. The scientific advances of the late nineteenth century were bearing fruit. Thomas A. Edison and his fellow inventors had opened up a whole new era for man by setting in motion dynamic forces of incalculable scope. Electrical equipment, the telegraph, the telephone, the ocean liner, the automobile, farm machinery, the kinetoscope, were swiftly changing the tempo of life and civilization. The day after the Coolidge wedding the Wright brothers made a successful circular flight of 24¼ miles in thirty-eight minutes and three seconds at Dayton, Ohio, and seven months later took out a patent for their flying machine. The farms purred with new scientific equipment. The X-ray machine was holding out promise for man's physical ills. To all intents and purposes the businessman and the legislator, the farmer and the consumer, had common points of communication. Theodore Roosevelt was riding the crest of the wave after the landslide of 1904. George B. McClellan, the General's son, was Mayor of New York. The New York Public Library was close to completion. John D. Rockefeller, smarting under the attacks of a new breed of journalist represented by Ida M. Tarbell and Lincoln Steffens, had turned over ten million dollars to the General Education Board with a significant note that it was given "with malice toward none and charity for all." John R. McLean, who would share in Coolidge history, had bought the Washington *Post* from Beriah Wilkins. Andrew Carnegie was financing libraries. J. P. Morgan was collecting art on a mighty scale. Wall Street seemed the bastion of national strength.

Lillian Russell, playing in Proctor's vaudeville, swept through Churchill's with feathers, flounces and diamonds. George Arliss and Mrs. Fiske were appearing in *Becky Sharp*. Blanche Bates was playing *The Girl from the Golden West* and the nation was humming *Meet Me in St. Louis*. The automobile was a smash hit and the talk of the day among those who could afford it. The W. K. Vanderbilt Auto Cup Races aroused almost as much excitement as the traditional horse and yacht races. It was a year of dashing parties, with hostesses setting new records for extravagance and show. The costume balls, banquets and cotillions in New York and Newport sparkled with curious novelties. Golden swans and flocks of nightingales, dinners for dogs and monkeys, imported theatrical casts, favors and decorations of fantastic value, all helped to make the social circus spin. Mrs. Astor's ball and James Hazen Hyde's masquerade in 1905 became legendary social events.

A dignified Vermonter, Louis Sherry, presided with style and popularity at his Fifth Avenue establishment. The Horseback Dinner, with guests mounted as they dined, was one of the most discussed events of the year at his famous restaurant. Meanwhile, the Sunday supplements exploited the marriages of rich American girls to titled foreigners and spread from coast to coast the piquant details of New York's great parties. It was an era of yachts and country estates, of regattas, horse racing, grand opera, large staffs of servants and glitter unlimited—a world the Coolidges would touch in time, but never inhabit in spirit.

Under the gilded surface stirred the forces of social unrest. Wage laws, work hours, compensation, all were discussed with growing discontent. The reformers of the late 1890s had broken the solid Victorian pattern and created a network of vigorous protest that filtered through in different areas. Upton Sinclair was finishing *The Jungle,* which would be one of the most discussed books of 1906.

But all was quiet and orderly in Northampton as Grace Coolidge joined the great army of women who went about in high laced boots, wearing long braided jackets and skirts that swept the dust. She was the average American woman beginning her married life in the average American home. She already had many friends in Northampton and she corresponded eagerly with her family in Burlington. The stone tower memorial to Ethan Allen had just been dedicated in her native city. A young man named Franklin D. Roosevelt occasionally traveled on the Lake Champlain boats *Chateaugay* and *Ticonderoga.* His father, James Roosevelt, had followed LeGrand Cannon as president of the Champlain Transportation Company. Captain Goodhue wrote that the *Chateaugay* was a fine boat with a 220-foot hull. It had fluted cherry stanchions, and Japanese lanterns swung from the deck as the passengers danced at night.

The Coolidges lived at the Norwood Hotel for three weeks after their return until they found a small furnished house belonging to a Smith College professor. Grace later pictured herself sitting at the window waiting for Calvin to come home from his office on Main Street "in accordance with the procedure commonly accepted as becoming a young bride." One day he arrived with a russet leather bag, which he opened solemnly by unleashing a succession of gadgets. She watched with amazement as a mass of socks flowed out. He told her there were fifty-two pairs for her to darn, and more would follow.

Always expert with her needle, she did a neat and thorough job, although in later life she confessed that she found darning a boring task. She jestingly asked him if he had married her in order to get his stockings darned.

"No, but I find it mighty handy," he retorted.

Since this was a story Grace told on herself there is no doubt of its truth, although many of the Coolidge stories are apocryphal and have grown out of the legend that in time attached itself to him as an unconscious wit and a sphinx with homespun virtues. When Dr. Clarence S. Brigham, president of the American Antiquarian Society, asked Mrs. Coolidge after her husband's death if all the stories told about him were true she quick-wittedly answered: "The best of them are." But she was authority herself for some of the choicest.

She quickly learned that woman's place was in the home—no great shock to her, since she was well schooled in the Vermont tradition that a man was master in his own house, a situation that she never questioned. But she found she was up against an immovable force in many of the small details of daily living. It took her some time to adjust herself to the more rigid atmosphere in which she now lived.

In the late summer of 1906 they rented half of a two-family house at 21 Massasoit Street. This was to be their home for many years, the birthplace of their two sons, and the house to which they returned from Washington. They clung to it long after they were well enough off to afford a much larger place. When the Norwood Hotel closed and its stock was sold they bought linen and silverware which they used for years, with its alien insignia.

The house was a simple frame dwelling, with three bedrooms and bath, a parlor, dining room, kitchen and attic. The front room had bay windows, where Grace sat with her knitting and sewing. Their porch was Calvin's favorite sitting place in good weather. Their rent was $28 a month and it went as high as $40 when he became Governor of Massachusetts. Their first neighbors were Miss Imogene Prindle and her mother. After 1918 Dr. F. W. Plummer, principal of the Northampton High School, moved in next door. His son and daughter played with the Coolidge boys and Dr. Plummer observed that Mr. and Mrs. Coolidge "tempered and complemented each other to an unusual degree."

Coolidge bought an oak bedroom set and installed the oak bookcase he had used at Amherst. Captain Goodhue had built them a couch as a wedding present and Calvin liked to sit in a Morris chair. There were Axminster carpets, books, cloth-bottomed rocking chairs on the porch, some water colors and prints on the walls and over the white mantelpiece in the parlor hung the quotation:

> A wise old owl sat on an oak,
> The more he saw, the less he spoke;
> The less he spoke, the more he heard.
> Why can't we be like that old bird?

Grace had little to say about the furnishings, for her first child was due to be born when, in the words of Calvin Coolidge, they "walked over to the new house." There was a temporary maid to help with the housework and Grace's knitting and work basket were conspicuous features of her ménage. All was plain and durable but clematis wreathed the bay windows and she had put the last stitch to a beautifully sewn layette when their first child was born on September 7, 1906, and was named John after his grandfather. "It was all very wonderful to us," Coolidge commented in his autobiography.

He promptly wrote to his father informing him that the baby was born just as the clocks were striking six. Grace had had minor pains all day, but nothing severe until four o'clock. She went to bed at five and "had a very easy time of it." The boy was "real white and was born hungry," Calvin added. His hair was dark, his eyes were blue, he had Coolidge hands and his mouth "is like mine they say."

Grace's interest in her home doubled with the arrival of young John. She was a devoted and punctilious mother and Calvin saw to it that his own developing interests did not draw her away from the fireside. As time went on she recognized his ambition and accepted the fact that he was a persistent office seeker. Time and again she saw him succeed although he did not discuss his plans with her, even in their early married days. She would learn in roundabout ways what was going on. At no time did she impinge in any way on his public life. Walter L. Stevens, the young lawyer who followed him in the office of Hammond and Field, and knew both of the Coolidges well as long as they lived, said of her: "She was the right wife for him. She never rung him in on things he wished to avoid."

"She is going to be a great help to me," Mr. Coolidge remarked soon after his marriage. And Grace was, in innumerable ways, not the least of which was a sound understanding of his unique character. No two people could have been more unlike. In all respects Grace Coolidge was the opposite of Calvin Coolidge, except for their basic sincerity and high principles. She was gregarious where he was solitary. She was joyous where he was glum. She was responsive where he was aloof. She loved a good time. He took a dim view of social pleasures. She was impulsive. He was cautious. But both had wit, on two different levels. Grace's humor was open, friendly and joyous, like herself. Calvin's was wry, unexpected and often incomprehensible to bystanders because of his poker face. But his wife never failed to pick up his jokes, and he was amused by hers. It was one of the bonds that sweetened their life together.

In her last years she was asked by an intimate friend how she had come to marry Calvin Coolidge.

"Well, I thought I would get him to enjoy life and have fun but he was not very easy to instruct in that way," she replied.

A romantic union? Many thought not, but the Coolidges gave every appearance of being happy together for twenty-eight years. When a newspaperman once questioned Mrs. Coolidge about their early romance she looked at him with her gray-green eyes, usually so frank, but on this occasion inscrutable and replied: "Have you ever met my husband?"

Yet she never underestimated the depth and continuity of his devotion. Looking back from the 1930s, with the proved record of the years between them, he gave his own crisp estimate of his married life in his autobiography: *For almost a quarter of a century she has borne with my infirmities and I have rejoiced in her graces.* This was a rare tribute, coming from Calvin Coolidge. It summed up the essence of his feeling for the woman he chose as his wife.

CHAPTER II

A POLITICIAN'S WIFE

G RACE GOODHUE believed that she was marrying a country lawyer
when she took her wedding vows in Burlington but Calvin Coolidge had already begun his inexorable climb to fame. It took him
only fourteen years from the day he was installed as mayor of Northampton to reach the White house. In his own words: *Some Power
that I little suspected in my student days took me in charge and carried me from the obscure neighborhood at Plymouth Notch to the
occupancy of the White House.*

It was a quick, undeflected rise, with Mrs. Coolidge staying quietly
in the background while he served as mayor of Northampton, state
senator, lieutenant-governor and governor of Massachusetts. When
asked on one occasion what his hobby was he snapped back: "Holding office." Soon after John's birth he left home to serve two terms as
representative to the Massachusetts General Court. He conducted
his political affairs from his office and his gaslit inner bedroom at the
Adams House in Boston. He read history in the evenings and sipped
green tea with his political friends while they drank brandy. Occasionally he took a glass of beer.

Neither then nor later did he have his family join him, although

Grace visited him occasionally in Boston and he traveled home to Northampton nearly every week end. "She never had taken any part in my political life, but had given all her attention to our home," he commented. "It was not until we went to Washington that she came into public prominence and favor."

These were strictly her domestic years although she was always first and foremost a homemaker. She had no political leanings but her husband's associates were not unaware of the charm of the greenish-eyed wife with the encompassing smile and ready wit who livened up the scene when she visited Calvin. They plied her with violets and gardenias to pin on her furs and bought her fine dinners when she came to town. They took note of her husband's admiring glances in her direction although he barred her completely from the circle of political intimacy. He was doing his job. She was doing hers. No one questioned either role.

Mrs. Coolidge was neither politically inept nor politically uninformed. After marrying Calvin she merely adopted a policy of keeping her counsel about public affairs. But she was forced to revise her thinking in the early days of her marriage. Her father was as ardent a Democrat as Calvin was a Republican and she had grown up in the shadow of Andrew Goodhue's political philosophy. After her husband's death she confessed to a friend: "I am just a lost soul. Nobody is going to believe how I miss being told what to do. My father always told me what I had to do. Then Calvin told me what I had to do."

But however repressive her husband, he could not subdue her ready enthusiasm or her vivid interest in the world around her. The year 1906 was one of great excitement. There were major disasters at home and abroad. An earthquake in Formosa killed thousands and Vesuvius erupted violently in April. In that same month one of the most memorable disasters in American history all but destroyed the city of San Francisco. Caruso was singing *Carmen* at the Grand Opera House to an audience ablaze with jewels and the trappings of a golden age, when the city shuddered with the tremors of an earthquake and thick black smoke came funneling up from Market Street. Soon fires raged over a third of the city. The misty old buildings of brick and redwood went up in flames. Fountains of water geysered from tugs and fireboats. People ran frantically from point to point or died in the ruins. The score was unforgettable—nearly 700 dead, more than 200,000 homeless, and property damage estimated at $200,000,000.

Meanwhile, archaeological research was having a brisk revival, and exploration of the Polar regions was under discussion at a conference in Brussels. The Olympics were held in Athens and the suffragettes demonstrated violently in London. There were anti-Negro riots and lynchings in Atlanta, Georgia, and the city was under martial law. Harry K. Thaw shot Stanford White on the roof of Madison Square Garden in New York. The anthracite coal miners struck in Pennsylvania. Theodore Roosevelt was awarded the Nobel Prize for helping to end the Russo-Japanese War. He was advocating an inheritance tax and was wielding the big stick with soft words on several fronts. His daughter, the spirited Alice Roosevelt who had brought dash to the White House, married Nicholas Longworth on a bleak February day that year. This event was only a distant echo to Grace, who would count Alice among her closest friends when Calvin Coolidge became President of the United States.

But however far she was to travel in later years she learned at the start of her married life the folly of being a gadabout wife. When she heard indirectly that her husband was going to speak at their church she decided to keep him company. He watched her putting on her outdoor things and asked her where she was going.

"Oh, I thought I'd go out and hear you talk," she replied.

Calvin looked at her glumly. "Better not," he ruled.

She stayed at home and was not so eager after that to volunteer her companionship when business was on foot. Her husband at this time was attentive to all the political winds that blew. The years of family building for his wife were his years of political growth. When he finished his terms as representative he resumed the practice of law in Northampton but his ambitions were quietly crystallizing on the local front, as he rang doorbells and let people know that he would like to be their mayor. His opponent was a popular merchant but Coolidge won by 187 votes and promptly took his family to Montpelier to celebrate by visiting his father, then serving in the Vermont state legislature. He had written to the Colonel while at Amherst: "I should like to live where I could be of some use to the world and not simply where I should get a few dollars together . . . It is not in what I shall get but what I can give that I shall look to for satisfaction."

But he was already finding out that it took money to raise a family and make worldly progress. Their second son, Calvin, was born on April 13, 1908, and nearly two years later, when he took office as mayor, he was forced to write to his father asking for aid. His salary was only $800. Meanwhile he needed an overcoat, a business suit, an evening suit and a cutaway suit, he wrote with careful detail. Grace was in need of a suit, a dress, an evening dress, an evening wrap, and two hats. There were social events she must attend as the mayor's wife. As a music lover she particularly valued the free seats she had for the Academy of Music, the local opera house.

During his two terms as mayor Calvin Coolidge solidified himself with the local Republican leaders and acquired a reputation for probity, thrift and reserve. They recognized him as a hard worker, a quiet man whose silence suggested hidden reserves rather than vacuity. He did not stir up controversy or get into hot water. His zeal in reducing taxes was applauded and he worked to increase teachers' salaries. His native respect for education, and his wife's close interest in teaching, caused him always to pay attention to the needs of this profession. He had many friends in the opposite party and was told by a Democrat after one of his political victories: "I'm glad that you were elected, but I didn't vote for you."

Calvin Coolidge stared at him coolly: "Well, somebody did," he rasped.

But the years leading up to her husband's election as governor were not dull ones for Mrs. Coolidge. She took a brisk interest in community affairs. Her thrifty upbringing in Burlington had prepared her for the stringent economies she found she must practice. The Coolidges lived strictly within their income, which never exceeded $2,000. Calvin stoked the furnace before setting off for his office. They used a party telephone line. Grace cooked and cleaned, did the washing and looked after her children. But there was nothing remarkable about this. Her neighbors did the same. The Coolidges entertained very little and when they did Grace usually served simple New England suppers. Cooking for her husband was a problem, for he was a finicky eater with many whims about his food. Nor could he ever forget how skillful his grandmother had been at canning fruits, vegetables and pickles.

Although much has been written about the domestic skills of Mrs. Coolidge her most devastating critic was Calvin. In fact, her pies and biscuits figured among his stock jokes in the early days of their marriage. He was apt to drop one of her biscuits on the floor and stamp his foot to emphasize the thud. His wry comments before guests on pie crust that resembled cement failed to douse his wife's bright spirits.

"Don't you think the road commissioner would be willing to pay my wife something for her recipe for pie crust?" he asked two of her friends from Clarke School after he had urged her to serve them some of her pie.

"Only those who have been placed in a similar position can imagine my feelings as I sat and watched them eat that dreadful pie, my husband also looking on with an inward glee of which I alone was aware," Mrs. Coolidge later recalled. "At last the final morsel was consumed amid loyal exclamations of approval."

But the tendency to tease and play jokes worked both ways in the Coolidge family. No one made fun of Calvin Coolidge more readily than his wife, or went so far in mimicking him. She did it to his face, always in an affectionate way, and he delighted in the effect. She would imitate his nasal twang, his inflections, his expression, his clipped way of giving answers, his reactions to those around him. As the years went on and the Coolidge legend gathered strength she added her own good-natured touches to tales of his frugality and reserve. But she was watchful to see that he was in the mood for such raillery. There were times when she would not have dared.

Although in their early days he was censorious about family matters Grace could always laugh at herself and she cheerfully admitted her own ineptitude when called to account. As time went on she proved herself to be a capable housewife and hostess under all circumstances and was just as much at ease in the East Room of the White House as in the little kitchen at Plymouth; entertaining the Queen of Rumania, James Lucey, Madame Curie or Will Rogers; sitting at the right hand of the president of Smith College or leading the grand march at a policemens' ball. For she was always herself— candid, unaffected, seeing the humorous side of things, kind and vigilant for her husband's interests, diffusing charm against the opaque screen of his reserve. She took things as they came and never showed surprise, even when the President gave her vigilant assistance in the White House, prowling through the kitchens, tasting the broth and watching the bills. As mayor he had less scope for his curiosity.

The year in which he assumed this office William Howard Taft, whose grandfather was a Vermont farmer, was inaugurated as President and Theodore Roosevelt sailed off to Africa to hunt. There was revolution in Turkey. Robert E. Peary reached the North Pole and Ernest H. Shackleton got to within ninety-seven miles of the South Pole in the *Nimrod*. Louis Blériot crossed the channel in his monoplane. Princess Juliana was born to Queen Wilhelmina in Holland and Joan of Arc was beatified in Rome. The Hudson-Fulton celebration of that year was of particular interest to Mrs. Coolidge. New York and Vermont joined to commemorate the tercentenary of the discovery of Lake Champlain, her own favorite body of water.

Her father shared in the excitement when President Taft and the governors of New York and Vermont crowded into the pilot house of the *Ticonderoga* as Burlington celebrated a historic occasion peculiarly its own. In New York the "dazzling floods of light" along Fifth Avenue, the flag-draped streetcars and the lighthearted jubilation made the Hudson-Fulton parade one of the most memorable in the city's history. People sang *It's a Grand Old Flag, The Girl I Left Behind Me, Strike up the Band* and *There's No Place Like Home*. It was a carefree interlude after a severe business slump in 1907. Nickelodeons flourished. The young danced the Turkey Trot and the Bunny Hug to the rattle of pianolas. There was optimism in man's affairs, with Sunshine movements and Prosperity Leagues spreading the gospel of sweetness and light across the land.

In 1912 Mrs. Coolidge paid her first visit to Washington. She went to the capital as chaperone for the graduating class of the Northampton High School. Major Albert Beckmann, the local sheriff, was in charge of the expedition, and she enjoyed it fully as much as the students. Trolley cars rumbled along the streets. The sophisticates of the capital wore Merry Widow hats, gloves to their elbows, hobble skirts and enveloping veils. The White House looked just as she had always envisioned it. When the class trooped through the Blue Room she sat down at the piano and ran her fingers over the keys. A guide touched her on the shoulder and asked her to stop. It was improbably reported in later years that she said on this occasion: "Some day I will come back here and open that piano and play on it, too, and he won't put me out." But she sometimes recalled this incident as she played the same piano after she had become mistress of the Executive Mansion. When the class of 1912 had a reunion in Washington in 1937 she was their guest of honor.

The year of Mrs. Coolidge's first glimpse of the White House was one of dramatic headlines. A republic was set up in China with the abdication of the Emperor and the retirement of the Manchu dynasty. New Mexico was admitted to the Union as a state. There was great unrest in New England as the textile workers staged a long strike in Lawrence, with heavy rioting. A million coal miners walked out in Britain. But the most startling event of all was the loss of the *Titanic* when it hit an iceberg. Millionaires and many world celebrities went down among the 1,503 who were drowned, and tales of personal heroism held readers spellbound.

In the following year Woodrow Wilson was inaugurated as President and his daughter Jessie was married to Francis Bowes Sayre in the White House. Coxey's Army made its second march on Washington. Four gunmen were electrocuted at Sing Sing for the murder of Herman Rosenthal, closing the book on one of the more sensational crimes of the decade. Water entered the Panama Canal locks for the first time, opening up a new era in commerce. And the Cape Cod Canal went into operation. J. P. Morgan died and Dwight W. Morrow, who would prove to be an influential force in Calvin Coolidge's life, became prominent in the counsels of Morgan's banking firm.

Meanwhile life in the little house on Massasoit Street went on with a swift flow of light and shadow. Toward the end of the year young Calvin, aged five, became desperately ill and had to be operated on for emphysema. His father wrote to the Colonel just before Christmas: "He is very thin and weak, but you would be proud to see how much courage he has. He is a thoroughbred." Grace was so exhausted by the time he recovered that she had to go home to Burlington for a rest.

This was the year in which Mr. Coolidge became President of the Senate in Massachusetts. His family were now accustomed to his comings and goings on official business. Every Saturday he rode in the day coach to Northampton and was back at his desk on Monday. He usually sat alone, smoking a cigar, and discouraging all attempts at conversation. On Saturday nights he sometimes acted as baby sitter to let Grace go out with friends—but on several occasions she was summoned home in peremptory fashion. When one of the boys fell out of bed one night Mr. Coolidge got on the party line:

"Grace?" he said.

"Yes? What is it, Calvin?"

"Hop home."

She did, and with full awareness of the urgency of his call. She was never resentful when he used that tone of voice to her, for she understood him as his grandmother and stepmother did. Many demands were made on her by this time. She was an active worker at the Edwards Congregational Church and there were meetings to attend. She sewed for the Church Guild, went to thimble parties, to church suppers and bazaars. The Coolidges occupied Pew 10 halfway down the church and her contralto voice was admired by her fellow parishioners.

She and her friend and neighbor, Mrs. Reuben B. Hills, went to market together nearly every day. They shared their anxieties over childish diseases, planned parties for their boys, took them tobogganing, picnicking and for rides in Mrs. Hills' yellow-wheeled motor car. It was built for two but more often held five—two mothers and three boys. Although Mrs. Coolidge was a good manager, her husband set the family standards for thrift and discipline. They were all urged to save for a rainy day and once when walking with the boys past a Northampton bank where they had small savings accounts, he said: "Boys, listen here a minute and maybe you can hear your money working for you."

Young Calvin's lively imagination immediately conjured up a picture of the dollar bills in action. The youngest Coolidge son was apt to be thoughtless with his pennies, and when he squandered five dollars given him on his birthday his father turned a sermon on extravagance to account by impressing on him the enormity of his offense. They were visiting Swampscott at the time and Mr. Coolidge, who liked to catch his family napping, as they sometimes did in church, both literally and figuratively, started an interrogation.

"Mammy, what was the sermon about?" he asked Grace after the morning service.

"Mercy, don't ask me."

"John, what was the sermon about?"

"I don't know," said John blankly.

Then it was Calvin's turn. He knew very well but he squirmed, for his conscience plagued him about the squandered five dollars. "I don't know either," he said evasively.

"Yes, you do, too," his father insisted and kept up the barrage until Calvin saw that it was no use to hold out. "Aw, spending money!" he conceded.

They often discussed the sermons after church and one story that traveled far was that Mrs. Coolidge had asked her husband what the minister had said on the subject of sin, and he had replied: "He was agin it." But Mrs. Coolidge punctured this anecdotal balloon. "I happened to be present the first time the President heard it," she wrote. "He laughed mildly and remarked that it would be funnier if it were true."

When a Baptist preacher dined at their home before a revival meeting and scarcely touched his food, saying that abstinence improved his preaching, Calvin reported back to Grace after listening to him: "Might as well have et."

She learned early in her married life not to cast her pennies on the waters. A glib book salesman had inveigled her into paying eight dollars for the Dr. Spock compendium of the day. The book was called *Our Family Physician* and she thought it would help her in treating childhood maladies. As soon as she had made the purchase she knew that she had been wildly extravagant and had better not mention the matter to Calvin. She merely left the book in view on the parlor table, where he soon found it and deduced what had happened. "This work suggests no cure for a sucker," he wrote on the flyleaf. After that Grace was always cautious when salesmen came around. But this did not apply to her clothes.

Mrs. Ernestine Cady Perry, her husband's secretary, developed a great admiration for Mrs. Coolidge, who used to breeze into the office like a "ray of sunlight." One day she arrived looking particularly stunning in a rose-colored picture hat, which had cost $19.90 and was much beyond her means. Her husband had insisted that she buy it when they saw it in a shop window in Springfield. During these years of separation he would study the Boston shop windows for hats and shoes for Grace. On one trip home he took a hat out of her closet, measured the crown with string, slipped the cord into his vest pocket and on his return to Boston bought a hat he had fancied at Collins and Fairbanks. It was a wide leghorn with a pink rose. They were leaving for Plymouth at the time and he turned up at the station carrying the hatbox gingerly. Grace had to wear it every time she went out of the house, although it was quite unsuitable for rural surroundings. "I have no doubt the neighbors thought I was 'high-hatting' them," she laughed.

This was her husband's favorite hat and it set a standard for the future. In later years when she wished to please him particularly she always knew that a picture hat would help and a pink rose would be effective. Pink was one of her preferred colors in any event and pink or yellow roses and gardenias her favorite flowers. "Northern Lights Blue" was her official White House color.

The Coolidges sometimes went to Rahar's Inn in Northampton for Sunday supper, where Calvin had taken his meals for seven years before his marriage. The boys considered this a treat. They had the run of the place and here young Calvin had his first encounter with a finger bowl. A thin slice of lemon floated on the water. He looked up at his father and inquired about its purpose.

"To drink," said his father solemnly.

Calvin picked it up and drank until his mother explained the true function of the finger bowl.

This was much like the occasion after he became President when Mr. Coolidge gravely poured his coffee and cream into his saucer at one of his breakfasts for politicians. They looked dismayed and a few followed suit, waiting politely for the President to take a gulp. This was just the effect he desired. When he had accomplished his purpose he bent down and placed the saucer on the floor for his dog. The bewildered guests were left with their saucers afloat and another good anecdote to tell on Calvin Coolidge.

Both of the Coolidges were zealous about the education of their boys. They believed firmly in the public school and Grace thought that parents should visit it regularly and discuss the children with their teachers. Their father examined their reports with care and made tart observations when they did not do well. Calvin was handsome and the brightest boy in his class but he learned with such speed and ease that he was disinclined to make an effort. He soon got bored and started to cut up in class. When he was in the sixth grade his teacher, later Mrs. Helen Woods, gave him 100 per cent in all his studies but only 50 in deportment. This was not good enough for a Coolidge and soon his mother arrived to see what could be done about young Calvin's behavior.

She listened quietly to what his teacher had to say, then went home and exercised her own judgment in disciplining him. She made it clear that unless he behaved better there would be no reading period after supper, nor would he get the pair of skis he wanted for Christmas. This brought immediate results. His teacher had no further trouble with Calvin and Mrs. Coolidge had left an indelible impression on her of a "vivid, buoyant mother and friend" who backed up her husband in discipline but had her own quiet way of enforcing order.

Another observer recalled a sound smacking being administered in public when Calvin Coolidge leaned across the table and briskly cuffed the ears of one of his sons in the ornate dining room of the Touraine Hotel in Boston. A whimper followed from the boy in knee pants. The other guests sat up in their chairs and viewed this disruption of the peace with horror. The victim probably was John, who was chastised for his misdeeds more often than Calvin.

"My brother had a little more deviltry in him than I had," John recalled in later years. "But what he did was cute. When I did the same thing it was naughty."

On another occasion the boys were quelled by their father in church after they had staged some merry play with a knife given them for Christmas. Mrs. Coolidge had no fads in bringing up the boys but she was meticulous in seeing that they did their lessons faithfully, dried the dishes, mowed the grass, kept themselves neat and were frank and truthful. She wanted them to be stalwart boys and she encouraged the outdoor life. She had a tent put up for them in the back yard, and later she helped to build a playhouse from a piano box, sawing the boards and driving in nails with her strong, capable hands. After that she helped them build a toy automobile with cart wheels, a Klaxon horn and two shiny tomato cans with nails driven in for headlights. She would play baseball with them outdoors or parchesi indoors with equal willingness.

Both boys suffered considerably from having to wear to school copper-toed leather shoes from Plymouth, because their father had worn them in his youth. They endured this torture as well as they could, although their teachers would not let them play indoors on stormy days because of the noise the clodhoppers made on the floor.

Fond of music herself, Mrs. Coolidge had hoped that the boys would be musical. Young Calvin took banjo lessons but he objected strenuously both to music and dancing lessons. John was more amenable in this respect. He learned to play the violin. Jack Hills, who was about the same age as young Calvin and spent much of his time with the Coolidge boys, took both piano and violin lessons. John Coolidge remembered his father asking him to play *Turkey in the Straw* on his violin for a square dance. He never heard him sing although there were rare occasions when he whistled, but not as well as

his mother did. She loved to sing, particularly ballads and sentimental old songs, and she could whistle buoyantly.

Young Calvin was an insatiable reader. Mrs. Florence B. Adams,
another neighbor on Massasoit Street who would become an intimate friend of Mrs. Coolidge's in the last years of her life, remembered him as the child who was always coming to her door to ask
for a book. Her small daughter, Jane, was fond of the elder Calvin Coolidge. Mrs. Adams had mental reservations about him at
this time but little Jane said to her: "Well, Mother, I think you'd
like him if you knew him."

Later on, at one of his official receptions, Mrs. Adams walked up
to him and greeted him although he had never spoken a word to her
in their Massasoit Street days. He looked at her keenly and said: "I
know your daughter."

"I always loved that," Mrs. Adams recalled nearly half a century
later. "There was a sweet side to his nature, for a child knows and
my Janie was fond of him."

As the boys grew older they jumped at the chance to make a little
money. They did neighborhood errands and delivered papers. John
gave ten cents of his weekly earnings to the church. His mother cut
down some of his father's clothes to outfit him for a masquerade
party. These were the lean days for the Coolidges and although Calvin was advancing steadily in state affairs he viewed his own progres-
sion as "slow and toilsome, with little about it that was brilliant, or
spectacular." Yet he was serving his third term as state senator in
1914 when former President Taft visited Northampton and gave an
address at Smith College on Washington's birthday. Mrs. Coolidge
noted in a letter to her old college friend, Ivah Gale, that "Calvin
had a seat with the 'Honorables' and I was favored with a seat among
the faculty wives."

The discomforts of an uncommonly cold February were jestingly
discussed by Grace on this occasion. They had just had a severe snow
storm and the house had been so cold that she had put on her outdoor things and gone into the open to get warm. The high school
had burned down, she wrote, and Calvin "had poohed the idea of
running to a fire" when she and John had hurried to the corner to

get a street car, but before it arrived the two Calvins were at their heels. She had just been on a "bat" to Springfield, she added, and had dined there with Calvin and two friends of his from Boston. They had given her a large bunch of violets and had treated her to a choice dinner. She had seen them off for Boston; then she had caught her own train to Northampton. It was hours late and she did not get home until midnight. The night was bitterly cold but "I wasn't finding any fault," Grace confided cheerfully to Ivah. "I had had a good time all right. There were lots of people waiting for that same train— especially college girls who had been away for the holiday."

Now she was looking for a much needed evening dress, Grace went on, but young Calvin had been ill and her plans had been side-tracked. So she thought she would wait for the new spring styles. She had just made herself a red silk and wool crepe, with "peg-top drapery and the waist plain with peasant sleeves." The girdle, broad and loose, was of brocaded velvet ribbon. "Once I should have resembled a tub—or rather two tubs placed thus—but now I look more like a toothpick whittled at both ends," she jested. This was an allusion to her college days when she and Ivah had worried about her plumpness. She was now quite thin. She had been reading *The Broken Halo* by Florence Barclay, which she found good. She reminded Ivah that it was by the author of that best seller *The Rosary*. They were in the habit of exchanging notes about their reading. Grace's taste grew more catholic as the years went on and she had a greater supply of books.

By this time Calvin Coolidge was presiding officer of the state senate and his wife and Mrs. Hills sat often in the gallery and listened to the debates. They heard the speech he made in January, 1914, that became noted in Massachusetts history. It summed up for Grace much of her husband's political philosophy and was to be closely identified with his Presidential history. Among other things he said:

Self-government means self-support . . . It may be that the diffusion of wealth works in an analogous way. As the little red schoolhouse is builded in the college, it may be that the fostering and protection of large aggregations of wealth are the only foundation on which to build the prosperity of the whole people.

Large profits mean large pay rolls. But profits must be the result of service performed . . . Don't hesitate to be as revolutionary
as science. Don't hesitate to be reactionary as the multiplication
table. Don't expect to build up the weak by pulling down the
strong . . . Recognize the mortal worth and dignity of man.

At this time Frank Waterman Stearns, a wealthy Boston merchant,
moved decisively into the lives of the Coolidges and helped to shape
their future destiny. Coolidge had been coming steadily to the fore
in state Republican politics but when Stearns decided to back him
for the lieutenant-governorship things moved fast on the political
front. Although he had had no experience in politics Stearns was
an able businessman and an expert in public relations. He was a
quiet, sturdy figure, as rugged in build as Coolidge was lean and
sharply chiseled. In the years that followed he was sometimes scoffed
at for his devotion to the man he likened to Lincoln. But he remained
his constant companion and backer from 1915 until Coolidge's death.
In the President's own words:

> While Mr. Stearns always overestimated me, he nevertheless was
> a great help to me. He never obtruded or sought any favor for
> himself or any other person, but his whole effect was always dis-
> interested and entirely devoted to assisting me when I indicated
> I wished him to do so. It is doubtful if any other public man
> ever had so valuable and unselfish a friend.

Mrs. Coolidge was readily drawn into this combination and she
became the close friend of Mr. and Mrs. Stearns. But Frank Stearns
was only one of the powerful triumvirate that helped to propel Calvin
Coolidge toward the Presidency. Winthrop Murray Crane, a former
governor of Massachusetts and influential figure in Republican affairs,
and Dwight W. Morrow were the other two. Stearns was without
political power but he understood the true nature of Calvin Coolidge
as few did. Crane was mighty in the counsels of the Republican
party, and Coolidge considered him the most disinterested public
servant he had ever known. "What would I not have given to have had
him by my side when I was President?" he wrote, but Crane died
just before the election of 1920. Morrow was a link with the world
of finance. Coolidge had impressed him when they were fellow stu-

dents at Amherst, although he had not wholly understood him. When the question of getting his alma mater some attention on the national scene came up Morrow remembered the ambitious young politician with the frostbitten face and clipped speech who had already made a good start in politics. He joined forces with Stearns to push a promising Amherst graduate up the political ladder.

The boom began at a conference in the Algonquin Club in Boston. Although the first step was the lieutenant-governorship Stearns already had his eye on the White House for Coolidge. On July 23, 1915, he wrote to Dr. George D. Olds, of Amherst: "Just for the minute it does not seem best to push him for anything higher than lieutenant-governor of Massachusetts, but later, of course, he must be governor and still later President. Just think what a time we will have at Commencement when the President of the United States, a graduate of your Class, '95, comes back to Commencement." And this was what ultimately came to pass.

When Coolidge finally decided to run for lieutenant-governor he gave up a trip he had planned with Grace to attend the Panama-California Exposition held at San Diego that year. This dovetailed with her attendance at the 1915 convention of Pi Beta Phi, held in Berkeley. By this time she was a well-known member of the fraternity. Initiated as a charter member in Burlington on November 24, 1898, she represented her chapter at the Syracuse convention in 1901, and became first president of the Western Massachusetts Alumnae Club formed in 1910. At the Evanston convention of 1912 she was elected vice-president for Alpha Province, covering the area from Florida to Toronto, and became president at the Berkeley convention in 1915.

The delegates crossed the country to California by special train and Mrs. Coolidge kept them all entertained with her keen observations and bright repartee. "I still remember her sparkle," a Pi Phi recalled nearly half a century later. She shared in their tour of Stanford University, their Hawaiian dinner, their stunt program, and trip around San Francisco Bay, followed by a picnic supper. They all went to the theater and visited the Pan-American Exposition. Mrs. Perce H. Curtis planned a house party for them in Glendale. In the group were authors Sarah Pomeroy Rugg and Anna Nickerson, as well as other Bostonians. Mrs. Coolidge was reminiscing with another New England girl, Sophie P. Woodman, when a telegram reached her from Calvin announcing that he had decided to run for the lieutenant-governorship. Instead of joining the house party she returned home at once to help him in any way she could.

On this trip the Massachusetts group decided to start a round robin correspondence, in which Mrs. Coolidge joined. Up to the time of her death she never failed to write to the members three or four times a year. Her letters to the Robins usually were packed with incident and comment, and read like a review of her years in the White House.

When Coolidge was nominated ultimately for the Vice-Presidency Mrs. Rugg, who had first met Mrs. Coolidge in Northampton in 1909, called at the Adams House as editor of *The Arrow,* their fraternity paper, and wrote an intimate article on a little known woman who was on her way to fame. She found her as much at ease as on all the other significant occasions on which she saw her. Both Mrs. Rugg and Mrs. Nickerson were witnesses to her bearing at public functions as Calvin Coolidge rose from one political office to another, and on different occasions they visited her in the White House. On inauguration day in 1925 when Mrs. Coolidge, standing close to the President, spotted Mrs. Nickerson at the foot of the platform steps, she waved to her and called out: "Hello, there. I'm glad to see you." Later she told her old Pi Phi friend, whom she had known since 1901, that it was good to see her in that sea of strange faces. By chance Mrs. Nickerson was born in the same year and was married on the same day as Mrs. Coolidge.

On her return from California Mrs. Coolidge was forced to leave hurriedly for Burlington to visit her mother, who was seriously ill. She was there when she learned that Calvin had won at the primaries; and also that he had been knocked down in the street by an automobile as he crossed with his umbrella up. He was uninjured and he went to Burlington to join the wife who by this time had come to believe that he consistently won what he sought. There was a certain inevitability about the way he moved ahead, without seeming to exert himself unduly or to beat the drums in an ostentatious way. His inscrutability seemed to inspire trust in the voters. The campaign speeches he made were quietly effective, laced, as they were, with practical arguments.

"I shall be elected—probably by a large majority," he wrote confidently to his father toward the end of October. And he was. When it was all over Mr. Stearns wrote to Mrs. Coolidge, who had already become his confidante in matters relating to her husband:

> You and I have one thing in common, at any rate. You picked out Calvin Coolidge some years ago and gave him your endorsement; more recently I picked him out and gave him the most emphatic endorsement I knew how to. Of course many others can claim to have picked him out, but amongst them all I think we can shake hands over the proposition that yours was the most important endorsement and mine comes next.

By this time Grace's social outlook was broadening as Mr. and Mrs. Stearns showered bounty on her family. Their quarters at the Touraine Hotel were always open to any Coolidge and they frequently visited their Swampscott home. They entertained them lavishly, sent flowers to Grace, remembered their children, and brought them to public attention in many different ways, so much so that Mr. Coolidge cautioned Mr. Stearns about his favors and established a clear line of resistance to personal financial benefits. Reacting with pride to the overgenerous impulses of Mr. Stearns he returned a check for $5,000 with the comment: "I have everything we need and am able to save something. I do not think a man who cannot take care of himself is worthy of very much consideration."

He frequently warned the selfless Mr. Stearns not to expect any return for the many favors done him. "I have often wondered why the greatest merchant in Boston was giving so much attention to my welfare," he wrote, but he need not have worried. Stearns served him for years without thought of reward, and no one was more certain of this than Mrs. Coolidge, who never failed to pay tribute to her husband's friend and backer. She could talk to him about her husband as to no one else. He was her chief adviser in matters affecting Calvin's health and well-being.

She and her sons were present at the inauguration ceremonies on January 6, 1916, when Calvin Coolidge became lieutenant-governor. In morning coat and striped trousers he presented his usual unruffled and staid demeanor. By the nature of things his wife more often heard him speak now. It was a novel experience for her when she attended a dinner given by the Amherst Alumni Association on February 4, 1916. This was the first time Calvin had appeared as speaker at one of these banquets, and Mr. and Mrs. Stearns had invited his wife to attend. She sat with Mrs. Stearns in a box at the Copley-Plaza Hotel and was visibly amused when Calvin recited Josiah G. Holland's *Gradatim* in his most nasal tones. Knowing that he might look her way she ducked behind a pillar in the box so that her mood could not be detected from the head table. But she listened with gravity while he said: "The man who builds a factory builds a temple, the man who works there worships there, and to each his due, not scorn and blame, but reverence and praise."

As time went on she became more familiar with the elocutionary style he was developing and the biblical simplicity of his phrases. His twang was more exaggerated on the platform than in his home. Through his speeches she sometimes caught unexpected glimpses of what he thought. He called them his Works of Art and she knew that he wrote them in pencil on yellow foolscap in the evenings and dictated them the following day with great deliberation. "I never disturbed him when he was preparing a speech, nor did I know what was going into it," she said on one occasion.

In general his speeches were threaded with aphorisms and homilies, expounding the eternal verities. They were likened to "hard granite" by Mark Sullivan. The language was simple and direct. The thought was distilled. They seemed impressive and of high literary merit to some. Others found them trite and lifeless, words without echo. Dr. Claude M. Fuess, his biographer, wrote: "Coolidge was accused of talking platitudes, but they were only such in the sense that all basic truths have been uttered, indeed must necessarily be uttered, again and again. What he said always had some bearing on his essential theme."

Only once did Mrs. Coolidge feel that an address had been written for him. He was speaking at the celebration of the hundredth anniversary of the Chickering Piano Company. She and Mr. Stearns were amazed at the outflow of comment on composers and rare musical items. She knew that Calvin simply did not have this knowledge. When it was over and they faced each other, she burst into laughter, in which her husband finally joined.

"Do you still believe that Calvin will be President some day?" she asked Mr. Stearns by chance on this occasion.

With Mr. Stearns the answer always was yes. By this time Grace was beginning to listen, but without conviction.

In 1916 Mr. and Mrs. Stearns took the Coolidges to Washington. It was Calvin's first trip to the capital although his wife had been there before. Mr. Stearns' declared intention was to have him meet important politicians who later might remember him. They all stayed at the Shoreham Hotel and were shown the White House, the Washington Monument and the traditional sights of the capital. Coolidge was moved to say: "That is a view that would rouse the emotion of any man," when asked for his impressions. Speaking that year on July 4, his own birthday, at Marshfield, the home of Daniel Webster in New England, he said: "Democracy is not a tearing down; it is a building up."

With his election as lieutenant-governor he invited a young lawyer named Ralph W. Hemenway to enter into a law partnership with him in Northampton. It was a nominal arrangement, since all the work fell eventually to Hemenway, because of Coolidge's absences. Grace saw a great deal of the Hemenways after this and Mrs. Hemenway was Nan or Lady Hemenway to Calvin Coolidge, who had known her from his college days. They all belonged to a group of young married people who went dancing together at one another's homes. They practiced the new steps, waltzed and had square dances. In summer they played croquet and had outdoor roasts. On rare occasions Calvin Coolidge was inveigled into joining them on his trips home. He would solemnly watch proceedings, but without attempting to dance. In time he came to enjoy his visits to the Hemenways' country place and he encouraged his partner to breed cattle.

At this time the Coolidges acquired a permanent housekeeper,

Mrs. Alice Reckahn, who was to stay with them until her death some time after they returned from the White House. Her presence eased Mrs. Coolidge's burden in some respects, for Alice was a notable cook and she had a firm grip on family affairs. Her presence enabled Grace to take more trips to Boston in Mrs. Hills' car, or by day coach. Although she delighted in these jaunts she was reluctant to leave the boys. At this time she learned to the full the disadvantages of being a politician's wife. She had endless waits while Calvin held conferences and attended to state affairs.

On January 2, 1917, two months after her husband had been re-elected lieutenant-governor, she wrote in mild exasperation to her friend Mrs. Hills about a journey she had been forced to make on New Year's Day. Grace addressed her as Perkins and signed her letter Hawkins, their nicknames for each other at that time.

Here I am and hungry, too, and come to think of it, I haven't the most remote idea whether that man o' mine expects to be here to dine with me or not. But I'd think a meeting at 5:30 would disperse for dinner and not "make a night of it." Now wouldn't you? I'll give him until 7, or possibly 7:15, and *no longer*. And I crocheted all the way down on the train, quite a stretch. Lots of folk travel on New Year's Day, don't they? . . . Wouldn't we just "do" this little old "burg" if you were here! There's no getting around it, we just have to do that little thing some time soon . . .

But the world that Grace knew was changing rapidly at this time. The storm that had swept over Europe with the outbreak of the first world war had finally stirred up the United States to action. The sinking of the *Lusitania* on a May day in 1915 had shaken the policy of neutrality. The drift into war against the Central Powers became stronger, and the era of preparedness set in. New England, like every part of the country, was galvanized into action in 1917 as war was declared and soldiers were shipped abroad with the declared aim of making the "world safe for democracy," a phrase that left taunting echoes down the years. Soon American soldiers were marching to the tunes of *Over There* and *Tipperary*. More than 2,000,000 men were overseas. Of the ninety-three combat units organized, forty-two reached France and thirty saw service in the line. Excitement mounted in every hamlet and city. Then came the casualty lists, the tales of victory and defeat.

Mrs. Coolidge was involved at once in Red Cross work, in benefits and entertainments for service men. She and Mrs. Stevens were co-chairmen of the women's war committee in Northampton. There were Victory Loan drives and campaigns of one kind and another. Both she and Mr. Stearns worried about Calvin at this time as he worked long hours and sweltered through the hot summer months in his tiny room at the Adams Hotel. By 1918 a severe influenza epidemic was sweeping the land, to add to the problems of a nation at war. Northampton blossomed with gauze masks. Churches and places of entertainment everywhere were closed. Mass meetings were canceled.

But the end of the war was in sight by the time the epidemic subsided. Soon ships were coming and going with lights ablaze for the first time in three years as the Allied drive went on and the German empire finally crumbled. Quietly, in Massachusetts, Calvin Coolidge was elected governor on November 5, 1918. But this inconspicuous headline was quickly lost in the crashing streamers that followed six days later: *Armistice Signed, End of the War! Berlin Seized by Revolutionists; New Chancellor Begs for Order; Ousted Kaiser Flees to Holland.*

People poured out from their homes to dance, laugh, kiss and make bedlam in the city streets and country hamlets. There was high excitement in Times Square, on Boston Common, along Main Street in Northampton, at Plymouth Notch, and on crossroads throughout the nation. Woodrow Wilson was wildly cheered when he solemnly announced in the House on November 12: *The war thus comes to an end.* In his formal proclamation he added: "Everything for which America fought has been accomplished. It will now be our fortunate duty to assist by example, by sober, friendly counsel, and by material aid in the establishment of a just democracy throughout the world."

The Coolidges had gone to Maine for a few days of rest after the heat of the election. They were wakened in the middle of the night to learn that the Armistice had been signed. They hurried back to

Boston to take part in the jubilation. November 12 was Victory
Day and Coolidge reviewed a parade and spoke at a victory meeting
that evening. He and Grace were welcomed back to Northampton
with a regimental band, a parade and a proud populace. The war
was over and a favorite son had taken another important step up the
political ladder.

Grace, Colonel Coolidge and young John and Calvin were interested onlookers as Coolidge was inaugurated governor of Massachusetts on January 2, 1919 after three terms as lieutenant-governor.
They were accustomed by this time to his unbroken stream of victories. On this occasion he hammered out with nasal emphasis one of
his more memorable sayings: "Let there be a purpose in all your
legislation to recognize the right of man to be well born, well nurtured,
well educated, well employed, and well paid. This is no gospel of ease
and selfishness, or class distinction, but a gospel of effort and service,
of universal application."

Mrs. Coolidge led the grand march at the inaugural ball with a
public official and Mr. Stearns, watching her, was moved to say in
a letter written to Mr. Morrow a few days later, urging the need to
raise funds for Coolidge's further advancement: "One of his greatest assets is Mrs. Coolidge. She will make friends wherever she goes,
and she will not meddle with his conduct of the office." But she
was none too pleased when the round-robin group she had invited
to the Governor's inauguration was denied admission except for
one member of the party. There had been a slip-up in the arrangements. "I guess you'll have to grin and bear it!" Calvin said. Grace
answered promptly: "Evidently I have to bear it—but I won't grin."

Mr. Stearns was now consciously steering the social fortunes of
the Coolidges and he told his wife to arrange a luncheon for a carefully selected group of prominent women in order to introduce Grace
properly in Boston. At the same time he strongly advised the Governor to rent a suitable house and to bring Mrs. Coolidge from
Northampton to preside as Governor's wife. It should be on Beacon
Hill but not on Back Bay, he advised, and if it were a historic house
so much the better. Meanwhile Mrs. Coolidge should engage a lady
to take care of the boys and to help her with her correspondence. "I

think they should entertain constantly," Stearns wrote to Mr. Morrow. "He makes friends, and she will, just as quickly as he comes in contact with people. . . . Four years intimate association with him has convinced me that he has many of Lincoln's strongest qualities . . . quietly and steadily we want to make him known outside of Mass . . ."

Calvin Coolidge listened but paid no heed. His salary was then $10,000 and he had no wish to be under obligation to anyone. He saw no occasion for social frills and Grace knew better than to argue the point. But he made one concession. He took two rooms instead of one at the Adams House and his family life went on as before. He and Grace journeyed back and forth between Boston and Northampton. "Mr. Coolidge may be Governor of Massachusetts but I shall be first of all the mother of my sons," she announced. But she made their hotel rooms homelike with books and photographs, her tea table and handiwork.

When the Women's Republican Club of Massachusetts gave a banquet in her honor just before the election that took her to Washington one speaker observed that "Governor Coolidge has faith in Massachusetts and Massachusetts women have faith in Mrs. Coolidge." Mrs. Corinne Douglas Robinson, Theodore Roosevelt's sister, was a speaker on this occasion. Mrs. Coolidge had her Pi Phi group at a special table and before sitting down she paused to wave to them. The Robins gave her a luncheon at the College Club in Boston before she left for Washington and prophetically attached a card reading "Eventually, why not now?" to a can of White House coffee.

But the die-hards of Back Bay looked coldly on a ménage so alien to tradition, style and convenience; to temporary quarters in the Adams House instead of a substantial home; to a charming wife who showed up only occasionally. It was a chill that never quite lost its edge where the Coolidges were concerned. Such parsimony was deplored in the inner social circle and Henry Cabot Lodge, who had written to Theodore Roosevelt a few months earlier that Coolidge was a "very able, sagacious man of pure New England type," curled a cynical lip over the Coolidge way of living. The proper Bostonians did not warm to the taciturn Vermont touch. The Coolidge ways were not their ways. When the time came for Mrs.

Coolidge to preside at the White House she said to a friend with an unwonted touch of bitterness: "I don't know what they expect me to do. Hang my wash in the East Room, like Abigail Adams?"

But when Calvin, unruffled, settled into his stern working mold as Governor, she backed him up and cheerfully explained: "Although my husband has moved up, it makes no difference in our mode of living. Why should it? We are happy, well, content. We keep our bills paid and live like everybody else." She was beginning to show great social skill, however, and to dress well. Early in 1920 Calvin wrote to his stepmother: "I wish you were here to see the dresses my wife has. Folks who see them know why I cannot pay very high rent."

Mrs. Coolidge had been campaigning openly for some time for a Ford car. "I have been talking it up to the Governor," she confided to a friend. "I shouldn't wonder if, some day, as soon as we can afford it, we might really own one." Now, at last, they had a car of their own. It was a source of great delight to her although she was never allowed to drive it.

With the governorship an accomplished fact, Mr. Morrow—back from Europe and negotiations with Lord Robert Cecil—talked matters over with Mr. Stearns at the Metropolitan Club in New York. He had finally decided that the Boston merchant was right about Coolidge. Both men agreed that he should now be presented to the public as Presidential material, and in a more human light. Although his taciturnity was understandable to New Englanders it was chilling on the national front. But the human aspects of his life and character invited attention. Bruce Barton, an expert in public relations, was called in to create the new image and to get some publicity for "our Amherst Governor in Massachusetts." He did the job effectively.

After a talk with Coolidge at the State House in Boston he took the view that he was a *rara avis* in political life, a man who read history and kept his own counsel. He decided that his cue was to play up the picturesque in Calvin Coolidge. He reported back to Dwight Morrow that he considered him a political novelty and that novelties were rare in public life. Barton predicted that he would become an important figure. The article he wrote for *Collier's* at this juncture had national impact. It dramatized the life and character of the quiet Governor of Massachusetts. This was the first major piece to appear about him, precursor to hundreds more. Soon Coolidge became so familiar with publicity requirements that he turned to Mr. Stearns one day as they were having their pictures taken and observed: "Let's spruce up a bit. And let's talk. It looks more natural and makes a better picture." In time he would even advise his highly photogenic wife on the poses she should strike.

Governor Coolidge was now so occupied that he made few trips to Northampton. And when Grace visited him he was so busy that he sometimes assigned a member of his staff to take her to social functions. The year 1919 was one of excitement and relief. The country was ablaze with the afterglow of victory, and politicians were beset by unfamiliar problems. Soon the soldiers were returning. War songs were sung with a cheerful swing. The Armistice was followed by relief, excitement, reunions, mourning in many homes, and a wider look through the windows of the world. General Pershing led a great victory parade up Fifth Avenue in the city's last war pageant of that era. Boston, too, had its share of military parades and returning veterans. All the governors of New England assembled for the parade of the Yankee Division and Grace Coolidge watched her husband receive the salute from the portico of the State House, as for five hours seasoned soldiers filed past in review.

On his return from the Peace Conference Woodrow Wilson landed in Boston, to be welcomed by Calvin Coolidge. The President was heading into a stiff fight for the League of Nations, with Senator Lodge and Hiram Johnson girded for action against him. Among those who greeted him in Boston was Assistant Secretary of the Navy Franklin D. Roosevelt. Another noted Roosevelt—Theodore—had died peacefully in his sleep at Oyster Bay while the Peace Congress was meeting in Paris in January, 1919.

The years Calvin Coolidge passed as governor were a time of transition from war to peace. Again he emphasized economy. Departments were reorganized. The street railways got relief. He vetoed a bill allowing the sale of beer with a 2.75 alcoholic content. He signed a forty-hour-week work bill for women and minors. "Nothing was natural, everything was artificial," he commented. "So much energy had to be expended in keeping the ship of state on a straight course that there was little left to carry it ahead."

But overnight the Governor was catapulted from state to national fame and the hopes and prophecies of Frank Stearns seemed closer to realization. The East was having its hottest September since 1881 when the Boston police strike threw the city into chaos in 1919. One faction of the Boston Police Department had organized a union, contrary to departmental rules, and nineteen men were promptly dropped from the rolls by Commissioner Edwin U. Curtis. The police force struck and Boston was under mob rule.

This was the most crucial political emergency in Calvin Coolidge's otherwise placid career. He kept a cool head under pressure, said nothing at first, and waited for developments while panic spread through the city. Years later he admitted that he should have ordered out the state militia when the trouble began. "A stone image would have viewed the impending calamity with the same composure," William Allen White commented.

As it was, the mob took over the ancient and historic city. Thugs and gangs of boys looted, burned, smashed windows, rang in false fire alarms, raided and destroyed. Shops, restaurants and theaters closed down. The city militia was helpless to control the spreading terror. Coolidge stood firm behind the Police Commissioner and sent Samuel Gompers, who had asked for the reinstatement of the union policemen, his famous message: *There is no right to strike against the public safety by anybody, any time, any where.*

Mrs. Coolidge was rarely apprehensive when her husband was faced with a political emergency. She usually knew about it only through the newspapers but all of New England, and indeed the nation as a whole, was stirred up over the menacing situation in Boston. Calvin was uncommonly quiet when he visited their Northampton home on a Sunday night in the midst of the crisis. On his return he ordered out the state militia and the strike was broken.

He had become a headline figure and was discussed as a Presidential possibility. When pressed in an interview at this time to comment on his proverbial taciturnity he said: "I've usually been able to make enough noise to get what I want." But he did not raise a hand to campaign for himself and snappishly told the press that he was busy enough being governor. Other Bostonians worked powerfully in his behalf, however, and when the Republican Convention met in Chicago in June, 1920, he was one of the leading possibilities. Stearns had scattered far and wide among the electorate a little book of Coolidge's assembled speeches entitled *Have Faith in Massachusetts*. Through this the delegates all had a timely chance to digest the views of the silent man from Massachusetts. Stearns circulated among them, pushing the Coolidge cause. Morrow stayed in the background, lest his Wall Street aura prove prejudicial in the grass roots areas. But he had already written to one of the delegates: "I am sure Coolidge would make a good President: I *think* he could make a great one." Calvin Coolidge, he pointed out, had tolerance, knowledge and character, qualities for which the world hungered.

But the plans of Governor Coolidge's backers went astray. Lodge failed to support him at the crucial point although originally he had been slated to make the nomination. Crane was desperately ill at the time and was at deadly odds with Lodge over the League of Nations. The Coolidges showed neither surprise nor dismay when Calvin missed first place on the ticket but was nominated as Vice-President to run with Warren G. Harding, whose campaign had been managed by Harry M. Daugherty.

When the news reached Coolidge in Boston that Harding had won the nomination he took a thoughtful walk across the Common and down some of the surrounding streets before rejoining Grace at the Adams House. She talked to him cheerfully while he smoked cigars and came face to face with the unfamiliar thought of political defeat. Then the telephone rang and he answered it. Without the slightest change of expression he laid down the receiver and called across to Grace:

"Nominated for Vice-President!"

"But you're not going to accept it, are you?"

"I suppose I shall have to."

Grace had understood that Calvin had no interest in second place on the ticket. Stearns was bitterly disappointed but Coolidge in the long run thought it a blessing, since he had his indoctrination before becoming President. His wife recognized it as a crucial point in his career but she had many qualms about the social demands that would be made on her should the Republicans win. Would she still live in Northampton or would Calvin take her to Washington? She could not help reflecting that everyone discounted the Vice-Presidency as a negative office, whereas Calvin was soundly established as a powerful figure in mighty Massachusetts.

In his acceptance speech Coolidge, talking from the familiar grounds of Smith College, was ambiguous on the League of Nations issue which was stirring up the country. He was less emphatic in his opposition to it than Harding and pointed out that the Republican party approved the principle of "agreement among nations to preserve peace." All around Mrs. Coolidge on this occasion were familiar faces. When the ceremonies were over a friend suggested that they should rest after such a tiring day. Grace laughed. "Calvin says it's about like any other day," she said. "We are going right back to Boston."

Coolidge met Harding in Washington late in June and was told that the "Vice-President should be more than a mere substitute in waiting." He intended him to be a helpful factor in the Republican administration as well as an active campaigner. Although Coolidge was quite ill with severe indigestion early in July, by the middle of the month he weathered an all-day gathering of two thousand Vermonters at Plymouth. They had come with picnic lunches to establish neighborly relations with the Coolidges. They listened to Republican speeches and engaged in friendly chat with Mrs. Coolidge. She proved herself a skillful campaigner on this particular day, as she shook hands with hundreds and struck the right note with a great variety of types.

But both of the Coolidges missed Mrs. John Coolidge at the farmhouse. In May, just before the convention opened, Calvin's stepmother, whom he had loved almost as much as his own mother, died at the age of sixty-four. She had had a long, lingering illness and both of the Coolidges had written to her often to cheer her. Now she was absent from the scene as the press swarmed around to drum up piquant impressions of the Coolidge family. Aurora Pierce, the Colonel's housekeeper; Miss Florence V. Cilley, who presided at the combined store and post office; Miss C. Ellen Dunbar, who had taught Calvin in school; and his aunt, Mrs. Don C. Pollard, all dug deep into their recollections for incidents that made lively newspaper reading.

The balky cow that refused to be milked by Calvin out in the open because it usually underwent this ceremony in a barn; the blue smock belonging to his forefathers that he sometimes wore in the fields; a day's fishing in the rocky, mountain streams of the Notch, all gave the public a spirited view of the family moving toward national prominence. But when the mocking note came through Mr. Coolidge firmly declined to don the smock for camera purposes and never wore it after he became Vice-President, his wife disclosed in later years.

The Republicans swept into power in November and bells chimed in Boston and Northampton for this fresh honor to a favored son. Grace thought that they were received like royalty when they returned to the graceful little city she now regarded as home. They were deluged with messages. "Please accept my sincere sympathy," wired the seasoned and witty Thomas R. Marshall, whom Coolidge would follow as Vice-President. Later, when he asked his law partner what he thought of the appointment, Hemenway replied, more prophetically than he could have dreamed: "With your luck I wouldn't want to be in the President's shoes for anything in the world." After Harding's death Coolidge recalled this grim jest.

He walked alone down the steps of the State House on a January day in 1921 to prepare for the inauguration in March and a shift to the Washington scene. According to custom he did not wait for the installation of his successor, Channing H. Cox, but he plucked a blossom from one of the incoming baskets of flowers to take to Grace. The guns had scarcely ceased roaring their welcoming salute for the new Governor when the two quiet Coolidges settled themselves in coach seats and rode through the familiar countryside to Northampton, conscious that strong new forces had entered their lives. Grace was happy because Calvin had weakened to the point of letting his family join him in Washington. "He really seems to need me," she wrote cheerfully to Mr. Stearns at this time. Medals, awards, honorary degrees now came his way. His movements were watched and Grace was studied as a promising new hostess for the incoming administration.

Just before Christmas they had gone West to visit the Hardings in Marion, Ohio. The President-elect, discursive, expansive and cordial toward the silent Governor and his beaming wife, discussed Cabinet prospects with Coolidge. Grace found her bearings with brisk, sharp-faced Florence Kling Harding, who was noted both for her business acumen and her ambition. They returned to Massachusetts with some slight knowledge of the pair who would now loom large in their destinies, and proceeded to sea-swept Plymouth just before Christmas to share in the three-hundredth anniversary of the Pilgrim landing.

It was a strong New England moment and Coolidge fitted curiously well into the ceremonies, muffled up in scarf and overcoat as he spoke. He was not feeling well and the weather was bitterly cold. But both were pleased with the letter that came from Mr. Stearns that Christmas. It contained a choice tribute to Grace: "You must have foreseen coming events fifteen years or more ago when you chose Mrs. Coolidge to be your helper in the work for others that you have done and are destined to do."

In the weeks between the election in November and inauguration day in March Mrs. Coolidge made preparations for the family move to Washington and ordered some clothes for the many functions she would now attend. She accompanied Calvin on several brief trips and was greeted everywhere as a person of some importance. They went to Montpelier, where he spoke before the Vermont Historical Society. They paid brief visits to New York and Atlanta, and then had two weeks of rest in the Grove Park Inn at Asheville, North Carolina. On the last day of February they set off for the capital, accompanied by Colonel Coolidge, the boys and Mr. and Mrs. Stearns.

The Marshalls met them at the station and Grace and Mrs. Marshall, a fellow Vermonter, established friendly relations at once. They found their suite at the New Willard buried in flowers and immediate social demands were made on them. Calvin worked calmly on his speech while his wife coped with a stream of callers. Mrs. Nickerson, present on this occasion, noted that she was just as easy with the first of the ambassadors to call as with a woman urging a charitable cause. "Mrs. Coolidge was her usual friendly self—poised, unaffected, perfectly natural," she observed. "Under any circumstances she approached people without any frills or affectations—no gush, no condescension."

Her wardrobe came under discussion the day before inauguration when the women reporters surrounded Mrs. Stearns and pressed her for facts.

"I'll show you," said Mrs. Stearns. "It's all here."

She went to a clothes closet and pulled out five or six dresses—a red homespun, four or five simple day frocks and one evening gown. The reporters were busy taking notes when Mrs. Coolidge appeared at the door of the suite. She saw her clothes spread out on the bed, with a group of strangers around them. For a moment her face was the picture of dismay. Then she laughed and joined the group.

"Goodness!" she exclaimed. "What's going on?"

"Do you like entertaining?" she was asked.

"We haven't entertained much," she replied. "We never could afford it, but I'm sure I shall enjoy it."

The Coolidges dined quietly in their suite on the night before inauguration, with all the social flurry of a changing administration swirling around them. From the moment they stepped off the train in Washington Grace was aware that they had shifted from state to national focus. The sight of the Capitol dome reminded her of Calvin's responsibilities. For the first time she would be steadily at his side to share in his official life. It was a fresh experience for her and she was keenly responsive to her new surroundings.

CHAPTER III

MIDNIGHT AT PLYMOUTH NOTCH

THE SKY WAS a brilliant blue, the air was tangy and the wind blustered around the Capitol when Warren G. Harding was sworn into office on March 4, 1921, as twenty-ninth President of the United States. Amplifiers carried his resonant voice to the fringes of the watching crowd. His silver hair and raven eyebrows, his handsome features and genial manner created a new Presidential image. The physical ruin of Woodrow Wilson was plain for all to see as he rode to the capital with Harding but could not share in the actual ceremonies. Champ Clark, former Speaker of the House, had died the day before.

The new President took the oath on the Bible used by George Washington in 1789. He called for a return to "normalcy," a word that slipped that day into the language of the period. The first to shake hands with him as he finished was Calvin Coolidge, who had already been sworn into office as Vice-President in the Senate Chamber, with his wife, his father and his two sons looking on. His was the briefest inaugural speech on record, delivered in a voice of startlingly nasal timbre. He described the Senate as a "citadel of liberty" for the constitutional structure of the United States. To onlookers he seemed slight and insignificant beside the massive and voluble Harding. The New York *Times* noted that he was "inducted with stately form" in the presence of a distinguished audience, with Harding applauding his speech from a big armchair in the Senate. But the *Daily Hampshire Gazette,* with New England restraint, disclosed that the Vice-President felt less important than on the day he was graduated from Black River Academy. He made no secret of the fact that he thought the ceremonies lacked order and unity by being held both outdoors and in, and he sharply reminded the awestruck that he had already taken a leading part in seven inaugurations.

Both Mrs. Harding and Mrs. Coolidge watched their husbands attentively throughout the ceremonies, conscious of the black-robed justices, the gold-braided diplomats, the representatives of the Army and Navy, the solemnity of the inaugural vows. John and Calvin sat with their mother, who looked around her with a radiant smile, and a faint suggestion of disbelief.

There were few bands and no parade for a war-weary generation and the crowds went home talking of the flatness of the occasion and the shocking appearance of Woodrow Wilson. Until they saw him riding beside the impressive figure of Warren Harding they had not realized how shattered he was. The full story of his incapacity was made public soon after that. Calvin Coolidge never saw him again except at a distance, although he received a sympathetic letter from him when he became President. "Such was the passing of a great world figure," he noted in his autobiography.

The day had begun for Mrs. Coolidge with breakfast at the New Willard with her husband, sons and Colonel Coolidge. It wound up with a dinner and ball at the home of Mr. and Mrs. Edward B. Mc-Lean, since President Harding had ruled out an inaugural ball that year. She suddenly found herself standing at the foot of a wide staircase in a historic mansion, being introduced officially to Washington society. Her hostess wore a Paris gown of brocaded white satin and Mrs. Coolidge had on what she later described as a simple dress made by a village dressmaker. But she enjoyed herself from the start. "It was all very gay and I had a wonderful time," she wrote.

General Pershing, the military hero of the hour, was her dinner companion and they found a common bond at once in their sons. "My training," she commented revealingly, "had been in the direction of avoiding subjects which dealt with matters in which public men were professionally engaged." Therefore neither one talked of military matters. The schools and interests of their growing sons kept them fully engaged. She was won by the General. He was won by her. "It has been my experience," she later recalled in talking of him, "that those who are truly great are the most simple people at heart, the most considerate and understanding, with a decided aversion to talking about themselves."

Mrs. Thomas R. Marshall, wife of the former Vice-President, took her in tow and introduced her to the ceremonial rites of the capital. She indicated the pitfalls, outlined the feuds, and showed her where it might be best to conform to custom. Mrs. Coolidge felt that she could not have had a more seasoned adviser and she always credited Mrs. Marshall with giving her the training that served her well when she found herself mistress of the White House. Mr. Marshall made no secret of the fact that being Vice-President was much like being in a cataleptic fit, conscious of all that was going on around one, yet without being able to move hand or foot. But there was no gainsaying the fact that the Vice-President and his wife had status on the social front and were invited to all the major events in the capital. Grace was quickly swept into a brisk whirl that did not confuse her in the least. When she gave her first reception it was noted that she "kept her wits at the end of her tongue" and was the "college type of woman." She was under keen and skeptical observation but she weathered the most jaundiced scrutiny.

The Vice-President had decided that they could not afford a house of their own on his salary of $12,000 a year, nor would he accept Frank Stearns' offer to give him one. "More hotel life, I suppose," Grace commented resignedly as they took up residence in the New Willard. But she soon gave the homelike touch to their suite of two bedrooms, dining room and reception room, and turned out chafing-dish suppers for the boys when they arrived from school. Joseph McInerney was their official chauffeur. Edward T. Clark, known to his friends as Ted, became Mr. Coolidge's secretary. He had filled the same role for Henry Cabot Lodge and had been recommended to the Vice-President by Mr. Stearns. Everything fell into place quite smoothly.

Mrs. Coolidge became president of the Senate Ladies Club founded by Mrs. Marshall originally for Red Cross work. She warmed up the Tuesday meetings with her frank and often witty approach to the day's events. No two women could have been more unlike than Mrs. Harding and Mrs. Coolidge, just as no two men could have differed more than their husbands. Mrs. Harding was the first woman voter to preside at the White House. She was also the first out-and-out politician, although other presidential wives had wielded influence in public affairs, including Mrs. William Howard Taft, who watched the initiation of Mrs. Harding and Mrs. Coolidge with considerable interest.

Both women had come from smaller towns and were alien to the hard drive and social maneuvering of life in the capital. Mrs. Harding was stilted in manner, unsure of herself, and could be strident and excitable at times. Like Mrs. Coolidge, she was modish and expertly groomed. Her silver hair was tightly marcelled. She ordered her clothes from New York *couturiers* and wore a black velvet band around her throat to hide the inroads of age. She lacked the unaffected amiability of the Vice-President's wife and had none of her husband's easy knack of making friends. He was quick to shake hands, to make promises, to play the good fellow. But onlookers soon suspected that she pulled political strings in the background.

On the surface she and Mrs. Coolidge had friendly relations but Mrs. Harding did not genuinely warm to the Vice-President or his wife. Her attitude toward them was crystallized in a chance remark she made in 1922. When Mrs. John B. Henderson, widow of a Missouri Senator, offered her house and grounds to the government as an official residence for the Vice-President, a bill went before Congress to accept the gift and make an appropriation for upkeep. Dr. Nicholas Murray Butler and his wife were guests at the White House while the matter was being debated. They expressed the hope that the bill would pass. Mrs. Harding showed great impatience and finally, according to Dr. Butler, "burst into flame and almost shouted,

'Not a bit of it, not a bit of it. I am going to have that bill defeated. Do you think I am going to have those Coolidges living in a house like that? An hotel apartment is plenty good enough for them.' " The bill was defeated but "those Coolidges" soon were residents of the White House itself.

Mrs. Coolidge had already felt the chill of Back Bay, even though she and her husband exemplified the best New England traditions of thrift and simple taste. In her early days in Washington there was some of the same hauteur among the sophisticates toward the austere Coolidges, and one New England hostess icily inquired: "How do you suppose they will adapt themselves to using an automobile?" But this point of view was lost in the chorus of approval when it became apparent to all that Mrs. Coolidge, although inexperienced, adapted herself easily to her new social setting.

She was wholly unconscious of any calculated coolness on Mrs. Harding's part as the new First Lady sought to banish the gloom and silence that had enveloped the White House during Woodrow Wilson's long illness. Flowers abounded everywhere. Bulbs were planted on the lawns. Birdhouses were installed in the trees. The doors were opened wide and the public was again drawn into the Executive Mansion. The Hardings held receptions almost daily. It was always Old Home Week as the smiling President and his noncommittal wife shook hands with an interminable stream of visitors.

The nation as a whole was relaxing in the freedom of its postwar mood. The days of stringency and sacrifice ostensibly were over. International issues were beating against the foundations of government, but the country still was isolationist in spirit. Calvin Coolidge gave much thought to these matters in his days as Vice-President. Aside from the social round, he had never had so much time to think, to read, to study, and many of the views that crystallized later in his acts and speeches were developing at this time. A parliamentarian at heart, he enjoyed presiding over the Senate in the early days of the Harding administration, although his intimates felt that he got bored as time went on. His functions in New England had been more potent, stimulating, and to his taste than the negative functions of the Vice-Presidency. But he traveled about, made speeches and was a silent onlooker at Cabinet conferences. His colleagues found him a good listener—a bystander on the political front.

All manner of demands were made on Mrs. Coolidge—for teas, benefits, balls, receptions, dinners and concerts. She went to Mrs. Henderson's weekly dancing class and enjoyed the tea dances that Mrs. Thomas F. Walsh gave in her ballroom. Her own parties drew a thousand callers at a time and she wrote blithely to the Robins that anyone was free to come to her At Homes and some odd ones turned up from time to time—"a few draw a chair right up to the tea table and proceed to make a 'square meal.' "

But the Coolidges relished the natural touch and were on guard from the start for any touch of the snobbishness that they abhorred. When they were invited to dinner by someone not in the *Social Register* Mr. Coolidge drawled: "No conclusion can be drawn from that. I have been in it myself only half an hour." Mrs. Coolidge dined out nearly every night, sat beside the celebrity of the hour, chatted with diplomats and politicians, observed the frills and frivolities of an extravagant era, and sometimes rescued her husband from social gaffes. The Vice-President did his best to maintain his ten o'clock bedtime and he would drag Grace away from functions regardless of how much she seemed to be enjoying herself.

The Senate ladies soon learned that Mrs. Coolidge liked to come to functions early and stay late, but that when ten o'clock struck and Calvin announced "Grace, we're leaving," she made her getaway as fast as she could, so as not to keep him waiting. On one occasion when she stayed late at a tea he telephoned her at the house she was visiting. "Grace," he said, "I've come home. You come home, too." Six o'clock was her deadline for teas.

His early bedtime eventually caught the fancy of the nation's comedians and cartoonists, so that later Groucho Marx, appearing in *Animal Crackers* in Washington strode to the front of the stage and looked straight at President Coolidge, who was seated in a box.

"Isn't it past your bedtime, Calvin?" he quipped.

The orchestra conductor thought that he saw the President smile. Assuredly Mrs. Coolidge must have laughed. He was equally peremptory when it came to early rising. When President Wilson landed in Boston after attending the Peace Conference Governor Coolidge burst into the bedroom where his wife and Mrs. Hills were sound asleep and barked "Get up" at them. The day's ceremonies had been pushed forward by two hours and he wanted to be sure that his womenfolk did not create any delay or complications.

For one who had held himself so aloof from the social scene Calvin Coolidge went through his paces as Vice-President with a willingness that surprised Grace. Within two weeks of inauguration day she wrote to Mr. Stearns: "All goes well here. Calvin was saying tonight that he had felt very well since he came so I think he feels that the climate here agrees with him. He is becoming quite a 'social butterfly.' (Of course I do not speak so disrespectfully of him except in the 'heart of the family')."

Mrs. Coolidge was then preparing to receive the Diplomatic Corps, a major ordeal, but she was in high spirits. Forsythia had just begun to bloom, she wrote, and she was eagerly awaiting the blossoming of the Japanese cherry trees. Always responsive to nature, she was alert to the rush of early spring that gave the capital its annual touch of magic. In April she was hostess at a "most alarming reception," she wrote to Foster Stearns, son of Frank Stearns. "I'll never dare to be 'at home' again for fear somebody will be crushed to death. Calvin says we'll serve tea on the sidewalk next time. Well, why not? If Mrs. Harding has garden parties why shouldn't I have sidewalk parties?"

Mrs. Coolidge found the garden parties entrancing, with women in diaphanous gowns strolling against a background of boxwood hedges and blossoming rambler roses, the Marine Band a circle of scarlet, blue and gold, and the fountain shedding a curved diamond spray. A "small dinner" given in her honor by Mrs. McLean at Friendship caused a stir and she wrote to the Robins that they had a "real thrill" when the film of the Dempsey-Carpentier fight was flashed on a movie screen out on the lawn. The moon was up. Fountains played nearby. The music of the 1920s whined through the groups of guests who roamed over the terrace and lawn.

However, it soon was apparent to the more worldly hostesses that the new Vice-President was a dead weight at the dinner table. One guest after another complained of the lengthy silences, the lack of small talk, the absolute impossibility of breaking through his glacial reserve. One flippant hostess was much quoted for her bon mot that every time he opened his mouth a moth flew out. Another spread the news that he would talk about Vermont, if nothing else, and those who were eager to please promptly primed themselves on the politics and vegetation of his native state. Mrs. Frances Parkinson Keyes, wife of Senator Henry W. Keyes of New Hampshire, did not find it difficult to talk to Calvin Coolidge. Acknowledging that he had no small talk and was impatient with persiflage she found him discursive on education and current literature.

Mrs. Coolidge had long ago learned that the best way to cover up her husband's social deficiencies was to laugh about them, and this she did, freely and often, in the Vice-Presidential days. She would have saved him from embarrassment if she could, but since Calvin was an individualist immune to social guidance she turned them to excellent account and helped along the growing legend of his aloofness. She liked to tell the story of his encounter with an important hostess who opened their dinner-table conversation with a direct challenge:

"You must talk to me, Mr. Coolidge. I made a bet today that I could get more than two words out of you."

"You lose," said the Vice-President with a poker face, and let it go at that.

It was noted that the Coolidges never turned down an invitation and when asked about this the Vice-President snapped: "Got to eat somewhere." But the varied menus played havoc with his delicate digestion, and on one occasion he remarked: "Sometimes I don't know whether I'm having food or soda mints, I have to mix the two so often." In the May following inauguration he was quite ill and "would hardly let me out of the room in which he was sitting for three days," Grace wrote to Mr. Stearns.

Mrs. Stearns had sent her a copy of Lytton Strachey's *Queen Victoria* "because she thought it ought to be seen upon my table." Mrs. Coolidge took another view of this. "I thought a book that was as good as that might bear reading and it is very much worth while," she wrote to the Robins. She had not read *The Sheik,* she added, but she had seen the film and liked it. She urged them all to read *The Career of David Noble* by Mrs. Keyes. It interested her particularly because David had begun his career on a Vermont farm. The Senate ladies were all chattering about Mrs. Keyes' *Letters of a Senator's Wife,* then running serially in *Good Housekeeping.* When it came out in book form Mrs. Coolidge was guest of honor at a Women's National Press Club party but although they had been close friends in the Vice-Presidential days she chilled off to Mrs. Keyes when she moved into the White House.

Mrs. Coolidge was instinctively averse to publicity of any kind and she had been coached not to play favorites among the women writers. "It has been my unbroken policy not to see newspaper writers or give interviews to anyone," she wrote to Mrs. Hills in the later days of the Coolidge administration. "At the word interview spoken or written my ears go up and my chin out." But the Keyes boys, Henry and John, continued to see a good deal of John and Calvin Coolidge, sitting with them in the President's box at matinees and seeing movie previews at the White House. Mrs. Keyes' admiration for Mrs. Coolidge remained undiminished and in later years she wrote of her:

> She gave everyone a sense of ease and enjoyment because she was so richly endowed with *joie de vivre* herself. I doubt if any Vice-Presidential hostess has ever wrung so much pleasure out of Washington or given so much in return. Everybody liked her, and because she went everywhere and did everything she became a familiar as well as a popular figure. She is the one woman in official life of whom I have never heard a single disparaging remark in the course of nearly twenty years.

With the shift to Washington the Coolidges gave careful thought to schools for their sons. Phillips Andover, the Hill School and the Kent School came under discussion but Dr. Joel Boone, White House physician, tipped the scales in favor of Mercersburg Academy. Mr. Stearns offered to send the boys to camp that summer but their father wanted them to go to Plymouth, as usual. However, they visited the Stearns family for a few days early in July, taking Jack Hills with them. Mr. Stearns wrote enthusiastically to Mrs. Coolidge about the boys and she replied in modest vein: "Jack Hills is certainly a fine boy and I think myself that John and Calvin do pretty well considering how they have had to get along." To the Robins she wrote: "It is only ninety-eight miles from Mercersburg to Washington so I can get at them once in a while. The hardest thing for me in going to Washington was seeing less of my boys and this plan seemed the best that could be worked out. We shall keep our home in Northampton open."

Mrs. Coolidge paid a brief visit to Northampton early that summer and went downtown marketing with Mrs. Hills, as of old. She was glad to be back in New England. "I love every stick and stone," she wrote. *Mrs. Coolidge, Unchanged, Finds It Good to Be Home* ran a headline in the local paper. Full of pride in his wife the Vice-President wrote to his father at this time: "Grace is home as you may know from the papers. She is wonderfully popular here. I don't know what I would do without her."

She shared in the impressive ceremonies at Arlington when the Unknown Soldier was laid to rest in the great mausoleum in November, 1921. A faint haze dissolved into brilliant sunshine as she looked around her from the platform where she stood with President Harding, her husband and Mrs. Harding. Ropes of laurel looped to the fluted columns of the amphitheater were linked with the wreaths of every state, each containing a leaf of solid gold. After the trumpet sounded, two minutes of silence initiated a national custom. "I think the two-minute period of silence and bowed heads was the most impressive single event of the whole day," Mrs. Coolidge wrote to the Robins, "especially when I realized that all over this great land of ours people were standing thus. Never have I experienced such a long two minutes."

Attentively she watched the foreign decorations being pinned to the casket cover. Admiral Beatty alone said nothing, saluting in silence as he laid down the Victoria Cross and a sheaf of palms and lilies. General Jules Jacques, defender of Dixmude, in an impassioned gesture as he thought of stricken Belgium, tore the Medal of Valor from his tunic and added it to the other decorations. Mrs. Coolidge thought that the American Indians made a touching picture as they stood in a little group by themselves while their leader laid down his totem pole and his "wonderful war bonnet."

She observed that Woodrow Wilson looked better than he had on inauguration day, and that President Harding was almost late for the ceremonies because of the traffic jam. He arrived greatly perturbed and admitted afterward to her that he "used language which was not for publication." She liked him greatly at this time. "He is a dear and so human!" she wrote.

Almost from the start Mrs. Coolidge found herself in conversation with the statesmen and warriors of the world. The leaders of nine nations assembled in Washington for the Conference on the Limitation of Armaments in the winter of 1921-1922. Briand, Foch, Beatty, Balfour—great names of the war—one after another became living persons to her in the receiving line and at the dinner table. She attended the first and the third of the plenary sessions, sitting in a box with Mrs. Harding and Madame Jusserand, both stiff as pokers. Alice Longworth ripped off her mushroom hat with zest the minute she was seated and Madame Wellington Koo surprised them all by vanishing for a few days and returning completely *soignée* in her Chinese gown and sable cloak, having given birth to a baby in the interim.

One day Grace was so late leaving the New Willard that she arrived at Continental Hall without her ticket. She announced that she was Mrs. Coolidge.

The doorman looked blank. "What's your husband's first name?"

"Calvin."

"What's his business?"

"He's Vice-President."

"Vice-President of what?"

The President's reception on New Year's Day, 1922, was particularly brilliant, with the delegates to the Arms Conference investing it with special interest. Pink rose bushes and ferns banked the staircase. Autumn leaves and palms made flaming patterns in the East Room. Pink carnations abounded and old-fashioned frilled bouquets gave a period touch to the Blue Room. Whenever Mrs. Coolidge shared in events of more than ordinary interest she incorporated full accounts of what went on in her Round Robin letters. She wrote of sitting beside Arthur Balfour at dinner and enjoying his sense of humor. Both Lord Beatty and he had persuaded her that the English did not lack this quality. But René Viviani was "always disgruntled about something and then peeved because nobody cared."

He baldly told one hostess that she had too much to eat. At one dinner he sat between Alice Longworth and Mrs. Minot, who is Senator Lodge's granddaughter, and they tried their best to be nice to him and interest him and he acted like a spoiled child. Mrs. Minot asked him, in French, of course, since he does not speak English and has no patience with anyone who does not speak French, if he was amusing himself in America and he replied that he did not come to America to amuse himself. Lord Beatty said that the retort courteous to that would have been "Nor anybody else either." . . . Gathered together about the table are these men of affairs governmental of whom we have all read and talked since we can remember and one feels oneself highly privileged to be able to sit and study these people all at once at such close range and later to sit next them at dinner and find they have a delightful sense of humor and are just folks with the rest of us.

Mrs. Coolidge, who dined with Calvin in the Senate restaurant during the Four Power Treaty debates in the Senate and then sat in the gallery listening afterward, was sorry to see the delegates go. "It is said that Mr. Balfour, now Sir Arthur, has become so Americanized that they do not like it very well at home," she wrote to the Robins. "He says 'Sure,' just as if he were one of us. Well, any time they want to kick him out we will be only too glad to take him on."

She was uncommonly scathing about Mrs. Herbert Asquith and her lecture tour. Her name should be "Ego not Margot," she wrote. In particular, Margot's comments on President Harding offended the wife of the Vice-President. After a visit to the White House the Englishwoman remarked that his education left much to be desired. She was reminded by a fellow guest that he was a college graduate. "With a toss of her head," Mrs. Coolidge wrote, "she discounted that, saying—'Oh, your American colleges.' " On the whole, she was glad that she had neither met Margot Asquith nor listened to her lecture. She warned the Robins not to read *I Have Only Myself to Blame* by Princess Bibesco, Margot's daughter.

Mrs. Coolidge stood in the East Room as Madame Curie, small, shy and speaking perfect English, received her precious gram of radium from President Harding. Mrs. Coolidge warmly clasped her hand and studied with interest the woman scientist who was helping to shape history. She was a striking figure at a dinner given for Madame Curie in New York. Mrs. Coolidge was always pleased to catch a passing glimpse of the metropolis and she enjoyed its soaring excitement. The postwar building boom was under way. The air was electric. Uniforms were everywhere. The shops were filled with glittering baubles. Women wore deep turbans, black satin coats and neat little Eton suits such as she had sported when Calvin was courting her in Northampton.

The elder John D. Rockefeller had just given Herbert Hoover two million dollars for his relief work in Europe. Judge Elbert H. Gary was denying that there was profiteering in steel. For the first time in history the United States was a creditor nation. And people of Irish descent in America were stirred up over the Sinn Fein agitation in Ireland. Caruso had just undergone a serious operation. Rachmaninoff was playing at Carnegie Hall. Pavlova was dancing at the Manhattan Opera House and Walter Damrosch was waving his baton over the New York Symphony Orchestra. The names of Gigli, Heifetz, Homer, Galli-Curci, Mary Garden, Geraldine Farrar, Alma Gluck and Zimbalist all were on the billboards and Toscanini was working magic with the La Scala Orchestra at the Hippodrome.

The 1921-1922 social season in Washington had just got under way when one of the worst disasters in the history of the capital took place. A great snowstorm had lashed the city for twenty-eight hours, leaving twenty-nine inches of snow behind it. Suddenly the roof of the Knickerbocker Theater, strained beyond capacity, collapsed, bringing down the balconies. Ninety-five died in the ruins and the city was plunged into gloom and mourning. The White House canceled all social engagements for a week.

Actors everywhere were moved by this disaster. It was an era when Doris Keane was playing in *Romance.* Laurette Taylor was plucking the strings of sentiment in *Peg O' My Heart.* Marilyn Miller as *Sally* was enchanting audiences at the New Amsterdam Theater. Ina Claire was young and provocative in *The Gold Diggers.* Lionel Barrymore was playing *Macbeth.* George Arliss was in *The Green Goddess* and Holbrook Blinn was having a lusty success with *The Bad Man.* Summer brought *Abie's Irish Rose,* which opened to poor notices and ran for the next five years. Will Hays was appointed czar of the cinema world as Hollywood and sin became synonymous terms, with the murder of William Desmond Taylor and the Roscoe Arbuckle scandal cornering headlines.

President Harding practiced golf shots on the White House grounds with Laddie Boy, his airedale, retrieving the balls. Coolidge tried the game a little later but decided that it took too much time and callers at the White House might wonder why the President was not on the job. Bill Tilden, Little Bill Johnston and other tennis stars appeared from time to time on the White House courts. Ring Lardner and Grantland Rice were entertained by the Hardings and Broadway stars came and went at random.

As Mrs. Coolidge's popularity in Washington increased, the wear and tear of official life, or perhaps the boredom of his minor duties, began to tell on her husband by the spring of 1922. He was depressed over criticism coming from Massachusetts. The Lodge and Coolidge factions were at odds and he was deeply wounded over attempts to undermine him. "I do not understand the attitude of certain persons in Boston," he wrote to Mr. Stearns. "I supposed I was here keeping quiet and doing what I could without harming anyone."

His Boston friend warned him bluntly that he should show more cordiality to the electorate. He must make people feel that he was interested in them and "I know you are," Stearns wrote, adding: "Why not be glad to see folks, let them know that you are glad to see them and try for six months to take it for granted that just plain common folks, the backbone of the country, feel it an honor to meet the Vice-President of the United States."

Plainly Coolidge was feeling restless in his secondary role. Mr.

Stearns had many talks with Mrs. Coolidge on this particular subject. Both understood the importance of warming up the electorate but Calvin answered tartly on this occasion: "I do not think you have any comprehension of what people do to me. Even small things bother me." But big and evil things were going on behind the scenes, too, and none close to the Harding administration could be dead to the growing air of uneasiness and suspicion that enveloped the Cabinet. Whatever Calvin Coolidge may have heard or observed of the subterranean scandals that exploded after Warren Harding's death he was too discreet to mention. Although he rarely shared in Cabinet discussions he listened attentively and was never absent from meetings. When the corruption was aired in the early days of his own administration he stood aloof from it all and never disclosed what he may have thought or heard of the machinations of the men close to Harding. Nor did either of the Coolidges ever share in the gossip that swept over Washington about the heavy drinking, dissolute habits and poker playing for high stakes indulged in by some of the men closest to Harding. They went their way quietly and minded their own business.

By the end of 1922 it was apparent to all that President Harding had changed. He looked ill and haggard. His eyes were sunken. His easy affability had a hollow note. Mrs. Harding, too, had been ill. With only one kidney her health was comparatively poor and the President had done some worrying about her, but Calvin Coolidge wrote to Mr. Stearns on November 18, 1922: "Mrs. Harding is resting better and he is much encouraged about her."

The Vice-President took Harding's place in delivering the budget address that winter. When the House recessed in March the Coolidges went to White Sulphur Springs for a few days of sunshine, then returned to Massachusetts. Mrs. Coolidge was greatly worried about her father at this time. She had made a quick trip to Burlington in February when she learned that he was seriously ill. He died at the end of April and Calvin and she went north for his funeral. Grace hid her desolation in the days that followed. Her father had never ceased to be a much loved figure in her life.

The scandals of the administration were about to explode in the open when the President left in June, 1923, for a trip to Alaska. Albert B. Fall, Secretary of the Interior, ultimately convicted in 1929 for accepting a bribe in the Teapot Dome oil scandal during the Harding regime, had quietly resigned. Colonel Charles R. Forbes, head of the Veterans Bureau, had been sent abroad on an official mission, with the understanding that he, too, would bow out. When the Senate began its investigation Charles F. Cramer, the Bureau's legal adviser, killed himself. The news reached President Harding in Florida in March and Colonel Starling watched him turn ashen as he read the letter. Jess Smith, Attorney General Harry M. Daugherty's handy man who was deeply involved with lobbyists and fixers, was another suicide as the air thickened around the White House. After that the President's decline seemed rapid. The ripples were widening around him. Mrs. Harding insisted on accompanying him on his trip to Alaska. He felt depressed and made his will before leaving. Coolidge, who had observed him closely throughout, left his own brief estimate of the situation in his autobiography:

We left the President and Mrs. Harding in Washington. I do not know what had impaired his health. I do know that the weight of the Presidency is very heavy. Later it was disclosed that he had discovered that some whom he had trusted had betrayed him and he had been forced to call them to account. It is known that this discovery was a very heavy grief to him, perhaps more than he could bear. I never saw him again. In June he started for Alaska and—eternity.

That same month Coolidge broke ground for a new chapel at Mercersburg Academy. He urged honesty, obedience, industry, thrift and faith on the students, among whom were his own two sons. He and Grace attended the Centennial Celebration at Amherst, the most notable occasion in the history of the college. They went to the Devon Horse Show in Philadelphia where Calvin insisted on having Grace with him in the enclosure, contrary to form. It was remarked at this time that he refused to let her out of his sight.

In July they settled at Plymouth for their customary rest in the mountains. Their sons joined them and helped Colonel Coolidge on the farm. The radical press at this time was belaboring the Vice-

President as a picayune man, a midget statesman, a politician with an "icy hand and a heart of stone." There were others who already recognized him as a personality on the national scene, and his wife's smiling face had become familiar from coast to coast. News of the President's trip to Alaska came over the wires but it took time to penetrate Plymouth Notch. The Coolidges were cut off from the world. They had no telephone. The newspapers arrived a day or two late. It was some time before they learned the details of his grueling trip, the speeches delivered in the burning sun, his sleepless nights and restless pacing about, his frenzied bridge playing and nervous manifestations. Toward the end of July he became ill in Alaska and he blamed his indisposition on tainted crab. He was in poor condition all the way to San Francisco and there he developed bronchial pneumonia.

The seriousness of his illness was conveyed to the Coolidges by reporters who had gathered at nearby Ludlow, to be on hand for any emergency. By this time George B. Christian, Harding's secretary, was also sending them news of Harding's condition. Telegraphic messages had to be relayed through the post office. Because he had not seen the Sunday papers it was July 31 before the Vice-President fully apprehended the situation. But he expressed confidence then that Harding would recover and he told the visiting reporters: "It is my opinion that he is the truest friend that our country has."

On August 2 the papers reported that although the President's pneumonia had been checked and he was rallying from a slight case of indigestion he would be an invalid for a considerable period. He had five physicians in attendance, including Dr. Boone. On that same day John Foster Dulles came in from Europe on the *Majestic*. He was then a member of the Reparations Commission and expressed pessimism over France's ability to pay her war debts to the Allies. Fifteen thousand aliens had arrived at Ellis Island on sixteen liners, in an effort to beat the quotas.

And Calvin Coolidge, on his remote farm, helped a neighbor, D. P. Brown, finish his haying by awkwardly operating a horse rake. His wife took her usual daily walk, helped Aurora Pierce in the kitchen, and did some reading during the hot August afternoon. The clapboard homestead gleamed white in the sunshine and Aurora's geraniums gave it a dash of color. John and Calvin had just left in the car with Joe McInerney, the family chauffeur, John to do military service at Camp Devens, Calvin to work on the tobacco farm of Dickinson and Day at Hatfield, Massachusetts.

The Coolidges retired at nine o'clock that night, believing that all was well with the President. The latest word had been reassuring. The valley lay in the deep stillness of a hot summer night. But Warren Harding was already dead in the Palace Hotel in San Francisco. His wife had been reading to him Samuel G. Blythe's piece in the *Saturday Evening Post* entitled "A Calm View of a Calm Man." It was about the President. He was enjoying it and was urging her to read on when suddenly he shuddered and fell back on his pillow dead. Confused and contradictory reports followed about the exact manner of his death, but the medical verdict was an apoplectic stroke.

The focus of political interest quickly shifted to the lonely farmhouse at Plymouth. Close to midnight a car came whizzing up the roadway from Bridgewater and stopped at the Coolidge house. The Colonel, who slept downstairs, opened the door and was handed a message by W. A. Perkins, a telegraph operator, who could not refrain from telling him the news it contained. For once the Colonel was shaken. He hurried up the stairs, calling his son's name and urging him to get up. Calvin came to life at once, knowing from the trembling note in his father's voice that the President must be dead. Later he wrote: "As the only times I had ever observed that before were when death had visited our family, I knew that something of the gravest nature had occurred."

The Colonel read aloud George Christian's simple announcement that the President was dead. Mrs. Coolidge wept quietly. Before going downstairs both she and Calvin knelt and prayed. In his own words he "asked God to bless the American people and give me power to serve them." He carefully selected a black sack suit and black tie to wear. Grace donned a black and white dress and white shoes and stockings, for she was already in mourning for her father. By this time a second car had arrived from Bridgewater and Joe McInerney, back from leaving the Coolidge boys at their destinations, stepped into the house in time to see Calvin Coolidge coming slowly down the stairs and to detect the tears that still ran down his wife's cheeks as she followed him. Joe had picked up a message from the telephone outside his hotel room in Bridgewater and had started off posthaste for the Notch with Erwin C. Geisser, the Vice-President's stenographer, and William H. Crawford, a newspaperman. They arrived almost as soon as Perkins, and Geisser handed Coolidge a message from Christian.

Mrs. Coolidge fetched an oil lamp and her husband sat down at the table and carefully studied the message he had received. His first thought was to send off a telegram to Mrs. Harding which read: "We offer you our deepest sympathy. May God bless and keep you. Calvin Coolidge. Grace Coolidge." By this time the outside world had already begun to batter at their door as cars converged from Bridgewater, Woodstock and Ludlow. The difference in time between the East and West coasts and the lack of a telephone at the Coolidge house had caused obstruction and delay. Christian's messages came over the wire to White River Junction and were telephoned from there to Bridgewater.

A carful of reporters next drove over from Ludlow and Congressman Porter Dale came speeding in from Springfield with L. L. Lane, a Vermont mail official, Joseph H. Fountain, the twenty-two-year-old editor of the *Reporter* of Springfield, Vermont, and Herbert P. Thompson, an American Legion Commander from Springfield. The Congressman was deeply concerned because the United States for the moment was without a President. He kept emphasizing the emergency. But Calvin Coolidge and his father soon saw to that.

"Father, you are still a notary?" Calvin asked.

"Yes," said the Colonel.

"Then I want you to administer the oath."

The Colonel took his mug and went off to the kitchen to shave. The news spread fast that things were happening at the Coolidge place. The valley quickly came to life. Oil lamps were lighted all through the rolling green hills. The warm summer night was charged with excitement. But events moved inexorably in the little farmhouse, without hesitation on the part of Calvin Coolidge or his father.

McInerney went to the nearby store to waken Miss Cilley, whose telephone would be needed. It was the only one in the valley. Then Mr. Coolidge walked over and put in a call for Harry M. Daugherty, the Attorney General, for advice as to the oath. He could not reach him at once, but soon Daugherty called back. Charles Evans Hughes, Secretary of State, next gave him advice as to what he should do. Both thought that no time should be lost. But the Colonel had done some exploring on his own account in the Constitution of the United States. He found the precise wording of the oath but no guidance as to who should administer it. However, his son had made his decision. In later years Colonel Coolidge was asked, "How did you know you could administer the Presidential oath to your own son?" He replied: "I didn't know that I couldn't."

While messages were going back and forth on the national front and preparations were being made for the ceremony Mr. Coolidge busied himself dictating a statement to Geisser. Grace had brought a second lamp from their room so that he could work with his secretary in the adjoining parlor, a room with horsehair furniture and a piano where the Colonel sometimes held church services. Meanwhile she seated herself on the arm of the rocking chair in the sitting room and spoke softly of Mrs. Harding. "She bears up wonderfully well under difficulties," she said. "She will need all her courage now."

Suddenly her husband appeared in the door with the sheets. She sorted them out, arranged them in order and handed them to the waiting reporters who quickly absorbed the text:

> Reports have reached me, which I fear are correct, that President Harding is gone. The world has lost a great and good man. I mourn his loss. He was my Chief and friend.
>
> It will be my purpose to carry out his policies which he has begun for the service of the American people and for meeting their responsibilities wherever they may arise.
>
> For this purpose I shall seek the cooperation of all those who have been associated with the President during his term of office. Those who have given their efforts to assist him I wish to remain in office that they may assist me. I have faith that God will direct the destinies of our nation.

The reporters raced off with this statement and missed the actual ceremony itself, except for Joseph Fountain, whose story was carried by the Associated Press. Soon an emergency telephone line was installed on the front porch, with wires running into the kitchen through an open window. The instrument was placed on a chair, since the Colonel had no intention of having a telephone in the house once the immediate crisis was over.

The swearing-in scene caught the imagination of the American public as it reached them in detail through the press. It was Americana of the simplest and most dramatic kind—a few minutes of intense drama, without precedence or artifice. A son of New England taking the Presidential oath by the light of an oil lamp in a farmhouse, with his father swearing him in, and his wife by his side. The room in which the oath was taken was called the sitting room and later it became known as the Oath of Office room. It was charged with memories for Calvin Coolidge. His sister Abigail and his stepmother had died in it. His own mother had rested there during most of her invalid years, although she had died in the adjoining room.

It was seventeen by fourteen feet, and had three bay windows, a door opening on the porch and another leading to the kitchen. It was only eight feet high. The wallpaper was faded. The Wilton rug was threadbare. It had a large wood stove with a pipe running along the ceiling, a rocker, two straight chairs and the desk on which Coolidge wrote a prize-winning essay on the causes of the American Revolution during his senior year at Amherst.

No American woman had ever shared in a parallel scene and Grace Coolidge fully realized the solemnity of the moment but kept her presence of mind. It was she who placed the lamp on the center table beside the Bible that had belonged to Calvin's mother, and set the stage for the simple ceremony. She went thoughtfully about her tasks, her eyes still large and melancholy with the aftermath of tears. When all was in readiness Calvin and his father faced each other, two men endowed with simple dignity. Mrs. Coolidge stood at her husband's right, a little behind him, and Congressman Dale, tall and imposing-looking, faced him across the table. Lane, Geisser, McInerney and Fountain completed the group of witnesses, their faces thrown into faint relief by lamplight. Although the Bible lay on the table it was not officially used, since Calvin knew that it was not the practice in Vermont or Massachusetts to swear on the Bible in administering an oath.

Grace's face was pale and solemn as the Colonel read the oath and his son repeated it with hand upraised, adding after a pause: "So help me God." The time was 2:47 A.M. The United States had its thirtieth President. The Colonel affixed the seal and Calvin turned to Grace. They exchanged a long look. The President said "Good night" to the waiting group and the Coolidges retired for the night without another word. The President went back to bed and later said that he promptly fell asleep. But the Colonel roamed about, stirred out of his native reserve by the night's events. His son was the sixth Vice-President to attain office through a President's death. The others were John Tyler, Millard Fillmore, Andrew Johnson, Chester Arthur and Theodore Roosevelt.

No one was more conscious of the drama of the event at the time than Mrs. Coolidge. It was an awe-inspiring thought that she now was the wife of the President of the United States. In after years both Mr. and Mrs. Coolidge were sometimes asked how they felt on that historic night. Mrs. Coolidge always recalled her faith in Calvin, her deep sense of the responsibilities ahead, and her sympathy for Mrs. Harding.

"I thought I could swing it," the President told Charles Sydney Hopkinson in jest when the question was put to him. The artist happened to be painting his portrait at the time and he hoped to strike a spark in Coolidge's unresponsive face. But a deeper emotion comes to light in his autobiography. It pleased him to think that his father was the first to address him as President of the United States. "It was the culmination of the lifelong desire of a father for the success of his son," he wrote. "I do not know of any other case in history where a father has administered to his son the qualifying oath of office which made him the chief magistrate of a nation. It seemed a simple and natural thing to do at the time, but I can now realize something of the dramatic force of the event."

Whatever elation his father may have felt about the night's events he weighed his words cautiously to the reporters who soon closed in on him. He conceded that he thought Calvin would do fairly well. He was no genius, he said, but just an average country boy who did not care too much for play. He fished in the rocky brooks near his home, went to husking bees, watched the sap being drawn from the maple trees and celebrated his birthday with a picnic. "I think of him just as a good and honest boy, who will do his best with any job given him," the Colonel remarked judicially. "He always has been that way and I guess he always will be. A trusty kind of a boy who always attended to whatever he had in hand."

The question of awakening Aurora had arisen during the night but Mr. Coolidge said: "Let her sleep. She will need to be up early to get us our breakfast. She will have a busy day tomorrow." Aurora, who had to pass through the Coolidge bedroom in order to get downstairs in the morning, was stunned to find that the man peacefully asleep had become President of the United States overnight without her knowledge or participation. However, she quickly put together a hearty breakfast of bacon, potatoes, rolls, coffee and doughnuts. The President had his regular dish of cereal and by seven thirty they were on their way to a new life, a new world.

As they were leaving the farmhouse the President noticed that one of the stone steps leading to the porch had been knocked out of place. "Better have that fixed, Father," he advised. Mrs. Coolidge kissed the Colonel affectionately and said: "You'll come to Washington." He went straight back to his farm chores as the car drove off. As they turned on to the main road the President asked Joe to stop at the cemetery and not to let anyone approach them. He and Grace walked up to the family graves and bowed their heads in prayer. In his own words:

When I started for Washington that morning I turned aside from the main road to make a short devotional visit to the grave of my mother. It had been a comfort to me during my boyhood when I was troubled to be near her last resting place, even in the dead of night. Some way, that morning, she seemed very near to me.

"Drive carefully," the President warned Joe as the car got under way again. It was fortunate that he did, for five miles along the road a pig ran in front of them. Joe slammed on the brakes and missed the pig, but skidded a few feet. Mrs. Coolidge later cited this incident as proof of his skillful driving. They were half way to Rutland to catch their train when the Secret Service men drove up and accompanied them the rest of the way. The President had declined the offer of a special train to take him to Washington but used a private car instead.

By this time the nation had wakened up to a realization of the fact that Harding was dead and Coolidge was President. John got the news at camp and young Calvin learned of it as he set out for his day's work bundling tobacco leaves and putting them on lathes to dry. He was earning $3.50 a day and was working hard. When he arrived at the farm his employer said to him: "Well, think of it, you are the son of the President of the United States."

Young Calvin quietly responded: "Yes, sir. Which barn do you want this tobacco put in?"

The boys were not summoned to Washington for Harding's funeral or the events that followed. The public caught only a glimpse of Mr. and Mrs. Coolidge as they drove from Grand Central to the Pennsylvania Station on their way through New York. Mr. and Mrs. Stearns had joined them en route. They reached Washington after nine o'clock on a stifling August evening and were met at the station by Charles Evans Hughes and Postmaster General Harry S. New, among others. By this time the Harding funeral train was on its way across the continent. At every stopping place crowds gathered and at many points groups of Masons in full dress uniform sang *Lead Kindly Light* and other hymns in low, rolling tones. Mrs. Harding asked that the train travel slowly through Ohio, with many stops. They reached Washington on August 7 and Warren Harding lay in state first at the White House, then at the Capitol. The Marine Band played for the slow procession along Pennsylvania Avenue and school children tossed flowers in the street as they sang *Nearer My God to Thee*. A day of mourning was declared throughout the nation. Governor Alfred E. Smith called Harding a "noble type." Henry

Cabot Lodge described him as a "thorough American" and Calvin Coolidge recalled him as a "high-minded man of distinguished ability, clear-sighted, wise and courageous."

Chief Justice Taft wrote to his wife that Calvin Coolidge seemed "cool and self-possessed" in the midst of all the ceremonies. He accompanied him to the station when the funeral train arrived. Hughes told Taft as they rode back together from the station that he would not run for the Presidency under any circumstances. They discussed Harding and Coolidge, and Hughes pointed out that Coolidge had never failed to attend a Cabinet meeting and was well primed on the details of the executive branch. He described Mrs. Harding as an able woman and marveled that Harding had withstood the wear and tear of such long stretches "of work or exercise or social enjoyment to the 'wee sma' hours.' " Taft thought that Harry Daugherty looked sick. In his opinion it would have been wise for him to resign, but he did not think that he would.

On the day of the funeral Woodrow Wilson was unable to get out of his car either at the Capitol or at the White House. Mrs. Harding and her party left that night for Marion after impressive services in the rotunda. The Coolidges followed next day, accompanied by Taft and various members of the Cabinet. Going out to Marion the officials were all invited into the Presidential car to pay their respects to the President and Mrs. Coolidge. "As I had no office to seek I kissed her hand to show my foreign training and she did not seem to dislike it," Taft noted in a letter to his wife on August 11, 1923. "I told her that I thought there would be no suspicion of an impression of a spirit of royalty in the function because of that. *She is very nice.*"

Already the politicians were speculating on the likelihood of Coolidge's nomination. The feeling was strong that the Republican regulars would support him in the convention against Hiram Johnson. Taft noticed both Ford and Edison at the funeral. "Of course Ford came to advertise himself," he informed his wife. "A funeral or a joke book are all the same to him."

The weather was insufferably hot when they reached Marion and were driven to the home of Dr. George T. Harding, father of the dead President. All the windows were closed and Taft expected someone to faint. As it was, Harry Daugherty collapsed suddenly into a chair. Mrs. Coolidge stood close to Mrs. Harding in the stuffy little room and Taft noted that the widow "bore up wonderfully, indeed, she directed everything." She shook hands with everyone present.

The funeral cortege moved slowly through the streets of Marion on the way to the cemetery. Thousands stood in silence as it passed familiar landmarks and particularly the office of Harding's paper *The Star,* where his wife had once been his assistant and had bicycled daily to work. At the cemetery Coolidge stood beside Taft, who had been President a dozen years earlier. Together they bowed their heads as taps was sounded. Mrs. Harding stepped into the mausoleum and after a while came out, dry-eyed. "Her face was lifted, and her eyes shone with a light I had not seen in them before," Colonel Starling observed. "She walked away, and the others followed her."

The Coolidges returned to the New Willard to give Mrs. Harding time to leave the White House. They were instantly caught up in a flood of publicity and appraisal. The papers welcomed the new President and commended his Puritanical simplicity and the austere quality of his family life. He was described as being modest, reticent, self-effacing, patient and firm. It was noted that he was the first President to come from New England in seventy years, and that his history was closely linked with the rugged traditions of Vermont. He injected a simple and pioneer note into Republican politics and arrived at the White House without smothering strings or party obligations. He was an unknown quantity, except for an already established reputation for silence, thrift and simplicity.

But his wife made an instant impression. From her first day as mistress of the White House she presented a picture of dignity and warmth. Every move and gesture were noted. The limelight beat fiercely on her manner, her history, her clothes, her family. It was a novel experience for her and one that she did not welcome but she was found to be "alert, kindly, gracious and entirely natural." Mrs. Marshall had prepared her for the barrage. And Mrs. Stearns, who considered her a woman of brains as well as a fine homemaker, was there to support her. Her own common sense and her desire to back up her husband in every way guided her past the early pitfalls. It was a fortunate circumstance for her and for the President that her friendly and spontaneous nature endeared her so readily to the variety of people whose paths now crossed hers.

CHAPTER IV

THE WHITE HOUSE

WHEN MRS. CALVIN COOLIDGE walked into the White House on an August day in 1923 as the President's wife she was beset by a feeling of unreality. "When I reflect upon my Washington career I wonder how I ever faced it," she wrote twelve years later. As she passed through the doorway into the columned corridor, the sun shone through the south windows. A soft summer breeze stirred the leaves of the magnolias in the grounds. The Washington heat spread its faint miasma over everything.

"There was a sense of detachment," she wrote. "This was I, and yet, not I—this was the wife of the President of the United States and she took precedence over me; my personal likes and dislikes must be subordinated to the consideration of those things which were required of her."

Mrs. Coolidge, always modest in her estimate of herself, felt that she had little preparation for the role she would now fill, except that her months as wife of the Vice-President had given her some knowledge of the official set, of the political alignments and personalities. "I was more proficient in setting up and operating miniature tracks and trains on the dining-room floor than in receiving and entertaining

87

guests in the drawing room," she wrote. Now the full burden of being the President's wife had fallen on her shoulders and she took up her task with diffidence. "We all know Calvin will make good," she wrote to Mrs. Morrow on August 14, just before they moved into the White House. "I have been somewhat doubtful of my own ability but if you say I can come through I know I can."

Coolidge was quietly sworn into office a second time at the New Willard by Justice Hoehling of the Supreme Court, D. C. Daugherty after further investigation had raised the point that Colonel Coolidge, as a state official, could only swear in officers of Vermont. This seemed a startling anticlimax after the solemn moment in the farmhouse but it escaped public attention. Daugherty noted in his autobiography that "no publication of the fact was ever made." The following Sunday they took communion at the First Congregational Church in Washington. The President, who had sent for the Rev. Jason Noble Pierce on his arrival in the capital, had been voted into membership. His wife was accepted as an associate member of the church.

Mrs. Coolidge made a smooth transition from her limited role as Vice-President's wife to the full responsibility of the White House. In later years she could not recall any moments of genuine embarrassment. Her husband took office at a significant period in the nation's history. The world was settling down after the first world war. There were earnest gropings for international unity. In spite of much internal opposition the United States was moving slowly into the center of the picture. The echoes of Woodrow Wilson's Fourteen Points could be heard through the land as he sank closer to death.

A great social upheaval was under way on the home front as the postwar generation kicked up its heels. It was a time of freedom from restraint after the shock of war, aggravated by a general revolt from prohibition as the law of the land. The years from August, 1923, to March, 1929, which the Coolidges passed in the White House, were a prosperous but rowdy period in American life. The old social order was changing fast. Silent forces soon to explode were at work behind the lurid front of the Jazz Age. As the span of the Coolidge administration ran on, with profits ever rising, the First

Lady found herself curiously poised in stable silhouette against a maelstrom of spendthrift gaiety, strange fashions and calculated lawbreaking. By 1926 the Jazz Age had reached its peak of fever and frenzy. The pace was wild; the times were out of joint.

Never was the White House more at variance with the mood of the hour. A quiet family life, based on the spirit of New England Puritanism, prevailed. Mrs. Coolidge embodied the established virtues of moderation, domesticity and reserve. "We New England women cling to the old way," she said early in her husband's term of office, "and being the President's wife isn't going to make me think less about the domestic things I've always loved."

Yet she was not censorious of others, or narrow-minded in her outlook. She was not unsympathetic to the women who were breaking the shackles and finding a working place for themselves in the world and a voice in political matters. Writers of the day kept fitting the Coolidges into their native setting. The President seemed even further removed from the madness that swept the land. The very dissidence of his type gave emphasis to his austere personality in a nation geared to excess. He was thrifty in an hour of extravagance, silent in a period of verbosity. To William Allen White he seemed like a "wineglass elm in a Vermont meadow." The Coolidge significance to the period in which they lived was defined by the New York *Herald Tribune* when Mrs. Coolidge died in 1957: "But what was austere and withdrawn in Calvin Coolidge was warm and gracious in his wife. As symbols they complemented one another, and as symbols they were necessary to an America which was spinning far too fast down the ringing grooves of change."

One of the first to applaud Mrs. Coolidge was the powerful Alice Roosevelt Longworth, who wrote of her ménage: "I recollect that the first time we went to the White House after the Coolidges were there, the atmosphere was as different as a New England front parlor is from a back room in a speakeasy." The Longworths were abroad when President Harding died. Alice was angry when she learned on her return of the gossip that surrounded his death. She had often been critical of the Hardings and they had not been fond of her. Mrs. Harding considered her contemptuous and condescending. But they had all played poker together and she had often watched Mrs. Harding, who was known as The Duchess, mix drinks for her husband's friends. She considered her an excitable, high-pitched woman, a First Lady who kept a little red book for purposes of retaliation, with the names of those who had not been civil to her. Mrs. Longworth's view of Harding was summed up in two crisp sentences: "Harding was not a bad man. He was just a slob."

Her slight knowledge of Calvin Coolidge before he became President was based on a trip they all took by private car to Bath, Maine, for Senator Walter Edge's wedding to Miss Camilla Sewall. She was amused when the sharp-faced Vice-President stayed up for hours on the train watching them all play poker. She knew Mrs. Coolidge slightly better, since the wives of the Vice-President and the Speaker inevitably met at functions. Alice thought that Mrs. Coolidge enjoyed her position, was amused by all the official functions and attentions, yet was absolutely natural and unimpressed by official Washington. Mrs. Longworth defined Grace Coolidge's attitude as a gift for making others happy because she enjoyed life so much herself. As an articulate and hard-hitting critic in her own right, and one who had stirred up many a political brew, Mrs. Longworth observed that Mrs. Coolidge "put no feminine finger into affairs of state, made no speeches, gave no interviews." But she thought that the President's wife kept a good many White House parties from lapsing into deadly silence.

Mrs. Longworth was generally credited with coining the much quoted phrase that Mr. Coolidge looked as if he had been weaned on a pickle. Actually her doctor had picked up this bon mot from a patient. When he told her about it, she found it irresistible and flashed it around Washington. It was soon attributed to her, since her reputation for wit and stinging sarcasm was well established.

When Mrs. Longworth left her doctor's office one day with confirmation of the fact that she was pregnant the first person she told outside of her family was Mrs. Coolidge, but the President apparently had prior information. The Speaker must have been looking into the future, too. Mrs. Coolidge later told the story with hearty enjoyment to William Allen White and other guests when they were all cruising down the Potomac on the *Mayflower*.

Alice had telephoned for an appointment, saying she had important news. Mrs. Coolidge had a delegation of women arriving for luncheon so she tried to put her off. But Mrs. Longworth, never one to be deflected from her purpose, rushed to the White House with an urgent plea: "Where's Grace? I must see her at once." Mrs. Coolidge was delighted to hear the news and passed it on to her luncheon guests, since Alice obviously wished to have everyone know about her baby. In fact, she whirled Irwin (Ike) H. Hoover, Chief Usher, off his feet and left him breathless on her way out as she told him that she was headed for motherhood.

"When will it be?" one of the luncheon guests asked, for everyone knew that Mrs. Longworth longed for a child.

"Now if that isn't like me!" Mrs. Coolidge exclaimed. "In all the excitement I just forgot to ask."

The President, who was the only man present, quietly volunteered: "Some time in February, I understand."

Grace turned to White and exclaimed: "How would you like to live with a man like that? He had known it two weeks and never a word said he to me!" Months later, when the baby was born, Mrs. Longworth, who had hoped for a boy, telegraphed Grace: "It's a nice girl."

The President kept a tight grip on the guest list, on the kitchen, and even on his wife's mail. There were invitations he would not let her accept. He had a keen remembrance of things past, when the sophisticated set was disposed to patronize the simple Coolidges. He appeared before Colonel Starling one day with the old unruly lock of reddish hair showing from under his hat. The reigning social queen of the capital had invited them to her house. But he recalled that she had cold-shouldered them when they lived at the New Willard Hotel and he was merely Vice-President. "Now that I'm President they want to drag me up to their house for one of their suppers and show me off to a lot of people," he remarked. "I'm not going and I'm not going to let that wife of mine go."

He was apt to change the seating list arranged by his aides and was disposed to favor the Budget Department whenever possible. Miss Mary Randolph, Mrs. Coolidge's social secretary, was appalled to view the Budget Chief being pushed in ahead of Justices of the Supreme Court at the New Year's Day reception. Nothing of that sort had ever occurred at the White House. However, the Tafts were always honored guests during the Coolidge regime and Grace shared many a jest with the Chief Justice. At first he considered her over-anxious to please and a little uncertain of herself. But he predicted in a letter to his daughter, Mrs. Frederick J. Manning, that she would be a worthy First Lady when she felt more at home and he fully expected the Coolidges "to do all that is required of them."

He felt that they had been unjustly criticized in some quarters for the hurried swearing-in, for dining at Friendship with the McLeans on the night that Mrs. Harding left for Marion, and for taking Mr. and Mrs. Stearns, strangers from Boston, with them to Marion for the funeral. However, he did not feel that Mrs. Harding shared this feeling.

Mrs. Coolidge particularly endeared herself to the Chief Justice through her understanding of his half brother, Charles Taft and his wife Annie, both of whom were deaf. She knew just how to converse with them and they chatted together about earlier days in White House history when Taft was the Chief Executive. "Annie felt that the President was most uncommunicative, and sympathized with his wife because he was so silent," Taft wrote to his wife.

Grace gave him a merry glance when he tripped twice on Mrs. Taft's train at a White House reception and muttered: "Drat the old thing." But the Chief Justice kept a close and perceptive eye on the new regime. He had been won by Mrs. Coolidge when they all went together to Ohio for the Harding funeral. He had yet to make up his mind about Calvin but within a month of his inheriting the Presidency Mr. Taft sent his wife a blueprint of the future after a satisfactory talk with Mr. Coolidge on judicial appointments and other matters. He left the White House with the impression that the new President would ignore political considerations when it came to the selection of judges.

After the first reception for the Judiciary he reported that Mrs.

Coolidge "looked very pretty and was most gracious. Coolidge is Coolidge, and he does the pump-handle work without much grace and without a great deal of enthusiasm." But Colonel Starling decided that the President had developed a sound technique in sweeping the victim ahead as he shook his hand. When he saw a bejeweled dowager approaching he was apt to stop the line with a deadpan expression and go off for a ten-minute rest.

By this time the country had heard from that trusted seismograph of public affairs in the 1920s—Wall Street. It showed neither nervousness nor hesitation with the advent of Calvin Coolidge. The stock market indicated that all was well. The *Wall Street Journal* characterized the new President as a sound and conservative figure and its publisher, Clarence W. Barron, a fellow New Englander, considered him a man of destiny. Elbert H. Gary, czar of United States Steel, said that he "stood for protection of property and welfare of individuals alike." The radical press piped another tune and the Republican *Emporia Gazette* ruffled the Coolidge front considerably with an impolite reference to this "runty, aloof little man who quacks through his nose when he speaks" and seemed to be a master of the platitude. Later William Allen White, editor of the offending paper, was entertained frequently at the White House and on the *Mayflower*, wrote two books about the President, showed great admiration for Mrs. Coolidge and became a family friend, if also, in the long run, a penetrating critic.

The press was united in its applause for quiet Mrs. Coolidge. Her friendly face brought warmth to a picture that had long been chilling. She was said to match Dolly Madison in charm and tact, to be "quick at repartee and full of fun," to be an accomplished dancer and better informed on baseball than most men. Actually she had Presidential orders not to dance in public "but when John comes home I just keep him busy dancing with me," she confessed. Another prohibition that she felt keenly was her husband's ban on riding. For the first time in her life she had an opportunity to learn to ride. Dwight F. Davis, then Secretary of War, aided and abetted her in her secret plan to take lessons at Fort Myer in Virginia. She joyfully bought her riding togs and he accompanied her to the riding hall for her first lesson. It was a happy morning. But the press got wind of the story, with predictable results. They were breakfasting when the President noticed the headline: *Mrs. Coolidge Takes up Riding.* She was described as looking more like a debutante in her jaunty tan habit and boots than like the first lady of the land.

He stared across at her with a look of surprise, mingled with anxiety and disapproval, and quickly dashed her adventurous spirit with the flat announcement: "I think you will find that you will get along at this job fully as well if you do not try anything new." Ten years later she wrote feelingly—or perhaps with her tongue in her cheek—of this moment that it had the "semblance of a death notice."

Those who knew Mrs. Coolidge intimately felt that there were times when the compromises she had to make must have hurt. She had no lack of pride and independence but Mary Roberts Rinehart, a perceptive friend who frequently visited the White House, detected strain in her efforts to stabilize an uneven situation. Others felt that no ruling of her husband's ruffled her deeply except where the boys were concerned. Calvin's word was law. She believed in him. She respected him. Moreover, she was deeply aware of the responsibility of her position. Once he became President she would have gone to any reasonable length to save him embarrassment. Generally she found it expedient to lapse into total silence when his anger flared up, for his nature precluded argument or discussion. Her own disciplined approach to life, in any event, had made her a conformist and her free and ranging spirit found other forms of expression.

She was enterprising by nature and liked to try new things, but in addition to the ban on riding Calvin would not let her drive a car, or fly (even with Colonel Charles A. Lindbergh), or have her hair bobbed when she longed to adopt this fashion, or wear culottes for country hiking, or express her views on politics, or in any way step out of character as wife and mother. Not that she showed any disposition to do so, and whatever views she may have held she kept to herself. Never once did she embarrass her husband with a malapropism in the political field, and many times she saved a social situation with her tact and intuition. She was unfailingly loyal to the Republican party.

When genuinely annoyed she found relief and placidity in her long walks and her vigorous knitting. One intimate who often watched her needles flashing on the *Mayflower* remarked that if her knitting could speak it would reveal the inner thoughts and true heart of Grace Coolidge. She owned up to this herself: "Many a time, when I have needed to hold myself firmly, I have taken up my needle. It might be a sewing needle, knitting needles, or a crochet hook—whatever its form or purpose, it often proved to be as the needle of the compass, keeping me to the course."

But whatever her inward mood she seemed fresh and unwearied when exposed to public inspection and she enjoyed herself in a natural, wholehearted way. Unconsciously she spread a certain radiance that soon became manifest as an asset to President Coolidge. The public felt it. Many of the politicians remarked on it. She had appeared so little with him in official life until he became President that her success surprised even his intimates. James J. Davis, Secretary of Labor, once told her that if he could run for the Presidency of the United States, he would like to have her for his campaign manager. She had the instinctive touch for handling assorted types. When a party of five hundred Grangers drove up to the White House by auto caravan to proclaim their support to Calvin Coolidge for reelection he received them briefly and then retired from the scene. But Grace knew that country people liked to visit and to feel at home. She drummed up a quick lunch for them, made them warmly welcome and mellowed the situation.

A congressman had only to tell her that a county constituent wished to meet her, and he would be invited to tea and would find his hostess alert to his family situation, his state background, his pet political philosophy. She had a well-trained memory for names and faces. She would remind a farmer of the fine peaches he had sent them from Vermont the previous summer. "How's the boy?" she would ask a passing figure in the receiving line, and he would leave the White House wondering how on earth Mrs. Coolidge remembered that his child was a boy, since she scarcely knew him. She would dig up unexpected jokes to fire at someone who looked lost and uncomfortable. She was remarkably successful with the Cabinet wives and the great variety of women she had to meet in a public capacity.

The diplomats were struck by her spontaneous and buoyant approach to her official duties. It was good leavening for their formal rounds. At one of her garden parties an English-speaking emissary asked a colleague who did not understand the language if he had followed what Mrs. Coolidge had said.

"That is not necessary," was the reply. "To look upon her is gladness enough."

Her understanding of the role she must play was a masterly feat in public relations, perhaps unconscious in an era when publicity and advertising had only just begun to blossom and soon would flower to an extravagant pitch. But its effect on the Coolidge regime was incalculable. "She did the front door job," an observer wrote. And she did it so well that the cynical found more stimulation in the acid bite of Alice Longworth's critical wit than in Mrs. Coolidge's unfailing grace and encompassing smile.

But things moved smoothly on the social side during the Coolidge administration. There were no major storms at the White House, although the staff did an uncommon amount of grumbling about the President. A steady routine prevailed and it all seemed orderly after the strange parade of Harding visitors. One day merged into the next in smooth procession. The new order was economical. It was sometimes dull. But it was always correct. The quiet family life was emphasized. Rigid economy was enforced on the household side. Plans were made well in advance. There was no confusion or crowding, no lavish display or deviation from established custom. The staff were afraid of the President but were warmed by the compliments Mrs. Coolidge paid them for every special effort they made. Occasionally magnificence prevailed for the scintillant guests who walked across the Washington stage during the boom era of peace and plenty.

Grace settled her family comfortably in the private rooms on the second floor. She had never lived in spacious quarters and she took delight in arranging furniture, brightening up the rooms with chintz, deep tufted sofas, family pictures, bird cages and her own disposition of the flowers that came in abundance from the White House gardens and greenhouses. Her bedroom was sunny, large and dramatically furnished, for she had the historic Lincoln bed installed there although she frequently pointed out that there was "no authority which established this as a correct designation." She immediately began to crochet a spread for it that took two years to finish. The President's seal was the central motif and she toiled to get the eagle worked in symmetrically. The Harding twin beds were moved into the boys' bedroom and the Coolidges slept in a double bed in the President's room.

Mrs. Coolidge controlled eighteen domestic servants, as well as special cleaning men, a valet for the President and a maid for herself. This was a long step from the services of Miss Aurora Pierce and Mrs. Alice Reckahn. But the White House machinery moved like clockwork, regardless of Presidential shifts, and only the personalities of new occupants disorganized the routine to any extent. Mrs. Coolidge left executive detail to those equipped to handle it. Ike Hoover presided at the White House for forty years and knew as much of what went on as anyone. Mrs. Elizabeth Jaffray was the housekeeper and a cold war soon developed between her and President Coolidge. Miss Mary (Polly) Randolph, already well indoctrinated in the social customs of Washington, followed Miss Laura Harlan as Mrs. Coolidge's secretary and stayed on for a time with Mrs. Hoover. Colonel Edward Starling, chief of the Secret Service detail, kept a discerning eye on all family matters and incorporated many of his observations later in book form. He was a Presbyterian from the hills of Kentucky and he felt that he understood the Congregationalist from the hills of Vermont. He considered Calvin Coolidge "honest, brave, religious, and stubborn."

Usually the President was up at six thirty. In nightgown and slippers he would peer out the window to see if Starling was waiting for him on the lawn. Occasionally he would elude him by heading for the most unlikely exit. But one day Starling turned the tables by hiding in the police box at the east entrance, a favorite trick of the President's. "His appetite for pranks was insatiable," the Colonel reported. The Coolidges breakfasted in their apartment at eight after the President had exercised on his mechanical horse and had taken a brief walk. The introduction of the horse provided much amusement for Mrs. Coolidge, who was asked to press the button and see what happened. Colonel Starling had told her that on the first try the horse had jumped and the President had lost his hat, and almost his seat. After that, they exercised like cowboys and Mr. Coolidge swore by his mechanical horse. He considered its use a valuable health measure and the family had many jests about father's horse. The press, too, let the nation know that Calvin Coolidge rode a mechanical horse instead of a real one.

He usually read the morning papers right through breakfast, which consisted of a hot cereal made from a special blend of unground wheat and rye, bacon, muffins or pancakes and coffee, either clear or with condensed milk. Mrs. Coolidge would eat whatever was provided but she was fond of doughnuts with her coffee. Often she would go downstairs at eleven with Miss Randolph and have more coffee. If her husband seemed to be in the mood to listen she talked gaily right over the newspaper standard he held. If he wanted quiet—and she always knew—she would sit in absolute silence.

After they had been in the White House for two weeks she felt she needed some clue to his movements. "Calvin, I wish you would have your secret service men give me your engagements," she told him mildly.

"Grace, we don't give that out promiscuously," he replied.

A communication from Vermont, however, was apt to draw a comment, as when letters poured in protesting a ban on Vermont trees because of the gypsy moth. Alice M. Lockwood, an old schoolmate of Coolidge's at Black River Academy, wrote in early in the administration, protesting the ban and recalling him "as though it were yesterday, crossing the assembly room to Greek and Latin classes, also skirmishing with Lena across the lawn from our house . . ."

Mrs. Harding often boasted that she "had made Warren Harding." Mrs. Taft attended important conferences in the White House until she became an invalid, and she was always deeply interested in her husband's political career. Mrs. Wilson was a power behind the scenes in her husband's last days. But although members of the household considered Mrs. Coolidge an important part of the administration, she scarcely knew from hour to hour what she was expected to do. She was always ready with her hat on, waiting for a last-minute summons to accompany the President anywhere. When Ike Hoover would ask her if she were going with her husband on a certain mission she would reply: "I do not know, but I am ready."

When the President left for the executive offices in the morning Mrs. Coolidge settled down to the routine of the day. She arranged the flowers in their private rooms, attended to her birds, and kept the radio or phonograph going as she worked. At nine o'clock Miss Randolph arrived with the mail and immediately became a fine buffer for all contingencies. She had to mollify Senators on social requests, crowd Mrs. Coolidge's calendar with fifteen-minute appointments, cope with crank mail, and handle requests for money, for clothes, for favors, for autographed photographs, for appointments, for jobs, for clemency, in addition to a vast amount of social correspondence and personal assistance. There was also the all-pervasive press. Would the gold service be out for the upcoming dinner? Would the flower decorations be Ophelia roses and freesia? What would Mrs. Coolidge wear?

Letters of political implication addressed to the President's wife were automatically turned over to Rudolph Forster in the executive offices. Sinister and threatening communications never reached her. At all periods of her life she was an enthusiastic letter writer. Even while in the White House she wrote more letters personally than any President's wife up to that time. Eventually she used a typewriter as efficiently as any secretary. She had a small, substantial desk in her sitting room and she dashed off notes on the slightest provocation, often sending them to friends in Washington by special messenger. Her handwriting was clear and unaffected, with generous loops and even spacing. She held her pen between her first and second fingers and wrote swiftly and spontaneously. It was her custom to cut out poems and enclose them in letters to those she thought might like them. Her spelling and punctuation were precise and she had a chatty, humorous style that was expressive of her personality.

Mrs. Coolidge wrote regularly to members of her family, to friends in Northampton and elsewhere, to strangers across the country and to the members of the round robin, who soon had an inside view of the White House direct from the First Lady. The first she sent them after her husband became President was begun at the New Willard and finished in the Executive Mansion. "I thought maybe you'd all like my contribution to be the first letter I wrote in the White House," she addressed them on August 21, 1923. "Just now it occurred to me that I would begin my letter here in the only home I have known in Washington, take it with me as I go and finish it in that great White House on Pennsylvania Avenue—one which must now become home to me for a year and a half. I wish I could tell you all that is in my heart at this moment—but there is so much that even I am bewildered. I want you all to just love me and pray for me." Then from the White House she added: "Alice in Wonderland or Babes in the Woods—however you wish to regard me—I'm here and nothing has happened to me. I wish I could describe my varied sensations as we came in and took up our residence here." Three weeks later she sent a card to Mrs. Rugg: "Being wife to a government worker is a very confining position."

One of her first acts was to settle on a suitable token to give to organizations that appealed to the mistress of the White House for donations. Mrs. Harding had always sent an embroidered handkerchief. Mrs. Coolidge chose an autographed engraving of the Executive Mansion. When a correspondent asked her to autograph a quilt in which a large flag had been embroidered she returned it without a signature. It was destined to be auctioned off and she did not consider this an appropriate use for the national emblem. Later she sent the woman a plain white quilt with her autograph.

The President was just as interested in his wife's mail as he was in her engagements, her clothes, and all that concerned her. He would often prowl into the alcove where Miss Randolph worked in order to see what was going on. Gifts were a problem. They ranged from a kangaroo to a ukulele, and a cherry pie five feet in diameter. They poured in on the Coolidges and the President insisted on poking into parcels against the counsel of his guard. He had no sense of alarm in days of well-founded peace, and he liked to sample the cheeses, jellies and sweets that arrived from different parts of the country. Cheese was an old Vermont taste of his and he ate it by the slice like pie.

The gifts were usually spread out on a large table in the steward's room and on his way to the executive offices the President always stopped to examine them. He was particularly pleased with a large salted cod from a Maine admirer and pronounced it a "mighty fine gift" that was to be kept for his personal consumption. One well-known statesman arrived one day with a dozen canvasback ducks. He had expected an important appointment which he did not get. A few hours later he departed—and he took the ducks with him. Mrs. Coolidge made a practice of keeping gifts in her room for a day or two at least, so that she could honestly say that she had enjoyed them. The great baskets of fruit that streamed in were usually kept in the family living room for a time before being sent to the kitchen.

The President was an indefatigable nibbler and bowls of nuts and fruit were always in his bedroom and on his desk. He liked to buy his peanuts from the vendor outside the White House gates. On their walks together Colonel Starling gave him dimes and nickels for peanuts, magazines and newspapers, although Mr. Coolidge, unlike some of the other Presidents, always carried money on his person. Both he and Mrs. Coolidge liked sweets. Walking with the Colonel one day he stopped in front of the Martha Washington candy shop.

"Do they make good candy here?" he asked.

Before the Colonel could reply the President added: "They must. My wife likes it." But for years his preference was for Jensen's confections bought in Springfield. Mrs. Hills kept him supplied with these sweets, and particularly with the old-fashioned chocolate drops that he had enjoyed as a boy. They arrived at the White House with a special code and so did not have to undergo scrutiny.

There was none of the mad scramble in the kitchens and elsewhere created by the Hoovers when they followed the Coolidges into office and brought in crowds of guests with little warning. The family routine was static. The President slept an average of eleven hours a day. He went to bed at ten and invariably took a long nap in the White House after lunch. At times he would lie down and sleep on his office sofa. He was like Taft and Wilson in this respect and could sleep at will, whereas Harding, plagued by his worries, was an insomniac.

Starling was as devoted to Calvin Coolidge as Ike Hoover and Mrs. Jaffray were cool to him. Mrs. Jaffray pegged the Coolidges as the "strangest couple that have ever occupied the White House," although she conceded that Mrs. Coolidge was the happiest of First Ladies and was "warm, friendly and talkative, a champion smiler." The President, on the other hand, rarely smiled or talked although he was known to tip his hat to the all-important cook. He prowled through the kitchens regularly, peered into the pots, inspected the pantries and knew what Mrs. Jaffray was buying and planning. These trips sometimes caused consternation. Harry Waters, a Negro who served the Coolidges as substitute valet, doorman, keeper of the kennels and pantry man and was still at the White House in 1960, banged into President Coolidge while he was being chased out of the kitchen by the cook, wielding a batter spoon. On this occasion the President actually smiled at the discomfited Harry.

It was his custom to check and initial the bills personally. He did not leave this to Grace or to a secretary. He was credited with saving more than any other President while in office and the actual household expenses during his term averaged less than $1,000 a month. The White House bills and receipts in the Forbes Library today testify to the economy of the Coolidge regime.

Mrs. Jaffray shopped by carriage long after the automobile was an established institution. Food prices, even after a war, were then at a comparatively modest level. She bought butter by the tub at forty-seven cents a pound, potatoes by the barrel, and fruit and vegetables by the crate at the public market. The White House coffee cost forty-three cents a pound. Mrs. Coolidge sometimes served as mediator between the lavish touch of Mrs. Jaffray and the frugal instincts of her husband, and was the unhappy witness to a sharp encounter one day when she invited the housekeeper in to her bedroom to show her the gown she would wear that night at an important function. When the President walked in Mrs. Coolidge asked him if he had seen the dining room.

"Yes," he said.

"Didn't you think it was beautiful?"

"Yes, it's all right."

"Did you step downstairs into the kitchens?"

"Yes, and I don't see why we have to have six hams for one dinner. It seems an awful lot of ham to me."

"But, Mr. President, there will be sixty people here," Mrs. Jaffray protested. "These Virginia hams are small and we cannot possibly serve more than ten people with one ham and be sure of having an abundance."

"Well, six hams look like an awful lot to me," the President persisted.

The White House pies came under fire at once, and particularly the custard pies. Mr. Coolidge did not like them. Mrs. Jaffray asked if there was a recipe that would please him. Mrs. Coolidge knew that she had never been able to satisfy him with her own pies, but she wrote to an inn in Massachusetts for a favored recipe. This brought peace to the kitchen. The President also liked corn muffins but not the White House kind, so again Mrs. Coolidge sent to New England for help. Baked beans were added to the menus and fewer hot breads were served. It was the custom to send up the menu with the First Lady's breakfast tray but Mrs. Jaffray soon had orders for two. The President wished to add his own approval to his wife's. But in the spring of 1926 Mrs. Jaffray and her brougham disappeared from the scene and Miss Ellen A. Riley took over the household management. She had worked as cafeteria director in hostess houses for the Y.W.C.A. during the first world war and had later organized the cafeteria of the R. H. Stearns Company in Boston. Mrs. Jaffray later turned her experiences to account in a book and Mrs. Coolidge did not like it.

She confided to the Robins that it seemed a pity she could not write something interesting, since she had seen fit to break into print. She deplored Mrs. Jaffray's comments on the Hardings and expressed the opinion that Mrs. Wilson was merely showing consideration when she had the housekeeper show Mrs. Harding over the White House. "Her attitude at times was amusing and at others very trying," Mrs. Coolidge wrote. "She had come to consider herself the permanent resident and the President and his family transients. For her to presume to tell how much a President saves from his salary is, of course, ridiculous and I suppose that the reason the Coolidge family seems so strange to her is that they are rather normal and didn't appreciate her."

Miss Riley fitted smoothly into the picture. Efficiency and economy prevailed and she got on well with Mr. Coolidge. He complimented her on the "very fine improvement" in food costs and noted a saving of more than $2,000 in six months. "Everybody likes her," Mrs. Coolidge wrote. "Peace and harmony reign over all that department. Everybody marvels at my carefree air and seems surprised to find me looking so well. To Miss Riley I give much of the credit." She soon became custodian of the plate, furniture and property in the White House, as well as housekeeper. The President taught her the combination of the vault where the gold and silver services were kept, but she promptly forgot it and he grinned as he showed her all over again how to get at President Monroe's gold service.

Mrs. Coolidge usually approved Miss Riley's menus without comment, but sometimes she wrote little notes, such as "when the ham is carved tomorrow will you see that it is cut so that the President can have that little round piece which lies near the bone?" She was always vigilant to see that the things he liked came his way. He was particularly fussy about his griddle cakes and one day he showed up in Miss Riley's office holding a dainty griddle cake between thumb and forefinger. "Why can't I have big ones like they have downstairs?" he demanded. To save time in the kitchen the servants used pancakes as large as dinner plates.

Everyone stood automatically when the President entered a room but one day he turned to Miss Riley and snapped: "Don't *you* keep gittin up." When films were shown in the evening he would sit in a big chair, smoking a cigar, and usually with Rob Roy beside him. When the picture was particularly amusing Mr. Coolidge would jab the collie in the ribs with his elbow and Rob would wag his tail. Although things were less lavish than they had been previously at the White House, Mrs. Coolidge quickly established a pattern of graceful hospitality. The Cave Dwellers took note and approved, and the more progressive elements found her vital and buoyant. She gave four state dinners and four musicales in her first winter in addition to a number of other functions. Early in the administration she leaned to musicales after the formal dinners. As many guests as could be accommodated comfortably in the East Room were seated on small gilt chairs to listen to the artists of the day. The President and Mrs. Coolidge occupied two large armchairs in the center of the front row.

They attended twelve official dinners during the season and as many as 3,500 invitations would be issued for one of their receptions. Mrs. Coolidge was always at her most effective when she came through the grilled iron gates at the foot of the stairway and progressed to the Blue Room at the President's side. The Cabinet members and their wives followed in a slow procession, while the Marine Band played *Hail to the Chief*. After the presentations the Coolidges would retire to their own quarters and dancing would begin in the East Room. The President's own view of these affairs and of his wife's part in them appears in his autobiography:

> While the President has supervision over all these functions, the most effective way to deal with them is to provide a capable Mistress of the White House. I have often been complimented on the choice which I made nearly twenty-five years ago. These functions were so much in the hands of Mrs. Coolidge that oftentimes I did not know what guests were to be present until I met them in the Blue Room just before going in to dinner.

Nevertheless, it was Mr. Coolidge who insisted on the most meticulous observance of all the established rules while he was on public view. But after a particularly stuffy event one of his aides was astounded to catch him bowing from the waist to Mrs. Coolidge while she mockingly danced a slow minuet. She had inveigled him into a hilarious interlude after the guests had gone. It took her only a short time to find her bearings with the parade of diplomats and judges, of Senators and financiers, of newspaper owners and railroad czars, of doctors and scientists, of writers, artists and musicians, of celebrities from all parts of the world who now moved into her sphere. It was an era of exploration and adventure as well as of high living and she relished these brisk encounters with world figures more than her husband did. Henry L. Stoddard, author and editor of the New York *Evening Mail,* who knew Calvin Coolidge well, thought that he hewed to the ways of his ancestors, preferring the family dinner table with his own carving to formal banquets, neighbors as his guests to "leading citizens," the intimacy of local chitchat around the home fireside to the frigid atmosphere of state occasions.

Mr. Coolidge talked business in his office only. He gave a series of breakfasts that baffled and sometimes bored the Senators and Congressmen who attended them. Mrs. Coolidge met the Cabinet wives on the last Wednesday of every month for friendly discussion of plans and projects. She gave small receptions that brought visitors from all parts of the country into the easy, informal atmosphere she created. Although she met fewer large groups than Mrs. Harding she succeeded in getting closer to her guests, leaving with them a vivid impression of her own personality. Delegations and groups of visitors were usually received at noon and were photographed with her at the foot of the flight of stone steps leading down from the south portico to the flagging. She thought that the iron railing with its entwining Virginia creeper made a flattering background for everyone.

But her afternoon teas in the Red Room were the functions which conveyed the most warmth. When the social season was at its height she usually held them on Mondays and Fridays, with from twenty-five to thirty guests. She was always ready to invite the relatives of politicians for these occasions. It was an informal and flexible arrangement. She would go round the circle greeting everyone and would then sit by the fire drawing out her guests and giving the best of herself to their entertainment. The Red Parlor on a winter day was a warming sight, with its deep red brocade walls, the gilt frames of the paintings of former Presidents gleaming in the firelight, the prisms of the crystal chandeliers glittering, flowers scenting the air, and the hostess seated by the fire, gowned in forest green or burgundy velvet, and glowing with interest. She used rich colors in her gowns to good effect.

Mrs. Coolidge was having one of these teas when Paul Pry invaded the Red Parlor, cleaned up the plates on the tea stand and dashed off with cream and chocolate dripping from his whiskers. When she told the President later of the dog's misdeeds she saw a familiar look on his face.

"I wonder how he got out?" she speculated, knowing full well.

"I don't think that little dogs like to be shut upstairs when there is a party going on," said the President.

This was one of many fond tricks that he played on his good-natured wife, and they usually caused her to laugh. At one of her teas she calmly watched a politician's wife stuffing a White House Madeira napkin into her purse. Realizing that her guest had mistaken it for her handkerchief Grace jestingly remarked: "You may as well bring it out for I saw you put it in." Her guest held it up with dismay. "It was filled with holes, too," Mrs. Coolidge observed.

The society reporters of Washington gave her gowns, her entertainments, her equable manners their due. They particularly admired her as she received the diplomatic corps, representing forty-nine nations, on a December night in 1923. She was gowned in white satin, without ornaments or jewels, but she held a bouquet of white roses that set off her lustrous looks. Great bowls of white carnations stood in the East Room and there were lilies and pink carnations in the Blue Room. The sharp-eyed press noticed a thinning of the elaborate arrangements of the past. The blossoms, ferns and trailing vines profusely used during the Harding administration were supplanted by a low bank of Australian ferns in the state dining room, with Madame Butterfly roses in the epergnes. Soon the twenty-two simple flower arrangements of the Coolidge administration became standard reporting.

The First Lady had to bow to a certain amount of this sort of observation. The President had no objection to specific news items involving official appearances, but no personality stories, quotations or personal interviews were permitted. The day of the free interviews with First Ladies had not yet arrived. Once when she was giving the newspaperwomen a luncheon under the giant magnolia tree planted by Andrew Jackson in memory of his wife Rachel, she was asked for a speech. Without any change of expression she raised her graceful hands and gave a five-minute talk in the language of the deaf, but without uttering a sound.

Maud Howe Elliott, Julia Ward Howe's daughter, was present on this occasion. She had not been in the White House since the time of Nellie Grant and she and Mrs. Coolidge had much to say to each other. When told that she had looked bridelike in her white satin gown at the diplomatic reception, the First Lady laughed and remarked that she had probably looked more so than on her wedding day, when she had worn gray. She was asked if she feared to stay in the White House, since its roof had been condemned. At this point Mrs. Coolidge quoted her husband's remark that he was quite willing to take the chance, and that a good many others seemed to share his feeling. She never hesitated to share a kindly joke at his expense on the entertaining end. When a prominent Washingtonian hurried up to her at tea one day with the news: "Oh, Mrs. Coolidge, I'm so delighted. I am going to have the honor of sitting beside your husband at dinner tomorrow evening at Mrs. So-and-So's."

"I'm sorry for you," said his wife. "You'll have to do all the talking yourself."

On another occasion a guest at a White House reception eased up to the President and remarked: "Mr. President, I'm from Boston."

His blue eyes rested only briefly on her as he said: "You'll never get over it!"

When the Coolidges retired for the night the lights in the public rooms went out and the doors were locked. A guard made regular rounds all night, giving signals every half hour. Mrs. Hills caught the full force of the system when she stayed out late one night at a party. She created uproar when the doors had to be opened. To make matters worse the dogs began to bark as she tiptoed to the guest room in the blue suite. She felt as if she had disturbed the nation. Next day at lunch the President dryly remarked: "Some people come home quite late in this house, Lady Hills."

Three bells signaled the President's emergence from the private apartment and one bell chimed for his wife, so that ushers, secret service men, the police and all other employees were on the alert. The President sometimes set off the alarm for fun to watch the reaction. Mr. and Mrs. Stearns came and went as members of the family, and Mrs. Hills was often at the White House to keep Mrs. Coolidge company. Guests liked to sleep in the Blue Room in the southeast wing which was once the Presidential office where Abraham Lincoln signed the Emancipation Proclamation. Every newcomer was informed of the legend that when the great light over the front door was dimmed for the night the ghost of Abraham Lincoln was supposed to pace silently to and fro on the North Porch.

At first Mr. Stearns was regarded as a second Colonel House in the administration but the press soon learned, and they in turn informed the public, that he had no political influence whatever, nor did he seek any. But Mrs. Coolidge was constantly grateful for his presence. He seemed to give great assurance to her husband, even if they only sat together for hours in silence, as they sometimes did on the south porch. Whole days would pass without a word being exchanged between them. "Mr. Stearns knew and understood the President as no other man knew and understood him," she commented. "As a contact man he was an excellent Boston merchant . . ."

Grace felt that she and Mr. Stearns were in the same situation as recipients of Presidential confidences. Often they put their heads together and figured out that two and two made four, "only to learn later that we had been adding the wrong numbers." The President always addressed his friend by his formal title, as he did Dwight Morrow, although he was inclined to give nicknames to the staff and to say Ol' Starling, or that "long-legged Haley man," or "The Mink," for John Mays, the doorman, and "The Ambassador" for another imposing doorman named Green. Mrs. Jaffray was always "The Duchess" to President Coolidge. He prowled around the White House grounds when he had an odd moment to spare but the squawking of the crows annoyed him. His walks were short compared with Mrs. Coolidge's, and he told a friend that window-shopping relaxed him after his day's work. Colonel Starling was distressed to find that the new President did not play golf, ride, hunt, swim, bowl or play billiards. He also thought that he walked with a slouch and he finally advised him that since he took constitutionals for his health he should not defeat this end by his posture.

Mrs. Coolidge walked with a natural swing and she could whistle for the dogs with the greatest of ease. In rain or shine, summer or winter, she kept up her routine, and the *Daily Hampshire Gazette* proudly reported that she refused to be "jailed" in the White House, preferring to walk five or six miles a day. She varied her course and there were few streets in the neighbohood that she did not traverse at one time or another. She walked to the Union Station with John when he was returning to college. Children hailed her in passing. She was often drawn to the pellucid basin at the Lincoln Memorial, returning home as Washington was bathed in the lavender mist of twilight.

Her first Christmas in Washington was a happy one. She was enjoying her role to the hilt. Her stately backdrop was beyond her dreams and she had deep respect for the traditions of the White House. "To me the House of the Presidents is sacred ground, hallowed by the memories of those men whom our country has chosen for the high office," she wrote, at the same time deploring the souvenir hunters who stole tassels from the curtains, silver ash trays and other removable objects. Settling down on the couch before her fire in the room "which I call Abraham Lincoln's room, for it was his long before it was mine" she wrote on another occasion to the Robin group:

Daily, I am impressed anew with the responsibility and opportunity which has been given me in coming to this wonderful old mansion. In no sense does it overwhelm me, rather does it inspire me and increase my energy and I am so filled with the desire to measure up to this God-given task that I can almost feel strength poured into me. . . . In the months that I have lived here in the great white house I have become greatly attached to it and there is much that is sacred about the associations connected with it. The one thing that is uppermost in my mind is the wisdom and great foresight of those who built it over a hundred years ago.

Her two sons were home from Mercersburg Academy for the holidays in December, 1923. Both were growing uncommonly tall, so that they towered above their parents. Mrs. Coolidge had just heard her husband address Congress for the first time and had felt proud of him. There had been a demonstration for her, too, as she walked in with Mrs. Charles Evans Hughes and Miss Ailsa Mellon. As she looked around she could see Mrs. Theodore Roosevelt, Mrs. Woodrow Wilson and Mrs. Herbert Hoover. Alice Roosevelt Longworth studied her with an experienced eye. Mrs. Coolidge had made special arrangements for the seating of the Cabinet wives instead of the usual jostling and crowding.

Mrs. Morrow had invited her to New York to shop for clothes. Although she felt she had found the nucleus for the season's wardrobe in Washington she did not believe Calvin would feel that "the thing has been properly done if I do not make a shopping trip to the 'big town,' " she wrote to Mrs. Morrow. But in the end he was satisfied with her selections and she did not go to New York. Mrs. Morrow and Elizabeth Morrow sent her a handsome brooch for her first Christmas in Washington. Up to this time Mrs. Coolidge had had no valuable jewels.

The White House that year had a true New England Christmas. The President took young Calvin window-shopping. Mrs. Coolidge explored stores for gifts for her family and friends. A spruce tree was set up in the Blue Room and there she gave a dance for sixty boys, doing a turn with each of them. She distributed gifts at Salvation Army headquarters; visited the Walter Reed Hospital to cheer the veterans; sent sixty poinsettias to her church; and she and the President shared in Christmas greetings to all the children of the United States.

It was Mrs. Coolidge's idea that carols should be sung at the White House by the vested choir of the First Congregational Church. Sixty-five choristers sang on the north porch, while the public was admitted to the grounds to listen, inaugurating a new custom. She and John joined the choristers and sang with them. Dr. Pierce had composed a hymn, *Christmas Bells,* which he dedicated to Mrs. Coolidge. On Christmas morning the family all attended church after the gifts had been unwrapped. They dined at seven, with Mr. and Mrs. Stearns as guests.

On New Year's Day it took three and a half hours for the line of 3,500 to shake hands with the President and Mrs. Coolidge. This was only the second New Year's Day reception at the White House in a decade and Washington enjoyed it. So did Mrs. Coolidge, who was a vivacious hostess in ruby red chiffon, one of her favorite colors. The diplomats in court attire added sparkle to the gathering and General Pershing, a war-worn hero, came smartly to attention as he passed the President. Military elements were strong in Washington, with the first world war still fresh in the memory of everyone. Mrs. Coolidge soon came to know many of the veterans at Walter Reed Hospital. When summer came she gave a garden party in their honor and the soldiers in wheel chairs and on crutches were warmed by her interest. She continued to entertain them outdoors although she soon abandoned garden parties as a White House form of entertainment. They were not in the Washington tradition and she had bad luck with the weather. But the smell of June roses after rain, the Marine Band on the terrace, the diaphanous hats, the chattering guests all left pleasant memories with Mrs. Coolidge.

During her years in the White House she opened rest clubs for veterans, attended concerts, laid cornerstones, planted trees, and sat in the gallery while her husband harped on his favorite theme— the need for economy in all areas of public life. She rode in parades, welcomed heroes and held receptions. She worked ardently for the Red Cross and backed up work for the deaf. Among many weddings she attended were those of Stuart Symington to Evelyn Wadsworth, and Ailsa Mellon to David Bruce. But one of the more somber memories of her early days in the White House was the death of Woodrow Wilson. The news was conveyed to the President while he was in church. He and Mrs. Coolidge called at the Wilson home at once and left cards. Four Presidential wives—Mrs. Coolidge, Mrs. Wilson, Mrs. Taft and Mrs. Harding—attended the funeral, driving up the hill to the unfinished cathedral on a bleak day in February.

In spite of her aloofness from politics Mrs. Coolidge soon found herself the guest of various Republican women's organizations. When the President went to New York in February, 1924, to make a Lincoln Day address he sipped tea somewhat gingerly in the afternoon at the Women's National Republican Club. A group of attractive women, including Mrs. Charles H. Sabin, who was then leading the women's fight on prohibition, surrounded him and chattered through fifteen minutes of silence on the President's part. Mrs. Coolidge, all in beige with a pink carnation at her collar, seemed to be doing better, as she managed "tea and cakes and sandwiches, introductions, greetings, hand shakes and a constant stream of animated conversation with the utmost grace." Finally she eased her way to the door after Calvin touched her shoulder and gave her a beseeching look. But the evening was all his. Seated with Mrs. Stearns in a ballroom box she listened attentively to his speech at the Lincoln Day banquet in the Waldorf Astoria. The new President had made headway. Others besides Mr. Stearns found points of comparison with Abraham Lincoln in his strongly native quality. The public was already embracing him as a man of dignity and silence, with an odd capacity to make them smile.

Mrs. Coolidge always made good use of her time on her infrequent trips to New York. She had seen little of the metropolis in her entire lifetime, so she enjoyed the streets, the theater, the shops and museums. The strands linking past and present were slackening visibly at this time. Dusty victorias creaked through Central Park with the aroma of the past. Soon the gray ghost of the Vanderbilt mansion at Fifty-Seventh Street would be leaning lopsidedly over the whirling crowds, its turrets gone, its walls crumbling. But for the moment the millionaire's world seemed firmly based and indestructible.

In April the President was back in New York, making a speech that caused Elbert Gary to compare him to the Rock of Gibraltar. "Altogether he is getting a strong position with the businessmen of the country," Chief Justice Taft observed in a letter to his wife. At this time the President was wrestling with three tough problems—the bonus bill, the immigration bill, and the tax bill. Taft hoped that he would veto all three. He believed that this would establish him as a man who not only spoke his mind but acted on what he said.

One of Mrs. Coolidge's most interesting functions that spring was the Easter egg-rolling with nearly 100,000 children cavorting in the White House grounds. Chief Justice Taft could see only the stomach-aches from hard boiled eggs and the "dreadful mess on the greenswards" that followed. But Mrs. Coolidge led the Cabinet wives down from the south portico and chatted gaily with the children as they crowded around her, patted her white collies and teased Rebecca, her pet raccoon. On May Day she welcomed groups of children bearing flowers, an annual event that gave her great pleasure. Charles Henlock, chief horticulturist in charge of the White House greenhouses, thought that she cared more for flowers than any other President's wife. Close to the rear entrance of the White House were two small gardens laid out originally by the first Mrs. Wilson. One was filled with rose bushes and closely hedged; the other was a colonial garden with lilies of the valley, pansies, nasturtiums and other simple flowers. Every morning Mrs. Coolidge strolled out to see what progress the flowers in these gardens was making. She touched a blossom here and there, wielded a trowel as the spirit moved her and sometimes plucked flowers for her private quarters. In June the fragrance from the giant magnolia tree was wafted across the colonial garden. The McKinley oak, the Wilson elm, the Coolidge birch all became part of this picture. In time Mrs. Coolidge had a water-lily pond added to the charms of the White House grounds.

There were times when she needed the solitude and refreshment of the gardens, for 1924 was a year of uneasiness on the political front. The President was deeply worried over the revelations made before Senator Thomas J. Walsh's committee on the corruption of the men who had surrounded Harding. One slashing blow followed another as the Teapot Dome scandal roared around the Capitol. The President was slow to demand the resignations of the men implicated. He had no wish to rock the boat but one by one they went. In March Edwin Denby, Secretary of the Navy, who had permitted the transfer of naval oil reserves from his department to the Department of the Interior, resigned under pressure. Harry M. Daugherty, who regarded Coolidge as a man of "friendly, peaceful instincts . . . a real man, honest, sincere, unaffected, strong" had a furious interview in the President's office, bounded out, "his jaw set and his eye like flint" and eventually resigned.

In 1927 he was acquitted on charges of conspiracy to defraud the Government. But by June of 1924 Albert B. Fall, who had been Secretary of the Interior; Harry F. Sinclair, to whom he had leased government oil properties; and Edward L. Doheney, accused of bribing Fall, had all been indicted. Fall was convicted. Sinclair was acquitted of charges of conspiracy to defraud the Government but served a term for refusing to testify on the Teapot Dome leases. Doheny was acquitted. Edward B. McLean was drawn into the picture for having lent $100,000 to Fall. He lost control of the Washington *Post,* battled his wife in the courts, and was declared insane the year that Coolidge died. Throughout the Coolidge administration the specters of the Harding regime churned up the political scene, with post-dated glimpses of Jess Smith, Daugherty's lieutenant; of Roxie Stinson and the Little Green House on K Street where lobbyists, fixers and hard drinkers foregathered and hatched their plots. Harding's reputation was further assailed in Nan Britton's book *The President's Daughter* and Gaston B. Means' distorted tale *The Strange Death of President Harding.*

With an election coming up Coolidge stepped warily in the trail of mud left by his predecessor, but it was highly embarrassing to his administration. There was no stemming the tide of gossip that swept over the shifting Washington scene. Many asked why Coolidge had held his peace while dubious moves were being made right under his nose in the time of Harding. Some found it difficult to understand his delay in getting rid of Daugherty.

He had other serious issues at stake all through 1924. He vetoed the Soldiers' Bonus bill, an unpopular move which was ignored as he was triumphantly overruled. He signed the bill restricting immigration, a hot issue, and one that involved Japan directly. Meanwhile, the Ku Klux Klan was rising to power in the South, with murders, kidnapings, floggings and threats. The ills of prohibition were shaking the foundations of law and order. The murder of Bobby Franks in Chicago by Nathan Leopold and Richard Loeb, with Clarence

Darrow's sensational defense of the two youths, drew international attention to a peculiarly unsavory crime on the American scene.

But neither the political revelations nor the scandals of prohibition enforcement had any effect on the election. The country prospered after the hard days of the war. The Coolidges had brought quiet and dignity to the White House. The President announced his intention of running for election at a Gridiron dinner held in December, 1923. By January he wrote that he was certain of success. In June he was nominated at the Republican National Convention in Cleveland. The Democrats were meeting in Madison Square Garden when the President and Mrs. Coolidge came face to face suddenly with the major sorrow of their lives.

CHAPTER V

DEATH OF A SON

M RS. COOLIDGE was playing the piano in the oval room on the second floor of the White House on a July day in 1924 when Dr. Joel Boone, who was one of several present, asked: "Where's Calvin?"

"He's lying down," she responded. "He isn't feeling well. Would you have a look at him?"

Dr. Boone found the sixteen-year-old boy suffering from a badly inflamed foot. With typical family reserve he had said little or nothing about a blister on top of his right toe that had developed after he had played tennis in sneakers, without wearing socks. When he saw the damage done, he had taken a hot bath, applied iodine and ignored the matter. But it was observed around the White House that he seemed tired and listless in the next day or two.

Soon pains were shooting up his leg, which quickly stiffened. He lounged about, listening to the Democratic Convention in New York on the radio, then became drowsy and lost interest even in this. He did not let his parents know how ill he felt. Now Admiral Boone saw at once that his foot was in a serious condition. He called Mrs. Coolidge and applied antiseptic dressings. Then he drove to Walter Reed Hospital with Miss Randolph, taking blood specimens along with him for tests. When he came out his face was grave for Calvin had a serious infection. A medical consultation was held in the night and by morning the entire household was alerted although the public was still unaware of the youth's critical condition.

The President kept his engagements that day and spoke before the National Education Association on "Education: The Cornerstone of Self-Government." It was July 4, his fifty-second birthday, but the most miserable he had ever spent. "Calvin is very sick so this is not a happy day for me," he wrote. Grace was calm and resourceful, although every hour brought deeper dismay. She worked swiftly and efficiently in the sick room, helping the nurses, staying close to Calvin with cheerful, comforting words. Guests left the White House. The boys' room was turned into a hospital ward. One medical consultant after another was called in. Every measure was tried but the age of sulfa and penicillin had not yet arrived. On the fifth it was announced that young Calvin had a fighting chance to live. By this time the nation knew that death hovered over the White House and all political barriers were swept away in sympathy for the two suffering parents. Bulletins on his condition were read at the Democratic Convention. It was remembered that Willie Lincoln had died in the White House as his father coped with the problems of the Civil War. "Terror clutched at all our hearts," Miss Randolph recalled.

The President went back and forth between the executive offices and Calvin's room. At first he kept appointments and stared blankly at papers that he must sign. He was suffering the most intense anxiety, while the best medical aid he could summon was applied to his son. His aides thought he had the bearing of a stricken man. When he noticed a rabbit hopping about among the plants near a fountain in the garden he picked it up and took it to Calvin. "A lovely smile, and a look of happy interest in the wan young face rewarded him," Miss Randolph noted. Colonel Starling, appalled by the seriousness of Calvin's illness, added: "He would have carried him the whole of the White House grounds, a handful at a time, if it would have done any good." Only that March he had told a group of young people: "There are only two things necessary for boys—to work and behave yourselves." Now his world was crashing in with the collapse of his son.

All day long the White House telephones rang with inquiries, suggestions, offers of aid. Joseph McInerney, the chauffeur who had been present at the swearing-in of the President, and many others offered blood, but Calvin was beyond help. White-faced and exhausted, Mrs. Coolidge rode in her car behind the ambulance that took him to Walter Reed Hospital where an operation was performed on July 6 in a desperate attempt to drain off poison. Artificial respiration, saline injections, blood transfusions, all manner of measures were tried. Seven physicians were at work on him by this time, including Dr. James F. Coupal and Dr. Boone, the White House regulars. His parents stayed all night at the hospital and returned to the White House for a few minutes in the morning before returning for what proved to be the final vigil. The mood in official circles was mirrored by Chief Justice Taft who wrote to his wife:

> The whole country is at the deathbed of young Calvin Coolidge in deepest sympathy of the stricken parents. Talking with Dr. Lockwood makes me think that it was a case that was hopeless from the first in the malignant character of the infection which by chance affected the blister. It was as if he had been bitten by a poisonous snake. It would seem as if the White House always carries domestic burdens for the occupants.

During the last two days of his life Calvin was in and out of delirium. His parents watched in silent anguish. "In his suffering he was asking me to make him well. I could not," the President wrote in his autobiography. He was always to feel that had he not held the office he did his son might not have been stricken. But Calvin put up a sturdy fight and his mother could scarcely accept the fact that it was a losing one. She had seen him through many crises in his childhood days, and in particular the operation for emphysema when he was five. On that occasion she had stayed with him at the hospital and their family physician, Dr. Edward W. Brown, had a vivid recollection of Calvin Coolidge, holding John by the hand, standing in the middle of the street looking up at the window with the most profound concern. "I am a poor man but I could command considerable money if you need it," he told Dr. Brown.

He was not a rich man now, but he was President of the United States and could draw on the best medical skill in the country. It was of no avail, however, and his parents were speechless when the sick boy looked up at them trustfully as they were about to leave the room and whispered: "Good night, Father and Mother. Don't worry any more."

On the last night of his life he fancied he was leading a charge of troops and winning a battle. His father thought that this buoyed him up until near the end. "He must have had some premonition, some intimation," he speculated when it was all over, "for suddenly his body seemed to relax and he murmured: 'We surrender.'"

"No, Calvin, never surrender," Dr. Boone exclaimed urgently, but the youth had slipped into a coma, from which he never revived. He died on July 7, only four days after the severity of his illness was recognized. Extras were shouted along Pennsylvania Avenue and a murmur swept the floor of the Democratic Convention when the news was announced. Franklin D. Roosevelt subsequently read a resolution of sympathy for the family. Next morning the entire nation learned of the death of the youth who had become a familiar White House figure.

Miss Randolph broke the news to John, waiting alone in one of the White House sitting rooms. It had reached her by telephone. Mr. and Mrs. Stearns, who regarded John and Calvin as they did their own sons, had come on from Boston. A month earlier Mrs. Coolidge had gone with Mrs. Stearns to Mercersburg Academy to see John graduate. The President had decided to spend that summer in Washington, taking frequent trips on the *Mayflower* for recreation. Calvin, who had always been more delicate than John, had grown beyond his strength. He had been shooting up and was five feet eleven when he became ill. He weighed 115 pounds and was frail in build.

Their older, and now their only, son went out to meet the President and Mrs. Coolidge as they returned from the hospital, weary, spent, speechless. Major Coupal stayed at hand all night and soon after sunrise Calvin's body was brought back to the White House and placed in the East Room with a guard of honor. The official death verdict was staphylococcus septicemia with pulmonary edema as a contributory cause. The nation sorrowed with the Coolidges over a youthful and most unlikely death.

With dignity and courage they faced the services in the East Room. Bare-headed, her face white and grave, Mrs. Coolidge walked between her husband and John. Others showed their grief openly but all three of the Coolidges went through the service with fortitude and calm. The President "did not let the storm of his heart reflect itself upon his face," William Allen White commented, but Mrs. Harry S. New noticed that he touched his wife's hand gently as Dr. Pierce spoke feelingly of young Calvin and read the Twenty-third Psalm. She thought that his gesture told more than words or tears.

Diplomats, statesmen, the nation's official dignitaries were present. Young military and naval aides were lined up in white summer uniforms. Many of the White House staff and the clerical force from the executive offices wept for Calvin, who had been a bright young spirit among them. The *Mayflower* orchestra played with special feeling, since every one of its musicians had known him well. Both of the young Coolidges were genuinely liked by the entire White House staff. Calvin resembled his father in appearance and had a touch of his dry wit. That night the funeral party, including Cabinet members, went by special train to Northampton where another service was held on July 10 in the Edwards Memorial Church, which young Calvin had attended from childhood. Here were the friends of his early boyhood. Children lined up along the entire route from the station to the church, where Dr. Kenneth B. Wells conducted the service. The Smith College chimes rang out and mothers who had gone shopping and baby-walking with Mrs. Coolidge stood on the sidelines and watched her with sympathy.

Her final ordeal was in the small cemetery at Plymouth Notch where she and the President one day would be buried beside young Calvin. Late afternoon sunshine slanting down from the Green Mountains burnished the group at the open grave. Mrs. Coolidge held the President's arm and tears coursed slowly down her cheeks as Dr. Pierce read the committal service and taps was sounded. The

Washington quartet sang *My Faith Looks up to Thee, Saviour, Like a Shepherd, Lead Us* and the Mercersburg Academy hymn *Jesus, I Live to Thee*. At the last moment Mrs. Coolidge bent down and tucked the Testament she had given Calvin as a small boy into the blanket of pink roses that covered his coffin.

Mrs. Coolidge's own description of the funeral and her emotions, written on August 3, 1924, to Mrs. Hills, the friend who had shared in his upbringing and whose son Jack had played with young Calvin, tells its own story:

> It is a beautiful spot and it was lovely the day we left little Calvin there. Before our train got to Ludlow there had been a thunderstorm shower which had laid the dust and made everything fresh and green. As we stood beside the grave the sun was shining, throwing long, slanting shadows and the birds were singing their sleepy songs. Truly, it seemed to me God's acre. There was a prayer, a few passages of scripture and two hymns, and the Mercersburg hymn which I have seen Calvin sing with the other boys at school and I could seem to hear and see him there. "Taps" never sounded as it did there, echoing and reechoing from mountain to mountain. I came away filled with a "peace which passeth understanding," comforted and full of courage. I remembered Calvin as I saw him last in that hallowed place helping Grandfather cut the grass and rake it, hardly more than a year before. Yes, he did love Plymouth, even as a little fellow when he was out on a rise of ground in the morning with his Grandfather and looking around said "This is a great place, Grandfather."

Mrs. Coolidge had sent daily telegrams to Mrs. Hills on Calvin's condition. The last one read: "Tell Mother little Calvin is at rest" and she immediately went to Mrs. Goodhue's home and broke the news to her. Both of Calvin's grandparents attended the funeral services. He had spent much time with his grandfather on the farm. The President took John out to the back porch and measured his height against the door jamb, an old custom of his. Like Calvin, he had grown uncommonly tall. Mr. Coolidge made a notation of his height with pencil and marked it "J.C. 1924."

"How tall was Calvin?" he asked John.

"Just an inch shorter than I am."

He drew a second line an inch below John's and wrote "C.C. 1924, if he had lived."

Mrs. Coolidge could not bear to let John return at once to Camp Devens, although the President thought he should go. "But everybody else backed me up," she wrote. John was "brave and fine" but she saw from the look in his eyes "there is sadness and loneliness in his heart," and added to Mrs. Hills: "John and I seem to need each other just now."

She and John and Colonel Coolidge drove to the lime kiln and dug up a small spruce tree about five feet high. They wrapped the roots in burlap and took it back to Washington. Next day it was planted in the south grounds near the tennis court, "where we can see it from the south portico and from the window of the President's room." She had a bronze plate made saying that it was brought from Plymouth and was planted there in memory of Calvin Coolidge, Jr.

The Coolidges were soon back in Plymouth, the only place where the President seemed to find repose. It was impossible to move in any direction without some reminder of the son he had lost. He summed up his own feelings at this point in his autobiography: *When he went the power and the glory of the Presidency went with him . . . I do not know why such a price was exacted for occupying the White House . . . Sustained by the great outpouring of sympathy from all over the nation, my wife and I bowed to the Supreme Will and with such courage as we had went on in the discharge of our duties.*

Mrs. Coolidge took it all in silence. She wore white all summer and winter, and assumed a cheerful manner although her buoyant laughter no longer was heard. "We are all of us well and keeping a stiff front, trying to be as brave and courageous as Calvin was," she wrote to Mrs. Hills ten days after his death. But the President's suffering was visible to all who knew him well. Alfred Pearce Dennis, who remembered him from his early days in Northampton, thought that his face had the "bleak desolation of cold November rain beating on gray Vermont granite." He was astonished to hear him say, as if his visitor might not have heard the news: "How are your boys? One of my boys has gone." John T. Lambert, a White House correspondent, quoted the President as saying of young Calvin: "He was a Coolidge with his mother's disposition."

Mrs. Coolidge passed many hours knitting in the gardens south of the White House. Every day she put a fresh rose in a vase in front of her son's picture in the sitting room and tucked a yellow one into the counterpane of his bed. She was not a sentimentalist but this was the major grief of her life and it dimmed the scene for her. John always sent her flowers on the anniversary of Calvin's death and in 1949, when he was married and had two children of his own, she wrote to him: "You are remarkable at remembering anniversaries, John . . . It seems hardly possible that twenty-five years have flown by."

Americans everywhere warmed to the Coolidges at this time and they became more firmly entrenched in the national consciousness. The social curtain was rung down for the time being but thousands of sympathetic messages reached them. Mrs. Coolidge answered as many as she could personally but the task was beyond her. Miss Randolph took over most of the correspondence at this time and many of the letters were acknowledged by a message of thanks engraved on a plain white card. Mrs. Harding, to whom Mrs. Coolidge had shown understanding and kindness at the time of her husband's death, wrote to her: "No matter how many loving hands may be stretched out to one, some paths we must tread alone." By the end of the year Mrs. Harding, too, was dead. Mrs. Coolidge kept in close touch with her as long as she lived, calling on her when others forgot her, seeing her off to Marion and being considerate of her in every way she could.

A letter written by Mrs. Coolidge to Mrs. Oliver Roland Ingersoll, of Brooklyn, was published as a general expression of her thanks to all who had sympathized with her. She hoped that it would "spread and make itself felt wherever a kindly thought had been sent out to me." She included the verse of a hymn that had comforted her:

I know not where His islands lift
Their fronded palms in air
I only know I cannot drift
Beyond His love and care.

But Mrs. Coolidge expressed herself more naturally to the Robins in a letter written shortly after Calvin's death in which she said she envied them because they could all come and go at will. She wished she could steal away without being seen and "have one day unaccompanied just to go about unrecognized all by myself." Then, in thanking them for their sympathetic messages, she wrote:

> No longer can we see and touch Calvin but in a very real sense he is with us and has his place in our family circle. Two years ago this year he taught me to swim—not because I wanted to learn but just because he wanted to teach me. He put his hand under my chin and I just had to do my best to please him. I'll never forget how happy he was when I took a few strokes, and heard his encouraging voice and I am not going to disappoint him.

The President's notes at this time were as always, brief and distilled. Typical was his letter to C. J. Hills: "The messages which come to me from the old friends are the best and most helpful, and I want to thank you for what you say, although shortness of time prevents a longer note. I am sure you will understand that my appreciation is none the less sincere."

Many stories that touched his parents deeply came to light after Calvin's death. One that they had known nothing about concerned a boy his own age who had addressed him as the first boy of the land. Calvin had replied on August 16, 1923: "I think you are mistaken in calling me the first boy of the land, since I have done nothing. It is my father who is President. Rather the first boy of the land would be some boy who had distinguished himself through his own actions." Mrs. Coolidge had this letter framed and she hung it in her room.

The summer Calvin died he had planned to help his grandfather harvest his crops at Plymouth. The President took pride in his zeal for work and he prized the memory of his son's response when one of his fellow workers said: "If my father was President I would not work in a tobacco field."

Calvin quietly replied: "If my father were your father, you would."

Soon after Mr. Coolidge became Vice-President the boys were urged by their mother to take dancing lessons. Calvin gravely asked: "Did my father take dancing lessons?" It was no surprise to him to learn that he had not, although he had shuffled about a bit at Amherst. "Well, if my father never did, I don't need to," he commented. But the President overruled him in this instance and he went to dancing classes with John, who took his lessons with enthusiasm and was much in demand at Washington parties. His father was scathing about the bell-bottomed trousers he wore in the tradition of the 1920s. "If you'd take some of the cloth out of those baggy-legged pants you'd have enough for a suit," he told John. But baggy pants or not, John did well at prep school and ranked tenth in his class during the three years he was at Mercersburg.

Although it was his habit to reprove the boys sharply and he had little patience with their shortcomings Mrs. Coolidge could remember only one occasion on which he punished one of them physically and then he used the hairbrush to good effect. Always he demanded prompt obedience and she considered him a strict disciplinarian. His propensity for teasing, under which they all smarted at times, was inherited from his forebears.

"He could never get a great deal of satisfaction out of teasing Calvin," she commented, "for his younger son entered into the spirit of it and enjoyed the encounter even more than his father did, but John was a more shy and sensitive child, and I could never get him to understand or adopt Calvin's method of outwitting his father. Occasionally John and I managed to turn the tables on him."

In his later years John admitted that although his father's teasing had wounded him at the time, in the long run he could see its humorous side and view it as a form of relaxation on the President's part. John conceded that most of the anecdotes attributed later to his father had a "degree of reasonableness." He also suspected that the President was just as amused as anyone else at the tales, both true and false, that clung to his name after he became famous. John was drawn more closely to both of his parents after his brother's death and he gave his mother great support and comfort. Calvin had been a student at Mercersburg Academy when he died and Mrs. Coolidge laid the cornerstone of the new chapel that October and served as a trustee on the board of regents for twelve years. The gold cross on the altar is a memorial to her son.

She sent personal notes to all the Mercersburg boys who had
written to her when Calvin died—"not only because I feel an interest
in every son of Mercersburg but chiefly because I think Calvin
would like to have me do so." In 1934 the students dedicated their
yearbook *The Karux* to Grace Coolidge with the inscription:

> The boys of the Mercersburg Academy most respectfully dedicate
> this annual book of the school to Grace Coolidge—a Mercers-
> burg mother and Regent, a graduate of the University of Ver-
> mont, recipient of the highest honorary degrees in American
> academic life, trusted counsellor of many noble enterprises, in
> simple, private life or exalted public station always the same
> genuine, gentle, gracious spirit. "She openeth her mouth with
> wisdom and in her tongue is the law of kindness."

Five years after his death, lying awake on the night of July 7
thinking of the son she had lost, Mrs. Coolidge jotted down a poem
which, in her own words, "wrote itself." She sent it to William F.
Bigelow, editor of *Good Housekeeping,* with a modest letter asking
if it interested him for publication. She conceded that it failed to
conform to rules of verse or prose and was an expression of the
heart, coming at a wakeful hour of the night, "quite a rare hour for
me." Her thoughts had centered on her son because the anniversary
of his death had come around again. Since she often received letters
from mothers who had shared her experience she hoped that the
poem might spread comfort if he did not feel that it was too crude
"to be worthy of its subject." In conclusion she wrote: "I feel confident that you will be quite frank and sincere with me, knowing that
I ask for your honest opinion, and I fully realize that the lines are
poetic in thought, but not in form."

Mr. Bigelow replied that true beauty did not have to conform to
definite standards, nor did real emotion have to be expressed in any
prescribed way. He felt that *The Open Door* had real emotion. He
promised that he would play it quietly, giving it a page of its own in
the magazine. To do more would be to exploit her and her sorrow.
He sent her a check for $250 to use as she saw fit. He assured her
that his readers would like it.

They did. The poem brought a tremendous response and was

reprinted in many forms. Mrs. Coolidge thanked him for his understanding letter and for using her tribute to her son in such an unostentatious way. She gave the check to John at the time of his marriage and told him to buy something for his home with it. She thought that Calvin would have liked that. The poem was much as she had described it:

> You, my son,
> Have shown me God.
> Your kiss upon my cheek
> Has made me feel the gentle touch
> Of Him who leads us on.
> The memory of your smile, when young,
> Reveals His face,
> As mellowing years come on apace.
> And when you went before,
> You left the Gates of Heaven ajar
> That I might glimpse,
> Approaching from afar,
> The glories of His Grace.
> Hold, Son, my hand,
> Guide me along the path,
> That, coming,
> I may stumble not,
> Nor roam,
> Nor fail to show the way
> Which leads us—Home.

But there was neither poetry nor song in Mrs. Coolidge's heart when she returned to Plymouth in the summer of 1924, a few weeks after her son's death. Although she knew that she might well be facing another four years in the White House, her spirits drooped. She threw her arms impulsively around Colonel Coolidge's neck as she stepped out of the car and kissed him. Aurora Pierce in her freshly starched gingham apron with deep pockets stood at the uncurtained front window watering her geraniums. Her tall, spindling frame looked stern and unyielding, but she turned with sympathy to Mrs. Coolidge.

Aurora was a family institution, guardian of the Colonel's welfare for sixteen years. A spinster from Shrewsbury, of independent spirit, she spoke her mind to the President as she did to everyone else. She had no hesitancy about ordering him around and telling him what he ought to eat. No Coolidge would ever have thought of interfering with Aurora's methodical ways. She was up at daybreak and had the laundry done before breakfast. She would wash the floor right under the President's feet as he had breakfast if the hour to wash the floor had arrived. Her geraniums were put out in the garden on Memorial Day and were brought in again on Labor Day. Aurora saved every scrap she could lay her hands on. She earned a dollar a day and died leaving thousands of dollars.

Her maple-frosted cake and blueberry and custard pies were stiff competition for the White House kitchens. She had great respect for Mrs. Coolidge and always welcomed her when the President's wife donned an apron and helped to prepare food for guests, or made up the beds, or sprinkled water on Aurora's thirsty geraniums. Everyone in Plymouth and Northampton were agreed that the White House had not changed Grace Coolidge. But it was clear that the death of their son had affected both of the Coolidges deeply and had left them apathetic about the campaign. The President sat for long stretches under the sugar maples that summer looking toward the hills. Or he would wander over to the cheese factory and sip whey. But the limelight beat constantly on the hamlet of Plymouth and both he and his wife, however reluctantly, were caught in its beams. Although Coolidge at this time stood aloof from political maneuverings and did no campaigning, Republicans from coast to coast worked to uphold the *status quo* of prosperity. And on the local front "Keep Cool and Keep Coolidge" became the official song of the Home Town Coolidge Club of Plymouth. A Coolidge-Dawes Caravan crossed the country with the Plymouth dance orchestra.

The fact that the President was in residence there brought an official touch to the hamlet. Executive offices were set up above Miss Cilley's store and post office. Great pouches of mail arrived and reporters came and went, prowling through the room at the back where Calvin Coolidge was born, and taking note of the old platform scales, the spice cabinet, the tobacco cutter, the kerosene pump and the cheese box that his grandfather had used in the store.

Five stout wooden tables were built for this rustic White House office and Violet Hickory Pelkey delivered hundreds of messages of considerable importance to the nation. Mrs. Coolidge gave Mrs. Pelkey, who inherited the store when Miss Cilley died, samples from her most glamorous White House gowns.

On a hot August day the Coolidges held a reception for the neighbors and people gathered from far and near. Farmers came in from the hills. Their wives brought their children to have a look at the President. Politicians arrived from New York and summer visitors drove in to the quiet little hamlet to view the family retreat. Mrs. Coolidge had a cut finger that day but she exchanged greetings until her hands were swollen. She was an instinctive campaigner. "I hope that I will look as young as you do when I am that old," she remarked to a ninety-year-old woman who passed in line. By this time the farmers in the valley had become used to the notion that the Man in the White House and the First Lady were two of their own. Colonel Coolidge sat in the hammock and nodded to familiar figures. The business of having a son in the White House pleased but did not dazzle him.

Every morning, while her husband conducted his official business, Mrs. Coolidge walked down the road to Calvin's grave, often carrying a pail of water to pour in the vases that held flowers. Sometimes her bouquets were wild flowers gathered as she walked along rugged woodland pathways. Sometimes they were peonies or roses from town. More often they were rain-drenched larkspur, pinks and sweet william from local gardens. Devil's paint brush flowed like wine over the surrounding fields and goldenrod burnished the heath. The rocky soil, too sterile for fruitful farming, was brightly checkered with field flowers. Usually in the afternoons they took drives through the surrounding country, past rocky streams of black water laced with foam, through forests where deer hid shyly amid the trees. Or else they called on Aunt Gratia, the President's aunt who had married John J. Wilder and lived in a mustard-colored house along the road.

The Coolidge family worshiped in the local church and on their first Sunday back after Calvin's death the Rev. John White talked on the spiritual and material values of simplicity—a quality with which both the President and his wife were endowed. The pews were hard benches, highly varnished. The pulpit was a platform. Mrs. Coolidge's voice could be clearly heard, rising rich and full in the hymns. The President made no attempt to sing but listened attentively. As stories of rustic living came out of Plymouth, Elisabeth Marbury, a veteran worker for the Democratic party, infuriated the Republican women with jeers at the tendency to present Mrs. Coolidge as a domestic and simple woman who could bake biscuits, do her own housework and make a shirtwaist for $1.69. "Milk-pail stuff!" said Miss Marbury scornfully. This was a misconception of the unaffected simplicity of the President's home life, her defenders chorused, as well as being a shocking violation of taste. But she could and did run up gowns for herself while in the White House, including checked ginghams with dimity collars and cuffs.

In spite of their desire for privacy the picturesque aspects of their life at Plymouth Notch were too compelling to be overlooked. Calvin Coolidge, like most Presidential candidates, was jockeyed into posing in odd garb which he wore so awkwardly that the cartoonists had every opportunity to make sport of him. When hacking at a tree he was apt to wear a city hat. When pitching hay he took off his coat but looked more like a chartered accountant than a farmer, although he had every claim to the role.

The President was too austere to indulge naturally in such demogogic gestures and the result sometimes bordered on the absurd. William Allen White was severely critical of these attempts to present him as the poor man's candidate. The aura of Wall Street was already strongly attached to the Coolidge administration. "He won, not because of this demagogy but in spite of it," the Kansas editor insisted. In actual fact, both of the Coolidges were deeply sincere and Grace was not prone to lend herself to artificial situations. Her sons learned early in life to protect themselves from the camera lens as their father became an important political figure. They were found hiding in the Y.M.C.A. on the day he became Vice-President. And now John was apt to head off to fish in a rocky mountain stream or disappear in the woods.

But election tactics were in the air when Henry Ford, Thomas A.

Edison and Harvey Firestone sat on the farmhouse porch with the President and Mrs. Coolidge that August and discussed the state of the world. The newspapers noted that this group was remarkably representative of modern American life—of its scientific advances, its industrial progress, its comforts, amusements and means of communication. Oil lamps were still in use all around them in the valley. Roads were rough. Creature comforts did not abound and the President and his wife slept in an old birch bed in a Spartan house. The pioneering touch was pervasive and the visitors who had worked their own way to success were not immune to its honest simplicity. The nation recognized this assemblage on Colonel Coolidge's porch as a symbol of the American tradition and it was widely publicized.

It was a bright day and the Green Mountains loomed in the distance. The valley was touched with glinting sunshine, its white houses sharply framed in the green sweep of the fields and hills. Kitchen chairs were brought out on the porch but Ford and Edison sat beside the President in the hammock. The conversation took a wide range, from reparations to diet. Quick to remember that Edison was a cat napper who survived with a minimum of sequential sleep Mrs. Coolidge discussed her husband's slumber habits with him. She expressed the opinion that Calvin had too much sleep by going to bed early every night and taking a nap after lunch.

The President gave Henry Ford an old maple sap bucket that had belonged to his ancestors. "My father had it, I used it, and now you've got it!" he remarked without any wasted words as he autographed it. Aurora had scoured it clean. She was not going to have it said that the sap bucket was dirty, a charge unjustly laid against her about the lamp chimney used on the night Mr. Coolidge was sworn in as President.

"The United States is lucky to have Calvin Coolidge," said Thomas Edison as he cranked a movie camera and exchanged jokes with the reporters.

"Calvin Coolidge will be elected President and the United States is assured continued prosperity," added Henry Ford.

The President escorted them around the property and showed them the nearby cheese factory. John, to whom Ford gave a compass that day, was to open a modern cheese factory on the family property at Plymouth in 1960, reviving a languishing industry in which his forebears had interest. Mrs. Coolidge was pleased to see her husband drawn out of himself that day, for the memory of Calvin obsessed him. She had set up the small wooden weather vane her son had made the summer before and it whirled on a fence post across the road from the Colonel's house. It had been taken down for the winter but he had asked to have it set up again, and Mrs. Coolidge found the nails and fixed it herself.

Toward the end of August they were back in another world. They had returned to Washington to entertain the Prince of Wales. The young heir to the British throne had captured the headlines on his visit to America and every move he made was watched with close attention. At the time he was still the idol of the British. But while preparations were being made for him at the White House Ike Hoover, who was devoted to John Coolidge, remarked: "Well, he may be the Prince of Wales but you're the Prince of Plymouth."

The Prince's visit was brief. He was in Washington for four hours only and was entertained at a family luncheon in the White House. Large crowds watched him drive from the station to the Executive Mansion but his visit involved no more ceremony than might have been expected from one of the Coolidges' Vermont neighbors paying a casual social call. The Coolidges found it altogether too casual. A telephone call had come through in the morning, asking if the Prince might come to lunch in informal dress. The President and Charles Evans Hughes, Secretary of State, promptly decided to wear business suits. Everyone knew that Mr. Coolidge was not only highly ceremonious himself in this respect but expected the same of others. He did not bend to the informal note in dress on state occasions.

The Prince wore his favorite pin-striped navy blue, with a deep-blue shirt, a soft collar, his regimental tie and a gray felt hat. The day was broiling hot and Mrs. Coolidge was informed that he had hurriedly cut off the cuffs of his shirt because of the weather. "The poor Prince," she wrote to the Robins. "Some day I will again be a humble citizen, while he can never be just himself."

He showed signs of being intensely nervous. Mr. Hughes presented him to the President in the Blue Room. Mr. Coolidge in turn presented him to his wife, and she introduced John. The tall, dark Prince of Plymouth towered above the golden-haired, blue-eyed Prince of Wales. John was a shy youth, too, but he had the Coolidge impassivity and seemed more composed. The Prince fumbled with his tie, buttoned and unbuttoned his jacket, smoothed down his shining hair, stood on one foot and then on the other.

The luncheon for four that followed was a memorably uncomfortable meal for all concerned. The President clammed up. The Prince, conscious of the fact that his host had recently lost a son, was ill at ease and said little. His usual smile and responsive air were absent. John was equally silent. The President ate abstractedly. Mrs. Coolidge created such conversation as there was and the Prince later pronounced her one of the most charming women he had ever met. There were references to his ocean trip, to the weather, to the international polo matches. It was the era of prohibition and the only drink served was White Rock.

After luncheon President Coolidge took the Prince to his study where they smoked and had twenty minutes of chat, with long intervals of silence. The Cabinet members and their wives were then presented to the Prince in the Blue Room but this, too, was an awkward interlude, without warmth or grace. When the Coolidges took their departure the Prince seemed to relax. His special train pulled out of Union Station in mid-afternoon and he was on his way back to James A. Burden's estate on Long Island.

As the year neared a close and the campaign gained momentum across the country the Coolidges sought solitude and rest repeatedly on the *Mayflower,* which became symbolic during the 1920s of the President's favorite form of relaxation. He was by no means a good sailor and they watched the weather predictions before going out. When reviewing the Navy at Hampton Roads in June, 1927, he was so deathly seasick that he was just able to take the salute before he collapsed on a sofa and watched the wind-up with his teeth gritted and his color pea-green. But he gamely observed the ceremonial rites and posed for pictures.

Although neither an instinctive yachtsman nor a lover of the sea he seemed to find refreshment in these periodical cruises. Mr. and Mrs. Stearns were invariably on board and Mr. Stearns, on ship or ashore, said grace before meals. Mrs. Coolidge was never consulted about the guest list. In fact, she usually had no idea who might be coming aboard, an omission that caused her to remark with considerable tact on one occasion: "I have never outgrown my childish enjoyment of the unexpected." But she was so gregarious by nature that this made little difference; she knew that she could handle any arrival.

Those in the inner Coolidge circle sooner or later were bound to cruise on the *Mayflower,* and reporters watched the guests for political implications. But the yacht was not used as a conference room for the Cabinet. Having picked his guests the President "avoided them and enjoyed them to the limit," said William Allen White, speaking from personal experience. The President relaxed to the point of wearing white flannel trousers and a navy blue blazer, with a yachting cap. Grace chose white silk accordion pleated skirts, trim navy jackets and berets for her seafaring costume. They were all piped on board with flourishes and ruffles and Dr. Boone was always on hand as family friend and physician. His wife and his daughter Suzanne were close to Mrs. Coolidge and the Boones were among her lifelong friends.

It was on the *Mayflower* that Dr. Boone helped Colonel Coolidge into his first dinner suit. The President had ordered the suit for his father and he sent Dr. Boone to his cabin to help him dress, since he did not wish to have the Colonel embarrassed even by the tacit admission to a servant that he had never before worn a dinner coat. Dr. Boone, handsome and always sartorially perfect himself, adjusted the Colonel's studs, knotted his tie, and gave reassurance to the reserved and able old gentleman whom he greatly admired. All through dinner that night Mrs. Coolidge kept smiling encouragingly across the table at her father-in-law who sat with dignity in what Dr. Boone described as the "silent loquaciousness" that characterized the devoted relationship of Calvin Coolidge and his father. The President sat for hours in silence on the yacht, his peaked cap slightly cocked, his frosted blue eyes turned to the sea. The Colonel was from the mountains. The sea was not his natural element and Mrs. Coolidge teased him gently about his ignorance of nautical language. They usually sailed at two o'clock on Saturday afternoons with a party of ten or twelve and returned on Monday morning. Sometimes they left on Sunday afternoon, returning late in the evening, but Taft noted that the President had a "deuce of a time having it made public that his trip on the river is after he goes to church." On the longer trips services were held on deck when the weather was warm and in the saloon on chilly days. A stringed orchestra from the Navy Band played the processional and hymns. They took these trips quite late in the season as well as in the summer months, cruising down the Potomac as far as Point Lookout, anchoring there for the night, then proceeding to Chesapeake Bay.

On warm nights a screen was set up on the fantail of the yacht and the Presidential party watched Buster Keaton in *The General* or other current pictures, while the sailors roared with laughter from their seats on the lower deck. *The Covered Wagon,* first of the Westerns to make a deep impression, was a popular selection and Harold Lloyd's antics as he hung from a skyscraper in *Safety Last* was breath-taking nonsense. The Sunday papers were brought out by hydroplane and were picked up by *Mayflower* surf boats. The President quickly turned to the headlines, which often involved himself. His humor for the day was sometimes determined by his Sunday morning reading. Although Mrs. Coolidge was convinced that Calvin was more genial on the *Mayflower* than ashore his dinner companions could scarcely detect the difference. Mrs. Frank B. Kellogg, a seasoned sufferer, and Mrs. Morrow made a determined effort one night to elicit some response. Mrs. Morrow was the first to give up but Mrs. Kellogg persisted. Next morning, knowing well the President's insistence on punctuality, she made a special effort to be on time for breakfast. But as she walked into the dining saloon she was just in time to hear him say:

"And where are 'my two fair ladies'?"

"Exhausted by your conversation of last evening," said Mrs. Coolidge briskly.

By this time Mrs. Morrow was quite won over by Calvin Coolidge, but she had been slow to appreciate his unique qualities. She was greatly disappointed in him when she first met him at a reunion of the Amherst class of '95 and sat with the Coolidges afterward watching a baseball game. For years she had been hearing her husband extol the remarkable Vermonter who had been his classmate at college.

"I don't see how that sulky red-headed little man ever won that pretty, charming woman," Mrs. Morrow remarked when they parted after the game.

"Don't be too hasty, Betty," said Morrow. "We'll hear from that man Coolidge some day."

"Yes," Mrs. Morrow agreed. "We'll hear from him—but we'll hear from him through *his wife.*"

"I couldn't have known then that my husband and I would both be right," Mrs. Morrow commented.

But her daughter Anne liked Calvin Coolidge from the start. When she visited the Governor with her parents in 1918 at the Touraine Hotel and his prospects as a Presidential candidate were under discussion on the way back to New York, she protested loyally when some one remarked: "No one would like him." Anne held up a taped finger. "*I* like him," she said. "He was the only one that asked about my sore finger."

Anne's father was delighted. "There's your answer," he said.

Mrs. Coolidge's devotion to baseball was quite marked on her *Mayflower* cruises. Radio was still something of a novelty and on Saturday afternoons she usually stayed glued to her set listening to the games. In the White House she would go to the telegraph room to pick up the score when a big game was in progress. She greatly endeared herself to the baseball-loving public in 1924, the year in which the unlucky Washington Senators won the World Series from the New York Giants. The President accompanied her to the game. The score was 3-3 in the ninth inning, with Walter Johnson pitching, when the President rose to leave. His wife clutched at his coat tails.

"Where do you think you're going?" she exclaimed. "You sit down."

Calvin sat down. The Senators went on to win the game and the series in extra innings. Had he left the field the fans would have been

slow to forgive him. This was one of many incidents that caused Mrs.
Coolidge to become known as the First Lady of Baseball. For
years she had rooted for the Boston Red Sox and had frequently
sat in the dugout at Fenway Park. Now she joined the Senators in
their dugout in Washington, and came to know the players personally.
She always kept her own record of the games on a score card and
followed the play closely. The President sometimes accompanied
her to games but he usually left early. His interest did not match
hers and he could not spare the time. But he went with her to the
wedding of Stanley R. ("Bucky") Harris, manager of the Washington
Senators and Miss Mary Elizabeth Sutherland, daughter of Howard
Sutherland, Alien Property Custodian. Mrs. Coolidge was a good
friend of Bucky's, as she was of Joe Cronin, manager of the Red
Sox.

There was nothing simulated about her interest in baseball. It
went back to the days when her boys were growing up and it stayed
with her until she died. In the last few years of her life, when she
went out little, she watched the games on television. Certainly no
President's wife before or afterward exhibited the same keen interest
in the national game as Mrs. Coolidge.

In November of that year she learned with mixed feelings that
she would have four more years of the White House. In October her
husband had written to his father saying that the outlook was promising. But with Calvin's death fresh in his memory he added that he
hoped he would never again be a candidate for office. "If only
Calvin were with us, we should be very happy," he wrote. On
November 3, just before the election, he talked on the radio, urging
citizens to vote and as he ended his speech he said good-night to his
father in Plymouth.

Coolidge and Dawes rolled up a heavy plurality at the polls and
Congress went convincingly Republican. Senator Lodge died a few
days later, an embittered man who had once tried to block the
nomination of Calvin Coolidge and had said of his Presidential prospects: "A man who lives in a two-family house? Never!" But
Coolidge had not been vindictive and had consulted him from time to
time on political issues. And in May, 1924, Lodge wrote that there

was no one in the country with any chance of being elected who was comparable to Coolidge in character or ability. In the same month Taft wrote to his wife, who was then in Paris, that "Coolidge's secret thoughts of Lodge are not fit to print."

In appraising the enthusiastic public response to the President at this time Dr. Claude M. Fuess, his biographer, who thought that Coolidge always sought a reform and never a revolution, wrote of him: "He was not magnetic, like the two Roosevelts, or ingratiating, like Harding and Taft, or intellectually dazzling, like Wilson . . . He had worked hard, he had been faithful to duty, he could be trusted as being safe and honest. The voters respected the purity of his private life, his simplicity, his freedom from sham and pretense."

And William Allen White, another biographer, read into his success the fact that he never lost his country-town view of life and never became a world citizen: "He has lived and will die, no matter where fate sends him, Cal Coolidge, of Northampton, of Ludlow and of Plymouth, the small-town American who is more typical of America than our cosmopolitan boulevardier. No boulevardier— Calvin Coolidge. One flag, one country, one conscience, one wife, and never more than three words will do him all his life."

In murky November weather Mrs. Coolidge christened the *Los Angeles,* America's converted dirigible, at Bolling Field. She pulled a red, white and blue streamer, releasing a flock of pigeons from a trap in the bow of the ship. The birds, with quotations from the Bible fastened to their legs, sailed aloft, circled the field and flew off to naval bases along the Atlantic seaboard. Much of the history of her husband's administration would be linked to aeronautics, from the first flight over the North Pole—Admiral Byrd's great feat—to Colonel Lindbergh's solo hop across the Atlantic.

In the following month Mrs. Coolidge was presented to the country in her more scholarly light. Boston University gave her an honorary degree when Mrs. Lucy Jenkins Franklyn was appointed the first woman dean in the history of that institution. The nation's First Lady was cited as student, teacher, daughter, wife and mother, a woman whose qualities of mind and heart "had gained the confidence, admiration and love of the American people." She wrote in humorous vein to the Robins that she found an LL.D. an overwhelming honor and that D.D., not for Doctor of Divinity but for Doctor of Domesticity, would have suited her case. She got "all wobbly" when she understood the magnitude of the degree she was receiving in the new Old South Meeting House. "It never occurred to me that I should rise to the heights of an LL.D," she added. The Robins were present for the ceremony and she caught glimpses of them at the tea that followed. "My life now seems made of tantalizing glimpses," she wrote. "It is terrible to have to spread out so thin."

As Christmas approached Mrs. Coolidge steeled herself against giving way to her feelings. "I shall not be sad at that happy time of year," she wrote to Mrs. Hills on December 9, 1924. "I found a quotation the other day which seems to me to express Calvin and something of what he is to me, one 'whose yesterdays look backward with a smile.' Always he seemed to be just ahead of me and I can see his smile. I shall have the Christmas carols this year as I did last, out on the north portico."

The President had arranged for Thurston, the magician, to give a performance at the White House and she wished John and Jack Hills might be there to see him. John was contented at Amherst. He sang with the Glee Club and the Chapel Choir. His father had warned him to remain in Amherst and "not go farther away than Northampton." John felt he could not afford the time or the money to go with a friend to the Amherst-Wesleyan game at Middletown. Jack Hills, doing brilliantly in Greek and Latin at this time, received an autographed photograph from the President.

The Morrows and the Bartons arrived for a visit at the White House early in December. Mrs. Coolidge seemed a graver, more thoughtful woman as she and the President faced a new term, esteemed and well established, irrespective of political storms. The public was beginning to quote and appreciate the tart observations made by Calvin Coolidge. After the scandals of the Harding administration the clean winds of austere living seemed to sweep over the White House. The static nature of the Coolidge policies had yet to come under heavy attack. The year was 1924 and prosperity washed the country like a tidal wave.

CHAPTER VI

RED DRESS, WHITE COLLIE

I T WAS ICY COLD but the sun shone brilliantly on March 4, 1925, when Calvin Coolidge was sworn in for the second time as President of the United States. The ceremony was dramatically different from the first swearing-in at the lonely farmhouse in Plymouth. Again his wife stood by but the family circle now was broken. The Colonel and John were present but only the memory of Calvin remained. The President had his mother's Bible open at the first chapter of St. John as Chief Justice Taft towered bulkily beside him, administering the oath. For the first time a President's inaugural address was broadcast and millions of Americans heard the thin penetrating drawl of Calvin Coolidge delivering the message: "I favor the policy of economy, not because I wish to save money, but because I wish to save people . . ."

The inauguration arrangements had been sternly made, with a view to the utmost simplicity. The dearth of pomp and pageantry was deliberate and Coolidge's grave face as he rode to the Capitol beside his smiling wife set the key for the day. But on the way back he relaxed and even waved his hat to the crowd. Mrs. Coolidge wore moonstone gray duvetyn with a high-crowned Milan hat edged with burned goose feathers, and she responded vivaciously to the cheers that greeted them.

The luncheon usually served on inauguration day was omitted. The Coolidges with Mr. and Mrs. Dawes lunched hurriedly at the White House on coffee and sandwiches before reviewing the parade. As the Richmond Blues swung around Fifteenth Street a spectator on the Presidential stand exclaimed fervently with raised hat: "God bless the Coolidges."

Mrs. Coolidge heard him and her face lighted up. "He has," she responded instantly.

The President had a brief nap before the reception for governors in the late afternoon. Mrs. Nellie Tayloe Ross, the first woman governor, was warmly greeted by Mrs. Coolidge on this occasion. Colonel Coolidge, Mrs. Hills, Mr. and Mrs. Frank Stearns, Mrs. Goodhue and Miss Laura Skinner were guests at the White House for dinner that night. John had arrived from Amherst for a one-day stay. At first his father had demurred; then agreed that he might come for the day if he was up in his work. But he was not permitted to bring any of his friends. Mrs. Coolidge wrote to Mrs. Hills that her husband could not extend the arrangements beyond the grown-ups. The President was in bed by 9:45 that night and seemed to be much fatigued by the day's events. It was thought that he was beginning to show the strain of office.

His wife had passed her forty-sixth birthday in January. By this time she was well known to the country at large. There were new Cabinet wives around her now as Frank B. Kellogg succeeded Charles Evans Hughes, Harlan F. Stone replaced Daugherty and Curtis D. Wilbur followed Denby. C. Bascom Slemp retired as her husband's secretary and she was the one woman at his farewell dinner. He insisted that he would not enjoy the party unless she were present. Mrs. Wilson had frequently attended stag affairs but this was Mrs. Coolidge's first venture of the kind. Everett Sanders, a lawyer and Congressman from Indiana, succeeded Slemp. More than six feet tall, with vigorous bearing and fluent address, he became an important member of the White House staff. The popular Ted Clark continued to serve the President.

A month after inauguration Coolidge put the quietus on an appeal to the public for gifts of colonial furniture to be used in lending grace and period atmosphere to the White House. Mrs. Coolidge had sparked a resolution adopted by Congress asking the public to dig out colonial treasures for the Executive Mansion. The response was meager—little more than an Adams piece from New England. Mrs. Coolidge had given much thought to the matter and had visited the American wing of the Metropolitan Museum with Mrs. Morrow and Mrs. Cornelius N. Bliss to study various effects. But she ran into trouble with architects over some of the changes proposed. However, a beginning was made and the Green Parlor was eventually furnished with pieces that seemed to her appropriate. Mrs. Coolidge took much delight in the White House china and cut glass. President Arthur had bought fish and game sets from Tiffany's. There was still a considerable supply of the purple-edged Lincoln china. Most of the cut glass with the President's seal engraved on it was purchased during the second Harrison administration.

Mrs. Coolidge was disappointed to find so little of the original furniture in the White House and she searched through the storerooms to see what she could dig up. One of Andrew Jackson's chairs was unearthed, scraped, rubbed and installed in the President's study. She found a large mahogany table with claw feet and twelve pic-shaped sections inlaid with brass. This was put in the family dining room but it collapsed. The President liked to use the large dining room, even when he, Grace and John were all alone. They invariably dressed, said grace, and sat looking rather lost in the expanse of the stately room.

Few new pieces were added to the furniture already in the family quarters but chintz covers brightened things up, and two large mahogany wardrobes were added. Mrs. Coolidge felt keenly the meager closet space of the White House. She had an uncommonly large and diversified collection of clothes and she needed more room. Above all else she admired the bronze doors of the White House and always noticed them in passing through the entrance. She was interested not only in the fate of the White House but in the other public buildings in Washington. Charles Moore, chairman of the National

Commission on Fine Arts, was a good friend of Mrs. Coolidge's and she often had him to tea. She was interested in the workings of the Public Buildings Act for the beautification of buildings in the capital. When General Pershing, serving as chairman of the Commission on Battle Monuments, brought the plans for a war memorial to show the President while he was summering in the Black Hills, Mrs. Coolidge studied them carefully, decided that they were too suggestive of a guillotine and the architect was asked to draw up a new design. This was one of the few known instances where Mrs. Coolidge quietly exerted power in the background. The President kept a watchful eye for any move that might be disturbing to the *status quo*. Once in a while his wife was led into innovations through enthusiastic friends. But she knew how to recede with tact.

Like Abraham Lincoln, Calvin Coolidge liked to wander in to his wife's room and look over her gowns for state occasions. But where Mr. Lincoln had only a vague conception of what Mary wore, and on one occasion remarked that some of the material in the train would be of more use around her neck, Mr. Coolidge was a precise and appreciative judge of his wife's attire. Miss Randolph observed: "I have never known any man more interested in his wife's clothes than Mr. Coolidge and the handsomer and more elaborate Mrs. Coolidge's dresses were the better he liked it."

This was his one indulgence and it sprang from his deep love for his wife. She could spend as much as she liked with nothing but applause from the President, who counted pennies in all other areas of their life together. His interest continued right through the preliminaries until he saw her in full panoply in the East Room. Sometimes he got in the way when fittings were in progress. Early in his administration, as his wife was having the last touches applied to a white satin brocade gown, he all but bungled the job. The fitter, on the floor pinning the dress, scrambled to her feet as the President walked in.

"What do you think of it?" Mrs. Coolidge asked.

He took a long, speculative look. "Very handsome dress," he conceded.

But his wife gave a shriek of horror and the fitter dropped to the floor and flung her arms protectively around the train as he deliberately walked along the entire stretch of satin to his wife's heels. He seemed to be pacing its length.

"Mr. President, get right straight off that train!" cried Miss Randolph, who was not afraid to speak up when the occasion demanded interference.

He meekly obeyed and the fitter, studying the satin inch by inch, reported that no damage had been done. Actually, there was not another yard of the material to be had. It was considered one of Mrs. Coolidge's most beautiful gowns. Without being at all extreme about her clothes she had the reputation of being a particularly well-dressed First Lady in a soft and feminine fashion. She liked trains and rich materials, fans and picture hats. Her husband had more or less kept her wedded to the picture hat and she had to win him over to the cloches, helmets and turbans of the 1920s. "The trouble with him is," she said, "that he likes the hats in which he first remembers me—in the years when a hat was no hat at all unless it had flowers and beads and feathers and bows all over it, weighed pounds, and was as big as a cart wheel in the bargain."

Hats and coiffures were undergoing sharp changes at this time. Berets and helmets were supplanting the cloche. "The higher the crown, the greater the chic," said Maria Guy. With Reboux she launched large drooping berets, casquettes with narrow brims, and towering helmet crowns suggestive of the Grenadier Guards. The severe bob with cowlicks down each cheek was softened by a fringe. Razors ran up and down the back of the neck shaping a peak, and men complained that the barber shops were taken over by women. The Eton crop was growing longer. A loose swirl was softening the shingle. The square Dutch cut had its own substantial following, particularly in literary circles. Large jingling earrings were worn with shingled hair.

Mrs. Coolidge had a mild struggle with the President over the new hats. She bought a batch of simple cloches with tiny bows and tried on one after another while he watched with disapproval.

"Where's the trimming?" he demanded.

Both his wife and Miss Randolph assured him that trimming was not in fashion. In the end he conceded that the small tight-fitting hats were becoming to Grace and he said no more about them, but he still registered approval when she donned a picture hat. Mrs. Coolidge, who had a modest conception of her own charms and did not consider herself particularly good-looking, never took as much pleasure in her clothes as her husband did. Long before she was in the White House and went in for elaborate and expensive gowns he would accompany her on shopping expeditions, and would hang on with tenacity until she had found what she wanted. She thought his judgment good and his patience much greater than hers. Although he had little time for this sort of thing in Washington and it would have been impossible in his position he still took note of gowns he thought might suit his wife as he went for his daily walks. Bright ribbons and glitter usually drew his attention. It was a period when fringes, paillettes and *diamenté* dripped and sparkled on the fashion front.

The President's fancy was caught one day by a black velvet gown with bright scarlet strips running from neck to hem.

"What do you think of *this* that the President has had sent up for me to see?" Mrs. Coolidge asked Miss Randolph.

Her secretary deftly tucked the streamers out of sight and remarked: "It wouldn't be bad without these."

"Oh, but that's what he likes about it; *that* is why it took his eye."

In the end Mrs. Coolidge, who tried never to hurt her husband's feelings, explained to him kindly that the dress was too large for alterations. Miss Randolph thought his interest both flattering and touching. He noticed other women's clothes too, and made comments on gowns he particularly liked, but no one ever looked more regal to him than his wife. Mrs. Coolidge was perfectly willing to wear the same gown on more than one formal occasion, but the President would stare down at the lamé or heavy brocade on the bed and remark reproachfully: "You've worn that dress before."

She usually bought her spring clothes in advance, so as not to be caught by a sudden heat wave. She was easy to fit, being slim and graceful in build. Most colors looked well on her and she wore pastels with effective results, as well as vivid reds and blues. Flowered

Mrs. Calvin Coolidge in the White House. Painting by Howard Chandler Christy in the Calvin Coolidge Memorial Room, Forbes Library, Northampton, Massachusetts.

Mrs. Coolidge with Calvin Coolidge on the day of his inauguration in
January, 1919, as Governor of Massachusetts.

Calvin Coolidge taking the presidential oath in the parlor of the Coolidge homestead in 1923. Mrs. Coolidge stands behind him. His father, Colonel John Coolidge, reads the oath of office. Painting by Arthur I. Keller in the *Ladies' Home Journal,* April, 1924.

Courtesy of Library of Congress

The Coolidge homestead, the barn, cheese factory, church and store at Plymouth Notch, Vermont.

The Coolidge family at the lily pond in the White House grounds shortly before the death of young Calvin. Left to right: John Coolidge, Mrs. Coolidge, young Calvin and President Coolidge.

President and Mrs. Coolidge at the opening game of the World Series in 1924.

Mrs. Coolidge welcoming three Washington children at the White House on May Day.

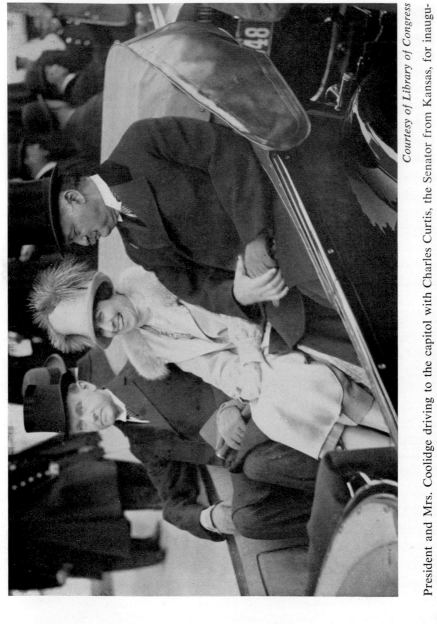

President and Mrs. Coolidge driving to the capitol with Charles Curtis, the Senator from Kansas, for inauguration ceremonies, March 4, 1925.

President and Mrs. Coolidge (at the President's left) with Charles A. Lindbergh and his mother, Mrs. Evangeline Lodge Lindbergh, at 15 Dupont Circle, during ceremonies following the aviator's transatlantic flight.

Mr. and Mrs. Coolidge at the Beeches in Northampton after they left the White House. With them are Rob Roy, the former President's white collie, and Tiny Tim, Mrs. Coolidge's red chow.

materials did not become her and she avoided black because of her husband's aversion to it, although it was an era when slinky black satin was high fashion. She was often dramatically turned out in white, even in winter snows, and after young Calvin's death she wore white, gray and orchid. For daytime she liked plain knitted dresses in different colors. Although she moved with the fashions she bought conservatively and was quite consistent about the length of her skirts. She picked up her clothes all over town and was just as prone to order an inexpensive little number from the ready-to-wear rack as a stately ball gown made to order. The President looked over the dress bills, just as he checked the White House kitchen orders. Typical ones for 1926 show her buying a green velvet dress for $200, a green hat for $35 and a rose velvet evening gown for $200 just before Christmas. A Boston paper noted that she spent $1,000 in a day for gowns. In general her hats ranged from $18 to $60 in price and her shoes cost up to $30. Her most admired gown was a gold brocade with a Persian design and shoulder straps of rubies and brilliants. She wore this at a state reception and there was much comment on the effect, with her flashing eyes and dark hair. She appeared in robes-de-style upon occasion, too. Ike Hoover thought that she loved clothes more than any other woman who had been in the White House in forty years but to him she always looked "young and sweet."

She had little expensive jewelry and would buy long strings of pearls for $20 or rock crystal earrings for $25 and wear them with style. She was much attached to a necklace of seven ivory elephants strung together, considering this a good luck piece. She had always given careful thought to her clothes but had matched her expenditure to a modest budget. In Washington she could indulge herself to some extent. She was much beloved by the salesgirls of Garfinckel's. She sent huge boxes of White House roses for the fifty seamstresses who worked on her first season's gowns. In her personal note to them she wrote of her "White House trousseau." The head dressmaker was invited to her next reception to see for herself how the gown looked on Mrs. Coolidge.

Although she shopped on an impromptu basis she never liked a fuss. However, she could scarcely swing into a Washington store without being recognized. She was amused when one salesgirl in Garfinckel's told her that she looked extraordinarily like Mrs. Coolidge, and then was left gasping when Miss Randolph told her that the parcel should go to the White House. However, she was annoyed when she went in to buy gloves and stockings on the main floor and a salesgirl arrived from upstairs with an armful of evening wraps. This made her conspicuous and she left the shop at once.

President Coolidge took considerable interest in his own attire during his years in the White House. He had always dressed with care and precision and he could not bear a wrinkle or a flaw in his tailoring. He was correctly, if somewhat stiffly dressed for any occasion that came up, but he did not wear informal clothes with ease. A dark blue, double-breasted coat which he kept buttoned up tight even on the warmest day was his usual choice. Because of his slim build he looked well in tails, which he called "shad-belly coats." He wore a pearl scarf pin on Sundays and had several watch chains. His valet had little to do, for he did not like to be waited on. He always knew what he wanted to wear and would sometimes have everything ready before the valet could function.

Chesterfield overcoats were popular during the Coolidge era. Trousers were long. Hat brims were wide, with deeply curved brims. Advertisements featured wide shoulders, deep lapels and high pockets. Casual clothes for sports were taking hold, as more golf and tennis were played, more motoring was done, and the country-life theme was emphasized. Gone were the days of the high iron collar, the square-set bowler, the funereal black suit and buttoned shoes. The tweedy age had arrived in a cloud of pipe smoke, but Calvin Coolidge was not geared to the casual effect. He usually paid $80 for his suits, $130 for his tuxedos and $150 for his overcoats. He averaged $5 for shirts and $2 for ties. He had small feet and he chose his shoes carefully, paying about $20 a pair for them. From time to time he had them repaired, resoled and stretched. Eight Secret Service men staged a hunt for one of his rubbers when the day of Herbert Hoover's inauguration dawned gray and damp. He announced that he would not leave the Executive Mansion until it was found, as it eventually was. When he bought his own cigars he chose Fonseca

Corona Fines de Luxe at $21 for 100, but as time went on he was inundated with cigars from different quarters.

Both he and his wife paid much attention to their hair. The President liked to have vaseline rubbed into his scalp and the unruly lock that had figured in his courtship was smoothly slicked down in his White House days. While staying at Swampscott during his first year of office he was persuaded to have some Harper hair treatments. His wife used this method for years. Her hair was long, lustrous and luxuriant. As women all around her had their hair bobbed she had a perfectly human longing to follow the fashion that swept the land. She considered it seriously when Queen Marie of Rumania was due to arrive, but she told a friend that although she would adore to have it cut the "President had his own ideas." After her husband's death she finally had it done on one of her trips to North Carolina with Mrs. Adams. But she continued to dress it so that few ever noticed the difference.

Mrs. Coolidge's coiffure was quite distinctive. It was called the horseshoe marcel and was made popular by Elsie Ferguson, the actress. It was stiff and formal, but it made an excellent frame for her broad features and wide smile. In Washington she went to a variety of hairdressers, as she did to dress shops, but she was particularly enthusiastic about the Harper method. She also went to Elizabeth Arden, Madame Anna Bute, Leon & Jules on H Street and Belle Pretty, who worked at the Washington Hotel beauty shop. Miss Pretty did her hair when Howard Chandler Christy was painting her portrait. But her most faithful hairdresser for twenty-eight years was Mrs. Evelina Flibotte of Northampton. Mrs. Coolidge had a standing appointment for Tuesday afternoons to have her marcel and shampoo done any time that she was in Northampton. She crocheted little caps to keep the marcel in place and preferred not to comb out her hair between appointments. She wore hairnets in the daytime and disliked intensely getting her hair wet when she went in the water.

The Coolidge picture of grace and dignity was far removed from the fashion absurdities of the era. The memory of the 1920s type lingers today chiefly in caricature, for the strange girl with the cowlick bob, skirts above her knees, waistline below her hips, bosom flat as a washboard, cloche hat jammed down to the eyebrows, and a dangling string of pearls, has become a period piece. Her strange habiliments matched the frenzy of the Charleston, the speeding roadster, the racoon coat and the furtive life of the speakeasy.

They all added up to the composite effect then known as Flaming Youth, which swooned over Rudolph Valentino and emulated Clara Bow. It was brightly cartooned by John Held, Jr., and became a likely target for puritans and preachers. The decline of family tradition, the antics of a jazz-mad generation, the devastation wrought by prohibition made current chitchat from coast to coast. Flags of alarm staked out the field.

Cheeks were highly rouged. Eyes were darkly kohled. Lips were raspberry red. New perfumes were wafted about, from Nuit de Noël to Chanel No. 5 and the deadly Chypre. It was a boom era for negligees, from fluffy marabou to Turkish satin trousers with smoking jacket. The "love nest" was a popular newspaper fable at the time, and the captive bird might be found slinking around in a chiffon velvet robe banded with deep cuffs of chinchilla, in satin trousers with a gold lace jacket, or in velvet brocade with frosted beading. Her décor was apt to be synthetic Empire, or semi-Oriental, with incense burning. Her boudoir was fluffed up with dolls, poufs and lacy cushions. She was half-mythical, half-real, but sometimes she hit the headlines with all the semblance of reality and ruin.

Black satin in the Theda Bara tradition was aped by the young and the fair. Chanel draped blonde models in black chiffon, tulle or taffeta, accenting their fragile beauty. By 1926 Lanvin and Lelong were pulling up the waistline. The shapeless sack was heading again toward contour. The two-piece costume was revolutionizing fashion, ranging from the stark *tailleur* of O'Rossen to Vionnet's plunging neckline with Alice in Wonderland bow. Women shone and glittered as they moved. Flexible rhinestone bracelets girdled the delicate wrists that juggled cocktails expertly at speakeasy tables. Dangling strands of pastel pearls went with long amber cigarette holders. Diamonds, emeralds, sapphires and rubies were still the best of form for those who could afford them. The plain gold wedding ring was becoming a period piece, having lost ground to the platinum and diamond circlet. Furs were flat, except for the enormous fox collars that reached from the pearl-encircled neck to the underslung waistline. Leopard had become the symbol of Gloria Swanson and other stars who stretched their languid limbs on tiger skins in movie sets.

The "ten best-dressed" was still a conceit of the future but Suzanne Lenglen's clothes were as much commented on as her tennis and temperament. Long before Gussie Moran's lacy pants were heard of, Suzanne was making fashion news on the tennis courts. Some of her competitors still sported old-fashioned bloomers that showed the elastic shirring at the knees as they leaped at the net. But not Suzanne, who brought tailored elegance and faultlessly groomed briefs to the tennis court. The body beautiful had already become the body streamlined when she defeated Helen Wills at Cannes in a contest of electrifying impact. The dash and glitter of a luxurious era were on display. The Mediterranean sparkled in the champagne sunshine of early spring. The flowers made vivid patterns over white walls and pink villas. The perfumed air, the clusters of parasols and gay printed frocks, the lounging men in flannels, all illustrated a carefree moment in man's affairs.

In general the wives of the Washington politicians played it safe in a dizzy era where fashions were concerned. Mrs. Longworth might appear in a batik blouse and look like an empress in so doing. Mrs. McLean might dazzle the public with her Paris gowns and Hope diamond but there was always the touch of New England conservatism about Grace Coolidge. Miss Vera Bloom, daughter of Congressman Sol Bloom, considered it ironic that she should be the President's wife to be represented in the Smithsonian Institution in a 1920 gown, for the spirit of the period was so utterly removed from her character. The Blooms were good friends of the Coolidges but Vera landed in hot water politically when she made the chance remark that Mrs. Coolidge was worth a million dollars a year to the Republican party. She was immediately accused of degrading the President's wife by setting a money value on her. The next time she was at the White House Mrs. Coolidge said: "Well, Vera, we've certainly had a lot of publicity together!"

"Yes," said Miss Bloom, "we've certainly had a lot of publicity together, Mrs. Coolidge, but I've had the trouble alone."

Both Mr. and Mrs. Coolidge enjoyed having their portraits painted. Taft and Harding were willing subjects but Wilson and Hoover both abhorred the experience. A room at the northwest corner of the White House was converted into a studio when this work was under way. Christy spent three weeks on the premises in February, 1924, and he soon decided that he had never seen such "unruffled harmony" as existed between Grace and Calvin Coolidge. But Mrs. Christy had some apprehensive moments after going to the White House kitchen and baking apple and custard pies for the President, a special skill of hers. Two days passed and nothing was said about them. She slunk around feeling much in disgrace. Then, when Christy asked the President what he thought of his portrait the truth came out:

"There's nothing wrong with that portrait. It's as good as your wife's pies—and they're the best I ever tasted."

Christy's painting of Mrs. Coolidge in a red dress with Rob Roy, her white collie, at her side, became a favorite on the walls of the White House. It was displayed for years in the pine-paneled China Room but in 1961 Mrs. Kennedy had it hung in the Red Room. She considered it one of the most effective paintings in the White House and decided that it looked particularly well in this setting. This was the first painting done of Mrs. Coolidge and it was the gift of Pi Beta Phi. She saw to it that the gold arrow pin of the fraternity was painted on to her gown by Mr. Christy at the last moment. The President showed great interest in all the preliminary arrangements and was consulted about Grace's gown. When Christy suggested that she wear red for purposes of contrast with Rob Roy the President held out for a white brocaded satin gown that he greatly liked.

"If she wears the red dress we'll have the blue sky and the white dog to make red, white and blue," Christy argued.

"She could still wear the white dress and we'd dye the dog," said the President with a solemn air.

Katharine Tower Barnes, a Michigan member of the fraternity, suggested that the painting be done of Mrs. Coolidge, as a popular figure and the first fraternity member to become First Lady. The plan was taken up enthusiastically by Anna Robinson Nickerson, grand vice-president of Pi Beta Phi, and arrangements were made to raise by popular subscription the $3,000 fee for Christy's work. Mrs. May Brodhead Wallace of Iowa, mother of Henry A. Wallace who later became Secretary of Agriculture, went to the White House to discuss the Christy project and the President gave his approval. Mrs. Coolidge stipulated that the arrangements should not involve any hardship for fraternity members. At this time the only paintings of First Ladies on the White House walls were those of Martha Washington, Elizabeth Van Buren, Letitia Tyler, Sarah Polk, Lucy Hayes, Caroline Lavinia Harrison and Edith Roosevelt.

The Christy portrait was unveiled in April 1924, when 1,300 college women—many of whom, like Mrs. Carrie Chapman Catt, had had distinguished careers—assembled at the White House for the ceremony. The presentation group consisted of Miss Amy Burnham Onken, grand president; Mrs. Nickerson, Mrs. Wallace, Miss Barnes, Dr. May L. Keller, dean of women at Westhampton College, University of Richmond; Mrs. Adele Taylor Alford, Emma Harper Turner, Grace Lass Sisson, Frances Evans, Irma Kerr Norwald, and Erminie Pollard, of the Vermont Beta, and a relative of the President's.

The guests assembled in the East Room, forming a semicircle around the curtained painting. Mrs. Coolidge appeared in soft gray georgette crepe trimmed with crystal. She wore a jeweled eagle on her shoulder, a chain with crystal pendant, a gold bracelet and the diamond-studded arrow she had received the day before from a group of personal Pi Phi friends to take the place of the simple pin with opals that she had worn since her college days.

"For the first time the nation has as its first lady a member of a national college fraternity," said Mrs. Nickerson. "From the days of Martha Washington until now never has it had as the wife of its President a woman more universally admired and loved. It seems distinctly fitting that to Pi Beta Phi, the first national college fraternity for women . . . has come the signal honor of claiming as its own Grace Goodhue Coolidge, first lady of the land."

The representatives of Vermont Beta and Michigan Alpha drew the silver-blue cords. The wine-red curtains parted and the Christy portrait was revealed. Colonel Clarence O. Sherrill, custodian of the White House, accepted the gift officially. The Marine Band played. Mrs. Coolidge sang the Pi Beta Phi anthem with the fraternity members and the group moved into the Blue Room, where she greeted them individually. They toured the White House grounds, abloom at this time with magnolias, pansies, jonquils and crocus.

The Alumnae Club in Washington sold copies of the painting to benefit the Pi Beta Phi settlement school in Tennessee and those autographed by Mrs. Coolidge were put up for a dollar extra. In 1927 she gave her original fraternity pin to be attached to her gown in the Smithsonian Institution. Four years later Kappa Kappa Gamma pinned a key on the gown of Mrs. Rutherford Hayes at the Smithsonian. She had been an honorary member of this group, whereas Mrs. Coolidge was a regularly initiated member of Pi Beta Phi.

Christy did a second painting of Mrs. Coolidge in white satin which now hangs in the Coolidge Memorial Room of the Forbes Library at Northampton, along with one of her husband. Mrs. Christy brought Mrs. Coolidge a siskin from New York while the work was going on. She named it Chatterbox because of the chip-chip-chip it kept up all day long in her dressing room.

On May 14, 1924, Mrs. Coolidge wrote to the Robins about their gift:

> I do not believe anyone here had a more enjoyable time than I when the fraternity paid me a visit. The portrait is now in place in the lower corridor with the other White House dames. Mr. Christy wants a light placed over it but, naturally, I would not so embellish my portrait when those of the other ladies must remain in outer darkness. . . . I wear my Robin arrow every day and love it for all that it expresses. When it comes to my position here, I feel very humble but when I think of my friends I am proud and haughty. How truly rich I am.

When Emil Fuchs painted her he posed her knitting on a period sofa in her private sitting room. He thought she had interesting hands. Her son John was particularly fond of the painting done in 1928 on Sapelo Island by Frank O. Salisbury, the English artist, while they were staying briefly in Georgia. The painting by De Laszlo, which hangs in the University of Vermont and shows Mrs. Coolidge in academic gown, was done in 1926.

Ercole Cartotto was like a member of the Coolidge household for a time while he did several paintings of the President. One was for Amherst College, another for the Phi Gamma Delta Fraternity and a third was for the State House at Montpelier. He and Mrs. Coolidge had many friendly exchanges about her husband's expression. Cartotto noticed that the atmosphere changed when she came into the room, and that the President seemed to relax. Grace was with him when he took a long look at one of the paintings and remarked: "Mr. Cartotto is the first artist who did not *create* a mouth for me."

Mrs. Coolidge had conferred with him about the image of her husband as a "fearsome man without a vestige of kindliness." But Cartotto was stubborn. He backed away from the canvas, and with illustrative gestures explained: "In New York people think of the President so." For the moment Cartotto wore the look of a spineless rabbit. "I show them tiger," he snapped. Mrs. Coolidge threw back her head with her customary hearty laugh but Cartotto caught the President as he conferred with the Director of the Budget, when his thin lips were clenched in a look of resolute firmness. He gave this particular painting to Mrs. Coolidge and she had it hung over the fireplace in Calvin's study. Cartotto also made a silverpoint of Mrs. Coolidge. When John looked at it he remarked: "It isn't much like my mother. Why did you make her look so solemn?"

The irrepressible Cartotto replied: "John, I once saw in your mother's face a look of resignation."

Joseph de Sigall painted both of the Coolidges and Charles Sydney Hopkinson did the official portrait of Calvin Coolidge that now hangs in the White House. It was painted in the year before his death and shows the strain of the years. Hopkinson found it difficult to arouse a spark of animation in his subject. In 1925 Edmund C. Tarbell did a full-length portrait of him at Swampscott which was destined to hang in the Massachusetts State House. Moses Dykaar, a Russian sculptor, made busts of the President and Mrs. Coolidge. He angered the President by pressing him for answers on the immigration question, then a burning public issue. Coolidge's jaw set and he assumed the stern expression revealed in this bust.

Mrs. Coolidge gave the social center of the American Red Cross at Walter Reed Hospital a painting of young Calvin, showing him sitting on the railing of the homestead at Plymouth with the Green Mountains in the background. Few Presidential families have been more photographed. Mrs. Coolidge was a remarkably good subject on all occasions. The President was usually willing to hand out photographs or give his autograph. But when Congressman Allan T. Treadway, visiting Plymouth, asked him for a copy of his latest photograph, he snapped: "I don't know what you want another for. I'm using the same face."

In April, 1925, the President opened the Woman's World Fair in Chicago with a five-minute radio address and his wife pressed the button that started the wheels turning. Mrs. Medill McCormick dedicated the Fair. Mrs. Coolidge wrote buoyantly to Mrs. Hills early in April that the weather was glorious and she was walking every morning from eleven to a quarter past twelve. She had a "fever to make a dress" and she longed to be riding along the roads in Dulcinea, her name for Mrs. Hills' yellow-wheeled automobile. "The time we've spent with our boys has been time well spent aside from the fun we have had. I wouldn't take anything for those memories, now," she wrote.

A year later the Coolidges were honoring the history of the past as well as of the present. The colonial spirit had been burning brightly in Philadelphia from the beginning of the year when a cushioned gold hammer tapped the ancient Liberty Bell, long silent, to usher in the Sesquicentennial ceremonies for the hundred and fiftieth anniversary of American independence. Its tones were wafted around the nation by that modern miracle, radio, firmly established in the American home during the 1920s as a new form of entertainment. Again the night watch, with staves and lanterns, paraded through Independence Square. Foot soldiers in Continental buff and blue formed a bodyguard for Mayor W. Freeland Kendrick as he hoisted the flag first used by George Washington in 1776. Actors representing Benjamin Franklin, John Hancock, Thomas Jefferson and the others whose quill pens signed the Declaration of Independence moved in the original setting and heard the historic document read.

Five months later the Sesquicentennial International Exposition opened to the public, a magic city of halls and exhibition palaces, covering great acreage. But its buildings stood unfinished, its outlines were blurred, as the opening parade passed under the Liberty Bell hanging symbolically at the entrance to the grounds. It was never to capture the blithe and memorable swing of the expositions of Chicago, St. Louis and San Francisco. Although thousands flocked to view its wonders, it stood as a white elephant in the months to come. But the President gave it his blessing in July, immediately after his fifty-fourth birthday, which he had celebrated on the Fourth with a quiet family dinner. "The things of the spirit come first," he said at the opening of the Fair. "Unless we cling to that, all our material prosperity, overwhelming though it may appear, will turn to a barren scepter in our grasp."

Mrs. Coolidge was in her element driving through the tiny thoroughfare designed to duplicate historic High Street. She used her imagination as she was greeted by women wearing the costumes of George Washington's time and saw replicas of the President's house, furnished by the D.A.R.; of Jefferson's house, cared for by the women of the South; of the Franklin Printing Shop and other historic buildings. The day was filled with interest for her. She became a focus of attention in the Stadium box—the "Lady All in White" who helped to make her husband smile at the photographers' behest. As they gathered around him he looked gloomy. Mrs. Coolidge came to the rescue. "Smile, Calvin," she said.

He turned to her but did not smile. She promptly lifted his high silk hat from his head and handed it to him. This made him grin and the cameras clicked. Later, the Girl Scouts of Philadelphia had a private audience with her, as their honorary president. The smallest handed her a basket of roses and larkspur. She turned to the President and said in her clear voice: "Do you see these girls? They are my scouts." A bell of her own yellow roses stood before her plate in the banquet hall of the Bellevue-Stratford that day, for Mrs. Coolidge had a rose, a sweet pea and other blooms named for her.

The Coolidges decided to set up a summer White House at Swampscott in 1925. There had not been one since 1916 when President Wilson stayed at Shadow Lawn in New Jersey. This was the only time during the Presidential years that Mrs. Coolidge expressed a preference in a major matter and she lived to regret it, for White Court proved to be the least satisfactory of all their summer homes. The President did not swim. He did not care for sailing, and there was no fishing, the sport for which he developed a "restrained enthusiasm in the summers which followed," said his wife. However, they all wished to stay close to Colonel Coolidge, who had been seriously ill.

Although Mrs. Coolidge found Swampscott beguiling it irked the President that he could not walk along the street without attracting attention. White Court, which was next door to Red Gables, the Stearns' summer home, was a long rambling white house with a stretch of lawn sloping down to the rock-bound coast. It had two swimming pools sheltered by rocks, as well as surf bathing. The house had a semicircular pillared entrance and strollers in the garden could see the President's back as he sat at his desk in the study. Mrs. Coolidge enjoyed the old-fashioned garden with heliotrope, petunias, larkspur, zinnias and other hardy flowers. She was made honorary president of the Swampscott Garden Club. But there was a slight chill in the air. When her husband was governor and they stayed with Mr. and Mrs. Stearns they were not accepted in the inner sanctum. North Shore regulars overlooked Calvin Coolidge as a social asset and he had no intention of responding to the overtures made now that he was President. He laid down the law for Grace although it was difficult for her to curb her friendly responses.

John, who was at Camp Devens during August, was showered with invitations which he scarcely heeded. He was doing his second year of military training and at the final review, when he was sent for by his commanding officer to salute the President, Mrs. Coolidge recalled that her heart "beat in time with his quick step." He was the tallest of sixteen youths in his platoon.

The summer executive offices at Lynn were three miles away from Swampscott. Cabinet officers and personal friends were entertained frequently at White Court. The *Mayflower* was in Marblehead Neck and they took several short cruises that summer and watched the sail-boat races from her deck. But in general their life was simple and restful. In May that year the President had alarmed his wife with the severity of one of his digestive upsets. In retrospect it was thought to be an early warning of the heart condition which ended his life. He had a special line installed to Plymouth and kept in close touch with Dr. Coupal, who was with his father after a serious operation. The Colonel had survived it but the Coolidges had reconciled themselves to the knowledge that his days were numbered. They visited him several times during the summer months.

On Sunday they went to the Congregational Tabernacle at Salem, where Mrs. Coolidge usually arrived with a single flower in her hand to give to some child. She had daily consultations with the Belgian cook and the Italian gardener. Mary Hernan, a swimming expert, taught her the Australian crawl at this time in one of the small cement pools. She slipped into the water with stockings, a long black bathing suit and the utmost protection for her hair. Every day she took a long country walk and on a hot July day four members of the Massachusetts state police, speeding to the Summer White House to drive the President to Cambridge, all but ran her down as they careened around a curve. James Haley, her Secret Service escort, shouted to her to watch out and she jumped aside just in time. "I was on the wrong side of the road," she cheerfully conceded as she told the culprits that they might say it was nothing at all if called to account by their superior officers.

On August 3 the President celebrated his second anniversary in office. He was lauded for his economy program and his measures for education. In Washington Secretary of State Kellogg was assuring the press that open diplomacy, as in the time of John Hay, was the rule of the State Department. The French Army had withdrawn after occupying the Reich for two years. Radicals were demonstrating in South China.

In Washington the Corcoran Gallery accepted Senator William A.

Clark's art collection. Gertrude Ederle swam the English Channel, establishing a record. The big names in sports that year were Red Grange, Bobby Jones, Bill Tilden, Babe Ruth and the two gladiators, Jack Dempsey and Gene Tunney. Floyd Collins died in a Kentucky cave while the whole nation followed for eighteen days the futile attempts made to rescue him. Tennis tournaments and horse shows made news at Newport. Like everyone else that summer the Coolidges followed the trial of John Thomas Scopes in Tennessee to test the validity of a state law prohibiting the teaching of evolution. William Jennings Bryan, fighting the Darwinian theory, battled with Clarence Darrow through the hot summer days. By August Bryan was buried at Arlington. He had played his last role before the public and won a decision, later reversed, while H. L. Mencken and other cynics kept the nation entertained with detailed accounts of the circus proceedings. The "monkey trial" went down in history as one of the major farces of a dizzy decade, the 1920s. The Lord Chamberlain of Britain banned Eugene O'Neill's *Desire Under the Elms* that summer. Charlie Chaplin attended the opening of *The Gold Rush* in New York. It was his first full-length comedy and was much discussed. Will Rogers and W. C. Fields were appearing with the *Ziegfeld Follies*.

The practice of entertaining stars at the White House received impetus during the Coolidge administration. Mrs. Coolidge was interested not only in a good play but in the personalities behind the scenes. Although she was a true devotee her husband was never wholly at ease in the theater. Occasionally she would prod him into attending. When they turned out for the opening of a new theater in Washington and the press was watching, the President put up his feet in front of him in the box. Mrs. Coolidge leaned over smiling and touched him gently. Without a flicker of expression he slowly withdrew his feet from public attention and planted them on the floor. He was a physically restless man and did not like to sit still for long. When he was Vice-President and Dawes was Director of the Budget Dawes often noticed how bored he became with an evening's entertainment and how anxious he seemed to be to break away. Mr. and Mrs. Dawes then lived on a higher floor in the New Willard than the Coolidges, and they liked to give entertainments after dinner. Mrs. Coolidge was the first President's wife who chose to sit in the orchestra as well as in boxes. She preferred seats four or five rows from the stage. Occasionally she attended a matinee by herself, or accompanied only by a Secret Service man. John always went with her when he was home from college and Mr. and Mrs. Stearns were often her companions. But in their early days in the White House the Coolidges turned down theatrical engagements, first because of mourning for Captain Goodhue, and then for their son Calvin. Charles Ray, the film star, wrote urgently to Mrs. Coolidge in August, 1923, offering a private showing at the White House of *The Courtship of Miles Standish*. He thought it would appeal to her because it "pictured the adventures of the Pilgrim Fathers, with its impressive lesson of the divine right of all high-minded men and the nobility of democratic ideals." But neither this film, nor *The White Sister* with Lillian Gish, were accepted at this time. And all such requests after young Calvin's death were met with the statement: "Mrs. Coolidge is not entertaining in any way at this time." But in other years she was noticeably enthusiastic about the cinema and took in a wide range of pictures, from *Hamlet* to Anita Loos' much discussed *Gentlemen Prefer Blondes*.

The President often scrawled "I don't think so" across theater invitations and Grace invariably took heed. When Holbrook Blinn was appearing in Washington in *The Dove* in February, 1925, he sought the President's attendance, mentioning the fact that his father was a Vermonter. But he was informed that the Coolidges were not going out in the evening at that time. Mrs. Coolidge was a devoted patroness of the National Theater Players and of the National Opera Association. Edouard Albion, the opera impresario, was on friendly terms with her and always delighted in seeing her walk into the Ambassadors' box, although all of her most intimate friends knew that she was not genuinely fond of grand opera. But she thoroughly enjoyed the symphony orchestras and was particularly devoted to Rachmaninoff. Returning from a performance of the Boston Symphony Orchestra in Washington she wrote enthusiastically to the Robins: "Oh, but I have just heard the Boston Symphony Orchestra play this afternoon and how they did play! I do hear lots of wonderful music and that makes up for a lot. Dr. Rachmaninoff came and played for me a week ago today. I had about three hundred in for the music and tea. As Mrs. [Adolphus] Andrews, wife of the Captain of the *Mayflower* says, 'He looks like a convict and plays like an angel.'" By March, 1927, he had played three times at the White House. Since music was a lifelong interest with Mrs. Coolidge one of the pleasures of her years in Washington was her easy access to the best artists of the day, and many of them appeared at her musicales, ranging from Madame Jeritza to John McCormack. She welcomed Chaliapin to her box when he sang *Faust* at the formal opening of the Washington Auditorium. She attended the performances of the Washington Opera Company regularly and listened to the Boston Symphony Orchestra whenever she could. She collected D'Oyly Carte recordings and wrote to the Robins: "Anybody who does not appreciate Gilbert & Sullivan ought to be taken out and shot at sun-up."

The music world was enriched during her husband's administration by the return of Arturo Toscanini to America after an absence of six years. He was welcomed as the master craftsman. Serge Koussevitzky presided with authority over the Boston Symphony Orchestra and Otto Klemperer made his debut with the New York Symphony Orchestra. The staid Metropolitan was undergoing the quakes and tremors of evolution, and Gatti-Casazza, its impresario, was hearkening reluctantly to the growing demand for native talent. John Alden Carpenter's ballet *Skyscrapers* jangled the nerves and stirred up discussion among large sections of the public. His opera was called the "essence of America, brilliant, swift, relentless." To many it was a nightmare of dissonance.

Another native innovation was the appearance on the Metropolitan stage of Mary Lewis, an ex-*Follies* girl. The entire country was interested in the debut of the minister's daughter from Arkansas who had both sung in a church choir and danced in the *Follies*. After seven years of hard training as a singer, and a debut in Vienna, she passed the acid test at the Metropolitan and made a brilliant impression as Mimi in *La Bohème*. Three weeks later she was followed on the same stage by a plump, pink-cheeked girl from Kansas City—

nineteen-year-old Marion Talley, daughter of a telegraph operator. Well billed in advance, her debut caused more excitement than Caruso could whip up at the peak of his career. Marion sang Gilda in *Rigoletto* and took eighteen curtain calls, more of a tribute to valor than to her voice. Mounted policemen kept the crowd in abeyance outside the Metropolitan and the telegraph wires were hot with stories about the girl singer. There was sentiment for the native girl who had blandly walked in the shade of the great divas. She did a broadcast on radio after her debut, so that her admirers in Kansas City were able to listen to her in their homes. She was invited to lunch at the White House and she sat in frozen shyness beside the silent President.

William Allen White was a fellow guest and between the soup and the salad Mrs. Coolidge, studying her husband's face, whispered urgently to White: "For Heaven's sake stir up those two at the end of the table." White immediately appealed to Miss Talley's mother and between them they "got the ice jam out of the conversational floe at the President's end of the table, and he actually made a quip or two, solemnly and with an uncracked face."

Gatti-Casazza at the moment was recognizing the spread of fine music over the airways. Madame Jeritza, who had brought Wagner back to the Metropolitan with high style, had just broadcast for the first time in her life. Orchestra leaders and singers were aware that the curtain was rising on a great new medium for the diffusion of their art. The public was learning to dial in for symphonic concerts and to pass personal judgment on a noble or shabby performance. A new form of rapport had been established between artist and listener, a miracle of communication, and Mrs. Coolidge was an enthusiastic participant from the start.

She struggled through one of the capital's major snowstorms to see Pavlova dance at the National, after lunching with sixty-nine of the Senate ladies. Jim Haley whispered to her that they must hurry home when the performance still went on at a quarter to seven. She had "to scoot" to be back in time for dinner, she wrote to Mrs. Hills. Otherwise she might keep the President waiting. When the Oberammergau Players were received by Mr. Coolidge she and John watched them from the doorway of the Cabinet room as they passed out. "I picked out Anton Lang but was not sure of the others," she wrote. "I think it was a mistake to bring them away from their own country."

Mrs. Coolidge made a point of having the Amherst Glee Club in for tea when the members visited Washington. In spite of the austerity of the Coolidges themselves they were by no means blind to the arts and the wide range of the 1920s in the entertainment field was reflected in the White House guest list, even to the appearance of a bevy of bathing beauties. But the chief emphasis was placed on the theater. John Drinkwater's *Robert E. Lee* was the first play attended by the Coolidges after entering the White House. The next was *Hamlet,* played by John Barrymore, and then they saw Jane Cowl in *Anthony and Cleopatra* and entertained her at the White House. Otis Skinner invariably lunched with the President when playing in Washington. They liked to compare notes about their boyhoods in the Green Mountains. After the Coolidges left Washington they were summer neighbors in Vermont. Mr. Skinner had a place called "Meandering Water" at Woodstock, only a few miles from the President's birthplace.

When Sol Bloom took David Belasco to call at the White House the dean of the American theater, impressive with his crest of white hair and clerical collar, remarked: "Mr. President, this is the greatest honor."

"No, Mr. Belasco," Coolidge replied, "the honor is mine. There have been many Presidents, but there is only one David Belasco."

During the Presidential campaign stage stars were drawn into the political picture. A group of forty breakfasted at the White House and then put on a show on the lawn. They assured the President that he had the support of the theater. John Drew, Al Jolson and Raymond Hitchcock led the delegation and Mrs. Coolidge was escorted in to breakfast by Jolson. The President's partner was Charlotte Greenwood, the immensely tall star of *Linger Longer Letty.*

She was dieting at the time and looked in dismay at the wheat cakes. But Mr. Coolidge urged her to try his favorite Vermont maple syrup. Charlotte promptly challenged him to run around the White House lawn with her for twenty minutes if she took the cakes and syrup. Mrs. Coolidge's merry laughter could be heard across the table at that point. On leaving the breakfast table Jolson remarked: "I ate everything but the sausages."

"Does that include the doilies?" Mrs. Coolidge asked.

"No, I have them in my pocket," said Jolson.

They all went out to the lawn where the leading stars of Broadway sang: "Keep cool with Coolidge" and put on a show and frolic. Mrs. Coolidge sang the campaign song. "Some note!" Jolson exclaimed approvingly as her voice caught his attention. This was a party she greatly enjoyed and she kept the ball rolling merrily with her talented guests.

She was quite at home receiving Mary Pickford and Douglas Fairbanks at the White House or chatting across the table with Ethel Barrymore. The theater was in a lush and creative state all through the Coolidge administration. In 1926 it had Eugene O'Neill and long-stemmed Ziegfeld beauties; Ibsen and *Lulu Belle*. There was something for every man's taste, from George S. Kaufman's sharp satire to Barrie's whimsy. Young Helen Hayes was bewitching her audiences with her tough but tender playing of Maggie Wylie in *What Every Woman Knows*. Emily Stevens, soon to die under hazy circumstances, was playing Hedda Gabler. Ina Claire was the suavest of crooks in *The Last of Mrs. Cheyney*, while off-stage she was earning the title of the nation's best-dressed woman. Lillian Braithwaite starred in a Noel Coward shocker *The Vortex*. Mary Boland made merry with *Cradle Snatchers*, while Alice Brady was earning great applause in *Bride of the Lamb*. Marilyn Miller in *Sunny* was the Mary Martin of her day, a graceful siren who smiled and danced in public, but wept at home that season over her breakup with Jack Pickford. *Abie's Irish Rose* was flourishing in its fourth year. The Marx brothers were whooping up lunatic fun in *The Coconuts*. *The Green Hat* was having a long run with Katharine Cornell, Margalo Gillmore and Leslie Howard earning laurels in a much-discussed but undistinguished play that seemed to epitomize the reckless spirit of the era.

"O'Neill's *The Great God Brown* was powerfully presented in the Greenwich Village Theater, and New Yorkers flocked downtown to view the combined efforts of O'Neill, Robert Edmond Jones and an inspired cast. It was a little-theater movement turning into galvanic professionalism, and was the breeding ground of much fresh talent. The play was baffling, for the public was only beginning to apprehend the strength of O'Neill. Between 1923 and 1929 the Theater Guild diffused good drama across the country, with subscription audiences in Baltimore, Boston, Cleveland, Pittsburgh and Philadelphia. Beginning its more successful period with *Pygmalion* in 1926 it had eleven hits in a row. By the end of the Coolidge era it had 200 actors, 75,000 subscribers, and had presented seventy plays and 9,000 performances. It had made such stars as Lynn Fontanne and Alfred Lunt household words across the nation.

The Guild became a pace setter for the American stage and by degrees repertory, the summer theater and the little-theater movement spread tendrils of independent enterprise in all parts of the country. The regional flavor became strong and effective and the Broadway stars who toured from coast to coast were conscious of this indigenous drive. The cinema was flowering so fast at this time that veterans of the legitimate stage felt that the theater was seriously threatened. Actually, the theater and motion picture industry were already at deadly odds. Everyone connected with the stage had taken alarm over the inroads made by films whose stars were now better known than those of Broadway. It was a complete change of pace in the entertainment world and one of lasting significance.

Ben Hur was the sensation of the hour on the screen. Audiences cheered almost continuously through two and a half hours of it. The sea fight and the chariot race roused fierce excitement in watchers not yet surfeited with cinematic sensation. The stars were Ramon Navarro, Betty Bronson, May McAvoy, Francis X. Bushman and Carmel Myers. Memories of the war made many weep as they watched John Gilbert and Renée Adorée in *The Big Parade*. It was a much loved picture, like *Stella Dallas,* a tear jerker then in circulation around the globe. John Barrymore was back on Broadway in his first picture since *Beau Brummell.* This time it was *The Sea Beast,* a free adaptation of *Moby Dick. The Black Pirate,* starring Douglas Fairbanks, was welcomed as the best example of technicolor up to that time. The tints were muted and did not shock with the garish quality common to the first pictures in color.

The stars of the era were known as vamps, like Theda Bara, or "It" girls, like Clara Bow. This bobbed-hair bombshell had made "It" the definitive term for the blaze of sex appeal, real or simulated, that fired the Hollywood scene. She aroused in the younger generation the screaming heebie jeebies later accorded to crooners and rock and roll exponents. The loves, romances and tragedies of the motion picture and stage stars had become a current passion with the public. Special magazines catered to this devouring taste, and snippets on the private lives of the screen darlings became popular everyday reading. Gossip was added to legitimate motion picture criticism. There was more to feed the fire than the stage had ever provided, with Wallace Reid, Mae Murray and, particularly, Gloria Swanson, who was then all the rage. Gloria's style was earnestly copied by flappers from coast to coast. Her fan mail was a paper hurricane that ranged from the parents of children trying to get their offspring into films to wild animal trainers who had noticed her addiction to leopard skin.

Gilda Gray, with frangipani in her hair, beads dangling to her waist and a rustling straw skirt, was inviting the public in a blatant advertisement to attend her first motion picture, *Aloma of the South Seas*. She had popularized the shimmy and, incidentally herself, but such was her vogue that she had been invited to do native Polish dances at Columbia University. She was only a mite less raucous than Texas Guinan, queen of the night clubs, whose brassy hair, clanking beads and stentorian greetings: "Give the little girl a hand" and "Hello, sucker" added another rowdy touch to the Broadway of the 1920s, as she rolled up a fortune of nearly a million dollars.

Visitors from Europe who had anything to offer in the way of entertainment, from lectures to grand opera, were in great demand. British authors filled halls and lapped up plaudits from women's clubs across the country. But the hardy native perennial, Burton Holmes, still fed the dreams of armchair travelers with his well-established talks and pictures. And people with knowing taste could still find the arts at their best in the 1920s. Mrs. Coolidge felt that she had much to be thankful for on all counts as the year 1925 came to a close. She had a wealth of new experiences to look back on and in a grateful mood she wrote to Mrs. Morrow on Christmas day: "Calvin and I are so delighted with the rare old engravings of Washington and Lafayette that I find it difficult to express our thanks. I am sure he would do it well but he is asleep, taking his annual Christmas nap."

And to the Robins she wrote: "This will be our third Christmas in the Nation's home. Every minute I grow more fond of it because of the many memories which cling about it and I try to picture those who have lived and worked and played within its high towering walls. And sometimes I make myself think that I hear the happy voices of the children of bygone days. Some of my happiest moments are those when the children come to see me."

Mrs. Coolidge was particularly devoted to little Paulina Longworth whose mother frequently brought her to the White House "in order that I may really see her develop." They had just been to see her and had tea with her upstairs. Paulina was then ten months old and she wore a new bonnet and cloak of baby blue silk with detachable quilted lining that the Baroness de Cartier had brought her from Paris. Mrs. Coolidge and Mrs. Longworth both got down on the floor to play with the little granddaughter of Theodore Roosevelt. "She looks uncannily like her mother and maternal grandfather," Mrs. Coolidge wrote to the Robins. "She seems to me to have the most real 'personality' of any child that I ever knew at her age. But that may be that she looks so much like her mother that I unavoidably see her mother's personality reflected in her."

Their third Christmas in the White House found both of the Coolidges looking younger than their years, in spite of the strain of their position. They had a smoother and more assured approach to their assorted duties than on the night of the swearing-in at Plymouth. The President looked less lean and anxious than a year earlier. All year he had been preaching thrift to a nation geared to lavish living and a carefree outlook. But his sermons on economy made small impression on the public consciousness in this era of delirious speculation. He urged cuts in state taxes and economy on all legislative levels.

A new revenue bill, providing a government income of $2,360,000,-000, and carrying tax reductions aggregating more than $387,000,000, became law that winter. The House and Senate voted $660,500,000 for defense, with the prospect that this would be fattened up to provide a five-year naval aviation program.

But this was the time when no one seriously believed that a second world war could follow the first. It was the interim of *dolce far niente,* with here and there a note of warning piercing the unruffled blanket of prosperity.

CHAPTER VII

A YEAR TO REMEMBER

PRESIDENT COOLIDGE AND MRS. COOLIDGE slumbered peacefully in the White House through New Year's Eve, 1926, leaving revelry to those who liked it. Next day they greeted 3,100 visitors and did a repeat performance for another 150 who arrived too late for the reception. The President broke precedent, ordered another fanfare of trumpets and marched back to the Blue Room accompanied by his wife, graceful in gray chiffon. With the utmost solemnity he went through the hand-shaking routine for the second time. But for once his inner thoughts could be judged historically from the revealing letter he wrote to his father a few hours before he faced his visitors:

> I suppose I am the most powerful man in the world, but great power does not mean much except great limitations. I cannot have any freedom even to go and come. I am only in the clutch of forces that are greater than I am. Thousands are waiting to shake my hand today.

Vice-President Dawes was spokesman for the administration in spreading traditional New Year cheer. "The advent of 1926 finds the world turning more eagerly and more definitely toward the paths of real peace than at any time since the end of the world war," he said. Andrew W. Mellon, another man of few words, admitted that the Treasury held a comfortable surplus and predicted continued progress toward world stabilization in the year to come. Only Mrs. Coolidge knew how much her husband felt the binding strings of his position.

In Pasadena 235 spectators were hurt when a stand fell at the Rose Fete on New Year's Day. Henry Ford, snowed in at his Wayside Inn in Sudbury, Massachusetts, enjoyed a concert of old-fashioned tunes played by eight New England fiddlers. John D. Rockefeller, another millionaire who had set his stamp on American civilization, started the new year with his customary round of golf at Ormond Beach in Florida, playing eight holes with zest. He was then eighty-seven. Helen Keller and Anne Sullivan Macy visited President Coolidge and the most noted of the blind read from his lips with her fingers his tribute to her: "You have a very wonderful personality, and I am glad to talk to you." Mrs. Coolidge, who had taught the deaf, quickly established rapport with her world-famous guest.

Charles Francis Jenkins, the inventor, predicted "radio vision" during 1926. He was a little ahead of his time but television was on its way. A less reliable seer, Robert Reidt, the house painter who had boldly predicted the end of the world, now saw New York going up in flames on February 6, 1926. But the city did not miss a heart-beat when the day arrived. The Daniel Guggenheim Fund was established for the promotion of aviation. Jewel bandits picked up $100,000 in a Fifth Avenue holdup. After three years of marriage, Rudolph Valentino was divorced by dark-eyed Natacha Rambova, the adopted daughter of Richard Hudnut. Mr. and Mrs. Franklin D. Roosevelt announced the engagement of their fair-haired daughter Anna to Curtis Bean Dall.

In New York the Wrigley brothers gyrated and sparkled over Times Square as horns, whistles and merry shouts welcomed the infant year 1926. More than 150 dry agents prowled the night belt, but the crowd soon thinned, scattering to speakeasies, to night clubs, to home parties, there to drink the strange potables born out of prohibition. Fast nips from hidden flasks hastened intoxication.

On the following day James J. Walker took office as Mayor.

Debonair and quick with wisecracks, he set the pace for the fabulous era in city politics that dawned as dour Mayor John F. Hylan departed unlamented from City Hall. The tilt of Jimmy's hat brim, his grin, his songs and sharp repartee matched the spirit of the heedless 1920s. At the moment he was Beau Brummell, the knight in still untarnished armor, who brought grace to the city administration. His after-dinner speeches were neat, witty and had punch.

All the Northeast was crippled by storms early in February. The White House grounds were deep in snow. New York was buried under a twelve-inch snowfall which brought out its icicled beauties but disrupted its communications. There had been few storms like it since the matchless blizzard of 1888. It rode in on a wind shifting from thirty to sixty miles an hour. The snow fell in stinging layers and piled up in drifts. Trains were stalled. Schools were closed. Milk deliveries were crippled. Mail was delayed. There were deaths and other mishaps. A great stillness lay over everything. Central Park was a gleaming expanse of beauty, with icy arabesques and frosted branches. The suburbs lay folded in the same deep hush, rooftops and cars capped with snowy mounds.

In March Colonel Coolidge died at the age of eighty-one in the Vermont house where he had sworn in his son as President of the United States. He had lived a simple and hardy life in the more rugged American tradition. His son, suspecting that the end was near, had written to him in the previous August:

It is two years since you woke me to bring the message that I was President. It seems a very short time. I trust it has been a great satisfaction to you. I think only two or three fathers have seen their sons chosen to be President of the United States. I am sure I came to it largely by your bringing up and your example. If that was what you wanted, you have much to be thankful for that you have lived to so great an age to see it.

All that winter Mrs. Coolidge had kept up close communication with the failing Colonel. Her letters had brought interest into his last days as she wrote of the President and John. There had always been perfect understanding between her and her father-in-law and one of his last public statements was a tribute to her. He told an interviewer: "She has always been helpful to Cal and kind to us. He was fortunate in getting such a fine girl for a wife. People take to her because she is so attractive, kind-hearted and thoughtful."

Now she hurried north with the President through a March snowstorm almost as severe as the one in February. They traveled by automobile and open sleigh from Woodstock to Plymouth, a distance of sixteen miles. Snow was cleared for the sleighs and pockets were cut along the roadside for two-way traffic. Hot bricks in the sleigh helped to keep them warm. As they reached the Notch they saw men hacking a path to the cemetery. They were too late. The Colonel was dead.

A biting wind whipped snow in their faces as they stood in deep slush at the graveside where he was laid to rest close to young Calvin. The train had stopped at Northampton to pick up John, who was then at Amherst. He, too, had drawn strength from his grandfather, whom he resembled physically in some respects. The story of the oil lamp, the old Bible, the dramatic swearing-in had enshrined the Colonel in American history. He was as honored by the public as by his family, and the fierce light that had been focused on him in the years that followed had never shown him at a disadvantage. Mrs. Coolidge was one of his most sincere admirers, and she helped him in many thoughtful ways when he was drawn into the nimbus of the Presidency. She returned to Washington saddened by the Colonel's death.

While nature created disorder all through the East with blinding snowstorms, man himself spread gloom in the South with a sudden rash of blue laws. Texas ordered a ban on all references to evolution in public school textbooks. But evolution was theory; strikes were fact, and at the moment the East was more concerned with the end of the five-and-a-half-month strike that had caused grim suffering in Pennsylvania. In March the whistles blew once more in the coal pits, and five hundred square miles of anthracite field came to life again. Weary of enforced idleness the miners tracked through the snow in overalls, their lamps in place, their dinner buckets slung over their shoulders. They were going down the shafts for the first time since August 31, 1925. They had accepted a five-year contract at the same scale of wages. It was the longest, costliest strike in the history of the industry up to that time.

But a shorter, more violent strike promptly broke out in the New Jersey textile towns of Passaic and Clifton. It came into national view when the police used gas bombs and fire hoses. They swung their clubs, charged a group of strikers, and broke newspaper cameras. Uproar followed, and they changed their tactics quickly, permitting orderly picketing by 3,000 men and women strikers and even helping the crocodile line to weave its way through traffic.

Mass picketing was comparatively new in America at this time, and had not been used on such a comprehensive scale. Reliance was placed on numbers, and the picket line swelled to inordinate proportions. For weeks the Botany Worsted Mills at Passaic were discussed across the nation. Students of economics and the social sciences gathered from Yale, Columbia, Dartmouth, Princeton, City College, Union Theological Seminary and other educational institutions, to study the methods used. No sooner was this strike settled in the United States than Great Britain was paralyzed early in May by a general strike. King George proclaimed a state of emergency and troops were called out to guard the coal pits. Public transportation was at a standstill and the streets were choked with motor cars getting people to work.

When Prime Minister Stanley Baldwin finally announced the end of the strike, he received an ovation in the House of Commons. The Prince of Wales, whom he would later help to topple from the throne, was an interested spectator on this occasion. He had hurried home from Biarritz when the strike began. An errant knight was in the making. By this time his hunting spills and riding mishaps were notorious. He was a popular figure at night clubs and cabarets. But he performed all his public duties with decorum, and his popularity was at its height. His failure to marry or to occupy one of the large royal residences gave concern to his family and to some of the statesmen around him.

Mrs. Coolidge, remembering him as her guest, read with interest of his doings. She took note of the birth of a daughter to the Duke and Duchess of York on April 21 of that year, just before the national strike threw London into chaos. No one at that time thought of the new baby, named Elizabeth, as having any serious claim to the throne of Britain. King George V was alive. His son, the Prince of Wales, was heir apparent. After him came his brother, George. Yet a mirror was held up to the future with such speculative headlines as: *Ducal Firstborn May Gain Crown as Elizabeth II,* and *Another Queen Elizabeth May Sit on the English Throne.*

But the Empire was uneasy. Imperialism was being questioned on all fronts. The race problem in South Africa was attracting discussion and criticism. There were mutterings in India, and a general unrest within the Empire, as new forces fomented and the man in the far outpost had more to say for himself. Women, too, were moving ahead and Mrs. Coolidge read with interest that Lady Astor had offered her seat in the House of Commons to Mrs. Emmeline Pankhurst. By this time American suffragists had become a more assertive force than the British, although there was no great rush to the polls. Jane Addams, founder of Hull House in Chicago, expressed the view that while women had been slow to take advantage of the vote, they were at last awakening to their responsibilities. Calvin Coolidge did not altogether agree. Addressing the Daughters of the American Revolution, he called on the women of America to bestir themselves in making better use of the privilege for which they had fought so strenuously. He bluntly stated that the American woman was apathetic toward the ballot, and reminded his audience that her forebears of the Revolutionary era shared the burdens of war with their men. He urged the women of 1926 to emulate this spirit and become good citizens by going to the polls.

Nevertheless, he deplored the aggressive campaign being waged by the National Woman's Party against protective legislation for women in industry. Led by Miss Alice Paul, the radical wing of the suffrage movement had stampeded a Conference of Women in Industry meeting in Washington. With another flourish they had marched through driving rain to the White House, brandishing the gold and purple banners of the old suffrage-picketing days. There they left a petition asking President Coolidge to help them in their fight. They demanded equal rights for women on the industrial front and specifically the choice of doing night work and overtime if they so desired. Among the marchers were veterans who had served on the picket line twelve years earlier, when the suffragists petitioned Woodrow Wilson for the vote.

President Coolidge gave their demands a chilly rebuff. Neither he nor his wife approved of their tactics. He emphasized the pleasure it had given him to sign the bills in Massachusetts which threw the blanket of protection around women in industry. "Women can never escape the responsibility of home and children, and the working woman as a mother and potential mother challenges universal interest," he commented.

Smith College, which always commanded Mrs. Coolidge's interest, had just established on its campus an institute designed to reconcile home interests with a career of intellectual activity. The women who had gone out to work during the war had set a pattern. Many did not wish to return to the home. And more and more of each year's graduates were combining marriage with careers. Ambition was an odd outcropping in this frivolous era. Mrs. Coolidge, the domestic-minded, conceded the trend of the times, but she was not an open advocate of woman suffrage: "Everyone talks of the restlessness of women since the war, of their dissatisfaction to return to the old kinds of life," she observed. "Of course they are restless. Soon there will not be an intelligent woman who is content to do nothing but live a social life."

In their assault on the larger world many were turning to sports. The Coolidge era saw a strong shift of emphasis in this respect. The more vigorous games, as always, had their own passionate following, with the addition of ice hockey, which had begun to draw large audiences in various arenas across the country. The new Madison Square Garden had only recently opened, and six-day bicycle races bolstered the prevailing fad for marathon sports. But Grantland Rice noted that tennis and golf, once regarded as effeminate diversions largely in the grip of the rich, had moved into the field of "red, he-man sport." Standards were changing all round. Athletics were pushed hard in schools and colleges. The young of both sexes were growing up to know, understand and participate in a wide variety of sports.

No one was sacrosanct. Young John Coolidge got a black eye and a sore chin boxing at Amherst that spring.

American sport in general was having a lively year. Jess W. Sweetser won the British amateur golf championship in Scotland that summer, and Bobby Jones took the British Open Golf title in a brilliant finish, with a score of 291. It was a chilly year and along the Eastern seaboard people shivered in the weeks when they usually swelter. Babe Ruth was worrying his fans with his Gargantuan stomach-aches and his romantic whims. Mrs. Coolidge, following the fate of the different teams, kept close watch on the Babe's professional performance. The public coddled him along but the sports writers rapped him sharply. The contract that guaranteed him the largest salary in professional baseball was soon to run out. It was vital for him to sustain his home run record in 1926.

Aside from professional sport big-game hunting drew devotees to various parts of the globe. Theodore and Kermit Roosevelt returned from the Himalayas with trophies for the Field Museum of Chicago. They had bagged eighty large animals, representing twenty species, and had brought home nearly a thousand small animals, birds and reptiles. They had killed *Ovis poli* at an altitude of 17,000 feet. The Roosevelt sons were carrying on in the tradition dear to their father.

News of historic importance beat against the White House doors as the Coolidges were close witnesses to the enormous progress made in aeronautics all through the administration. The first major event was the flight over the North Pole by Lieutenant Commander Richard E. Byrd and Floyd Bennett, first in the world to perform this feat. It took them fifteen hours and fifty-one minutes to fly there and back from Kings Bay, Spitsbergen. They circled the pole several times, solemnly shook hands at the climactic moment, and Commander Byrd saluted in honor of Admiral Robert E. Peary and the Navy. It had taken Peary eight months with dogs and sled to cover the ground encompassed by Byrd in a day. Roald Amundsen, Lincoln Ellsworth and Colonel Umberto Nobile sailed into the morning sun the following day with their dirigible, the *Norge,* heading for the same goal, but knowing that the laurels had already fallen to Byrd. They reached the Pole with equal certainty, and there Amundsen lowered the Norwegian flag, Ellsworth the Stars and Stripes, and Colonel Nobile the Italian flag, a triple gesture to the nations involved.

Commander Byrd and Floyd Bennett returned to a tremendous welcome as conquerors of the North Pole. Thousands cheered them in Washington and New York. President Coolidge praised their "superb courage" as he decorated both men, and Mrs. Coolidge gave them a warm welcome at the White House. But while glory was being wrung from the skies the ground forces were locked in combat and hamstrung with red tape. The black sheep of the flying world at this time was Colonel William Mitchell, who had risked his professional reputation by attacking his superior officers, and had lost. President Coolidge had just confirmed his suspension from the army for five years, giving out the statement that summed up contemporary official thinking on the rebel in army ranks. The theory of government, the President reminded him, implied that every official in office "shall deport himself with respect toward his superior."

But Billy Mitchell refused to be squelched, and he had a large public following. Two weeks after the President's pronouncement he was in New York advocating an aviation branch of the service free from army and navy control. He compared the military bureaucracy to an ostrich burying its head in the sand. Seven years after the war, and with $500,000,000 spent on flight operations, American airplanes were not up to combat with any other nation. They were not even fit to fly, Colonel Mitchell insisted. He promptly wrote a series of articles on the way in which the youth of America might be organized and trained for aerial warfare. He advocated a force of 3,000 crack flyers always available for instant action. A shrewd prophet had spoken!

But a saga of heroism at sea preempted the headlines at this moment. For the next three weeks British and American papers were filled with testimony to man's courage, when the *President Roosevelt,* skippered by Captain George Fried, picked up twenty-five men from the *Antinoe,* a sinking British freighter, in one of the most gallant rescues in sea history. King George wrote to President Coolidge, extending thanks. The American crew was welcomed with a harbor salute and a thrilling greeting at Plymouth, as the rescued were landed in England. Two weeks later Captain Fried, bewilderment in his blue-gray seaman's eyes, showed embarrassment as guns, cheers and plaudits greeted him on his return to America. It was not a one-man job, he protested, uneasy in the hero's role. But the music of bands, the whir of airplanes, the praise-laden speeches of dignitaries overwhelmed him as for a week Fried and his crew were feted, with the ubiquitous Grover A. Whalen acting as master of ceremonies.

The public warmed, as ever, to a tale of heroism. It was a welcome change from the shifting sands of world politics, a switch to human fundamentals. It was good for national morale at this time, too, for America, the vast, the dynamic, the progressive, was furnishing adverse headlines around the world. The British papers consistently played up the grotesque, the scandalous, the absurd. Rum-running operations made daily entertainment abroad. Gang killings abounded. Marathon dancing and flag-pole sitting had lunatic overtones. American motion pictures were credited with corrupting the young at home and abroad. Flaming youth was notorious, and the infection was pictured as springing from one great focus to the west of the Atlantic. Fast communications were telescoping time and space and making transmission easy.

But in spite of Coolidge prosperity and Coolidge calm the shadow of things to come clouded the financial scene early in March when the market took a deep and unexpected plunge. In a three-day convulsion it reached levels never before attained on the local exchange, in the volume and breadth of shares involved. Hundreds of weary speculators hung over tape machines in brokerage offices as stocks broke from 1 to 80-odd points, sweeping away fortunes. Markets from coast to coast reflected this first deep fissure in the economic structure of the 1920s. Heady speculation had become a national pastime on all social levels.

News of the first day's excitement brought crowds to the gallery of the Stock Exchange, anticipating another day of chaos. But no sooner had the market break become public knowledge than soothing syrup was spread around. The financial writers fell into a reassuring tempo. Both Andrew Mellon, Secretary of the Treasury, and Herbert

Hoover, Secretary of Commerce, gave interviews while the boat was rocking. The market rallied almost as rapidly as it had fallen. Fortunes were reaped as well as lost. Jesse Livermore, conducting his operations from Florida, sold short and made a killing. The seasonal exodus from Palm Beach was speeded up by the sudden news from Wall Street. Twenty-five bankers arrived on one train to try to salvage their fortunes. Soon all was quiet on Wall Street again, and three years of unprecedented prosperity lay ahead, to culminate in the historic crash of 1929.

That summer the Coolidges visited Burlington and the usual crowds gathered at the station to welcome Grace Goodhue, including many young women students at the summer school. Leaning over the car rail she grasped the hands of old friends and called out greetings. It was again like the week-long celebration of 1923 when she and Calvin traveled north for the 150th anniversary of the settlement of Burlington. He was not yet President at the time but he was lionized in Grace's native city. In reviewing the history of Burlington on that occasion he paid tribute to Ethan Allen and the Green Mountain Boys; to the University of Vermont, chartered in 1791; to the *Sentinel,* published in Burlington first in 1801; to the *Vermont,* a lake boat chartered in 1808. He finished with a warm tribute to his wife's city: "The same gleaming waters remain. The same shadowy mountains tower around us. The dream city rises from the shore, now a reality."

Speaking at Wheaton College, President Coolidge voiced his favorite political philosophy. "Individual initiative, in the long run, is a firmer reliance than bureaucratic supervision. When the people work out their own economic and social destiny, they generally reach sound conclusions ... We do not need more material development, we need more spiritual development. We do not need more intellectual power, we need more moral power. We do not need more knowledge, we need more culture. We do not need more law, we need more religion."

In the three years since he made those speeches the political wheel had been spinning fast and not in the direction of spiritual development or moral power. Now Grace visited the University and sought out friends of the past. On her return to Washington she started a quest for her round robin letter, which had gone astray at the White House. The chain had never been broken and the letter was searched for diligently. Eventually it was found in the Secret Service files in a folder marked "seemingly silly letters." Mrs. Coolidge was amused. She noted that all were "written by college graduates of some years' standing." However, their ingenuity in finding different forms of address had puzzled the Secret Service. Mrs. Coolidge tried a wide variety herself, including *Dear Robinettes, Sisters of the Skillet, Dear Knightdresses of the Robin Round, Dear Chirpers, Robins on the Wing, Members of the Charmed Circle, Dear Birdies* and *Members of the Force.*

Again in 1928 a round robin letter was mislaid at the White House, and Mrs. Coolidge gently chastised the Secret Service men for pigeonholing this valued correspondence. Writing to the Robins about his obtuseness she commented: "I explained to him that I was a human being before I was the wife of a President and counted myself fortunate in having friends who knew me before I came here and who still had the good sense to continue to regard me as a human being. Would he, therefore, not continue to regard with suspicion a letter arriving with a strange beginning such as Dear Honey-Elephant or Dear Mate or Dear Goody and signed all sorts of things as The Skipper, Your Ol' Pal, etc."

In August, 1926, the Coolidges went to White Pines Camp, an estate close to Saranac Lake, and owned by Irwin R. Kirkwood, a Kansas City publisher. This proved to be more of a success than White Court. The executive offices were at Paul Smith's and the President passed his mornings there. In the afternoons he tried fishing with Colonel Starling and developed zest for the sport. Mrs. Coolidge walked for miles over hemlock bark trails with a dog at her heels, enjoying the mountain paths and bracing air. Here she learned to paddle a canoe and to row a boat, although she was no more adept at this than at swimming. Miss Riley had to use ingenuity in coping with all the fish that reached the kitchen. The President caught them. The Secret Service men caught them. The guides and finally the servants developed the craze and spent their free time on the lake. In addition, gifts of fish arrived from Mexico and Canada, mostly for comparison with the fish the President was catching—a bigger muskie or a trout with more speckles.

The camp, a group of detached houses built of split logs, was situated on a low bluff overlooking Lake Osgood, where they had fishing, boating and fresh-water bathing. They were greatly plagued by mosquitoes in the Adirondacks and were often driven in to the great living room with its Oriental rugs and marble fireplace. When they worshiped in the tiny Presbyterian church at Saranac Lake the President was observed holding the hymn book for his wife.

Guests came and went constantly. Cabinet members, Senators, Governors, labor leaders, businessmen were entertained in this al fresco atmosphere. Among them were Julius Rosenwald, Owen D. Young, Frank Kellogg, and Bruce Barton, who was collecting material for an article on the President. A guest whom Mrs. Coolidge greatly enjoyed was Governor Alfred E. Smith, who drove over with Mrs. Smith to spend the day at White Pines. She had met the Governor only once before, at the time of Harding's funeral. Listening to the men at the luncheon table Mrs. Coolidge wrote: "They discussed problems of common interest and experience, and it seemed to me that their minds ran along parallel lines in many instances." The Governor later commented that he did not consider Coolidge a cold man and he was impressed with his true sense of humor.

When all four were out in a motor boat on Lake Osgood and they were discussing waterways the Governor said he would like to sell the Erie Canal to the federal government, because it was costing his state so much money. He feared that some day the state would be faced with a serious problem in supplying water to the people of New York.

"Why don't you sell *them* the Erie Canal?" the President demanded.

Governor Smith took away with him a four-pound pike caught by Coolidge and had it stuffed. There was much excitement when he made this catch. Waving the fish at his wife he walked up to the cabin calling: "Mammy! Mammy! Look what I've caught."

There were many flower beds and gardens scattered around the grounds of the camp at White Pines and Mrs. Coolidge delighted in cutting the flowers and arranging them in the various cabins. She had her birds and some of her dogs with her. The White House dogs and other pets played a large part in the family life of the Coolidges, summer or winter. Laddie Boy was identified with Warren Harding. Falla would be associated forever with Franklin D. Roosevelt. The public came to know a succession of different breeds during the Coolidge administration but Rob Roy and Prudence Prim, the handsome white collies so often seen with Mrs. Coolidge, were king and queen of the kennels.

It was frequently remarked that Mrs. Coolidge presented a dashing picture, swinging along the White House graveled pathways, her skirts blowing in the wind, her eyes sparkling, her color bright, while Rob Roy dashed ahead or marched in lordly fashion beside her. They made a dramatic combination and Rob Roy was used with striking effect in the Howard Chandler Christy portrait of her. There was so much life and vivacity in her bearing that the clerical staff in the executive offices, to whom she waved gaily in passing, would sometimes feel like cheering. The public watched for her coming out. "Why, you almost expected her to break into a race with the collie," said one observer.

The kennel master treated the dogs' coats with blueing—like a woman's hair—to keep them white, and Mrs. Coolidge always complimented him on the job he did. Harry Waters, serving in this capacity at the time, found that she never made any unnecessary demands and was uniformly pleased with his services. "She was a wonderful lady and always happy," he recalled. "Rob Roy was a wild one. He would dig into me, but she had no fear of him. Sightseers were sometimes more interested in the dogs than they were in the White House."

Harry was never so sure of the President's attitude to the dogs, or the meaning of his quiet jokes. He worried when Mr. Coolidge said to him on one occasion: "You can lose them one of these days if you want to." But the staff knew that he was just as devoted to the dogs as Mrs. Coolidge was. However, they had a hard time persuading their lordly collies to board the *Mayflower* for cruises. Both turned stubborn at the wharf. Immune to Presidential pressure the collies squatted on their haunches and refused to cross the gangplank.

Rob Roy was from Wisconsin. He was used to open fields and big barns and when first brought to the White House he feared the elevators. Mrs. Coolidge brought him in to the house for short periods, talked to him and gave him reassurance. Eventually he would walk the red carpet like a grandee with a bow of baby blue ribbon tied to his snowy coat.

Prudence Prim was brought on to keep him company. She was a creature of feminine wiles and graces, in Mrs. Coolidge's estimation. The dog accompanied her everywhere, stayed at her side in the house, and slept by her bed at night. At tea time she would go from guest to guest in the most mannerly way. Mrs. Coolidge treated both dogs like children. One day she made a straw bonnet for Prudence and trimmed it with ferns and green ribbons. The collie wore it to one of the veterans' garden parties and made a hit. But in the spring of 1927 she was ailing. They took her to the Black Hills with them but she died that summer. "Rob and I shared a common sorrow," said Mrs. Coolidge.

Rob Roy was closely identified with the President, sleeping in his master's room, attending press conferences with him and often lying at his feet as he entertained the men of the hour and talked politics. Occasionally guests thought that Mr. Coolidge paid more attention to Rob Roy than he did to them. Like his wife he often took tidbits upstairs from the dinner table for the dogs. "He was a stately gentleman of great courage and fidelity," the President wrote of Rob Roy in his autobiography. "He loved to bark from the second-story windows and around the south grounds."

One of Mrs. Coolidge's little jests was to have a calling card engraved for Prudence Prim and to leave it at the homes of her more intimate friends with her own card. She liked to think that the White House pets had personalities of their own, and in time the public came to know their characteristics and to take a lively interest in them. She let her friends know that Prudence Prim always bounded into the room while she and the President were having breakfast, established herself in a chair and shared Calvin's cereal with him. One Christmas she addressed a card to Mrs. Hills' cat, Mr. Nansen Pussy-Cat, with greetings from Paul Pry and from Peter Pan, their first dog in Washington. He was a wire-haired fox terrier who was fidgety and nervous and they soon got rid of him. But Paul Pry was a wild airedale who was half-brother to Harding's Laddie Boy. He was jealous of Rob Roy, and all of Mrs. Coolidge's efforts to teach him the amenities were fruitless. But she wrote to the Robins that she was devoted to him. "He is like some people, always keeping you guessing and always being funny. True to his breeding he assumed charge over one individual, that one in his case being me and he will not let my maid come into my room to pick up my things if I am not there."

The servants made so many complaints about him, one of them carrying a long-handled duster in her hand to defend herself if attacked, that Mrs. Coolidge finally banished him to the *Mayflower* but he did not like the sea and soon ran off, finding a home ultimately with a Navy family. Tiny Tim, a gift on the President's birthday, was known as Terrible Tim and he earned the title. He would have nothing to do with Mr. Coolidge. Calamity Jane chewed the electric wires at the summer White House in the Black Hills after being flown out there, and she had so many mishaps that the Coolidges did not know what to do with her. A collie puppy known as Diana of Wildwood followed Terrible Tim. Ruby Ruff was left at the door with a note that she had been bred specially for Mrs. Coolidge. She was tan and white, a small edition of a collie, but the other dogs did not like her. The next in succession was a coal-black Gruenendael known as King Cole.

Mrs. Coolidge was not particularly fond of cats but her husband liked them and they began their married life with three successive kittens from Vermont—Bounder, Climber and Mud. The President would hide Bounder, who liked to play in the water, and his wife would have to rescue her. At the White House he frequently walked into her sitting room from the executive offices with a kitten named Tige draped around his neck like a snake. The other White House cat was Blackie.

While the Coolidges were in occupation the White House was lively with the screech of birds as well as the pounding of dogs. Mrs. Coolidge had a succession of canaries, and guests always remembered the singing birds around her, the profusion of flowers, and her bright face turned up to a gilded cage. All the pets, like her friends, had nicknames. The favorite canaries were Nip and Tuck, Snowflake, Peter Piper and Goldy. Old Bill was a thrush.

But the bird with character was Do-Funny, a trained troupial from South America who sometimes lit on the President's shoulder and tweaked his ear, or jabbered madly at Mrs. Coolidge. He belonged to the oriole family and was about the size of a crow, with vivid flashes of yellow and blue in his dark shiny plumes. He was loud and raucous when annoyed, but Miss Randolph noticed that he had a flutelike whistle for Mrs. Coolidge. When let out of his cage he would eat from her mouth and whistle. He liked to catch food or little wads of paper in his bill. When she whistled to him from another room he delighted her by answering.

When the screens came down and soft autumn breezes fluttered the curtains birds sometimes flew in from the grounds. One night Mrs. Coolidge was awakened by an exclamation from the bathroom. Her husband had got up to spray his nose and throat. She rushed in and found a bat hovering against the tiles. Tying a towel around her head she dashed for a broom and on her return to the bedroom found an owl poised on the marble mantelpiece. Mrs. Coolidge thought she was having a nightmare but it developed that the owl had chased the bat into the White House. Meanwhile, the President had got rid of the bat and peace was restored.

But Rebecca, the raccoon intended as a gift for their Thanksgiving dinner, stayed on as an honored and amusing guest. The staff detested her, except Miss Riley, who made her her special care. The President found her crafty and amusing. She tore silk stockings, pecked holes in clothes with her small black paws and terrified Miss Randolph. Watching Rebecca climbing up her one day as she stood petrified with fright Mr. Coolidge removed the cigar from his mouth and drawled: "I think that little coon could bite if she had a mind to."

She was free indoors but was chained outside, with a fence around her for protection. She had so much personality that the President was reported to have escorted her around the White House on a leash and then to have asked her what she thought of it. True or false, this made her a front-page character. But it was a verified fact that when he returned from the executive offices in the late afternoon he would play with Rebecca as if she were a child. She would get into a tub and splash about with soap and water, making suds. She was a pretty little creature with black stripes and a fluffy tail, and could be worn like a necklace. Sometimes the President appeared in his wife's quarters with Rebecca, like Tige, draped around his neck. She ate her dinner on the tiled floor of Mrs. Coolidge's bathroom and liked persimmon, chicken, green shrimp, cream and eggs. When the family was staying on Dupont Circle she lived in a tree in the garden with a collar and chain to keep her in tow. But one night she broke loose and played hide and seek with four policemen. Finally the lure of a corn muffin brought her hustling out of the hedge, making the little crooning noises that indicated she was happy. She was kept in the cellar that night, but the President, on the prowl, discovered her under a packing case. Eventually she wound up in the zoo but she was one of the most distinctive of White House pets.

Since she was skillful with animals Mrs. Coolidge usually coped with emergencies, assisted by Miss Riley. She lived through a succession of animal gifts that had to be turned over to the zoo. Among them were a bear from Mexico, a wallaby from Australia, a hippopotamus from South Africa, five lion cubs from Johannesburg, a duiker and some Pekin ducks.

About this time the President's wife had just succeeded in downing a ridiculous story that she was expecting a baby. For months during 1925 caps, blankets, pillows, socks and afghans had been arriving at the White House. Mrs. Coolidge was more touched than angry by the good-will and interest of women in small places across the country. But the fact remained that she was forty-six and there was no truth in the rumor. Miss Randolph returned the gifts with a denial that a baby was expected. No rational explanation was ever found for the story and she helped to squash it in Washington as she circulated among friends.

It was just as far off the mark but less annoying than a later rumor that Mrs. Coolidge intended to divorce the President after she left the White House. The story was so persistent that Miss Randolph consulted family friends about it, but they would not take it seriously.

It seemed too absurd. They all went round quietly denying it but the story made headway, nevertheless, and lived on for the better part of a year. Finally, the matter seemed so serious that a decision was taken to have the Coolidges appear conspicuously together in public—not only at church and official functions—but walking through crowded streets at busy hours and driving on the most populated parkways. All this seemed ridiculous to Mrs. Coolidge but eventually the story died after the manner of Presidential gossip. "If ever a tale was made out of whole cloth that one was," Miss Randolph observed, "for even had they not been so devoted to each other, neither was of the type that would ever have considered divorce."

Actually, the President's love for his wife made a profound impression on Miss Randolph, who had watched them as intimately as anyone during their years in the White House. As soon as he stepped from the elevator on the second floor and approached their private apartments he would call for Grace. If she happened to be out he would go straight to Miss Randolph's alcove and ask where she was. Then he would watch for her from the window. Light would break across his grave face as he turned back toward the elevator to meet her on her return. "For she was the sunshine and the joy in his life—his rest when tired—his solace in time of trouble," Miss Randolph wrote. "Deep, indeed, went the roots of Calvin Coolidge, and they were close bound about that wife of his, and the children."

Mrs. Hills, another close observer whose knowledge of them went back to Mrs. Coolidge's earliest married years, was never in any doubt that he "worshiped Grace." She thought that his pat on his wife's shoulder was the equivalent of a bear hug from a more demonstrative man. It was clear to all that he liked always to have her near at hand. In private he usually addressed her as "Mammy" or "Mamma" and Grace occasionally varied "Calvin" with "Papa."

"The whole union seems cabalistic," said William Allen White, after he came to know them well. "She is a vital part of his success, of his life, of his happiness." He was struck by her candor, the strength of her face, her self-control in spite of what he deduced to be an emotional nature. He found her charming where her husband was silent, quick where he was slow, intuitive where he was logical.

When she went to Northampton to visit her ailing mother Colonel Starling observed how much the President missed her. They would sit on the back porch at night and smoke and talk, but more often the President would speak of his dead mother than his living wife. He invited the Colonel to share his breakfast hour. Meanwhile, he watched eagerly for Mrs. Coolidge's letters and would personally cut the twine on stacks of personal mail at the executive offices and search until he found the one he wanted. Then he would pocket it, walk at once to the White House and lock himself up for half an hour to read it, while Colonel Starling mounted guard outside his door. "He loved his wife deeply," the Colonel observed. "He was, of course, a very sentimental man, and a very shy one. He loved a few people a great deal, and he was embarrassed about showing it. Gradually, as time went by, I found him to be so human and thoughtful that I came to the conclusion his outward reticence and aloofness were part of a protective shell."

Mrs. Coolidge was well aware of this. He never kissed her when they met or parted, although he usually kissed his father and sons, and Mrs. Coolidge was given to embracing her friends with warmth and spontaneity. But this was no indication of the depth of his affection. It was her policy never to embarrass her husband in public, and a loving gesture would have been completely out of character for him. But she was photographed so often with her arms around children that she wrote jestingly to the Robins that she might eventually become known as the "National Hugger." A New York grandmother who attended one of her teas told her that her grandson had said to her: "I wish you would take me to Washington and let Mrs. Coolidge hug me." But Helen Keller, reading the President's lips, did not hesitate to hug him. "We had lots of fun about that," Mrs. Coolidge wrote. "I told her I was glad she did it because he thought I was the only woman who dared."

Mrs. Coolidge also liked to tell the story of the time she induced Calvin to kiss the bride at a wedding in Boston while he was still in the State House. A sister of one of the stenographers in the executive offices was marrying a Colonel Logan. As Mrs. Coolidge approached the bride and embraced her the girl said: "Your husband didn't kiss me."

" 'What!' said I. 'Well, we'll see about that' and I turned around and there he was just behind me," she wrote to the Robins. " 'Didn't you kiss the bride?' He said, 'No, I didn't know I had to.' So I took him by the hand and led him forth and he played up nobly—did a good job. It wasn't so funny when Colonel Logan spoke up and said 'I can't see why all this is so one-sided.' You can imagine the rest."

Jealous and possessive though he was where Grace was concerned, Calvin Coolidge added his own personal testimony as to their relations when he told Bruce Barton in 1926: "A man who has the companionship of a lovely and gracious woman enjoys the supreme blessing that life can give. And no citizen of the United States knows the truth of this statement more than I."

CHAPTER VIII

A JESTER AND A QUEEN

M RS. COOLIDGE was just about my 'Public Female Favorite No. 1,' "
Will Rogers announced at a time when the country was sensitive
to the pronouncements of the Oklahoma sage. Chewing gum, lazily
swinging his lariat, his comments on public affairs had aroused considerable public response and his jokes were quoted from coast to
coast. They added a dash of salt to the gaudy parade of the 1920s
and reflected the preoccupations of the hour. His brief newspaper
paragraphs combined shrewd satire with homely philosophy. Will
Rogers had become a national character, a wit with the astringent
touch needed in an era of extravagant nonsense.

His concentration on the President as a *rara avis* in political life
had not gone unnoticed in the White House. When he asked if he
might pay his respects during a visit to Washington he was invited
to stay with the Coolidges. The chance to hang up his hat in the
Executive Mansion was eagerly seized on by Will Rogers. He wrote
to Everett Sanders on September 30, 1926, that it was the greatest
honor ever paid him. It had the added fillip of being the "first meal
I ever had on the government."

But his train was late. He had no time to dress for dinner. When he ambled into the state dining room the President had already tasted his soup. However, Will Rogers wrung a jest from the incident: "This is what I call true democracy, the President and his wife waiting dinner on me, such as I am." His quip was enjoyed over other dinner tables across the country, although it was somewhat gingered up.

The President rose to greet him. For the first time Rogers stood face to face with Mr. and Mrs. Coolidge. "It's Mrs. Coolidge I want to meet," he had written to Sanders. And she did not disappoint him. She gave him plenty of assistance that night as he tried hard to live up to his reputation of being a wit. It was not easy to wring a smile from Cal. But Mrs. Coolidge laughed heartily at each sally. As they rose to leave the table he turned to her and drawled in an aside loud enough for her husband to hear: "I wish you would tell me if the President is going to run again."

"You find out if you can, and let me know," she replied in the same pseudo-confidential tone.

Later that evening he probed a little deeper and Mrs. Coolidge backed him up, but the most they evoked was the brief comment: "I got enough troubles now without looking forward that far." But Will Rogers appreciated the Coolidge wit. There were those who thought that they shared a similar strain of acid perception. "I wish I had a dollar for every good gag he has pulled that has gone over some politician's bean," the Oklahoman commented. "He pulls 'em— if you don't get 'em, that's your fault." He had hit on a basic truth about the President, for many of his jokes went unacknowledged because of his poker face. The turn of phrase was apt to be more pungent than the point of view.

After dinner they gathered around the jigsaw puzzle that was in the making. Both of the Coolidges were expert at this favorite pastime of the 1920s. But the President was a restless man and given to prowling. He would never begin a puzzle until his wife or someone else had set up the framework. Then he would insert a piece here and there in finicky, accurate fashion and wander away. He worked with particular tenacity on one that no member of the family could solve until they discovered that Mrs. Coolidge's troupial had made off with some of the pieces and left them on top of a door frame. When the bird screeched madly at him he remarked: "Don't seem to approve of me, does he?"

Tiny Tim and Prudence Prim both were present during Will Rogers' visit. When they all abandoned the jigsaw puzzle and settled down to talk Tiny Tim, usually so hostile to the President, pillowed his head on Mr. Coolidge's lap and had his ear scratched. Mrs. Coolidge knitted as she followed the unhurried stream of their guest's conversation. She talked to him about Queen Marie of Rumania, who was soon to arrive on a state visit. She questioned him about Lady Astor, with whom he had had a lively encounter. He decided that night that his hostess had certain points in common with the Virginia-born Member of Parliament, except that Mrs. Coolidge was more reserved—"but they both got humor and they are in for anything to get a good laugh."

Will Rogers considered that he was making headway, at least with his hostess, when half-past-ten came around. Like a bolt from the blue he learned that it was time to go to bed, although he had thought the evening was just beginning. Later the story circulated that Cal had gone to sleep on him but this was not the case. It was just his regular bedtime.

"Grace, where is Will going to sleep?" the President asked pointedly.

Mrs. Coolidge rose obediently and urged their guest to breakfast in his room at any hour he wished. The President escorted him halfway to his sleeping quarters. Rogers found the large room with the four-poster bed too awe-inspiring and chose a smaller room with a plain brass bed. Next day he found Mrs. Coolidge "just as alive and cheerful early in the morning as at dinner." But he felt lost in the corridors of the White House and paid morning calls on Mrs. Nicholas Longworth and James J. Davis, Secretary of Labor. His vogue at the time was so great that he was a welcome guest on his own terms. He lunched with the Coolidges, then flew off in the afternoon with a fresh store of anecdotal material. He was on his way to visit George Horace Lorimer and his White House stay made good groundwork for his articles in the *Saturday Evening Post*.

The encounter left a wake of conflicting impressions. The visiting philosopher characterized the President as "mighty friendly and nice, and talks a whole lot when he is with somebody that he feels can't tell him anything." The President in turn commented: "Oh, Will's all right." But he was far from pleased later when Will Rogers mimicked his speech and mannerisms over the air. Mrs. Coolidge later quoted him as saying that he "supposed he had to make a living the same as the rest of us and if that was the only way he could do it, he didn't think he ought to object to helping him." Many considered the buffoonery quite convincing and it served to strengthen the Coolidge legend. Some thought they were listening to the veritable voice of Cal. But during his visit Rogers was completely won by Mrs. Coolidge and wrote of her:

> We have been particularly blessed with the types of Ladies who have graced our Executive Mansion. But this one there now has the reputation, given her by everyone who has met her, of being the most friendly and having the most charming personality of any one of them all. She is chuck plumb full of magnetism, and you feel right at home from the minute you get near her. She has a great sense of humor, and is live and tight up and pleasant every minute, and Calvin is just setting there kinder sizing everthing up.

Ike Hoover believed that the Coolidges did not pay sufficient attention to their guests but let them wander about at will to find diversion for themselves, aside from the formal functions they attended. Miss Randolph viewed things differently. As the custodian of Mrs. Coolidge's calendar, which recorded a succession of fifteen-minute engagements all day long, she considered it imperative that guests should not linger about, waiting for the Coolidges to appear, but should attend to their own business and visit whom they wished. It was her task to attend to social etiquette, invitations, trunks, sightseeing and all contingencies that might arise, making certain that the guests were on hand promptly to lunch and dine with their hosts, or to attend any state functions that might occur during their visits.

She needed all her professional and social skill to cope with the unprecedented problems created by Queen Marie of Rumania, who arrived in Washington in October, 1926, right on the heels of Will

Rogers, and outmaneuvered President Coolidge in her determined effort to squeeze the full publicity value from her official visit. The Queen was a dominating personality whose looks, loves and intrigues had become part of the accepted picture in Europe. Her son, Prince Carol, was an exile from his kingdom, having abdicated the year before in favor of his young son Michael. Magda Lupescu at the moment was a new name, a new face, to the newspaper reading public. Princess Helen of Greece, whom Carol had married in 1921, was contemplating a divorce. Central Europeans watched the affair with skeptical eyes. But a tenacious romance had sprung from the mountain mists of the Balkans. More would be heard of it.

Queen Marie was one of a long succession of visitors from Europe who came to the United States in the 1920s to feather their national nests, spread some particular gospel, lecture for stiff fees, or merely to spread good will and see the country. From Coué, the apostle of cheerful assurance, to Ramsay MacDonald, the statesman, the invasion went on. Ticker-tape parades up Broadway and formal visits to the White House were key events for the more important.

The Queen sailed into New York harbor through fog and rain, pronounced the skyline Egyptian in character, and rode up Broadway with Mayor Walker, gratified to receive so rousing a welcome in so dazzling a city. Confetti floated down on her upturned face and settled on her tightly draped turban and muffling furs. She shared the front pages that day with Trotzky, who perforce had bowed out to the Stalin regime and after a few more political maneuvers would be on his way to obscurity and death.

Queen Marie was more dramatic, more overpowering and, in the long run, more troublesome than any of the other visitors from Europe. The White House was her prime point of attack but word had gone forth that she could not use the Presidential office to promote the publicity in which she loved to bask. When she stepped off the train in Washington she shed the aura of ancient European royalty although she prided herself on being a progressive monarch. To onlookers she seemed both stately and commanding as a fanfare of trumpets greeted her and Secretary of State Kellogg bowed over her hand with a fragile, courtly air. But the Washington crowds were curiously cool after the deafening din of New York.

The Queen's formal call at the White House was upsetting to the President's aides. She chose her own chair instead of seating herself in the appointed place, thereby forcing the President to camp uneasily on a small cane chair in which he sat sidewise while she deluged him with talk. Mrs. Coolidge, usually so articulate, could find few openings for her customary friendly comments. Her interest was piqued by what she had heard of Queen Marie. Reigning monarchs were a novelty at the White House but not then or later was she intimidated by any visitor during her husband's term of office. She turned her attention warmly to Princess Ileana and Prince Nicolas when the President asked that they be brought in from the Green Room.

One of the measures used to keep the Queen from exploiting the White House on her visit was a ban on photographs, and the grounds were cleared of cameramen. Marie was already signed up for syndicate rights and the press was getting uneasy. But on her return to the Rumanian Embassy from her official call she stepped grandly from the White House limousine and climbed into a touring car awaiting her there. Then she turned an expectant face to the grateful cameramen. The Rumanian chargé d'affaires had already been notified that the President did not wish to be photographed on his return visit. All was quiet in Sheridan Circle as the Coolidges drove in. Reporters were mysteriously absent. For half an hour the Queen and Mrs. Coolidge, gowned in black satin, a color she rarely wore because Calvin disliked it, chatted with great animation, while the President looked on silently. Her guests were about to leave when the Queen picked up her draperies and brightly interposed: "Just one moment."

From behind the palms trooped the happy cameramen, all ready with their flashlight bulbs and plates. The President, who by this time was well used to publicity and not particularly averse to it in the proper place, was moved to the kind of cold wrath that sometimes took possession of him. However, he accepted the inevitable with icy impassivity. "His anger and annoyance increased when he later viewed the unwelcome proof that this clever woman had outwitted him," Miss Randolph reported. "Queen Marie is a most determined lady, and was not to be outdone by a mere President of the United States."

All over the nation next morning Americans took interested note of their Cal looking grim beside the opulent Queen Marie. He had a severe cold at the time, unknown to the public, and was dosing himself with all his favorite pills. He was not in the mood for regal parade or for the overpowering personality of the Rumanian Queen. The state dinner that followed was a wearing affair so far as he was concerned. The Queen sparkled, from her diamond and pearl diadem to her rhinestone-studded slippers. Her Patou gown of heavy white crepe, threaded with silver and festooned with rhinestones, had a sweeping triangular train falling from one shoulder. She wore three ropes of huge pearls and a wide blue satin decoration athwart her bodice. Side panels helped to disguise the fact that her skirt was knee-length, and she confided to Mrs. Coolidge after dinner that she always used her huge ostrich feather fan in the evening to cover up her legs. She waved it to demonstrate.

Mrs. Coolidge solved this problem by wearing full-length gowns on formal occasions during the era of fantastically short skirts. Her husband preferred it that way and once told a pretty young guest on the *Mayflower* named Mrs. C. C. Glover, as she frantically tugged and pulled at her skirt in an effort to cover her knees: "What you need is a rug."

"What a thing to have to tell my grandchildren when they ask me some day, 'And what did the President say to you, Grandmamma?' " she later commented.

Although always fashionably turned out, Mrs. Coolidge was never seen in knee-length skirts and her daytime clothes were conservatively cut to mid-calf length. In her own words: "My shortest is 10½ inches from the ground. I'll not go any higher—not that I'm fussy, I just do not think they look well." Aside from her natural sense of the appropriate her legs were her least graceful feature. But Queen Marie looked no more regal than Grace that night as she appeared in a white gown brocaded with pastel-tinted velvet flowers and a long train lined with orchid chiffon. She wore modest strands of pearls and single-pearl earrings, and used virtually no make-up. The Queen's *maquillage* was overpowering.

They were a study in contrasts as they did the official circle in turn in the Blue Room before going in to dinner. The stringed orchestra of the scarlet-coated Marine Band played softly. The official and diplomatic sets were out in full panoply. Queen Marie's hand rested lightly on President Coolidge's stiffly offered arm as they marched into the state dining room with its silver chandeliers and gold service. The flowers were pink roses, white snapdragons and blue delphiniums. The menu was strongly native—caviar, consommé, lobster Newburg, filet of beef with mushrooms, potato balls, green string beans, cold turkey in aspic, green salad, ice cream with maple sauce, cakes and coffee.

Prince Nicolas was visibly nervous until Mrs. Coolidge took him in tow and put him at ease as he sat beside her at dinner. She was never at a loss with the young and her knowledge of her own two sons gave her special tact in dealing with youths of Nicolas' age. Princess Ileana, a jeweled bandeau flashing above her handsome face, was the partner of Andrew Mellon. The Queen made slow headway with the President but kept up a barrage of lively conversation while her bold dark eyes flashed in all directions. Every time the President looked across the delphiniums and pink roses so skillfully arranged in Greek figurines on the glass plateau centerpiece he could see Grace beaming at her partners.

After dinner the two women sat side by side in the Red Room and discussed their children. They were quite at ease with each other and soon grew confidential. Miss Randolph had coached Mrs. Coolidge on procedure and had warned her to stay beside the Queen on the sofa, so as to control the situation. "Don't let go of her for a moment," she implored. Marie was known to be a creature of impulse as well as being a shrewd manipulator. Miss Randolph brought up the guests in order of rank, four at a time, and they sat two by two in small gold chairs at either end of the sofa, chatting briefly with the Queen and their hostess. There was to be no kowtowing, but the full exercise of all the ceremony that the occasion demanded. Warm-hearted Mrs. Coolidge, observing that the ladies-in-waiting seemed to be left out in the cold, forgot for the moment Miss Randolph's injunction and crossed the room to speak to them.

The Queen went into action at once. She signaled to Alice Longworth to sit by her side. From then on she paid no further attention to the waiting guests but chatted with the brilliant daughter of Theodore Roosevelt, effectively garbed in Chinese red, without a single jewel. Mrs. Longworth could not break away and the impasse continued until the men arrived from the library and they all moved on to the Blue Room. There they remained standing and the Queen was quickly surrounded by men.

When the royal party had left, Mrs. Coolidge let her train fall to the ground with a sigh of relief. She noticed her husband standing by the open window and moved to his side. Dr. Coupal was already on his trail, ready to hurry him off to bed.

"Calvin!" she said reproachfully.

"I just wanted to see if the Queen had gone," he remarked as he turned away from the window.

He had not been his happiest that night and Grace knew it. But he had done his best in a difficult situation and she knew that he was not feeling well. There had been other occasions with women he knew more intimately when he had been far less gracious. One that made a lasting impression on his wife was a dinner at which both Mrs. Dawes and Mrs. Kellogg, seated to his right and left, had made vain attempts to hit on a topic that might draw a response. To her confusion and dismay she observed him getting up from the table before the dessert had been removed and the fruit and confections passed.

"Groping for my gloves," she related, "I was guilty of a grave social error in saying across the table: 'Your guests have not finished.' With a correcting smile in my direction he replied, 'I have.'"

Everybody promptly moved. Later, over the coffee cups in the Red Room Grace jested mildly with Mrs. Dawes and Mrs. Kellogg, both good friends of hers, about their inability to hold the President in check until the others had appeased their appetites. The joke was enjoyed all round. "As a dinner guest there is no denying that he was unsatisfactory," she wrote good humoredly. But she was not readily embarrassed when her husband put her in an awkward position. Usually she was ingenious in saving the situation. She could thaw a frost without any great effort. But Queen Marie was long remembered as the first European queen and the most pushing guest to visit the White House.

She continued to harass the press, and they her, as she conducted her cross-country tour by special train, with a growing tide of skepticism surrounding her. The crowds cheered but reporters missed train connections, got lost, and muffed their deadlines. Syndicates fought over the rights to her personal story. They could not silence the voluble queen or keep her thoughts and impressions exclusively to themselves. Given the least encouragement the dam broke loose until everyone knew what Queen Marie thought on all conceivable subjects. Her impulsive acts and comments encouraged headlines, which took on the withering note of satire. The feuds and entanglements in management reached a crisis in Portland, Oregon, and the royal Rumanian troupe, complete with Loie Fuller's dancers, dissolved in chaos. There was merriment in Europe over the Queen's adventures in America, although she scarcely qualified for the role of an innocent abroad. The regal image was slightly tarnished before she sailed for home in November, but her fulsome notes to the various state officials who had entertained her left a flavor of romance.

Crown Prince Gustavus Adolphus of Sweden fared better when he arrived with Crown Princess Louise. The six-foot Swede viewed Washington as the most beautiful of cities and he and President Coolidge found a common meeting ground. The state dinner went well. Princess Astrid of Sweden, a cousin of the Crown Prince, was being discussed at the time as a likely wife for the Prince of Wales. Beautiful, intelligent, domestic, she fulfilled the public image of a suitable mate for the most famous Prince of his day. But Edward was headed for exile and one of the prime romances of history. Astrid would die at the age of thirty in an automobile accident on a Swiss highway, while driving with her husband, King Leopold of Belgium.

The President and the Crown Prince of Sweden stood side by side at the unveiling of a memorial to John Ericsson in Washington while

Mr. Coolidge paid tribute to the Swedish settlers in America, and Gustavus responded in kind. The royal pair saw different aspects of American life. They visited museums and public landmarks. They played golf and went yachting and shopping. The Prince lauded American energy but exemplified it tenfold himself. The Princess paid tribute to the American woman and her attire. The flappers, the bobbed hair, the ultra-short skirts she saw all around had their counterpart in Europe, she said, and so did not shock or surprise her. Visiting Europeans by this time had stock answers ready for the stock questions asked them so unfailingly by the tireless press. Only now and again did an individualist like Lady Astor break loose and upset the *status quo* with tactless or sharp-edged comments.

While in office President Coolidge received a Prince of the reigning house of Japan as well as of Sweden, the Premier of France, the Governor-General of Canada, and the Presidents of the Irish Free State, of Cuba, Haiti and Mexico. But these were minor social links in a world where the means of communication steadily gathered speed. The year 1926 held the seeds of conflict at home and abroad, as well as moments of heroism and disaster. Americans set their own swift pace in enterprise and abundant living, but in the background loomed the distorted canvas of world affairs, and visiting statesmen were uneasy. The United States was now involved in the world picture, for better or for worse, but beyond all doubt for the full sweep of the unpredictable future.

Entry into the World Court was still a burning issue as the year began and late in January the Senate voted seventy-six to seventeen in favor of the final step. Mrs. Woodrow Wilson, who had listened to the debate for seven hours, walked up the gallery steps to make her exit with a look of satisfaction on her face. To her it was the voice of her husband speaking. To the country at large it was the technical, if not the spiritual, end of a seven-year battle against isolation. But the reservations voted by the Senate were unacceptable to the Court, the dream died and President Coolidge continued his efforts on behalf of international good will by proposing a conference of the leading naval powers to be held at Geneva in the following summer. Only Great Britain and Japan accepted and no agreement was reached.

Germany was fighting her way back into the family of European powers and was seeking to set her riven house in order. The shrill voice of Adolf Hitler was silent after his earlier bid for power in the Beer Hall *Putsch,* but *Mein Kampf* was off the presses, drafting the shape of things to come. Thunder would crash through Europe again when the brief solstice of German prosperity ended, as world recession set in by 1930. Dictatorship had struck a foundation in the chaos left by the world war. Black-shirted Italians cheered Benito Mussolini as he ushered in 1926 by proclaiming himself the modern Caesar. He promised that Rome would be restored to imperial grandeur within five years "as a marvel to all the people of the world —vast, ordered, and powerful as it was in the time of the first empire of Augustus." Within a matter of weeks he was bidding Italy prepare for its "hour," at the seventh anniversary of the birth of Fascism. Fifty thousand blackshirts, marching in Rome to the hymn *Youth,* hailed the Duce.

The tide of adulation rose ever higher, fed by his periodical speeches. Vivas followed him wherever he moved. A great fiesta on Rome's birthday involved civic ceremonies, colonial parades, trade union celebrations and sports gatherings. Chimes spilled melody from the belfries. Searchlights played on the Forum. Flares lit up the Tiber at night when Mussolini returned from a triumphal trip to Tripoli. His boundaries were expanding.

Meanwhile, the strings of dictatorship were drawing tight elsewhere in Europe in 1926. In Greece Premier Theodoros Pangalos seized power with the aid of the army. In Poland Joseph Pilsudski led a military revolution in Warsaw and established his dictatorship. Both Asia and Africa had battlegrounds as the year progressed. An uprising plagued Syria, and trouble raged in the oil-rich Mosul area, claimed by Turkey after the war. The Riffs were fighting their way to defeat in Morocco. Their warfare was picturesquely covered by the American press, but with an air of remote association. None of these struggles impinged seriously on the immediate sense of world security, as envisioned in 1926. A strong sense of the repetitive march of history was engendered as the golden casket of King Tutankhamen, removed from his tomb after 3,500 years, was borne down the rocky way from the Valley of the Kings to the Nile. The long-forgotten ruler was restored to contemporary fame from the dust of antiquity. Archaeology was discussed by the man in the street. King Tut jokes were passed across the footlights. The Egyptian motif was reflected in fashion.

World leaders made imposing pronouncements during 1926. On Washington's birthday President Coolidge interpreted the foreign policies of the first President as teaching mutual fellowship in international relations. The father of his country was no "small American" preaching hatred of all things foreign. On the contrary, he made large concessions for the settlement of disputed questions, said the thirtieth President of the first. And a much respected American sage and prophet, Chauncey M. Depew, nearing his ninety-second birthday, exulted over the new spirit of good feeling in the world. He expressed the hope that Locarno was the first step toward a confederacy of Europe, and recalled that in times of crisis Providence had supplied leaders such as Caesar, Napoleon, Bismarck, Washington and Lincoln. His words were weighted with hope and, in the light of subsequent events, with bad prophecy.

Thomas A. Edison, celebrating his seventy-ninth birthday at Fort Myers, Florida, commented on the state of the world with the optimism of the man who has lived long and richly. He saw things getting better, with increasing numbers of "fine, humane, honest people," the true test of civilization. He was sure there would always be little wars, but no big one for at least another generation. When asked to name the world's five greatest men, his rugged face creased into laughter. "You wouldn't know them," he said. "They are working around in laboratories and such places."

The way of the tyrant was becoming clear to many observers on both sides of the Atlantic but the front pages in America still had room for plenty of domestic items, and the emphasis lay on national news. A golden shower of prosperity gilded the land in 1926. The annual surveys were fat with profits. Coolidge and Mellon let the facts bear witness to the state of the union. Both were masters at maintaining silence. Wages and spending power were high. Taxes were low and tariffs zoomed. There was little unemployment and the major industries were having their greatest boom since the end of the war. Buildings were going up from coast to coast. The iron and steel industry was in high gear. But farmers were not so happy and the McNary-Haugen bill, which the President would veto in the following year as economically unsound, was in the making. It provided for the maintenance of prices at home by marketing surpluses abroad.

The automobile industry burgeoned with profits and new ideas. Americans boasted ten million automobiles, although eighty per cent were bought on the installment plan and the year's casualties on the nation's highways were 24,000 killed and 500,000 injured. One sixth of the national income was tied to installment buying. Refrigerators, radio sets, streamlined automobiles, modern furniture, motor boats, country homes, proclaimed the new prosperity. Great pounding waves of advertising washed around the public, with their insistent message of the skin you love to touch, that schoolgirl complexion, not a cough in a carload, reach for a Lucky instead of a sweet. Madison Avenue was whipping the buying public into action, conditioning the nation's tastes, stirring up the manufacturer's ingenuity, unloosening the family purse strings. During the Coolidge era magazine advertising almost doubled in volume. The total expenditure rose by 1927 to one and a half billion dollars.

Such, at least, were the visible and more garish signs of prosperity. Coupled with the quiet assurance that emanated from the White House, they were enough to deaden the tension and lull the anxiety that had plagued the nation since the end of the first world war. Yet the domestic picture, aside from its more innocuous frivolities, was one of great commotion, as prohibition undermined the legal machinery of the land, and headlines shouted crime. All through the 1920s the names of mobsters threaded the news of the day—Legs Diamond, the vain and agile crook with the nine lives of a cat; Dutch Schultz, industrious, businesslike, slangy and given to savage rages; Owney Madden, the soft-spoken racketeer who bred pigeons on the roof of a New York apartment house; Vincent Coll, the "mad dog" with ice in his veins who died in a telephone booth; Larry Fay, the manicured fop who specialized in rainbow taxis and fashionable night clubs; Arnold Rothstein, the master gambler and Broadway boulevardier who simultaneously moved in sophisticated circles and ran an underworld empire; and Al Capone, most notorious of all, whose operations cast dark shadows across the country from his stronghold in Chicago.

Their armor-plated automobiles and machine-gun raids, their political power and pervasive racketeering, their gang wars and art collections, their vengeance and mass killings, like the St. Valentine's Day massacre in Chicago, made lurid headlines. Most of the uproar grew out of prohibition, which was the law of the land, breeding hoodlum instincts. Gangsters drove through the streets with sawed-off shotguns. High-jackings, gang killings, gambling and prohibition raids were the prime scandals of the day.

In the spring of 1926 eight-column streamers proclaimed the state of the union to be rotten, as a special investigating committee in Washington probed into the workings of prohibition. The wet and dry forces had hearings in a full blaze of publicity, and newspaper readers shared in tales as curious as any ever heard in the capital. Wherever Mrs. Coolidge went that spring the talk was of prohibition, as the wet and dry forces battled it out in public. The law was observed to the letter in the White House although the President quietly told friends that "any law which inspires disrespect for the other laws —and good laws—is a bad law."

Emory R. Buckner, United States Attorney, told the startled Senators that bootleggers' revenue amounted to $3,600,000,000; that the prohibition law was ruining the country; that the courts were swamped with untried cases; that it would take $75,000,000 to dry up New York alone; and that more courts and judges were needed, as well as 15,000 additional men to patrol the Canadian border. It was argued that a broom was being used to sweep back an ocean as the dizzy operations of Rum Row went on unchecked. Lawlessness had reached the point where judges and police officials not only protected bootleggers, beer manufacturers and gangsters, but publicly attended the gang war funerals. This was the era when the murdered rogue was buried with pomp and circumstance. His power in gang circles was appraised by the showing of floral harps, crosses and anchors at his funeral.

The wets argued that college morale had been smashed through prohibition and that the young were drinking as never before. Lurid pictures were painted of speakeasies as elaborate as Arabian palaces and as dismal as barren little cells with checked tablecloths in dingy basements. The frenzy of the Charleston and Black Bottom, the petting in parked cars, the whine of jazz bands, the rudeness of the young, were all tied up with the evils of prohibition as a long parade of witnesses took the stand and gave startling testimony. But women representing nine national organizations with a membership of 18,-000,000 stormed the hearing to protest any modification of the Volstead Act.

Although much of the crime was linked to prohibition, there were still the solo bandits who played their own game for big stakes. Such were two of the most discussed criminals of the Coolidge era—Gerald Chapman and Richard Reese Whittemore, both to die for their crimes, both to accept their fate with reckless hauteur. Chapman, condemned to hang for shooting a New Britain policeman, after effecting a huge mail robbery and other crimes, wrote sonnets in his cell as he appealed four times for reprieve. But Governor Robert H. Trumbull, of Connecticut, who would later become John Coolidge's father-in-law, let the law take its course. "Death itself isn't dreadful," Chapman commented after he was sentenced. "But hanging seems an awkward way of entering the adventure. It was not I who was convicted but a super-bandit the newspapers had exploited."

By this time the country knew him well. It was an era when the criminal was built up by publicity, evil though the portrait might be. If he had the Robin Hood touch, was a poet, a gallant, or a man of some education, he became a rare specimen, the subject of countless columns of newsprint, as in the case of Whittemore, a murderer and jewel thief who was a veritable bombshell of sinister purpose. He was violent in manner and had none of the philosophical detachment of Chapman. He headed a gang of thieves who eventually turned on one another and talked. The story of their jewel operations read like an Oppenheim novel. Their combined confessions were described by the district attorney as a "textbook in crime." They worked with machinelike precision, rehearsing every move in advance. Each man had his part to play. Each robbery was carried out with lightning dispatch. When a job was finished they promptly went out on the town, visiting cabarets and carousing. With their capture many large jewel thefts that had baffled the police were explained. They gave the names of their fences and more arrests followed. Whittemore, a man of some education who came from an established Maryland family, was finally convicted in Baltimore.

But the murder mystery with enduring echoes down the years was the Hall-Mills case. When the Rev. Edward W. Hall, an Episcopalian rector, and his leading choir singer, Mrs. James Mills, were found dead beneath a crab-apple tree in a lovers' lane near New Brunswick, New Jersey, the case lapsed after a half-hearted investigation. But in 1926 it burst wide open with the arrest of Mrs. Hall, her brother Willie and her cousin, Henry Carpender, all of whom were charged with the crime. The trial that followed was one of the most sensational in the history of the American courts, with the dying Mrs. Jane Gibson, known as the "Pig Woman," being carried into court on a stretcher to identify Mrs. Hall as the woman she said she saw standing beside the dead bodies when she rode nearby on her mule. Willie, who had been pictured as a mental defective, confounded his interrogators from the witness stand and testified with dignity and conviction. All three were acquitted but the case remained one of the riddles of jurisprudence.

Another headline snatcher at this time was Edward W. Browning, a real estate operator who came to be known as Daddy Browning when he married fifteen-year-old Frances Heenan, familiar to the public as "Peaches." He was fifty-one years of age at the time, and such was the uproar attending his marriage that the Society for the Prevention of Cruelty to Children intervened on behalf of Peaches. She looked anything but a child, however, as she turned a limpid stare on the press and lisped out her love for Daddy. This was only the start of the four-ring circus staged by Browning as his marriage broke up and other protegées followed. He died in 1934 and Peaches found and lost four husbands within the next two decades.

A very different romance struck deep chords in public interest when Irving Berlin telephoned to Ellin Mackay on the spur of the

moment and urged her to marry him at once. She promptly made an
enduring choice. They had long been in love. Ellin had been taken
to Europe to break the spell. But Irving's love songs followed her
wherever she went. Family opposition was pulling them apart. They
were of different faiths. Irving was thirty-seven. Ellin was twenty-two.
He had been a singing waiter ·in Chinatown, an East Side boy who
had found dazzling success on Broadway with his natural gifts and
industry. Ellin had grown up in a conventional social setting as the
daughter of Clarence Mackay, president of the Postal Telegraph
Company. It was a love story of international interest, but nowhere
was the romance more relished than on Broadway. Berlin's theatrical
friends were certain that it would last. Ellin's debutante friends were
not so sure.

Lucretia Bori and Beniamino Gigli were singing at the home of
Clarence Mackay on the day the Berlins returned from Europe and
settled down to their married life in New York. His doors still were
closed to Ellin, but the years were to bring the Berlins lasting love
and happiness, three daughters, one son who died, world famous songs
and shows, many friends, and eventually, reconciliation with Ellin's
father. In the days of financial adversity after the crash Berlin gave
generous aid to Mackay. After thirty-five years the union still held
fast, and the songs Berlin wrote for Ellin, *Always, All Alone* and
others during the days of their courtship, became part of the national
idiom of love.

The Berlin furor had scarcely quieted down when another romantic
story caught and held the headlines. James A. Stillman, the banker,
and his estranged wife, Anne Urquhart Stillman, better known as
Fifi, were suddenly reconciled and sailed secretly for Europe on the
Olympic. Five years earlier, boarding the same ship, Mrs. Stillman
had been served with the papers that started the most sensational
divorce suit of the decade. Her husband had named as her lover
Fred Beauvais, an Indian guide she had met at her summer home in
Quebec, and her son Guy as the Canadian's child. She had counter-
sued, identifying Flo Leeds, a chorus girl, as her husband's mistress
and Jay Leeds as his child. Bitter litigation had raged between them

in the intervening years. Their affairs had become notorious throughout the land.

But the reconciliation did not last. In time Mrs. Stillman obtained her long delayed divorce and married Fowler McCormick, heir to the International Harvester fortune and a former friend of her son's. This final twist in the strange tangle of human passions passed almost unnoticed, as did the death of James Stillman on a January day in 1944. But their story was part of the shock background of the 1920s, when the older generation was reviving from wartime strain with corroding disillusionment. A spirited new generation was startling its elders as if it were the first in history to sidekick convention. Some blamed the young for the wild tenor of the times. Others hung the burden of guilt on their parents.

Tradition, established form, complacency, were under attack by a new school of artists and writers. They were committed to realism at all costs—the stark line, the lean phrase, the scorn for sentiment. The faith and habits of their fathers were anathema to this group of rebels, whose range extended from the Midwest to Greenwich Village and the Left Bank. Genius flowered among them, too. Meanwhile skyscrapers rose higher, science and medicine rested on the brink of extraordinary advances, and education shifted rapidly to progressive patterns. There were tales of heroism, noble purpose and discovery, as well as of lawlessness and crime.

The Coolidge era was one of sparkling vitality and controversy in American art and letters. Mrs. Coolidge took a lively interest in the literary battles that raged during 1926. Theodore Dreiser, Sinclair Lewis, F. Scott Fitzgerald and Henry L. Mencken were making headlines outside of the scope of their literary endeavors. When the Pulitzer prize went to *Arrowsmith,* its red-headed author rejected this "menace" and urged his fellow authors to follow his example. It was only a matter of weeks since Lewis had had a sharp taste of the headlines when he challenged God to strike him dead. In the years to come he was to revise his views on literary awards and accept the Nobel prize. But for the moment a paper storm whirled around him —headlines, editorials condemning his act, comment on his brash red-headedness. He was called the town bully and a smart aleck. He was chided for failing to appreciate the stable virtues of Main Street, and the inherent goodness in men like Babbitt. Midwesterners were wounded by his barbs, but they read their acid critic. He was discussed from coast to coast. In satirizing the conformist, he had stirred up waves of social self-analysis. Main Street and Babbit became generic terms in the language, springing directly from the Coolidge era. Sinclair Lewis shared the limelight with Theodore Dreiser, since the aura of genius and endurance surrounded *An American Tragedy* from the start. Dreiser's circumlocution might offend the stylists, but his vitality overpowered them.

By early summer the scene was rich with fresh talent. Best-sellers ran into substantial figures. A popular novel soon topped 100,000 and fiction was in its heyday. A revolution was in the making, for the Book-of-the-Month Club was just getting under way in the spring of 1926. Its significance was barely noted at the time. Authors became famous overnight by spontaneous public demand in a book-buying era, by advertising and by the potent offices of the critics. In *The Writing of Fiction* Edith Wharton was giving advice out of the riches of her own experience. In the much applauded stream-of-consciousness technique she could find nothing but a recrudescence of the old French method of reproducing small areas of life, with the added factor of mental as well as visual reaction.

The trumpets were beginning to sound for Ernest Hemingway, but not too loudly at first. One critic found him "a much more deft and finished artist than Sherwood Anderson, with a quiet irony beyond the scope of the older man." Others assailed the monotony of his prose, but Hemingway stunned them all by the end of the year with *The Sun Also Rises*. It was also the year in which F. Scott Fitzgerald's *All the Sad Young Men* was published. The handsome Princetonian was then busy building up the legend that was to flourish for a time, die and be revived three decades later. His ideal woman was pinpointed in this instance. She was fragile, rude, demanding and created an illusion. She was different from the John Held girl of the 1920s; from Sinclair Lewis's ruthless Carol Kennicott. She was the special Fitzgerald creation, reflecting his wife Zelda and life lived on a mountain peak of excitement.

More noble fare was offered by Carl Sandburg in *The Prairie Years,* received as a fine piece of Lincolniana. One critic noted that both were plain men from Illinois, admirable story tellers, rationalists, and Jeffersonian democrats, at times beset by melancholy moods. The later success of the popular type of medical book was foreshadowed in Paul de Kruif's *Microbe Hunters,* which was seized on by the public as a novelty. Charles G. Norris's *Pig Iron* was viewed with interest as part of a social crusade. Political memoirs, sharing newspaper and book publication, were causing a flurry of talk, in particular *The Letters of Walter Hines Page* and *The Intimate Papers of Colonel House,* loaded with startling revelations about Woodrow Wilson.

Early that year Rupert Hughes raised a storm at a dinner in Washington when he chose to throw darts at the impeccable conception of George Washington, describing the father of his country as a profane, irreligious and pleasure-loving man, who lied, gambled, swore profusely, brewed beer, distilled whisky, played cards, danced, attended horse races, played billiards and was never such a mollycoddle as to get himself embroiled in the cherry tree myth. The author repeated his inflammatory tale to a large crowd in New York's Town Hall. The nation viewed George Washington from a new angle. Some liked what they saw. Others were enraged.

This realistic approach to heroes spread. Debunking became a popular pastime in the Coolidge era. Mrs. Harry Atwell Colman, addressing the Susan B. Anthony Foundation, called Dolly Madison a frivolous, rouged, snuff-taking, card-playing woman. In fact, had she lived in 1926, she would have been known as a flapper, said this bold lady. Canada banned a magazine running a series entitled *The Heartbreak of a Queen,* which was thought to reflect on the character of King Edward VII and to misrepresent the life of Queen Alexandra. The era of royal memoirs had not yet cushioned the way for such revelations. The *Saturday Evening Post,* with a circulation of more than 2,925,000 and a solid grass-roots air, was running names that were part of the national idiom. Montague Glass, George Ade, Harvey O'Higgins and Rupert Hughes were much before the public. A typical issue of the *Post* featured Henry Ford on "Man and His

Machines," Will Rogers on "My Rope and Gum for a Democratic Issue," "You're on the Air" by Graham McNamee, "A Thousand in the Bank" by J. P. Marquand, and "Mopping 'Em up at Monte Carlo" by Frank Ward O'Malley. Humor was in demand, from the sharp satire of Ring Lardner to Finley Peter Dunne, advertised as a "jazz philosopher, a peppy, modern Plato."

A galvanic new influence was exerted by the *New Yorker*, a year old in the spring of 1926. In that time it had run up a circulation of forty thousand, and was already known to the public as a magazine unique in style, sprightly yet literary in content. It became the Bible of the initiate, a periodical exciting in tempo and substance. As time went on it took many friendly jabs at Calvin Coolidge.

In this period of peace and plenty a good deal of intimacy prevailed in writing circles and chitchat was fast, furious and often vitriolic. Authors were on view. They were beginning to come out of the shadows and circulate in public. They made speeches. They autographed books. They addressed women's clubs. In San Francisco, in Chicago, in Denver, in Boston, in the deep South there were vigorous literary stirrings and small groups devoted to fostering the arts. Edna St. Vincent Millay wove her delicate verse and burned the candle at both ends, to the delight of the younger generation. Elinor Wylie might be heard reading her poems against the stained glass of St. Marks-in-the-Bouwerie Church in New York on a Sunday afternoon. Robert L. Frost taught English at Amherst while he turned out sturdy verse. The regional touch was developing strongly, with Zona Gale writing of Wisconsin, Ellen Glasgow of the South, and Willa Cather endowing her novels with a strongly native flavor.

Newspaper columnists were beginning to exercise influence of a new kind. During the Coolidge era they ranged into the open field, away from the well traveled paths of sports and the problems of the lovelorn. The political commentator was gathering strength and influence. The wits like Franklin P. Adams, Frank Sullivan, H. I. Phillips and Don Marquis had long had their faithful followings. Park Row had its own philosopher in the shambling Heywood Broun and Chicago had its Line O' Type by B.L.T. Papers across the country were developing a new breed of columnist and the Walter Winchell era had begun, along with tabloid papers and news conveyed by picture.

Not since the eighteenth century in France had the average man undergone so much reappraisal as during this period of revolt and energy in American letters. The political picture might be static during the Coolidge administration but the arts blazed with creation. H. L. Mencken, one of the nonconformists, was leading his own iconoclastic campaign in the *American Mercury*. He lighted fires that burned across the country and did not soon go out. The Iowa farmer railed at Wall Street. The Anti-Saloon League spilled charges of treason. The morals of Broadway and Hollywood, the manners of the young, and the ethics of the business world provided weekly targets for the nation's pulpits.

The public moved swiftly into channels of travel and material expansion. The shift was felt from Greenwich Village to Nob Hill as expatriates settled in Paris and along the Mediterranean shores. The Left Bank was astir with the impact of creative forces from the Western world as young writers and artists from different parts of the United States browsed by the Seine, strolled under the chestnut trees, or studied the passing show from sidewalk cafés. Some went on to fame; others drifted into the shiftless sands of idleness and failure.

But all was effervescence while the boom was on. Tourists poured into Paris. In fashionable as well as in Bohemian circles the American influence made itself strongly felt and the accents of Georgia, Maine or Michigan were mingled along the Champs Élysées. The Charleston was strutted on the Place Pigalle. American jazz whined and shrieked out of every night club. With prohibition the law of the land at home, Americans were learning abroad to savor their wines and appraise their vintages. The grand tour of museums, galleries, nature's beauties and the continental shops went on. Travel was no longer limited to the well-off few. The low rate of currency in France was a big inducement. Old steerage quarters were converted into tourist class for teachers, students, writers and artists. Advertisements read: "Intellectuals Get Special Rates."

Horizons widened every day. Intercommunication had become a reality. At the time it added little to mutual understanding. The element of caricature and distortion remained strong on both sides of the Atlantic. It was not until after her husband's death that Mrs. Coolidge made her first trip abroad and by then the picture had changed beyond recognition. But the need for international understanding became a fast-developing issue during the Coolidge regime. Woodrow Wilson had set the machinery in motion and in a speech before the American Legion in the autumn of 1925 Coolidge urged tolerance at home and international amity and understanding abroad. However, in discussing disarmament on another occasion he expressed the opinion that "if the people want to fight, they will fight with broomsticks if they cannot find anything else."

But while significant changes were in progress around the world he was attending zealously to his homework and was urging the states not to shirk their rights. He advocated the expansion of local self-government and the contraction of federal rule in a speech delivered at Williamsburg on the hundred and fiftieth anniversary of American independence and his own fifty-fourth birthday. He envisioned the ideal state of the union as one in which the public looked after its own affairs with a minimum of interference from Washington. It was a popular conception at the time and represented the inner core of his theory of government. "The President shouldn't do too much," he told Bruce Barton. "And he shouldn't *know* too much." He sometimes said to his Cabinet: "There are many things you gentlemen must not tell me. If you blunder, you can leave or I can invite you to leave. But if you draw me into all your departmental decisions and something goes wrong, I must stay here. And by involving me you have lowered the faith of the people in their government."

Barton thought that Coolidge understood human nature and had a profound sense of the dignity of his office. Walter Lippmann expressed the opinion that inactivity was a "political philosophy and a party program with Mr. Coolidge." He defined it as a grim, determined, alert activity that kept the President occupied constantly, and was peculiarly suited to those who believed that government had become top-heavy. "The Coolidges are really virtuous people in the old American sense, and they have provided this generation, which is not virtuous in that sense, with an immense opportunity for vicarious virtue," said Mr. Lippmann. "There were no thrills while he reigned," commented H. L. Mencken succinctly, "but neither were there any headaches. He had no ideas but he was not a nuisance."

Charles Merz sought to prove that the Coolidge silence was a myth, although the public image of a strong and silent man in the White House had been built up convincingly in the public mind by the end of 1926. Actually Coolidge outdistanced the eloquent Woodrow Wilson two to one in the number of his public addresses. He spoke to seventy-five public gatherings in the course of a year and delivered 8,688 words a month into the microphone. The age of radio had arrived and he profited by having his talks, with all their nasal emphasis, reach directly into the homes of America.

Mrs. Coolidge was busy all through the winter and spring of 1927-1928 with fast-paced social duties. In February, just after the President had vetoed the farm bill and there were rumblings about what this would do to his chances of reelection, John D. Rockefeller, Jr. and his wife were guests at the White House. It was noted that Mrs. Coolidge gave the menu some personal touches on this occasion and ordered out the best linen, glass and plate. The President went out of his way to be considerate and offered his arm to Mrs. Rockefeller as they went into the dining room, although it was his practice in general to march in ahead of everyone, and hurry absent-mindedly to his seat.

He took little interest in the preparations for the state affairs but liked to appraise the results. Just before one state dinner he visited the kitchen and opened the refrigerator door. The cooking and decorating for this occasion had been under way for three days and the shelves were filled with elaborate hors d'oeuvres, aspics and salads. They looked like the illustrations in a woman's magazine. The President inspected them carefully, then turned to Miss Riley: "Mighty fine looking dog food," he said. He had chosen the pans of dog food on the floor on which to comment.

One judiciary dinner was rated perhaps the handsomest of the Coolidge functions. The pineapples and red plums in the gold fruit dishes, the red carnations and white freesias that decorated the table, were much admired, but Chief Justice Taft, the guest of honor, dined solely on two slices of whole-wheat bread. He was then on a rigid diet and would not break it even on such an occasion as this. No matter what main course was served to other guests roast beef was slipped into place before the President. This was a standing rule and it was so adroitly carried out that few ever noticed it. With his more intimate friends he might take what he called "steaky" but he was fully persuaded that beef was helpful when his asthma was severe. Actually pork was his favorite meat.

The most calamitous of all the Presidential dinners, however, was the one given for President Machado of Cuba. It was a stag affair and Mrs. Coolidge was just as glad afterward. First, the bow tie of one of the visitors fell into his soup. Then the President's military aide, who had been to the dentist that afternoon, lost a temporary front tooth and lisped his way through dinner. A naval aide lost one of his epaulets. The kitchen chimney caught fire. And the meal ended with one portly Cuban visitor solidly attached to his chair. He had gone through the seat as early as the fish course and had remained solidly wedged in without revealing his plight. It took two husky waiters to get him free as he finished his dessert.

When John came home for the holidays from college he was swamped with invitations. "The pace is absolutely impossible," Mrs. Coolidge wrote to Mrs. Hills. "The dances here begin at 10:30 and nobody really goes before midnight which means they dance until four or five. The social whirl was so intense that I knew it wasn't possible for John to get into it and return to college with any energy for his work so I didn't let him start."

But John enjoyed the tea dances and the jazz music of the era. One day when he had been to Annapolis with Mrs. Hills and had stayed too late at one of these functions he reached the White House private sitting room a few minutes before the dinner hour. His father looked thunderous. John respectfully asked him if he might dine without changing, since he was so late. Then the President spoke, in a way that neither John nor Mrs. Hills ever forgot: "You will remember that you are dining at the table of the President of the

United States, and you will present yourself promptly and in proper attire."

The valet had all his things out and John changed in two minutes flat. He understood that it was not vanity on his father's part but respect for the office he held. Mrs. Hills wore a dinner dress under her fur coat, so that she got to the table in the nick of time. She was used to being teased by the President and they had shared many a joke over quiet little family suppers in Northampton with Liederkrantz cheese and coffee. On one occasion he told her that he was calling on her with his wedding shoes, which were eight years old. Because she was of Norwegian descent he summoned her as a special guest when he entertained Nansen, the Norwegian explorer. He knew how much Mrs. Coolidge prized her companionship during their days in the White House. Mrs. Hills represented a familiar family touch in the midst of so much formality.

By the beginning of March, 1927, the President was reminding Mrs. Coolidge, when she complained of slushy weather conditions, that she "would soon be walking, riding in street cars and taxicabs." He liked to tease her about this but "no terrors lie therein for me— I am keeping my walking apparatus in good trim," she wrote to the Robins. By this time she had gathered up her canaries, her family pictures and intimate possessions and had moved her family to 15 Dupont Circle. A detailed report ordered by the President on the actual state of the White House had convinced him that the scare mongers were right. The building was in a dangerous condition, and although major renovation was not in keeping with his notions of public economy he told Grace to pack up her belongings and give the experts a chance to put a new roof on the White House. Demolition began in March and she often stopped in to see how things were getting on, and climbed the wooden stairway at the east end of the building for observation.

Her temporary home was one of considerable elegance. Stanford White had designed it for Mrs. Robert M. Patterson, wife of the publisher of the Chicago *Tribune* and it belonged to her daughter Eleanor, who had been the Countess Gizycka before marrying Elmer Schlesinger. It was four stories high and had thirty rooms and ten baths.

Its pink, white and blue ballroom was in Louis XVI style. Although she found the slantwise rooms "a little cramped after the big square rooms at the White House" she liked them, Mrs. Coolidge wrote to Mrs. Hills. "Like most of the Washington houses this one was built with more thought given to the entertainment side of it than to the living side. The second floor is taken up entirely with a large hall, a ballroom, library and dining room, with butler's pantry. The closet room is not very satisfactory but by spreading out we manage to be very comfortable." Soon after settling in her temporary home she wrote: "Dear Hillsy, I do not let myself think too much about all the things I am missing which I love, neither do I allow myself to think about the future as it concerns me. Rather, I am thankful for all the happy memories of the past and am content to live in the present as usefully as I know how. I told the President a couple of days ago that I thought I should go home for a few days in May but all the reply I got was a grunt which didn't sound like a sympathetic or an assenting one. No hope!"

Some of Mrs. Coolidge's most successful parties were given in the Dupont Circle mansion, and it was here that she entertained her most noted guest, Charles A. Lindbergh, and introduced his mother, Mrs. Evangeline Lodge Lindbergh to Mr. Morrow, thus opening the door to the most publicized romance of the period—the marriage of Anne Morrow and Lindbergh.

The two days that Lindy was her guest were the most exciting she had ever known as a hostess. The house on Dupont Circle was mobbed as the crowds chanted ceaselessly: "We want Lindy. We want Lindy." He had just electrified the world with his transatlantic flight in May, 1927. *Lindy Does It! To Paris in 33½ Hours* ran the New York *Times* headline.

He sailed up the Potomac on the *Memphis,* a golden-haired young man with the sun striking on his boyish features. All Washington was *en fête* to receive him. Mrs. Coolidge had invited his mother to be her guest and she arrived the day before her son. Morrow dined at Dupont Circle that night and afterward the Coolidges attended a meeting of the Bureau of the Budget, leaving Mrs. Lindbergh and Mr. Morrow alone together. "I think their conversation centered in that son who captured the love and admiration of the whole world and held it," Mrs. Coolidge later wrote.

It was agreed that Mrs. Lindbergh should be the first to go aboard and would greet her son in a private cabin, as she did not wish any public demonstration. Actually, there were stories at the time that she was not on the best of terms with Lindy. The *Memphis* steamed slowly up the river through deafening noise, attended by airplanes, cruisers and small craft. Of all the Washington ceremonies and parades for the noted of the world, the sight of Lindbergh engendered the highest degree of enthusiasm up to that time. For once the President and his wife played second fiddle and were scarcely noticed. Mrs. Coolidge watched her husband pin the Distinguished Flying Cross on Lindy's blue serge suit as great crowds roared their approval at the Monument Grounds. She did her best to put him at ease at the luncheon that followed although the crowds outside demanded attention. Then she and the President posed for pictures with Lindbergh and his mother on the steps of the house on Dupont Circle. He produced a dress suit from his single suitcase and walked into the dining room that night with Mrs. Coolidge on his arm. When he sounded her out about taking a short flight with him some time she shook her head and smiled: "No, I'm afraid not. I promised my husband that I would never fly."

Afterward they went to the library but yells from the street were so insistent that finally Lindbergh joined his mother and Mrs. Coolidge at the window. The crowds seemed delirious and he was mobbed again when he returned from the receptions of the Minnesota Society and the National Press Club. All next day he went through a series of official engagements with the excitement mounting wherever he appeared. Mrs. Coolidge remembered these hours as the most hectic of her years in the White House. She found Lindbergh a deeply fatigued and bewildered young man and her heart warmed to him. His romance later with Anne Morrow was of vivid personal interest to her.

Although the Morrows were in and out of the picture while the Coolidges were in the White House, the magnetic and vigorous banker was not influential in the President's counsels. But Dwight Morrow held no resentment, showed absolute loyalty to Coolidge at all times, and told friends on different occasions that he considered him the man best fitted to be the President of the United States. At the time of Lindbergh's return Morrow was offered the post of Ambassador to Mexico. "My relations with Coolidge are such that I cannot accept an honor from him," said Morrow. "But I *can* accept a job." Mrs. Morrow, a close friend of Mrs. Coolidge's, was not so sure that her husband should make this move. "It means giving up J. P. Morgan's and New York . . . I wish I thought it was an adventure!" she observed. But he took the post and functioned brilliantly as Ambassador to Mexico.

Meanwhile the country turned with genuine relief from tales of corruption and banditry to heroism and high adventure. New Yorkers threw eighteen hundred tons of paper into the canyons of lower Broadway as Lindbergh rode up to City Hall. A fresh young national idol had come into view. Immediately after entertaining him Mrs. Coolidge left Washington for the Black Hills of South Dakota, filled with enthusiasm for the shy young man who had been her most shrinking, reserved and gallant guest. A new era had arrived in world communications and the Coolidges had seen it happen.

CHAPTER IX

"I DO NOT CHOOSE TO RUN"

O NE OF THE most surprised persons in the country when Calvin Coolidge announced on an August day in 1927 that he did not choose to run again for the Presidency was his wife. She was also the most unquestioning. "Whatever Father wanted was all right with her," according to the testimony of their son John. He had kept his plans from her as successfully as he had from the public. On leaving that morning he had turned to her and remarked: "I have been President for four years today." That was all. She was used to comments without context and thought nothing of it.

In the end she did not get the news from him, but from Senator Arthur Capper, the Kansas publisher who was their guest at the summer White House in the Black Hills, when the memorable pronouncement was made. After personally handing out to the press slips of paper recording his dramatic piece of news the President returned from his executive offices in a high school in Rapid City to lunch with Mrs. Coolidge at the state game lodge, where they were staying. Senator Capper and a Congressman made up the group of four at the luncheon table. The Senator from Kansas was still affected by the scene he had witnessed in the President's office and he kept looking at Mrs. Coolidge, expecting her to make some comment on her husband's decision. But she chatted along in an unconcerned way while Calvin picked at his food and said little. As soon as he had finished lunch he went off for his afternoon nap, a rite that nothing was allowed to interrupt.

Mrs. Coolidge settled herself in a leather chair close to the massive stone fireplace. The setting was rustic in a majestic way—a heavily beamed living room with great buffalo skins on the floor and antlers on the walls. Tiny Tim, her red chow, snoozed at her feet. A novel by Harold Bell Wright lay on the table beside her. She looked the picture of placidity, little dreaming that within a matter of hours the entire country would be talking about her husband.

Senator Capper, who was leaving for Kansas that afternoon, could contain himself no longer, although he was a man of discretion and reserve.

"Quite a surprise the President gave us this morning," he volunteered.

Mrs. Coolidge looked up brightly from her knitting. Clearly she was uninformed. She listened attentively while he described the scene in her husband's office as he made his announcement.

"Isn't that just like the man!" she exclaimed. "He never gave me the slightest intimation of his intention. I had no idea!"

But the news did not dismay her. Later, when Colonel Starling asked her what she thought of her husband's refusal to run, she answered most revealingly: "I have such faith in Mr. Coolidge's judgment that if he told me I would die tomorrow morning at ten o'clock, I would believe him."

Paradoxically, when the Colonel became the President's chief guard and Mr. Stearns undertook to indicate some of Coolidge's likes, dislikes, whims and prejudices, he warned Starling that "in all things Mrs. Coolidge came first—something I found to be true without exception." But affection did not enter into the hard, cold world of politics in which Calvin Coolidge moved, and a woman's counsel was of small account. His wife bore no resentment and in the year she left the White House she wrote: "I am rather proud of the fact that after nearly a quarter of a century of marriage my husband feels free to make his decisions without consulting me or giving me advance information concerning them."

Actually Mrs. Coolidge was relieved to see his term of office come to a close. His health was poor at the time and so was hers. The White House had brought them strain and sorrow, as well as honor and gratification. But the nation was unprepared for the cryptic statement that came so suddenly over the wires. Its form proved to be as provocative as its substance. The President's press conference was usually scheduled for nine o'clock but on the morning of August 2 Everett Sanders, knowing what was in the wind, suggested postponing it until noon. Allowing for the difference in time this would mean that the news would not reach the public until after the stock market had closed for the day and would give Wall Street time to absorb the shock.

Sanders was the only person with advance knowledge of the President's move. He had seen an earlier draft of the statement and had questioned its phraseology without being able to budge the author from his original intention. It might not be clear to others but it was crystal clear to him. Just before the press assembled Mr. Coolidge picked up his pencil and wrote out the same statement, word for word: *I do not choose to run for President in nineteen twenty eight.* Sanders gave it to Geisser to copy. The White House stenographer turned pale with alarm. For the second time in his life he had history in his hands, for he had copied the oath at Plymouth on the night the President was sworn into office, dramatically and without forewarning. Now he was told to run off a number of copies, repeating five or six times on each sheet the message that ended the era he had seen begun. The President cut them up himself, snipping off two-inch slips which he handed personally to each of the waiting reporters.

They took one swift look and knew that they were on top of a crashing story. There was a rush for the door, which Sanders guarded, but Charles Michelson, of the New York *World,* paused long enough to ask: "Isn't there something else to be said about this, Mr. President?"

"No, that's all the news in the office this morning," Mr. Coolidge replied in a classic understatement.

The townspeople wondered if a fire had broken out as they watched the press race from the high school to the telegraph office. The impression prevailed that the inscrutable Coolidge was enjoying the commotion he had created and the scampering that ensued. He was in good humor as he drove back to the lodge and the minute he got inside he followed his invariable custom of calling for his wife. She responded promptly to his usual "Where are you, Mammy?" but it was another two hours before she accidentally learned of the step he had taken that morning.

She pinpointed her reactions to the President's failure to take her into his confidence, and his attitude to her on public affairs in general, in an article that appeared in the *American Magazine* after she had left the White House. "Sometimes I wonder if Mr. Coolidge would have talked with me more freely if I had been of a more serious turn of mind," she speculated. But he need not have feared that she would have betrayed his confidence, for she was noted for her discretion. She made no secret of the fact that her interests were domestic and humanistic rather than political. It was an old joke between them that Calvin would say to people who tried to assay her feeling for public life: "She has kept me running for public office ever since I married her."

He relished a jest of this kind and did not mind repeating it. It was always delivered with a straight face and sometimes with a grim expression. Actually, Mrs. Coolidge was completely consistent in her attitude to his political interests and although on friendly terms with the wives of his Cabinet officers she never discussed public issues with their husbands. On one occasion she wrote with some conviction that had she manifested any particular interest in public affairs "I feel sure that I should have been properly put in my place." Thus petticoat government was conspicuously missing from the Coolidge administration.

There were moments when Mrs. Coolidge had the impression that her husband thought ill of her education, although a First Lady who wound up with three honorary college degrees as well as a regular one, was something of a novelty in her generation. But he teased her when she could not tell him the year in which Martin Luther was born. Early in her marriage she recognized the fact that Calvin never discussed the abstract or philosophical with her, and she was not supposed to know too much about government, history or current events. In general he preferred to talk to her about family matters, to make jests, and to recall incidents from his boyhood days in Plymouth, the region that claimed his spirit. Actually, Mrs. Coolidge took a bright and intelligent interest in the world in which she lived and was a shrewd judge of people.

Cut off from direct communication on political issues she would have consulted Mr. Stearns at this point but he was missing from the scene when the President made his announcement at Rapid City. He had not gone West because of the altitude, and he knew no more of what was afoot than Mrs. Coolidge. He could scarcely credit the news when it reached him. No sooner had the President's decision become known than speculation began about his precise meaning. He faced the deluge of comment that followed without being drowned, or even moved, by it. Soon great debates were raging over his use of the word "choose" and political leaders were urging him to reconsider for the sake of the national economy. Did it really spell the end of the Coolidge bonanza? Would he be susceptible to persuasion? No one doubted that he could be renominated if he so desired. The country was cradled in riches. Although alien in all respects to the golden framework in which he moved the President's taut figure and unbending ways had become the symbol of prosperity. The contemporary view of Calvin Coolidge would be greatly revised in the years that followed, when the boom days ended and the depression set in, but at the moment he was a popular and reassuring figure, coming in for much less criticism than Presidents usually do.

As the man who believed in preserving the *status quo* and tightening the strings of the national economy at a time when speculation was reaching a dangerous peak, he loomed up before the public in a provocative way. His statement drew humorous comment in the clubs, business centers, theaters, farms and homes of America. The cartoonists and professional humorists pounced on "I do not choose to run" as a loaded phrase. His ways and sayings became further embedded in the national consciousness, strongly and lastingly, if not with wholesale approval. The name Cal Coolidge could evoke a strain of reminiscence or encourage a smile thirty years later as it stirred up echoes of an unforgettable personality.

In the months that followed his announcement Mr. Coolidge added a few words to the subject but not much enlightenment. He told friends at various times that a term of ten years was too long for one man to be President, that a new impulse was more likely to be beneficial, that it was a good idea to get out while the public still wanted him, and that he believed he could best serve the people by stepping down. He conceded that his election seemed assured if he chose to run again. Mrs. Coolidge remembered him telling a member of his Cabinet: "I know how to save money. All my training has been in that direction. The country is in a sound financial position. Perhaps the time has come when we ought to spend money. I do not feel that I am qualified to do that."

John Coolidge was convinced that the health of both of his parents was a factor in the President's decision not to run again, and that his father believed there were good and able men who could do the job as well as he. He had found it wearing and on more than one occasion had drawn attention to his wife's fatigue. "Four years more in the White House would kill Mrs. Coolidge," he wrote. By this time he had also had warnings that his heart might not be in sound condition.

Mrs. Coolidge's most intimate friends knew that the news was no great blow to her. Both she and the President seemed carefree after the announcement became public. Those who knew the President best never doubted the sincerity of his declaration. Colonel Starling viewed it simply as a native Vermont way of saying what he meant. He regarded Coolidge as a "long-headed thinker" who saw disaster ahead. Ted Clark, who followed Sanders as Presidential secretary, believed that Coolidge foresaw the economic collapse to come; that he was apprehensive over the decline of foreign outlets; that he viewed Russia, India and China as three "vast, potential powers."

Others felt that he might be available for a draft. When Andrew Mellon asked Dwight Morrow for an opinion the answer was: "The only way to find out is to nominate him." Taft, writing to his son Robert from Pointe-au-Pic in Canada on August 16, 1927, expressed the belief that Coolidge really wished to avoid running for the Presidency because "he has had enough." But he deduced from the nature of his announcement that he did not wish to be confronted with a prior statement that he definitely would not run, should his party insist on drafting him.

The Chief Justice appreciated Coolidge's unique qualities and on June 5, 1927, while still unaware that the President was about to bow out, he wrote to his son:

> Coolidge amuses me greatly. I think he is a very long-headed politician. I think he has made a very good President. My only criticism of him would be his selection of men, because I don't think he has good judgment in that regard, and he hasn't done as well by us in the selection of Judges as he might, although he has appointed some good ones. Still he would make a great deal better President than Al Smith and his continuance in office would give a stability to our Government and the progress of the country that would be worth a great deal.

The Chief Justice was even more devoted to Mrs. Coolidge. She sent him pots of Easter lilies and he gallantly kissed her hand upon occasion. When they left for South Dakota he predicted that "if it were not Coolidge, I should say that he would have a stupid time out there. I am sure that Mrs. Coolidge will." But he thought the change of scene might do the President good and would serve as a sop to the discontented farmers after his veto of the McNary-Haugen bill for farm relief. It remained for Ike Hoover to draw the most devastating picture of Mr. Coolidge's manner and motives in declining to run again. In his book *Forty-two Years in the White House* he commented mercilessly on what he considered the chagrin, grief, bad temper, frustration and actual illness on the part of the President when he was taken at his word and Herbert Hoover was nominated to succeed him.

All through the summer of 1927 the White House in the Black Hills was a source of unusual news, both personal and political. Colonel Starling had scouted the region with care, taking into account a climate that would suit Mrs. Coolidge, good fishing grounds and the absence of rattlesnakes. "I'm not worried about myself," Mr. Coolidge told him. "It's Mrs. Coolidge's health that bothers me. I don't think she can stand much more of this Washington climate and this official life."

The lodge in which they settled stood on high ground in the state game preserve, with a brook nearby and beyond that a ridge of pine-covered hills that reminded Mrs. Coolidge of the Green Mountains of Vermont. From their porch she and the President could watch mountain sheep, elk and Rocky Mountain goats grazing in separate enclosures. The lodge had twenty rooms and rustic log cabins for guests and staff. It was part-timber, part-stone, with crystal and mineral flecks shining in its rough surface. The rooms had curious names—Cecil Hyde, Elma Mary, Chimney Rest, Buffalo Den, Maiden's Rest, Deer Trail and other regional references. Their nearest neighbor was fourteen miles away but there were tourists' camps nearby and cross-country motorists stopped to stare at the summer White House, which was close to the highway.

Soon Calvin Coolidge, however unconsciously, was engaged in the most conspicuous showmanship of his entire career. He had whetted public interest with the dynamic use of a single sentence. The press was hot in pursuit of every nuance in his behavior that summer. They took delight in his visits to Indian reservations, mines, farmers' picnics, county fairs and rodeos. They photographed Mrs. Coolidge panning for gold and her husband in a variety of hats and postures. In August the Coolidges attended a great gathering of Sioux Indians at Pine Ridge. Twenty thousand tribesmen gathered around the President in the largest assemblage since 1875. They made him their honorary chief and with a tight grin he donned the feathered hat. It was recalled at the time that he had Indian blood in his veins. He addressed the warriors and they told him they wanted to recover the land on which the game lodge stood.

The public watched each move with intensified interest as the President who did not choose to run was photographed in Indian feathers, in Boy Scout and cowboy outfits, and as the dedicated angler of the mountain streams of South Dakota. As at Plymouth some of his intimates thought that the demagogic touch did not become him, since he was essentially a man of dignity and reserve. Skeptics like

Ike Hoover (who did not happen to be on the scene) thought it was done for political effect. He felt that every detail of the trip ran counter to Calvin Coolidge's instincts and natural way of doing things. But Colonel Starling, who fished and shot with him, felt that he was as pleased as if he were having a delayed boyhood.

Mrs. Morrow, who with her husband visited the Coolidges in the Black Hills during August, noted that some of his friends protested when he was photographed in a cowboy outfit. Their dismay was based on the knowledge that he always thought in terms of the importance of his position. However, he brushed aside their arguments on kindly grounds: "But I don't see why you object. The people here have sent me this costume, and they wouldn't have sent it unless they expected me to put it on. Why shouldn't I have my pictures taken with it to please them?" But on one occasion, as he yielded to the demands of the photographers, he turned aside and remarked to his wife: "Oh, Mammy, they're making a perfect fool of me."

"Nothing of the kind, Calvin," said Grace stoutly. "You're never that."

She was always quick to compliment him on a performance and she would turn to a group and say: "Doesn't he do things well?" She was aware of the jibes, jokes, cartoons and wisecracks that her husband's most innocent action evoked. By 1927 he was well used to the rapier thrust of the cartoonist and could study with quiet amusement the magnification of his own sharp features. No one knew better than Grace that he liked to try on odd hats and had often amused his family by parading up and down with assorted styles from a closet. But she wrote that a "man must needs have a heart of stone" to turn down the request of a delegation of cowboys who brought all their paraphernalia to him with the request: "Now, Mr. President, we'd like to have you put them on and have your picture taken with us." Under these circumstances it seemed the most natural thing in the world to her that he should don chaps, belt, boots and spurs to the delight of his young visitors. "And all the time," his wife commented, "I believe he knew he was making those boys happy at the cost of future criticism from friends who would remonstrate with him for appearing to act a part in order to curry favor with our summer neighbors."

She had no lack herself, however, of the touch that humanized. She already possessed it to a high degree and she made a strong impression on the people of the Black Hills as she stopped with the President at twilight for a cup of coffee at an inn at Sylvan Lake, exchanged recipes with a farmer's wife, or bought peanuts at a crossroads store on the winding mountain road to Camp Galena. She even broke one of her fixed rules and made a speech at the dedication of a log community building at Custer. She recalled that in 1922, when her husband was Vice-President, they had visited Sioux Falls and had thought the people much like their neighbors in Vermont. This had made them wish to return. The Black Hills women gave her a rose quartz necklace made with stones from a local mine. She wore it with feeling, as she did her lucky string of elephants.

Mrs. Coolidge was not particularly interested in fishing but she had the luck of the novice when she sat in a motorboat in front of a hotel and caught almost as many fish as her husband and his party did when they fished from a rowboat ten miles away. However, her finger caught on a fishhook and this involved a minor operation. The region was rich in trout streams and a miraculous supply of fish seemed to snatch at the flies the President dangled in the water, helped on by Colonel Starling's arrangements for the streams to be stocked at certain points with game trout, held in check by steel-mesh nets sunk across the stream, with logs concealing them. By this time the President had been converted to the use of flies. Professional sportsmen and the cartoonists had convinced him of the iniquity of using worms for bait. He returned to Grace day after day proud of his catch and the papers built up the popular conception of Cal Coolidge the Angler. Had he been angling for another term it might have passed as effective promotion, but as time went on it was increasingly evident that he intended to stand pat on his decision.

When they climbed a mountain trail in a lumber wagon to the summer cottage of Governor Samuel E. McKelvie, the Governor said that Coolidge in his ten-gallon hat made him think of the early Puritan fathers. Their wagon stuck in the mud on the way up and the

President got out and helped to push it. At first Mrs. Coolidge laughed heartily and egged the men on, but as soon as she saw Calvin puffing and showing signs of strain she grew grave. He was showing unwonted characteristics that summer and seemed to be anxious to prove his mettle. He proposed to ride a wild mare that had been given to him until Colonel Starling enlisted Mrs. Coolidge's assistance in blocking this venture. The Colonel, responsible for Mr. Coolidge's safety, did not think he rode well enough to handle this particular horse.

Mrs. Coolidge was sitting on the porch knitting socks for John when the President, wearing his ten-gallon hat and riding breeches, announced that he was going to ride the mare. Colonel Starling's protest was met with stubborn silence until Mrs. Coolidge interposed: "If Colonel Starling thinks the mare isn't safe, I think you should accept his judgment. I shall be very uneasy while you're away if you go against his opinion."

She could give him advice on a personal matter of this sort, if not on political affairs. But the President was visibly annoyed. "Well, what am I going to do?" he protested. "Just sit here on the front porch and ride back and forth to Rapid City?" But he yielded the point and rode Mistletoe, a horse that was considered safe even for the smallest child. They went cowboy fashion up Mount Rushmore to attend ceremonies at the memorial to Washington, Jefferson, Lincoln and Theodore Roosevelt, carved out of rock by Gutzon Borglum. On this occasion a mountain was named for the President and a stream for Mrs. Coolidge.

But the Coolidges provided some high-powered headlines while in South Dakota on another and more personal score. The President paced back and forth at the lodge on a June day, frantic with anxiety because Grace was missing. In Colonel Starling's estimation he registered "all the symptoms of intense suffering." She had started out at nine o'clock for her daily walk with James Haley, the Secret Service man assigned to guard her. Lunchtime came and they had not returned. First the President registered impatience, since he disliked unpunctuality; then he became worried about her safety.

He always liked to know where Mrs. Coolidge was and he was

reluctant to let her out of his sight. On this occasion he feared that she might have been bitten by a rattlesnake, a particular dread of his. A search party was sent out. They met Mrs. Coolidge and Haley on their way back. The Secret Service man was a city youth unfamiliar with the woods. They had walked farther than they intended and misjudged their time, since the road back was uphill. It was two fifteen when Mrs. Coolidge came swinging along the trail that ended at the rear of the house, and joined her husband on the porch. She saw at once how agitated he was and reassured him, explaining as she drank a glass of water what had happened. They went into the house together, and things quietened down.

But the repercussions were severe. The President emphasized the incident by transferring Haley shortly afterward to another post. He thought that the Secret Service man should have known his business better than to have let Mrs. Coolidge get lost in the woods The newspapers came out with headlines picturing him in the role of a jealous husband. The assumption was misleading but the damage had been done and for the only time in her career as First Lady Mrs. Coolidge was seriously embarrassed by unwelcome publicity.

Starling felt sorry for the handsome young man, blue-eyed and fair-haired, who was under his command. He had roomed with him on President Harding's trip to Alaska and had found him a devout youth who went down on his knees and said his prayers every night. At the time of the Coolidge incident he was deeply in love with the girl whom he later married. He wrote to her every night from the Black Hills. Haley had great regard for Mrs. Coolidge and expressed the opinion that she was universally liked because of "that million-dollar smile of hers."

After this incident the President issued orders that Starling was to be his wife's escort. Confusion followed. If Mr. Coolidge wished to go fishing the Colonel had to go with him, and Mrs. Coolidge was forced to stay at the lodge. However, she accepted the situation with good humor, just as she had relinquished a culottes hiking suit that she had rashly bought at a shop on Connecticut Avenue before leaving for the Black Hills. She was quite proud of this purchase. It seemed to be just what she needed for mountain trails. Since the President was always interested in her clothes she gave him a preview of the little number she had picked up for outdoor wear. He took one look at the bifurcated effect and his face froze. "No member of the Coolidge family ever appeared in anything like that," he snapped. "Take it back where you got it."

The suit was returned at once, since Mrs. Coolidge never fussed or argued when her husband laid down the law. If it did not please him it would not have pleased her. So she took her long daily walks in the Black Hills wearing a skirt, a white silk sports shirt, sweater and hiking boots. She thought nothing of walking eight miles a day and it took someone with the swift, long stride of Jim Haley to keep up with her. Curtis D. Wilbur, Secretary of the Navy, made one try and gave up. He estimated that they did six miles at the rate of a mile every fifteen minutes. His lack of enthusiasm for a second walk through the woods caused Mrs. Coolidge to comment in jesting vein that "although he might be a big Navy man, as a land hiker he left something to be desired."

The Secret Service men and police detail at the White House assumed new importance in the time of Calvin Coolidge. He was the first President who did not seem to resent their omnipresence. If they did not show up immediately as he left for a ride or a walk he would sometimes wait for them. Mrs. Coolidge was not so fond of being guarded, but she accepted the presence of the Secret Service men without any fuss and was always considerate of their feelings.

Early in September, as the Coolidges were about to leave South Dakota, Colonel Lindbergh swooped down over Rapid City in a salute to them during a cross-country flight. They had just returned from a trip to Yellowstone Park. The President was having one of his digestive upsets as they left and he decided to sit quietly and fish instead of sharing in the strenuous sightseeing. There was much comment at the time on his attitude of coldness and indifference. He was thought to be sulking when he turned his back on the Cody dam, and would scarcely look at the geysers. But Mrs. Coolidge and John thoroughly enjoyed the natural wonders of the region. John had passed his college exams and was in high good humor. He danced with farmers' daughters who were earning their way through college by waiting on table at Lake Hotel in Yellowstone National Park.

The President was noticeably tired, bored or unhappy. Actually, he was not feeling well and he was much disturbed over the publicity the Haley incident had had. Anything concerning his wife was of the deepest concern to him and Grace had been amazingly successful at staying out of the headlines. Although there was no doubt that Haley had irritated him, and he could find no excuse for a Secret Service man unable to chart his route and get back on time, no one felt happy about the scene he had made or the emphasis he had given the matter by transferring the culprit.

For once in her life Mrs. Coolidge showed some resentment, too, at being put in so false a position. Both members of the family were deeply upset at this time and it took some time for the ice to thaw. When Mr. Coolidge was displeased with any member of the family the punishment was sustained silence. This was trying for friendly Grace, particularly when it stretched into hours and even days at a time. The silence that followed the episode in the Black Hills was devastating. Again, when John was involved in an automobile accident in New Haven a year later his father would not even mention his name for days. Because he was the President's son and Wilfred Veno, the well known hockey player, was injured in the collision, the case received much publicity.

While the President was in the Black Hills the growlings about the fate of Sacco and Vanzetti would not be stilled either, and there was comment on the fact that he was sound asleep when these two men, whose conviction had whipped up severe repercussions in the state of Massachusetts and across the land, died in the electric chair that summer. The Citizens National Committee of Boston sent Dwight Morrow a last-ditch plea while he was visiting the President in the Black Hills, urging him to try to influence Coolidge to intervene in order "to calm opinion at home and abroad and save the nation from disgrace." The President was deluged with appeals but the execution went through, leaving questioning echoes down the years.

The Coolidges returned to a White House that had been reroofed and renovated from top to bottom. A new electric elevator had been installed and the house gleamed with fresh paint. The East Room had been finished in a soft cream. The Green Room had been furnished with appropriate pieces assembled by Mrs. Coolidge, and the new red velour hangings in the Red Room enlivened its *décor*. The third floor now had additional guest rooms with baths, as well as the maids' rooms. Mrs. Coolidge noted with satisfaction that not one blind spot remained as she surveyed the linen closets with mirrored doors, the cedar room, the sewing room, the storeroom for the President's personal effects and a great assortment of closets. She had also arranged for a water softener that made a difference to the servants in their work.

But the sunroom on the tiled roof over the south portico which she called her Sky Parlor had been specifically designed for her and was equipped with Vita glass. This was to be her own sanctum, invaded by none but her family and most intimate friends. It had a couch, a writing table, porch furniture, her phonograph and portable radio, her favorite pictures, books, and her work basket. She was in the Sky Parlor when the *Graf Zeppelin* glided over Washington like a monster cigar on its initial trip to the United States. Some of her friends were invited in to share in this spectacle.

As soon as the Coolidges settled down in the White House again they were subjected to a barrage of curiosity. The political leaders closed in on the President. Her friends asked Mrs. Coolidge incredulously: "Does he really mean it?" She remained as bland and noncommittal as she always was when anyone tried to sound her out about her husband. Both were studied with intensified interest after all the headlines and there was much chatter about Haley's fate as well as about the Presidential prospects. But the President, addressing the National Republican Committee at the White House, flatly announced: "My statement stands. No one should be led to suppose that I have modified it. My decision will be respected." On the more intimate level he commented that the country was in good financial order and others could carry on.

Mrs. Coolidge was bewildered herself after her return from their shattering summer in the Black Hills. She wrote to Mrs. Hills on September 19, 1927: "Did I have faith in those who claim to read the future I should certainly hie me to one now. Alas, what will be my next move? It begins to seem to me that my life has been bitten into job lots and having made three moves since last March I am wondering what next?" And on Armistice Day she wrote regretfully to Mrs. Hills that she could not go with her to the Army and Navy game. "Of course, if I went I should have to go with 'bells on' and there's no fun in that," she wrote. "Couldn't get permission, anyhow. I guess nobody but you has a real idea of how shut in and hemmed about I feel. Well, I'm not complaining. I'm only telling you."

In his 1927 Christmas message to the American people the President said: "Christmas is not a time or a season, but a state of mind. To cherish peace and good will, to be plenteous in mercy is to have the real spirit of Christmas." Thus the inscrutable Calvin Coolidge uttered bland words but not even Grace had a clue to the tenor of his thoughts at this important point in his life. She went on from day to day, sure only of one thing, that her days in the White House were numbered.

CHAPTER X

A TRIP TO CUBA

M RS. COOLIDGE stood on the deck of the *Texas* on a January day in 1928, observing the shore of Cuba as the President and his official party sailed into Havana to attend the Sixth Pan-American Conference. Three destroyers escorted them and the transport *Memphis* brought up the rear. Flags whipped in the breeze. Guns boomed to welcome the President of the United States, who was accompanied by Charles Evans Hughes, Frank Kellogg and Curtis D. Wilbur.

Thirty years earlier Grace Goodhue had celebrated the victory of Dewey in the Spanish-American War with a boat trip on Lake Champlain. Now she was seeing the old guns of Morro Castle, the royal palms, the snowy houses splashed with crimson blossoms. She went over the side of the ship to ride on President Machado's barge to the special landing place. The Presidential party stepped ashore to martial music, to gold-braided ceremony, to a rush of Spanish greetings. They rode through the streets over a pathway of roses. They had a seven-room suite at The Palace and Mrs. Coolidge slept in the Marie Antoinette Room, all pink and cream.

President Machado gave a memorable dinner in their honor. She wore a gown of silver cloth, its train lined with green chiffon. Communication was difficult since the Machados did not speak any English, but Mrs. Coolidge by this time had coped with the diplomats of so many different nations that she felt at home in the midst of all the ceremony. The President of the United States and the President of Cuba both made speeches at the conference held in the National Theater. They toured around Havana, visited a sugar mill, attended a special exhibition of *jai alai* and were lavishly entertained by official Cuba. The Robins soon received a detailed account of the trip from Mrs. Coolidge, who never failed to catch the humorous as well as the official aspects of a trip of this sort. She wrote:

> Every moment was crowded to overflowing but I think we all agreed that the drive to the President's *finca* or country place where we had lunch in a thatched covered pavilion provided the most interesting part of it all. The food we ate with the exception of the crab and the rice was grown and raised on the place. Can you imagine my eyes grow wide upon looking up to behold my dignified much better half with a mango firmly impaled on the tines of a spear made for the purpose, biting into its juicy interior, looking for all the world like a small boy caught at mischief. He was certainly having himself a time!

It was Mrs. Coolidge's first experience of a tropical island, a world of azure and gold, and she used her camera freely and enjoyed it all in her wholehearted way. But later that winter, on her return to Washington, she became seriously ill. The public never learned how critical her condition was. The President was distraught and after a week during which she had seen no one but nurses, doctors and her husband, he stood before Mrs. Hills with tears coursing down his cheeks and said: "Hillsy, I'm afraid that Mammy will die."

She recovered only slowly and for the first time the President had to appear without her at a reception that spring. It was the fourth state reception of the season and was given in honor of the officers of the Army and Navy. Mrs. Coolidge convalesced in her sky parlor. She listened to her favorite records and Mrs. Hills read to her by the hour. The President tiptoed along the corridor to visit her, trying to tread softly on the uncarpeted floor outside her solarium. After Mrs. Hills went back to Northampton Grace, bored with inactivity, wrote to her: "I am sitting in the sky parlor. The President sits here smoking. He delivered his Andrew Jackson address at the Capitol at three o'clock. I listened in—perhaps you did . . . I have taken no rest today. I am going to be an emancipated woman! . . ."

As soon as she picked up strength she strolled in the grounds, and went one afternoon to see *Rio Rita* with Mrs. Boone and Mrs. Stearns. That same evening the President accompanied her to hear Rosa Ponselle in *Norma*. But she tired quickly and they left after the first act. On another of her trips out she reported to Mrs. Hills that the President had not asked her "where she ate or what," but that the improvement he saw in her convinced him that wherever it was had been the right place. "It certainly did a lot for me," Mrs. Coolidge added. But she was impatient of all the restrictions placed on her and wrote to the Robins of her doctors that "once they get their clutches on you there seems to be no way of shaking them off."

By May she was moving about more freely, although her long walks were banned. She sometimes drove out to Silver Springs to visit Miss Stella Stewart, an old friend who had trained with her to teach the deaf at the Clarke School. When she wished to shed her official role and relax completely she was apt to seek out the little white cottage in Maryland where her old friend lived. Miss Stewart was a government employee by this time and Mrs. Coolidge would invite her to the White House from time to time, particularly for functions involving the deaf.

She was ailing all through the spring of 1928 and she listened to a great deal of music on the phonograph and radio and took in some of the new motion pictures. Young and old sang *Rio Rita* and *Ol' Man River* that year and Helen Morgan sat on a piano and wrung susceptible hearts with *Can't Help Lovin' That Man* and *Why Do I Love You?*—all from *Show Boat*. Libby Holman sang torch songs and Helen Kane's boop-boop-a-doop was the teen-age jargon of the hour. George Gershwin's *Rhapsody in Blue* was deliriously received when the New York Symphony Orchestra presented it, with Walter Damrosch conducting.

Greta Garbo and John Gilbert, romantically linked at the time, were the current heart throbs in *Flesh and the Devil*. Clara Bow was starred in *Wings,* the first big aviation film of the silent screen, with a tall youth named Gary Cooper coming shyly into view. On Broadway, audiences still close to the war were electrified by the tough realism of *What Price Glory,* the Laurence Stallings-Maxwell Anderson play. *The Cat and the Canary* was the most discussed thriller of the day. The Martin Johnson film *Simba* was popular at the moment and Mrs. Coolidge noted in her letters that she went to see it, but her interest at the time was languid.

By the end of May Chief Justice Taft wrote with authority: "Coolidge will not run. I don't think his wife is in good condition, and I don't think he is, and he does not want to run, and he is a man who ordinarily does not do what he does not want to." Although the question of President Coolidge's health did not enter strongly into the picture at this time, his intimates were aware that he was plagued by asthma and digestive disturbances. However, he presented himself as the "healthiest President that the country has ever had," in a statement he prepared for the St. Louis *Post-Dispatch* on its fiftieth anniversary. He attributed his condition to his daily walks, regular hours for meals and sleep, and his vibrating machines. But he proposed a retreat for Presidents within driving distance of Washington. Perhaps remembering the headlines that resulted from his summer in South Dakota he pointed out that the only place the President could enter without considerable preliminary disturbance was the White House itself and, once there, freedom of action was impossible. Then, giving thought to his wife, he added:

> While I have made no mention of the mistress of the White House, she is, of course, to be considered. The public little understands the very exacting duties that she must perform, and the restrictive life that she must lead. Fully as much as the President, she needs an opportunity for a change and some place where she can have the seclusion of the White House without a constant reminder of its obligations.

But Mrs. Coolidge had another view of the "healthiest President" down the long stretch of the years. His health had been one of her concerns from the day he married her, although outwardly he seemed to go along at a steady pace. In time she became used to his whims about food, to snacks between meals, to pills and potions, to the recurrent digestive disturbances that he called his bellyaches, to the spray he had to use for his allergic manifestations. At public functions she often disposed quietly of her bouquets of flowers when she saw Calvin's nostrils twitching sensitively. Some of his stomach aches were attributed by his staff to the unparched peanuts that he ate in quantity, and other indigestible snacks. He was often so dyspeptic that he had to lie down and rest, or he would return to the White House in mid-morning and his physicians would walk him up and down in the corridor, trying to ameloriate his distress.

He found some relief from his asthmatic condition in the mountainous Plymouth region. His electric horse in the White House saved him from the irritation of horse dander. When he was Vice-President the dust that rose from the matting under the carpet in his office gave him severe distress. There were times when he tired unaccountably. He showed danger signals in 1925 and again in 1928 and cardiograms were taken while he was in the White House. Outwardly he had the bearing of a healthy man but he was apt to dwell on the deaths of his mother, his sister and his son. In his early married days he was haunted by the thought that he might have inherited tuberculosis from his mother. In 1921, when he became Vice-President, Dr. Coupal took him in hand and gave him X-ray tests, which proved to be negative. Mrs. Coolidge wrote to Mr. Stearns, with whom she often discussed her husband's health in the spirit of mutual concern:

Dr. Coupal has taken a great interest in him and he feels as you and I have felt for some time, that he should have a thorough going-over. How far he will get with it I do not know but he made a beginning this morning by taking him to have his lungs X-rayed. I had quite a long talk with the Doctor yesterday morning and found he had "sized him up" pretty well. I told him of his tendency to take various sorts of pills upon slight provocation and he agreed that it was a bad habit. However, he doesn't do that as much now that he is making fewer speeches. He used to think he was keeping himself in speaking trim that way.

While at Brule in Wisconsin in the summer of 1928 an effort was made to keep from the public the state of the President's health. Mrs. Coolidge wrote to Mr. Stearns that instead of going to his office papers were being sent to him at the house. "He is beginning to get rested but is having quite a lot of trouble with his asthma, or whatever it is," she wrote. "This is not known outside. He was very, very tired when he arrived here."

They had gone to church in Brule on the morning that she wrote and the President had taken his spray with him in the car. Word had been given out that if they left the church before the end of the service the explanation would be that Mrs. Coolidge "was not very well and had to leave." However, the President was able to stay to the end of the service without having one of his attacks. "Every day, I think of how good you are to us and thank God for friends like you," Mrs. Coolidge finished.

By this time the Republican Convention had been held in Kansas City and Herbert Hoover had been nominated on the first ballot with 837 electoral votes. Eighteen had been cast for Calvin Coolidge in spite of his protestations that he would not run. Sanders had been sent to Kansas City with instructions to notify the leaders of state delegations not to vote for him. All through the winter and spring Coolidge had watched the political forecasts with interest and attention. He seemed to his staff to be out of sorts as the boom for Herbert Hoover developed.

The Coolidges were on their way to Brule when word of the nomination reached them. The President had caught the drift of events before leaving Washington. He was silent and morose when the final word arrived. He telegraphed at once to Herbert Hoover: "I wish you all the success that your heart could desire. May God continue to bestow upon you the power to do your duty." Mrs. Coolidge topped this with her own message sent from Brule on June 15: "The President and I send you and yours our love and best wishes."

For the first ten days at Brule the Coolidges were a miserable pair. The rain never ceased. The President was nervous and could neither sleep nor eat. They had been three days late in leaving Washington because Mrs. Coolidge was too ill to get out of bed. After their arrival she lay day after day on a couch on the porch and watched the rain come down. Dr. Boone had forbidden walks. Her health was showing no improvement. Colonel Starling had made careful soundings for their holiday ground that summer, taking climate into consideration. Finally, through Senator Irvin B. Lenroot of Wisconsin, he had hit on the H. C. Pierce 5,000-acre estate on the Brule River. The Colonel thought that the balsam-scented air would be good for Mrs. Coolidge.

But on June 28, as they all sat on the porch of Cedar Island Lodge watching the rain, the President told Colonel Starling that Brule was not the climate for Mrs. Coolidge. Dr. Coupal was insistent that she must have dry air. After talking things over they agreed that they would wait until July 4, the President's fifty-sixth birthday. If it rained that day they would move on. But it dawned clear and warm. The President fished every day after that and took up trap shooting, with Mrs. Coolidge applauding from the sidelines. Colonel Starling had argued strongly that the outdoor life would do more for him than his assorted pills. Before the summer was over the President had cleaned out his medicine cabinet of everything but aspirin and fruit salts.

The lodge was a one-story cottage covered with gray cedar bark. It was situated on an island bordered with barberry bushes. Pink petunias and trailing vines in the cedar boxes under the windows delighted Mrs. Coolidge. From the front and back porches they could look up and down the Brule River. Sightseers paddled past in canoes to stare at the summer White House, which was two miles from the main road. The executive offices were in Superior, thirty-six miles away, and when he felt better the President went there twice a week.

Mrs. Coolidge crossed the rustic bridge to the mainland several times a day and here she fed the game trout which were again more or less obliged to stay on the spot. The President named a hungry one Danny Deever. "I'll hang him in the morning," he would promise her. Meanwhile she fed him well while her husband, wearing a red mackinaw and a ten-gallon hat, dangled his flies in vain. Both worried about the dogs because of the porcupines that abounded in the region. Mrs. Coolidge sent Mrs. Hills detailed accounts of her daily doings at Brule; of Calvin posing for the photographers on his birthday; of his enthusiasm for fishing and the luck he was having; of John's arrival looking thin but with a hearty appetite; of the lovely view from the south porch down the river and the birds singing all around her; of the ducking John Fitzgerald, the Beau Brummell of the Secret Service detail, had when his canoe upset; of her dread of a forthcoming picnic for "you know the President is not a happy picnicker"; of the way "his eyes shone with delight" as he opened the Jensen candies that Mrs. Hills had sent him, delved at once to the bottom of the box, picked his favorites and went off to his room with them; of the hat she was crocheting out of shoe-thread such as she had used for the Lincoln bedspread; of the fact that she did not regard Brule as such a lonely place since John's arrival.

Mrs. Coolidge wrote on July 20 that she was doing more walking than Dr. Boone would approve. The entire household thought that she looked better and Colonel Starling had said to her: "You look like you did when I first knew you." In the jesting vein she used with Mrs. Hills she added: "We all know what a prize beauty I was then!" Two weeks later she was doing still better and was managing four miles a day, almost her old speed. But her heart was involved and she wrote to Mrs. Hills: "I guess my heart will last as long as my disposition and I know that would go to smash if I did not get some exercise. I am still going without coffee but I had a demitasse on the train the other night. How good it tasted!"

Mrs. Hills was going through a time of great anxiety over her son Jack, who was suffering from a severe infection following a soccer injury. Remembering her own Calvin, Grace wrote: "I'm praying, dearest, and holding tight. Keep up good courage, be out of doors all you can in order to keep as fit as possible for the long pull—not for yourself but for Jackie . . ."

When the Hoovers visited the Coolidges at Brule in July Mrs. Coolidge wrote to Mrs. Hills that after having been in the thick of things for so long she was thoroughly enjoying the sidelines. "It was interesting to have Secretary and Mrs. Hoover here," she wrote. "Awfully funny to see and hear him tell about some of the things he has to have and the annoying things which arise which we have been all through—he seems so surprised with it all." Mrs. Hoover's father had just died but Mr. Hoover was keeping the news from her, since he did not wish to worry her and they were moving along as fast as they could.

Mrs. Coolidge learned from Fitzgerald early in September that they were leaving at once for Washington and would then proceed to New England. Calvin had given her no inkling of these plans, she confided to Mrs. Hills. Three days later she deplored a published report that there were tears in her eyes as she said good-by to John. "You know I am not that sort," she commented. She was pleased because John had found a job in the statistical department of the New York New Haven and Hartford Rail Road. "Too bad the papers won't let him alone," she wrote. "Some one said he has crowded his father and the Presidential candidates off the front page." The press was now persuaded that with a job John would marry Florence Trumbull, daughter of Governor Robert H. Trumbull of Connecticut. He was upset when the photographers caught Florence coming out of church with his mother. This was letting the cat out of the bag ahead of time.

Wherever the Coolidges were they made a point of attending church. In the Black Hills they worshiped in a small timber chapel at Hermosa, where a twenty-one-year-old student named Rolf Lium faced the President apprehensively every Sunday and delivered a sermon—"quite a test for the chap but he did splendidly," Mrs. Coolidge noted. Well over six feet tall, and about John's age, Lium was studying to be a medical missionary. He was grateful for her sympathetic manner—"Mrs. Coolidge's smile every Sunday was a great help to me," he commented. "No matter how often I preached when the President came to church, I always had to overcome a slight nervousness and her wonderful smile steadied me."

In Brule the Coolidges drove to a simple country chapel where a blind pastor presided. Mrs. Coolidge found him "rather evangelistic in his preaching" and it took her back to her good old Methodist days. The church-going habits of the President's family were well known to the public. Mrs. Coolidge did practical church work from her early years in Burlington to her last days in Northampton. Her son John thought that his mother drew spiritual strength from her religious faith.

Ecclesiastical storms were as characteristic of the Coolidge era as the crime wave that accompanied prohibition. Religion was front-page news between 1926 and 1929, but more in the controversial than in the spiritual sense. Men of God battled over ancient dogmas. The Episcopal, the Presbyterian and the Baptist churches were most directly involved. Modernists and Fundamentalists clashed on such public issues as divorce and prohibition, as well as the fundamentals of faith. Students discussed religion and compulsory chapel attendance. The age-old theme of atheism was debated in the light of twentieth-century scientific revelation. Echoes of the Scopes trial would not be stilled. History was merely repeating itself, but the manifestations were widespread and violent. Luther Burbank publicly pronounced himself an infidel shortly before his death. This thirteenth child of a New England family of fifteen shocked many of his fellow countrymen with his denial of the divinity. Henry Fairfield Osborn, president of the American Museum of Natural History, took a public stand of another sort and urged the restoration of the teaching of religion in the public schools. "As a teacher of religion I am not afraid of science," he said.

The American Association for the Advancement of Atheism started a drive to have chaplains dropped from Congress, the Army and Navy. But evangelism flourished, and such preachers as Dr. Harry Emerson Fosdick drew great crowds wherever they spoke. John D. Rockefeller, Jr. was planning a suitable forum for his favorite Baptist preacher and from this came the Riverside Church. Bishop William T. Manning opened a drive for $5,000,000 to complete the Cathedral of St. John the Divine. Ten million dollars had already been raised for the Gothic pile rising slowly on Morningside Heights. But the Bishop was having trouble in his diocese. Dr. Percy Stickney Grant and Dr. William Norman Guthrie had openly flouted him on doctrinal and personal issues and been worsted. Bishop William Montgomery Brown, the unfrocked Episcopal Bishop of Arkansas who had been expelled from the ministry for heresy in 1925, was agitating in New York.

Church leaders pounded away at easy divorce. The ratio at the time was one to every seven marriages. But divorce, evolution, church attendance, birth control, the follies of youth, modesty in dress—all under discussion in ecclesiastical circles—paled before the burning issue of prohibition. When one faction in his church came out for modification of the Volstead Act, Bishop Manning declared himself opposed to any such move. Cardinal Hayes at the same time strongly criticized the prohibition enforcement act and made a counter plea for "real temperance."

Meanwhile, Dr. John Roach Straton, the lean and fanatical Baptist preacher who had created turmoil for years and stood for extreme fundamentalism on all social issues, was having a noisy row at Calvary Baptist Church in New York. He was accused of hippodroming the pulpit as he led the attack by the Fundamentalists on the "Rockefeller influence" in the Baptist church. The Presbyterians fought over parallel issues when the New York Presbytery split over ordaining students who had failed to affirm the Virgin Birth. Again the forces of modernism and fundamentalism were balanced one against the other, with Dr. Henry Sloane Coffin leading the liberal element.

Late in June of that same year a pageant unique in American church history drew enormous crowds to the twenty-eighth Eucharistic Congress, held in Chicago. With a blaze of color, of ceremonial robes and ancient habits, rites dating back to the days of the Caesars were performed in a skyscraper city ridden by gang warfare. Princes of the church sat enthroned on a gilt-domed dais, trumpets blared, and 62,000 children in white and yellow joined in the solemn pontifical mass at Soldiers Field. Airplanes buzzed overhead as the children sang *Mass of the Angels,* walled in by a crowd of 400,000 spectators. Hail pelted on the pilgrims and scattered them when a great storm broke during the pilgrimage to Mundelein that followed.

News of another sort was breaking in Los Angeles while the Eucharistic Congress was in progress. It had some relation to the religious world, but more to the theatrical evangelism peculiar to Aimee Semple McPherson. Her Angelus Temple was three years old, and the emotional orgies of her audiences were unique in their time.

Aimee had just returned from a European tour and was still a popular idol when news was flashed across the nation that she had disappeared. She was thought to have drowned, for she was last seen in a green bathing suit at Ocean View Beach near Los Angeles. For a month the faithful prayed in Angelus Temple and along the beach where she had vanished. Divers and airplanes joined in the search for the missing evangelist. When she turned up close to the Mexican border with an unlikely story of kidnaping she had a royal welcome on her return to Los Angeles. Her path was strewn with roses. The Temple band serenaded her through the streets. She pushed an investigation to find her kidnapers but her story lacked conviction and the grand jury let it drop. Eventually she was charged with conspiracy to obstruct justice. The legal proceedings that followed were of circus proportions. From being the Angel of Angelus, Sister Aimee had become a scarlet woman. She was to live until 1944, to write the story of her life, to travel and lecture, to engage in a number of lawsuits, to get involved in numerous curious scrapes.

But she was eloquent to the last, a tarnished angel who had won worldwide fame with her Gospel preaching, and worldwide ignominy when her own flamboyance destroyed her. She had become a music hall joke, the saint turned sinner, but at the end she was buried with pomp from the temple she had built. Thousands wept over Sister Aimee, who had given the 1920s its most curious brand of jazzed-up religion.

Nothing could have been more alien to the Coolidge way of living, to their inherited respect for religious faith than the unrest, skepticism and buffoonery that kept church news on the front pages during their regime. But Fundamentalists and Modernists drew together for a few hours when President Coolidge greeted 5,750 Baptist delegates on the White House lawn at a moment when the battle raged its fiercest in 1926. It was the largest denominational group ever assembled there and Mrs. Coolidge moved among the churchmen with ease and familiarity. She frequently entertained groups of churchwomen and she was greatly pleased when John taught in a Baptist Sunday school.

Religious controversy was just beginning to simmer down by 1928 when Alfred E. Smith, as Democratic candidate for the Presidency, became the focus of virulent attack. Hoover, the Quaker, and Coolidge, the Congregationalist, both broad-minded men on religious questions, deplored the injection of the Catholic issue into the campaign and called for fair play. But their voices were scarcely heard in the din.

The Hoovers welcomed the Coolidges back to Washington from Brule. "The President was never better and I am so well that I think I could work sixteen hours out of the twenty-four," Mrs. Coolidge wrote to Mrs. Hills. "We were both sad looking objects when we arrived." But Mrs. Goodhue's condition had grown much worse during their absence and the President sat by her bedside in the Cooley-Dickinson Hospital in Northampton with all the respect he had always paid Grace's mother. They moved on to Plymouth and toured Vermont to study the damage done by the recent floods. The President invited his cousins, Park and Erminie Pollard, to join them at Bellows Falls and accompany them north to Burlington. Every visit the Coolidges made to Burlington involved great acclaim, with old friends of Grace leading the welcome. Before they had finished their tour the President visited Black River Academy and made a speech at Bennington on September 21, 1928, that is treasured today as his tribute to Vermont:

It was here that I first saw the light of day; here I received my bride; here my dead lie pillowed on the loving breast of our everlasting hills.

I love Vermont because of her hills and valleys, her scenery and invigorating climate, but most of all, because of her indomitable people. They are a race of pioneers who have almost beggared themselves to serve others. If the spirit of liberty should vanish in other parts of the Union and support of our institutions languish, it could all be replenished from the generous store held by the people of this brave little state of Vermont.

Calvin Coolidge did not campaign actively for his successor. Coolidge prosperity spoke for itself. But at the last moment he talked over the radio in support of the ticket and he was photographed at the White House with Herbert Hoover. He was not well at the time. Ike Hoover pictured him in a state of nervous tension, leaving the

Cabinet dinner on November 8 before his guests had finished, but those who knew him best thought he was having another of his digestive upsets. Hoover had run up a popular majority of 6,432,612 and Coolidge was passing on the scepter.

After the election the Coolidges motored to Charlottesville for Thanksgiving, attended church there and lunched at the home of Dr. Edwin A. Alderman, president of the University of Virginia. Afterward they watched the annual football game played against the University of North Carolina. Their twenty-third wedding anniversary had passed in October with a minimum of fuss. Roy O. West, who was about to be appointed Secretary of the Interior to succeed Hubert Work, dined with them that night and noticed unusual flower arrangements in the family sitting room. When the President walked in, he looked around, noticed the flowers and said with a faint twinkle in his eyes: "Mr. West, what do you think of a wife who keeps from her husband the fact that it is their wedding anniversary?"

Without pausing for an answer he solemnly twanged "Dinner" and marched off ahead to the state dining room. But this was no surprise to Grace. Her husband rarely if ever gave her anything on anniversaries, birthdays or at Christmas. She made a point of not reminding him of special occasions and the only anniversary gift that she could recall was a flexible gold and platinum bracelet that he thrust into her hand as she crossed the lobby of the Touraine Hotel in Boston with Mrs. Stearns. They were on their way to the theater and at first she thought that Calvin must be playing a joke on her, for the package suggested a toothbrush.

On another of their anniversaries they were lunching with friends when he suddenly looked across the table at her and said: "Let's see, Mammy, when does our wedding anniversary come along?"

Mrs. Coolidge spoofed a little at this point, pretending uncertainty. She took off her wedding ring and read the date—October 4.

"That's all I want to hear about that," he said.

"Well, who is talking about it now?" she quipped.

And that was all that she ever heard about it, but she knew that he had not really forgotten the date. No one knew better than she that Calvin liked to add a few touches now and again to the growing legend of his wry wit. He played the game best with his family, and they responded to the fun. One Christmas he gave Grace five twenty-dollar gold pieces, along with a card engraved with Mr. Stearns' name and the words "Compliments of the Season." She spotted the card at once as one that had come a few days earlier in a box of neckties from Mr. Stearns. This was the full range of his gifts to his wife in twenty-eight years of married life, although she could be as extravagant as she wished where her clothes were concerned. She had full understanding of this quirk in his nature and wrote that he had "deeper sentimental feeling than most people whom I have known, but he did not reveal it in outward manifestation."

During her last days in the White House Mrs. Coolidge helped to lay the cornerstone of the D.A.R. auditorium. She attended the wedding of Princess Cantacuzène's daughter Bertha. The Princess, who before her marriage was Julia Grant, granddaughter of General Ulysses S. Grant, was born in the White House while he was President. She was a favorite with Mrs. Coolidge and saw her frequently. Both of the Coolidges at this time went to see Ethel Barrymore in *The Kingdom of God*. The President did not like the play. Even Mrs. Coolidge was doubtful about it. "To me, Miss Barrymore was not convincing in her part," she wrote to Mrs. Hills. "It seems to me she is unsuited to it." Her husband, as she wrote, was preparing his last message to Congress, in which he said that the country "can regard the present with satisfaction and anticipate the future with optimism."

In December they took a trip to Sapelo Island to visit Mr. and Mrs. Howard Coffin. Mrs. Coolidge wrote enthusiastically to Mrs. Hills about the harmonious house where they stayed, surrounded by huge live oak trees draped with Spanish moss. Two hundred peacocks strutted around and she delighted in her surroundings, although Secret Service men were still at their heels when they went outdoors. The primary purpose of the trip was a turkey hunt. The President went out the first morning and returned with two wild turkeys and six pheasants, three of which he had shot himself. Grace was persuaded to join in the hunt on the second morning but she did not relish the experience. She was roused at half past three in the morning and drove seven miles to the thicket where the hunt began. When word got out that the President was hunting turkeys he had to stage his customary performance for the camera men.

Frank O. Salisbury, the noted English artist who had been commissioned by the New York Genealogical and Biographical Society to paint the President and Mrs. Coolidge, had gone south with them. He found the festooned oak trees, with a glimpse of the sea in the distance, an admirable setting for his portrait of Mrs. Coolidge. Her chiffon draperies and shaded ostrich fan were done in orange tones. Salisbury thought that Coolidge resembled a parson when he posed for him first in a black suit. The President amiably donned a light suit to meet requirements. When Salisbury told him he looked distinguished in the light suit, he gravely responded: "This is a very distinguished suit."

The customary New Year's Day reception was not held in 1929. The curtain was coming down on an administration that was austere to the finish. In February the Coolidges went to Mountain Lake in Florida, where the President dedicated the Bird Sanctuary and Singing Tower that Edward W. Bok had given to the nation. The sense of national security was deep and strong at this time in spite of frenzied financial operations. Warnings of doom were strangely missing. Fortunes tripled overnight. Stocks were bought lavishly on margin. The small businessman speculated as well as the millionaire. But a sense of material well-being blanketed the land. Americans amassed possessions, traveled, made quick fortunes, had no fear of the future.

At the close of his administration the President stood out as the apostle of thrift, poised over a whirlpool of spending; as the voice of sobriety rising above the din of crime and frivolity; as the leader whose fortunes seemed tied to material prosperity and the power of Wall Street; as the man who would be remembered for what he had said rather than for what he had done; as the husband of the most popular First Lady since Dolly Madison.

Friends and observers burned candles at her shrine both during and after her years in the White House. She was one of the fortunate few in public life about whom none spoke ill. Anne Hard, who thought she had the eyes of an earnest child, compared her to a

"New England pond, serene, unruffled, bland, bright in the sun," with a great capacity for making friends. Alice Booth, in *Good Housekeeping,* pronounced her the perfect wife for Calvin Coolidge. "With miraculous wisdom she accepted the fact that here was a man— not in the making, but made," she wrote.

Gamaliel Bradford in *The Quick and the Dead* expressed the belief that "she was at the heart of the whole movement of Coolidge's life . . . The man would not have been what he was without the woman, and most of all precisely because of her infinite, exquisite tact in effacing herself." William Allen White, who saw both of the Coolidges in relaxed as well as in official moments, thought that "she was as dear as he was wise." He added: "To what extent Mrs. Coolidge has influenced her husband's judgment only two persons may testify. One is too silent to say, even if he realized it; and the other too smart! But Mrs. Coolidge has accepted her husband's ideals and striven with him to realize them . . . But for Mrs. Coolidge, her husband would not have traveled the path he has climbed." Samuel T. Williamson, writing for the New York *Times Magazine,* found her utterly natural in all situations. He felt sure she enjoyed her White House experience to the full and had only just begun to live after "considerable repression for most of her life." Her son John also believed that she enjoyed her days in Washington but that when she left she put it all behind her and neither looked back nor indulged in nostalgia. It was a closed chapter in her life.

When Mrs. Hoover invited the Washington newspaper women to tea at her house on R Street after the nomination of her husband they found a photograph of Mrs. Coolidge displayed on a table. By chance each reporter's glance seemed to light on it with unmistakable affection. Mrs. Hoover watched them with interest. "If, four years from now," she observed at last, "even one of you looks at my picture as you all seem to look at Mrs. Coolidge's, I shall feel I haven't lived in vain."

Colonel Starling considered her the personification of charm, "amazingly successful as a hostess, being gracious and friendly without an air of worry or flurry." Princess Cantacuzène decided after a few days' stay with the Coolidges that they enjoyed "as perfect harmony as is possible for two fine natures." She observed how often the President looked at his wife, how quietly he smiled at her, how simple, sincere and magnetic she was, how keen her sense of humor. She noticed that the President always walked a step ahead of Grace, that his silences were not unsympathetic, that he laughed quite freely at jokes. Together the Princess and Mrs. Coolidge studied the room on the second floor where Julia was born while Ulysses S. Grant was President, and they talked of the days of Mrs. Grant and her daughter Nellie. Together they attended a memorial service for Woodrow Wilson. Together they sat in the Senate gallery and listened to a debate on Teapot Dome.

But Dr. Boone saw deeper than most. As family physician, and the man who stood at her side while young Calvin was dying, he had watched her in moments of stress and storm as well as on parade. Like others, he acknowledged her vivacity, charm, thoughtfulness and warmth, but behind the smiling mask he also recognized the sincerity and fortitude of Grace Coolidge. "She didn't wear her feelings on her sleeve," he commented. "She didn't spend herself on trivialities but went to the heart of an issue. She could take a good strong stand and often did, particularly where the boys were concerned. She never spoke out of turn. She knew when to be silent with her husband, and when to speak. She would encourage him to talk and when he wouldn't she quickly filled in the gaps."

Mrs. Boone and her daughter Suzanne were frequently at the White House and Mrs. Coolidge typed out for Suzanne's parents a detailed account of one of the child's overnight stays with her. "This was the sort of thing she did naturally and easily," Dr. Boone recalled. "It was fortunate for our country that she walked this way, and fortunate for any individual privileged to have had her friendship and her love."

CHAPTER XI

FAREWELL TO WASHINGTON

M RS. COOLIDGE watched the raindrops falling on the manuscript held by Herbert Hoover as he read his inaugural speech on March 4, 1929. The skies were pewter gray. The day was chilly and Mr. Coolidge wore a fur-collared coat and his most inscrutable expression as he made his last political gesture before leaving Washington for good. When told earlier that morning that it might rain he answered solemnly: "Well, I hope not, but it always rained on my moving days."

A whole lifetime seemed to have intervened since Mrs. Coolidge had seen him take the inaugural vow. Now interest had shifted to his successor and the new First Lady. Mrs. Hoover, pale and dignified in plum-colored velvet and broadtail, listened attentively to her husband and seemed remote from the proceedings. The Cabinet wives had said good-by to Mrs. Coolidge at the White House that morning. She had arranged the private rooms as she thought Mrs. Hoover would like them, leaving the stamp of her own presence on everything. She had checked the boxes and trunks that had taken seven weeks to pack. All was in order. She would answer the last of her mail from Northampton, she told the President the night before, as she

255

gaily waved a bundle of letters in his face. Many friendly messages had reached them during these final hours in the White House.

They had received the Hoovers in the Blue Room before leaving for the Capitol. Mrs. Coolidge had given the Lincoln bed with its coverlet "a loving pat" as she left. She and Mrs. Hoover found that they were the forgotten participants as they exchanged pleasantries in the Senate gallery while the new Vice-President was being inducted. Describing the scene to the Robins she wrote:

> So many people were "looking out" for Mrs. Hoover and me that we nearly missed this part of the proceedings . . . I began to feel a little uneasy and finally I heard the Marine Band strike up "Hail to the Chief" and I made a break and grabbed Mrs. Hoover saying "Come on, I'm going." We made a joke of it and going out the door I said, "I don't know who precedes the other because I don't know whether your husband or mine is President, now." Well, of course, we arrived in due season but we should have been there before.

Now involved in her last appearance as First Lady, Mrs. Coolidge looked about her, relieved that she had ceased to be a focal point of attention. But many friendly glances were cast in her direction and she saw familiar faces all around. Cheers swept the crowd of fifty thousand, huddled under umbrellas, after President Hoover took the oath and Calvin Coolidge, white-faced and stern, stepped down from office. The burden had shifted from his own frail shoulders to a man of sturdier physical build. There was less contrast between the incoming and the retiring First Lady than between the two men who stood dramatically side by side. Like Mrs. Coolidge, Mrs. Hoover was a woman of dignity and reserve, educated, thoughtful, and concerned for her fellow men.

Back in the White House all was activity and bustle. The new era had already begun, as two thousand guests swarmed in for a buffet luncheon. The staff had mixed feelings about President Coolidge's departure. His silences had baffled them at times; his tempers and teasing had sometimes been abrasive. But all were sorry to see Mrs. Coolidge go. Soon her sitting room would be turned into a semitropical bower, with plants and ferns, wicker furniture and grass rugs. Guests would pour into the Executive Mansion in great numbers and the spirit of expansive entertaining would prevail. But Calvin Coolidge was leaving a strong impression of himself as a personality, if not as a President. His image was firmly rooted in the consciousness of the public. Later Mrs. Coolidge was to comment on the chill winds which left the outgoing President the forgotten man in the moment of inauguration. But it was their own wish that they should go as simply as they had come, without fuss or ostentation.

Crowds cheered them intermittently all the way from the Capitol to the station as they left the scene the moment the Hoovers had driven off. The outgoing President had asked his Cabinet members to accompany his successor instead of going with him to the station. The White House secretaries, Everett Sanders and Ted Clark, along with their wives, went with them and faced the crowd that had gathered to see the last of Cal and his popular wife. In a final radio message from the station Calvin Coolidge said that he had enjoyed his stay in Washington and he expressed appreciation that the $2,000,000 fund for the Clarke School for the Deaf had been fully subscribed.

Mrs. Coolidge, holding Tiny Tim in her arms, looked down from the rear platform at the friendly faces watching her. "Good-by, good luck," they cried and cheered lustily as she came out five separate times by demand, like a stage star. The flags, the crowds, the cheers were fading now. Life would be still and quiet by comparison. "Good-by, folks," she said into the microphone, with a final wave to the receding crowd.

Her husband later wrote of this significant moment in his life: "We draw our Presidents from the people. It is a wholesome thing for them to return to the people. I came from them. I wish to be one of them again." And Mrs. Coolidge gave her own view of this moment of farewell:

> As we turned and reentered the car, I suddenly realized that I had come back to myself, that my husband was no longer the head of our great nation, and that he and I were free to come and go and order our lives according to the dictates of our hearts, responsible only to ourselves for the outcome of our decisions.

Gone were the men of the Secret Service, the aides, the valet, the maid, and we were homeward bound.

The crash of 1929 was only seven months away but all seemed fair and promising as President Hoover took over the reins of office. There had been peace and prosperity with Calvin Coolidge. There was also a record that historians of the future would debate with considerable heat when the final accounting was in. But no great crises were in view on the day they went back to Northampton, except in Mexico, where the army had revolted in eight states, seizing Veracruz and Nogales. Dwight Morrow was functioning with skill in a difficult situation. His daughter Anne was the girl of the hour, with a twofold claim on public interest. She had just become engaged to Colonel Lindbergh and their plane had crashed in Mexico, with the conqueror of the Atlantic as pilot. Since the Morrows and the Coolidges were close friends and Mrs. Coolidge had watched little Anne grow up she heard of this engagement with the greatest interest.

But if the Coolidge departure from Washington left them with a sense of flatness their welcome to Northampton was stirring to Grace, who now regarded the Massachusetts town as her true home. A great cheer went up as they stepped off the train and the American Legion band played *Home Sweet Home*. The Mayor and a reception committee were there to greet them, and a smile hovered faintly on Calvin Coolidge's face. He had asked that there be no ceremony, but flags and welcome-home banners flew along the mile and a half route they followed to their old home on Massasoit Street.

Friends and neighbors lined the streets and pressed around their slowly moving automobile. Smith College girls in double rows cheered as they passed and the college chimes pealed out. Chapel had been held early so that they could welcome the Coolidges home. The Clarke School children watched Mrs. Coolidge with devotion as they waved their flags.

"The privilege of being a private citizen again," her husband murmured as they stepped down at the house to the strains of *America* and were immediately mobbed by photographers.

"Hello, boys," Mrs. Coolidge called to a group of children clinging to the porch rail. Wherever she turned there were familiar faces, friendly handclasps and greetings. A cold drenching rain was falling. Slush lay underfoot. Things had not changed at 21 Massasoit Street, although their own lives had broadened out into a wider stream. Mrs. Coolidge went from room to room, climbed the familiar stairs and buried her face in the masses of flowers that friends had sent her. The whole house, she cheerfully remarked, could be fitted into the state dining room of the Executive Mansion with room to spare. But for the moment she felt that it had "grown dearer through the years of absence, the years of living in larger, grander houses."

But the fitting-in took ingenuity. She had written to Mrs. Hills in advance with instructions about her various boxes and crates. "Please treat me rough when I get home and kick me about a bit so I'll realize I'm human," she jested. But Mrs. Hills found it hard to forget that Calvin Coolidge had been President.

"Good morning, President Coolidge," she addressed him.

"I am not President any longer," he said, with a thin smile.

"As long as you live you'll be President to me," she assured him, and continued to use the title.

Northampton had changed and grown. Its graceful white houses glimmered through the leafless trees of March. Late winter winds ruffled the topaz surface of Paradise Pond. The Smith College girls went bicycling around the campus and ate hamburgers and ice cream at the corner drugstores while they crammed for exams. Mrs. Coolidge smiled at them as she swung along on her daily walks or drove downtown to shop in the same fashion as before she became mistress of the White House. One of her first orders was for a pot roast, which she longed for after so many elaborate dinners. Mrs. Reckahn was still on hand to give it the touches that Mr. Coolidge liked. She had cooked for them for fifteen years and had grown a little lame with age. But the Coolidges considered her cooking as fine as ever, and she addressed the master of the house with the same bluntness as Aurora Pierce. No one except Aurora and Mrs. Coolidge knew better than Mrs. Reckahn how to cater to his idiosyncrasies in food.

The Coolidges sought to resume life on the old basis, but from being a comparatively obscure New England couple they were now known around the world, and their lives and habits had been presented to the public in the most intimate detail. Mr. Coolidge settled in his chair on the porch, his back to the street, but he could no longer find relaxation in this, for he was now besieged as cars rolled past, sometimes at the rate of one every six seconds. The people of Northampton were not the sinners. Except for a friendly interest they let the Coolidges alone, but passing motorists knew that Calvin Coolidge lived in the plain house on Massasoit Street and they thought it a good chance to see at close range the curious man who had recently left the White House.

He was also coming to grips with a new and vastly diminished way of living. "What will I do with him?" Grace asked Mr. Stearns, knowing how hard the transition would be for her husband. In all respects she seemed the same Grace Coolidge the town had always known—simple, natural, unaffected. Yet her vistas, too, had widened. She was now a woman of the world, who had entertained some of the most famous figures of the day. When she walked forth people noticed her. Out with her dog one evening after dark she heard a voice from a passing automobile exclaim: "Not in half of that house!" Letters reached her accusing her of making a laughing stock of the country by living on such a simple scale.

"I haven't any idea what he has in mind," she wrote to the Robins about the newly retired President. "I always did like the unexpected and am awaiting with intense interest the next jump." It came fast when she was told that they were off to California. They had long wished to travel but they had not counted on the mob scenes that they would encounter along the way. Early in 1929 they went from Florida to New Orleans. Mrs. Coolidge expected her husband "to turn on his heel and walk out" of the old French restaurants with all the rich food but "something had tamed him, perhaps one or two of those charming southern women, and my anxiety for his behavior at an end I gave myself over completely to enjoyment of the highly seasoned viands and a few good swigs of perfectly poisonous coffee," she wrote cheerfully to the Robins. But the mob scenes were alarming, now that they no longer had a solid guard around them. They were warmly greeted all the way from New Orleans to Los

Angeles where they were suddenly projected into the cinema world, under the guidance of Mary Pickford and Douglas Fairbanks. Calvin Coolidge made a hit with the movie colony and an occasional grin brightened his impassive face as the stars paid him their own particular type of homage. From Hollywood the Coolidges moved on to the theatrical splendor of William Randolph Hearst's castle San Simeon, where they stayed for a week. Grace wrote enthusiastically to the Robins about this experience:

"We lived in a medieval castle like the knights and ladies of old—a marvelous experience. Really, I did feel queer around there in modern garb, the only objects that were not at least five hundred years old." She told Mr. Hearst that his castle lacked nothing but medieval costumes and an organ. He replied that an organ was out of place anywhere except in a church or cathedral.

"Very good," said Mrs. Coolidge. "Bring over a cathedral next."

Privately she thought when she saw his choir stalls that they, too, belonged in a cathedral. She and Calvin occupied the Doric suite running across the front of the château on the third floor. Instead of using the circular stone stairs she decided one day to try the elevator hidden in the center of a huge column. But it stuck between floors as she was going down for lunch. The alarm gong did not sound, so she resigned herself to a long stay in the "rather small dungeon." She had to stand up but she kept on knitting in the dark. With her usual touch of humor she wrote:

I thought I should eventually be missed but time passed and there was no sound except from workmen on the roof, workers in stone who seemed diligent in plying the chisel and unable to hear the call of a woman in distress. After a while, I decided to try my voice at yodeling and was rather surprised at my own performance. However, I was the only one to enjoy it. After half an hour of knitting to my own yodeling, a voice from above was heard to inquire, "Somebody call?" My liberator!

She assured him that she was not at all afraid but only cold and hungry. The man, appalled that a former First Lady should have been trapped in Mr. Hearst's elevator, began elaborate rescue operations. No one, not even Calvin, had missed her and she did not tell her host what had happened until it was time to leave, lest she make him uncomfortable. She greatly enjoyed the films shown in his private theater and if she chanced to mention any she cared to see her host had them flown in from Los Angeles at once. "The whole experience rivaled Alice in Wonderland," she wrote. "But Alice woke up and we went home."

At this time Mrs. Coolidge undoubtedly was enjoying her newfound freedom. She assured the Robins that by degrees she was becoming more emancipated and hoped to make plans for herself. "During the time that my husband held a responsible and exacting office, I made it my business to be on hand in case I could do any little thing to ease the burden," she wrote. "I guess I spoiled him and I know I got myself into the habit of making no plans for myself until I had made sure that he wouldn't need me."

In June of that year Mrs. Coolidge was a star in her own right when she received an honorary degree from Smith College. Shortly afterward *Good Housekeeping* named her one of America's twelve greatest women, not for any professional accomplishment but for her outstanding place in the nation as a symbol of home and family life at its best. Others on the list were Willa Cather, Martha Berry, Helen Keller, Grace Abbott, Jane Addams, Cecilia Beaux, Mrs. Carrie Chapman Catt, Mrs. Minnie Maddern Fiske, Dr. Florence R. Sabin, Madame Schumann-Heink and Mary E. Woolley. Mrs. Coolidge's third honorary degree was bestowed by her own alma mater, the University of Vermont in June, 1930, with the citation: ". . . all ours when the schoolgirl lived and worked among us; ours still though not unshared, when the First Lady cast her kindly spell of act and speech and manner over the hearts of a nation; ours now when we honor in her guise the crown of achievement, the art of all arts, the power of grace, the magic of a name."

Consternation developed at this time over the gown to be shown on the model of Mrs. Coolidge in the Smithsonian Institution. Vera Bloom and her mother, Mrs. Sol Bloom, both campaigned for something more striking than the white satin brocaded gown originally chosen for this purpose. Mrs. Coolidge promptly sent them the coral red velvet dress that she wore at her last reception, explaining that it was not the one used for the Christy painting. She added red velvet shoes. Fifteen years later Mrs. H. Whitwell Underwood, whose husband, Captain Herbert W. Underwood, commanded the Waves at Smith College, was aghast when she saw the Grace Coolidge figure at the Smithsonian. "It was so plain—no jewels, no gloves, nothing, just a dress of that decade and not very becoming, but a nice color," she wrote. The skirt was in tiers and was comparatively short in front, with a long train behind. Again Mrs. Coolidge assisted cheerfully in the embellishment of her wax image. She sent Mrs. Underwood a string of pearls, gloves, handkerchief and an immense fan of coral-shaded feathers, all of which she had used with this gown. Crowds gathered at the Smithsonian Institution to see the transformation of Grace Coolidge's image.

Two dozen of her gala gowns with fans and other extras were later kept at Plymouth and cherished by her daughter-in-law, for the major event in Mrs. Coolidge's life immediately after leaving the White House was John's marriage to Florence Trumbull, which took place six months after the Coolidges' return to Northampton. John had waited a long time for his bride. For nearly three years he had concentrated on her as whole-heartedly as Calvin Coolidge had on John's mother. He had graduated from Amherst in 1928 and was now well established in his job with the New York New Haven & Hartford Rail Road. He felt he could support a wife, if not quite in the fashion to which Florence was accustomed.

A tall dark youth, reserved in manner and dignified in bearing, with a strong touch of the Coolidge nature, John was plugging along at Amherst when he first met Florence on the train going to Washington for his father's inauguration. As the son of the President and a likable youth in his own right John had been much sought after by hostesses. All the White House staff liked the unpretentious and grave young man who had a mixture of his mother's affectionate impulses and his father's reserve. Florence was a popular girl, used to official routine as the daughter of the Governor of Connecticut. She was tall and lithe, with reddish-blonde hair, a quick bright manner and a wholesome relish for life. Soon John was inviting her to the proms and was meeting her at South Hadley, Massachusetts, or at her father's house in Plainville, Connecticut. There was much traffic between Mount Holyoke and Amherst and his enthusiasm for dancing reached its peak at this time.

Mrs. Coolidge was sympathetic to their romance and saw to it that Florence had choice White House orchids for her gala corsages. When she went abroad just before their engagement in 1929 his mother wrote sympathetically to John from Massasoit Street: "Dearest Johnny, I guess you are missing Florence but you will have her soon for always and then you will not have to miss her." Florence regarded Mrs. Coolidge as a second mother but she was a little afraid of the President at first, until they began to make jokes together. She had one memorably embarrassing moment at the White House when she sat at his left at dinner one night. She was in Washington as a page at a D.A.R. convention. By some mischance she dropped some fish in her lap. Without a pause Mr. Coolidge looked across at his wife and announced in clear and nasal tones for all to hear: "Mammy, Miss Connecticut has spilled on her lovely gown."

Mrs. Coolidge came to the rescue in a practical way and sprinkled talcum powder on the mess. But Florence and the President got on well after that. He always called her Miss Connecticut. On one occasion he staged a performance for Florence's benefit at Plymouth, digging into a closet and walking up and down before her in a succession of old and somewhat comical hats. "How would that look?" he kept asking as he tried on each new one. Very funny, she thought, and burst into hearty laughter.

There was speculation about the young pair as early as 1926. The papers had got wind of their romance although there was nothing official about it. There were stories that Florence's life was in danger when Gerald Chapman was hanged at Wethersfield Prison in Connecticut and her father did not intercede to commute his sentence. The President did some worrying about John, too, as the jazz age reached its full momentum. This was the Roaring Twenties, and stories of hip flasks, joy rides, and bathtub gin were disturbing to the quiet occupants of the White House. Both John and Florence engaged mildly in the diversions of the 1920s. They went to tea dances and could Charleston as nimbly as the rest of their generation. John wore the traditional raccoon coat that befitted the New England climate and he had been known to drive his car at racing speed. But neither he nor Florence came under the blanket heading of Flaming Youth.

Although he plied a steady course his father thought that his marks should have been better, so he assigned Colonel Starling to join him at Amherst. "At the tender age of fifty I was going to college," the Colonel reported indignantly, hating his assignment. "John was embarrassed and so was I. He was a thoroughly decent chap, however, and had inherited his father's sense of humor. He decided to make the best of it and I made him realize that I had no intention of sticking his nose into a book and holding it there."

Every Saturday night he and John took the trolley to Mount Holyoke and while the young pair courted Starling managed to kill time as best he could. In the mornings he and John, who roomed together, dressed to the tune of *Alice Blue Gown* on the portable phonograph. But when they returned to Washington for the Christmas holidays the President listened to Colonel Starling's plea for deliverance and a younger Secret Service man was assigned to John. So strong was the feeling about the Sacco-Vanzetti case at this time that there were rumors that John had to be guarded. As the President's son every move he made came under scrutiny.

Florence was discreet about her devotion to John. All their friends were aware of their love for each other and from time to time reporters pursued her for confirmation. She admitted freely that she liked to go about with John Coolidge but she would not be pinned down on the subject of marriage. Actually, she wore her engagement ring on the third finger of her right hand when she came in from Europe and thus fooled the vigilant press. But immediately afterward their engagement was announced by Governor and Mrs. Trumbull. The President and Mrs. Coolidge were resting at the time in the Swannanoa Country Club, high in the Blue Ridge Mountains, near Waynesboro, Virginia.

John was twenty-three and his bride was twenty-four when they were married on September 24, 1929, in the Plainville Congregational Church. Florence, looking stately beside her six-foot bridegroom, wore a princess gown with a scarf of duchess lace, given her by Mrs. Coolidge, draped as a veil on her glinting hair. Her jewels were pearls and she carried Easter lilies. She was attended by her sister, Jean (later Mrs. Alric R. Bailey), wearing peach chiffon with ecru lace, and her bridesmaids wore bouffant yellow gowns and horsehair picture hats. Stephen Brown, son of the Coolidge family physician at Northampton and a classmate at Amherst, was John's best man.

More than a thousand yellow chrysanthemums flown from California adorned the white-steepled colonial church. There were eighty-two guests. One governor, four former governors and two senators were present, as well as the former President of the United States, who wore a gardenia in his buttonhole and looked pleased with the day's events. Mrs. Coolidge was beamingly happy in beige lace with a brown velvet hat, a sable scarf and a corsage of orchids. Young Jack Hills was with her.

An aviator dipped low over the Trumbull house as the wedding party gathered there. Six miniature silver airplanes decorated the wedding cake, for Governor Trumbull was an enthusiastic flyer. "Talkies" were taken of the wedding and Mr. Coolidge was surprised to find a microphone at his feet beneath the Oriental rug and demanded that it be taken away. When asked by the press if he chose to say what wedding gift he had given the young pair he answered blankly: "No, I do not choose to say."

Mrs. Coolidge gave them colonial furniture for their bedroom. The young pair settled in a four-room apartment in New Haven, paying $78 a month rent. Florence buckled down to simple housekeeping, while John went to work every day for the railroad. In her letters to friends Mrs. Coolidge reported that they were "deliriously happy" and that she had the "nicest daughter that a son ever presented to his mother." Mrs. Trumbull was "a peach and nothing seemed to bother her at all."

This letter was written to the Robins on Mrs. Coolidge's twenty-fourth wedding anniversary. Calvin, she wrote, had just told a woman reporter from the New York *Times* that they never planned anything in particular for their anniversaries but "preferred rather to celebrate every day." Mrs. Coolidge was not so sure of this. "In accordance with this custom we separated as soon as breakfast was over," she added. "I do not know how he spent the day but I went to the cattle show, a grand affair, visited my mother at the hospital, poured tea at the nurses' home . . . then went to a tea at a private house."

A month after John's wedding, which was a front-page event in the metropolitan papers, Mrs. Goodhue died in the Cooley-Dickinson Hospital after a long illness. She was eighty-one and had been cared for by Blanche N. Cole, a nurse who kept Mrs. Coolidge closely informed of her mother's condition while she was in the White House. Coley, she wrote, gave her peace of mind and quietude of heart because of the faithful care she gave her mother. Going about her official duties she would clip out inspirational verses for Coley to read to Mrs. Goodhue, and often she sent them mementos of White House functions—feathers from a peacock fan, a swatch of silk, a menu or dinner list. Thus she kept alive a brisk flow of communication between the Executive Mansion and her mother's sick room. Later, when Miss Cole in turn became an invalid, Mrs. Coolidge maintained close links with her and with Miss Edith Hill, whose companion she became in later years. Both were invalids and lived in Northampton. Her letters and visits cheered them and Miss Hill helped Mrs. Coolidge with her correspondence.

A few days after Mrs. Goodhue's death news of the Wall Street crash swept the country, with particular implications for Calvin Coolidge, who caught the full impact of the disaster as he quietly studied the newspapers in Northampton or fished at nearby Goshen. Day after day the headlines roared the collapse of the structure that had grown to dangerous proportions during his term of office. The entire country was caught in the storm. It affected every channel of business and blighted the lives of thousands. The small speculators were pushed to the wall as inevitably as the big traders.

President Hoover's message to Congress early in December called for the restoration of confidence. He pronounced business sound, urged speed on tariff legislation, and pledged an income tax cut. But his words fell on barren ground. Brokerage houses were suspended. Banks closed. The volume of money going into brokers' loans from banks across the country had increased by 68.7 per cent in the four years preceding the crash. Now these scattered bankers called in loans to meet withdrawals. They realized on securities and refused fresh credits, with demoralizing results to the economy as a whole. Small businesses were stifled for lack of credit. A dozen Oklahoma banks failed to open after the death of the man who controlled thirteen banks in the state. The legend of panic suicides grew, beginning with the shot that killed J. J. Riordan, a New York banker, a few days after the crash and reaching its crescendo with the suicide of Ivar Kreuger in 1932. The picture of the ruined jumping from skyscraper windows was overdrawn at the time but the score was grim enough, from Worcester to Wisconsin, from Philadelphia to St. Louis.

Relief money was raised with speed in Chicago, Detroit, Cleveland, Birmingham and other cities where the emergency was acute. The drought of 1930 brought added misery to rural areas. Tens of thousands of farm families had their savings swept away. They learned all over again to live off their farm produce, to use their smoke houses and root cellars, or else to starve. Grain prices dropped. There was bartering at the cross roads. By the summer of 1935 a total of 730,-000 farmers had been aided through cooperative associations. Nomads grew in number, riding the rails, drifting along the highways, creating their own derelict shelters in vacant city lots. In the autumn of 1932 it was estimated that two million Americans were on the move. The unemployed in Georgia were put to work in public fields. State prisoners grew their own food in Tennessee. Hooverville villages mushroomed across the country. Breadlines were no longer a novelty and malnutrition was recognized in a nation normally geared to abundance.

The world of mink coats, diamonds, servants and yachts had come down with a crash but so had the world of the average man. New cars were manufactured but none could buy them. Homes were sold with heavy losses. Debts went unpaid. Theaters, shops, restaurants, night clubs went into eclipse. Many of the young gave up all thought of college and even the ice cream fountains in drugstores felt the pinch. The fantastic building boom of the 1920s came to a sudden halt. Luxury apartment houses stood empty except where big concessions were made. Florida real estate values faded like a mirage.

By the summer of 1932 fifty per cent of the workers in Chicago were unemployed and in the following year the total production of the American economy was estimated at a third less than in 1929.

The former President watched the rush of events with silent concern as the years of prosperity he had known gradually telescoped into the dwindling spiral of depression. He turned to his books and his writings with added concentration as the blackout followed the crash and people of all social classes were faced with joblessness and defeat. But he wrote optimistically for the *American Magazine* of February, 1932: "We have had a tremendous spiritual awakening concerning our duty to relieve human suffering. There is scarcely a hamlet in the land where there is not an organization and active public effort for the relief of the unemployed."

Mrs. Hoover kept up friendly exchanges with Mrs. Coolidge. They had always liked and understood each other. But both of the Coolidges felt far removed from the scene as President Hoover coped with the devastating problems of the hour. Coolidge made only one return visit to Washington. He attended a luncheon in 1929 celebrating the signing of the Kellogg pact, one of the major diplomatic feats of his administration. At the time it was considered a valiant step in international relations, with sixty-two nations pledging themselves to renounce war. On this occasion Mr. Coolidge called on Mrs. Hoover. His wife was not with him but both appeared at an American Legion convention in Boston in 1930 at which Mr. Hoover was the speaker. There were shouts for Coolidge when he stepped into view. He seemed embarrassed and delivered a one-line speech: "Gentlemen, I charge you to be true to the laws and Constitution of the United States." Mrs. Coolidge recorded her own reaction to this occasion in one of her Robin letters: "It was so interesting to see all the old guard around the President and Mrs. Hoover when we went to call on them at the hotel and then to walk out a free man and woman leaving them to their misery, if you see what I mean."

By this time another wedding anniversary had come around and much to her surprise Mrs. Coolidge learned that they would celebrate with a brief visit to the Wayside Inn at Sudbury when on their way to Boston for the American Legion convention. Calvin had liked the cottage cheese there when he stopped for tea en route to the Republican state convention the week before. It was closed over Sunday but special arrangements were made for the Coolidges. They occupied the Henry Ford suite and a special dinner was prepared for them in the old inn kitchen. The roast was baked in a Dutch oven, the vegetables in iron pots on the crane, hoecake was done in the ashes, and Indian pudding and pumpkin pie in the brick oven. They ate at the old tavern table and were served by a kitchen maid in a period print dress. The sap bucket the President had given to Henry Ford hung on the wall. Mrs. Coolidge commented that it was not difficult to turn back the pages of the years in these surroundings. "Another adventure into dreamland," she wrote to the Robins.

In the spring of 1930 the Coolidges moved into a larger house. Much as they valued their early home they had never felt so much like goldfish. Their overcrowded quarters and the everlasting scrutiny were interfering with their way of life. They bought The Beeches, a shingled house buried in magnificent trees. It was built for Dr. Henry Noble MacCracken while he taught at Smith College before becoming president of Vassar. It had eight acres of land, a tennis court and a small swimming pool. Its sleeping porches to the rear overlooked broad meadows that swept down to the Connecticut River, with Mount Tom visible in the distance. Here the former President could sit in the evenings, his feet on the fender (a favorite trick of his), smoke and read without fear of observation. Iron gates at the entrance, flanked by tall stone pillars, set up a barricade against invasion and he had the property fenced to keep out intruders. There were two acres of lawn, with tall hedges and the beech trees that gave the house its name. It was a verdant, secluded spot and it gave the Coolidges more space for their possessions. On Massasoit Street Grace had had to squeeze the choice antique desk that the ladies of the Senate had given her on leaving Washington into the dining room. But at The Beeches she had her own work room upstairs, where she typed her letters, sewed and knitted, read and attended to her pets.

"We do most of our living on the meadow side of the house," she wrote to the Robins. "Down below is the swimming pool and a summer house—a fine place for picnics when the mosquitoes have had their fun . . . Path and steps lead up and down, in and out among the trees on the slope. The high net around the tennis court is covered with lovely vines, Virginia creeper, clematis, Dutchman's pipe and another vine whose name I do not know. There are lilacs, syringa, brides wreath and forsythia. The perennial gardens are lovely, also the rose garden. There are three arches covered with Dorothy Perkins and Crimson Ramblers." As time went on Mrs. Coolidge experimented with the garden but "my life-partner makes strange, snorting noises when I talk about flowers and gardens—and my ambitions along these lines. At times I think I detect a note of mirth amid the snorts." When Will Rogers called on her at this time he told her that he was making the trip East because he wanted some money to pay for moving a hill on his ranch. "So here I am and when I get back there's goin' to be some hill-movin' in California," he observed.

In the summer of 1930 both of the Coolidges were involved in literary effort. Even before the President left the White House he had taken to jotting down his personal reminiscences, but he would do nothing with them until he stepped down from office. Then he contracted to write articles for three magazines. A series that he did for *Cosmopolitan* developed into his autobiography. He had not intended to have an office but he was soon back in his old quarters with Ralph Hemenway. The binding strings of his position could not be cut in a day. Letters flowed in on him in great heaps. "A former President is hardly less set upon by nuisances and notoriety seekers than when in office," Grace wrote. "Some go so far as to say that they are a sister or brother. Sometimes I think there is little truth left in the world."

Mr. Coolidge was finally persuaded in 1930 to write daily newspaper paragraphs for the McClure Syndicate, with a contract that netted him more than $200,000 a year. Nearly a hundred newspapers subscribed at the highest rate paid up to that time for a feature of this kind. The paragraphs were from 150 to 200 words long. He called them his "chore" and he never misjudged his space. Here was a spot where his economy in words was an asset. He chose the topics himself and labored over them mightily, writing them in pencil at night in his study, then dictating them to Herman Beaty in his office next day, with one foot planted on a half-open desk drawer and a cigar between his lips. He was never late or missed a deadline. No interruptions were permitted until he had finished. Then he would talk to callers.

His first paragraph dealt with the depression and had a note of exhortation: "My countrymen, it is time to stop criticizing and quarreling and begin sympathizing and helping." But from then on he deliberately avoided political comment, saying "I refuse to be Deputy President." This was a disappointment to his readers. Some considered his paragraphs lifeless bundles of platitudes, lacking in the wry humor that the public had come to associate with Calvin Coolidge. They were done with a simplicity that led his critics to dismiss them as trite and as loaded with self-conscious aphorisms. He worried considerably over them and was distressed by the scoffing remarks that they sometimes evoked. He said impatiently to Bruce Barton: "Perhaps some day I'll write one on 'The Importance of the Obvious.' If all the folks in the U.S. would do the few simple things they ought to do, most of our big problems would take care of themselves."

As usual Grace knew nothing of what might be coming from day to day but she always picked up her New York *Herald Tribune* with interest in the morning and saw what Calvin was thinking and saying. Somewhat to her own surprise she, too, began tapping out articles on her typewriter. They appeared in the *American Magazine* in 1929 and later she did some writing for *Good Housekeeping*. She confided to the Robins the spontaneous way in which this had begun, and the help Calvin had given her in having them placed. He had even approved of her literary endeavors. During a long evening passed alone in a hotel room in Springfield, while he was attending an Amherst trustees' meeting, she picked up a pencil and began to scribble. Her letter to the Robins went on:

I sewed and wrote in turn until I became rather more interested in the paper than in the cloth and by midnight I had covered a surprising number of sheets of paper. For several weeks, I wrote on in spare moments, unknown to anyone, even my best friend and neighbor. Not even my husband knew that I was entering his "field" . . . Finally I said that I was trying my hand at it but did not feel very confident of my ability in that direction particularly since he did it so well. I felt that the comparison would be a bit hard on me, an inexperienced beginner.

But he thought well of what she had written and "was even willing to have them follow his articles—in fact he had established himself my manager without request and without commission, and took the articles with him when he went to New York and submitted them to his publisher." But Mrs. Coolidge was realistic. She finished by telling the Robins that she was well aware her articles would not have been worth the paper they were typed on, had she not been First Lady. In her own words, she skirted the outer edges, "carefully avoiding the section given over to the mature fruits of philosophical education." She left that to Calvin while she gave bland treatment to "When I Became First Lady." She added two more poems to the one she had written about young Calvin, and when *Watch-Fires* was reproduced in the *Outlook and Independent* of January 14, 1931, after appearing in the New York *Herald Tribune,* the editors speculated on the possibility that Mrs. Coolidge was a frustrated writer. "What does Calvin Coolidge think about this poetry writing, anyway?" they asked.

Actually, Mrs. Coolidge wrote fluently all her life and even in her early days at the University of Vermont she liked to dash off verse. She never pretended that it was good, but it gave her pleasure to turn it out in spontaneous fashion, as the spirit moved her. The poems that appeared during these first years at home, while her husband was busy meeting demands from magazines and newspapers, were characteristic:

THE QUEST

Crossing the uplands of time,
Skirting the borders of night,
Scaling the face of the peak of dreams,
We enter the regions of light,
And hastening on, with eager intent,
Arrive at the rainbow's end,
And there uncover the pot of gold
Buried deep in the heart of a friend.

WATCH-FIRES

Love was not given the human heart
For careless dealing.
Its spark was lit that man
Might know Divine revealing.

Heaped up with sacrificial brands,
The flame, in mounting,
Enkindles other hearts with love
Beyond the counting.

Reflected back into each life,
These vast fires, glowing,
Do then become the perfect love
Of Christ's bestowing.

Writers circulated around The Beeches and political reminiscences were eagerly sought but no revelations were forthcoming. His newspaper paragraphs wearied Calvin Coolidge, and he refused to renew his contract at the end of a year in spite of a heavy demand, but his autobiography gave him quiet satisfaction. It was written with grace and economy of words and held no surprises for anyone. It cost three dollars and sold well. Grace persuaded him to autograph copies for an extra dollar apiece at Northampton bookstores, the proceeds to go to the missionary society of their church.

Various business overtures were made to Calvin Coolidge in an economy that was hurrying downhill. His name was still identified with prosperity and big business. He considered becoming the Judge Landis of the oil industry and wrote to Everett Sanders for his advice: "I cannot find any peace, even writing, where there are not problems and criticism of what I am doing." This came to nothing but he became a director of the New York Life Insurance Company and attended the monthly meetings in New York with unfailing regularity. Another of his interests was the American Antiquarian Society in Worcester. He was a trustee from 1925 and became president in 1930. Mrs. Coolidge always accompanied him to the council meetings, which were held four times a year, and they invariably lunched with Dr. Brigham, executive head of the Society, and his wife. While the meetings were in progress Mrs. Coolidge usually sat outside knitting. Dr. Brigham persuaded her on one occasion to visit the famous Worcester Art Museum. But she was so afraid of keeping Calvin waiting that she hurried back. When she expressed a wish to visit Elm Park, Dr. Brigham asked her: "Have you time?"

"No," said Coolidge promptly.

He had little to say at the council meetings but was listened to with much respect when he voiced an opinion. Presidents were under discussion at the first meeting he attended, and specifically Washington and Jefferson. Dr. Brigham found him loquacious when he had him alone, and at different times they discussed prohibition, with side allusions to bourbon; political speeches, life at the White House, Washington correspondents (he had his pet detestations), book collecting and topics of the day.

When Dr. Brigham showed him a rare copy he had in his home of Dante's *Inferno* and observed: "I don't suppose you ever read that," Coolidge looked at him grimly and replied: "I read it in the original Italian. When I was courting Grace I thought I would look up foreign languages and I read twenty books in Italian and twenty in French. German I never could stand. But I read Dante's *Inferno*."

True enough, Grace could remember seeing the *Inferno* among the books he kept at hand when she first married him, along with the Bible and *The Life and Letters of Charles E. Garman,* an Amherst idol. Five shelves in a golden oak bookcase fronted with a sateen curtain held standard classics—Shakespeare, Hawthorne, Whittier, Longfellow, Tennyson and Kipling, as well as Latin, Greek, French, German and Italian grammars and various textbooks.

When Dr. Brigham visited the Coolidges at Plymouth in 1931 Calvin took him to the barn to look over some of his early favorites. He picked up Bancroft, then turned to an unabridged life of George Washington and remarked reflectively: "It is strange, but the character of Washington never appealed to me as a boy. He was too wise and serene and omniscient." Ethan Allen was more his boyhood hero. They discussed books from many angles. When Dr. Brigham asked about the books he had found on his arrival at the White House, Mr. Coolidge replied: "Files of *Blackwood's Magazine*."

"And what did you leave?"

"Files of *Blackwood's Magazine.*"

But in the intervening years he had acquired a fine library, with many autographed copies from the authors themselves. The Coolidges had arrived in Washington with only a few personal effects. They left with two pianos, furniture, rugs, china, glass, silver and fifty-five cases of books, with close to four thousand volumes, which were stored temporarily at the Forbes Library. David C. Mearns, chief of the Manuscript Division of the Library of Congress, had personally catalogued the books for Mr. Coolidge in the White House, with the dogs now and again getting in the way. At times the President autographed books himself and in one, inscribed to Edward K. Hall, who had lost a son, he expressed his own private grief: *In recollection of his son and my son, who had the privilege by the grace of God to be boys through all eternity.*

Like everyone else, Dr. Brigham observed the harmony that existed between Calvin Coolidge and his wife. He noticed that at first the President, from force of habit, walked ahead of Grace and Mrs. Brigham, but he soon dropped this Presidential custom and let the wives go first. He was hospitable when friends visited him at Plymouth. While Grace busied herself in the kitchen with Aurora he took Dr. Brigham to the sink to wash his hands. Twice after her husband's death Mrs. Coolidge returned to the Antiquarian Society—once to help Mrs. Adams look up material on her ancestor, Fanny Fern, whose biography she was writing, and once to track down a genealogical question.

Mrs. Coolidge may not have appreciated the *Inferno* as a prop for Calvin's wooing but, like him, she was a reader all her life. She followed the current novels, and leaned to biographies, memoirs and travel books. But when asked about her favorite books she had a stock reply: "People. I have been fortunate in being placed where I had an opportunity to gratify my taste by meeting great numbers of them." However, books loomed large in the Coolidge household and after her husband's death she gave the Forbes Library part of his collection. Special cases were bought by the city government to hold them, along with other Coolidge mementos. Mrs. Coolidge was at

Cap Martin on the Riviera when she heard about this and she wrote at once to J. L. Harrison, librarian of Forbes at the time, expressing her appreciation of this civic act.

The Beeches, with its leaded windows and reposeful air, made a good setting for the Coolidge books, although the library could house only 1,500 of the 4,000 volumes they owned. Mr. Coolidge liked to arrange them himself, so that he would know where each one was. Bruce Barton, who had seen the Coolidges in Washington, in the Adirondacks and New York, found them comfortably settled at The Beeches in 1931. He admired the iris beds, the well-filled bookcases, the steel engraving of George Washington over the fireplace, the Salisbury portrait of Mrs. Coolidge and an oil painting of the *Mayflower*. On the piano were photographs of all members of the family and one of Mrs. Hoover with her first grandchild. French doors led to the sun porch which overlooked a shady lawn. Barton thought the President looked more relaxed and cheerful than he had ever seen him. And Mrs. Coolidge was the picture of serenity. "It surely agrees with you to be home," he told her.

"You just can't imagine how good it is," she replied.

She seemed young and slim to Barton and he watched with amusement when she came swinging into the kitchen with a tin of crackers and some apples while Calvin stirred up hot chocolate for a late supper for his guest. Much banter passed between them and Barton had the impression that although she did not talk about what went on, little escaped Mrs. Coolidge. She picked up the tail end of a conversation in which Barton had quoted an insurance director as saying that Coolidge was *always* right.

"Send him up to talk to me," said Mrs. Coolidge briskly.

When Calvin groped around for a forgotten name she gave him a playful push toward the stove where he was solemnly stirring chocolate and exclaimed: "And he's the one who is supposed to know everything."

"From the hotel room to the White House; back to the home library and the kitchen," Barton wrote after this visit. "This is our Democracy . . ." He found the law offices enlarged from two to five rooms and Coolidge sitting behind a flat-top desk, with oak bookcases around him, and on the walls a steel engraving of Lincoln and facsimile copies of the Declaration of Independence, Shakespeare's will and the warrant for the execution of Charles I. Barton went with the Coolidges to church. As the son of a minister this was a rite that he understood, but the day was hot and he was overpowered with drowsiness. "I mustn't go to sleep in the pew of the former President," he kept telling himself, but in the end he did, and snored into the bargain. When he apologized afterward Mr. Coolidge looked at him in a measuring way and remarked: "It's natural. The ventilation usually isn't very good. Preachers' voices tend to be singsong."

But before he dozed off Barton wondered what might be passing through Coolidge's mind as the young pastor pleaded for the abolition of armies and navies. Only a few months earlier he had been commander in chief of these forces for the United States. The former President glided out immediately after the service without speaking to anyone, while Mrs. Coolidge and Barton stopped and chatted with the parishioners. Both felt much at home in these neighborly circles. After dinner that night Mrs. Coolidge talked of the younger generation. To her they seemed straightforward, genuine and wholesome, in spite of all the madcap publicity. She cited the case of John and Florence, happy on their small income, and working hard.

Barton went up to the attic with the Coolidges and saw a great array of boxes and bundles, scrapbooks of the White House days, pictures, books and a billiard table. After watching Coolidge as he poked among these possessions he wrote optimistically: "Perfectly contented. No more dress-suit dinners. No more handshaking. No further political ambitions. No regrets." As he drove away from The Beeches and saw its owners framed in the doorway, waving good-by, he thought that they seemed uncommonly happy. "It was peaceful there under the trees, in front of their own house—just he and she, and Beauty and Tim," he later wrote.

The family routine at The Beeches was simple. Mrs. Coolidge had drawn up a precise schedule for the household to follow. Meals were served promptly at 7:15, 12:30 and 6 o'clock. She detailed the fare for the dogs as carefully as for the family. Beauty must have her muffins broken up in her dog food. Rob Roy did not like his muzzle,

for it tickled his nose. Two dozen eggs were bought every week
from a Vermont farmer. Mr. Coolidge liked soup and Mrs. Coolidge
went in for salads and light desserts. His cereal had to be cooked for
five hours in a double boiler. "Do not hesitate to try new recipes,"
Mrs. Coolidge wrote. "We like surprises."

In the evening she and Calvin read by the light of the Coolidge
lamp. By this time the oil lamp used for the swearing-in at Plymouth
had been copied by Mrs. Helen Woods, who had once taught young
Calvin. Mrs. Coolidge had sponsored her when she opened a lamp
studio in Northampton and sought the President's permission to put
a Coolidge lamp on the market. He pondered over Mrs. Woods'
proposal when she visited The Beeches with her plan. Then his wife
remarked: "You know if Helen does this she will do it beautifully."

Mr. Coolidge thought for a while and asked a few questions. Then
he gave his judgment: "I don't know why she shouldn't. I know it
will be right. I hope she makes a lot of money."

When she was at Plymouth that summer Mrs. Coolidge made
detailed sketches of the original lamp for the benefit of Mrs. Woods,
even counting the little swirls. Later she dug out old pictures from
the attic that would present an interesting view of the homestead and
the country round about. Among them was a little picture of Calvin's
windmill. Mrs. Woods' idea was to adapt the old lamp to modern
usage, at the same time suggesting the spirit of the swearing-in at
Plymouth. Mr. Coolidge gave her a letter to a New York manufacturer who helped her with the glass-molded chimney.

When Mrs. Woods gave a showing of her lamps in Northampton
Mrs. Coolidge, who was still in the White House but happened to
be at home at the time, appeared with her Secret Service escort. When
a much larger showing was given later at the Savoy Plaza in New
York both of the Coolidges were present. By this time they had left
Washington, and *The New Yorker,* in "Talk of the Town," took
sprightly note of Mr. Coolidge's presence there with a number of
other notables:

Some people complain that we write too much about Calvin
Coolidge. They say he isn't worth the space. That simply isn't

true. Coolidge is as American as the dollar; he is one of the greatest of our nationals; and he is worth every inch of space we can allow him. This week, we are eager to report a small occurrence that throws light on the marvellous diversity and vigor of his post-presidential activity. We have just learned that, on Monday, March 31, busy though he must have been with his writing, his life insurance meetings, his fishpoles, his dogs, and with meeting publication date, he was not too busy to be one of the patrons of a lampshade exhibit at the Savoy Plaza.*

Mr. Coolidge was pleased that a lamp should become a symbol of his life. He put the reproduction on display in Plymouth, since the original was being saved for historical purposes. He used one with a copy of the original chimney on his own desk. And Mrs. Coolidge wrote often about the pleasure her lamp shades gave her. She was touched when Mrs. Woods made a shade with a tiny silhouette of young Calvin for Christmas, 1930, and she wrote to her at once: "I love it and the little silhouette! I knew, at once, that it was my Calvin. How sweet of you to think of that!"

Now that he was at home again a fresh crop of legends grew up around Calvin Coolidge's name. He was never the forgotten man, but he was not being used in an advisory capacity and his loneliness grew. He suffered from the emptiness that comes to the President when he has stepped off his pedestal. Ralph Hemenway was one of those who thought that he was never happy after his return from Washington. Mrs. Coolidge obviously was much more contented than he during those days at The Beeches. She had her friends, her community work, her flowers and dogs, her letters, her books, her doublecrostics, and her days were filled with bright activity. As of old she sewed and knitted socks for John and Calvin, with the radio gently purring beside her while she listened to the news, to baseball, or to Mozart, as the case might be. She followed baseball in her private sitting room, for Calvin did not share this interest. But she was frozen out when the Northampton Literary Club met at The Beeches. This was an ancient club, dating back to the time of the Civil War.

* From an article in *The New Yorker;* copyright © 1930 The New Yorker Magazine, Inc.

It had a small and exclusive membership of men and no woman had ever dared to stampede it. But Mrs. Coolidge had listened to so many jests from other wives about the sacred club that she volunteered to go out in the rain one night and peep through the dining room window of The Beeches to see what might be going on. "Such a quiet, restrained aggregation I never did see," she reported back. "Not a smile on one face."

Calvin could be genial enough upon occasion but he continued to baffle the neighbors. He disliked group conversation and when Grace's friends came in he would say "Glad to see you" and add "Going to take a nap." Then he would amble off to his own quarters to smoke in peace, or to enter in the small memorandum book he kept a record of every check made out and every bill paid. He refused to share in casual criticism of the government and he particularly disliked the scoffing utterances of expatriates or visitors from abroad who chose to snipe at American ways.

Every day he walked past the home of Dr. Melville L. Eldridge, who kept goldfish and pond lilies in a little pool in his garden. When the doctor halted him on one occasion to point with pride to the beauty of his lilies, Mr. Coolidge dashed his enthusiasm with the crushing comment: "I never did like stagnant water."

With the election looming up Otis Skinner, entertaining him at Meandering Water, remarked: "Oh, Mr. Coolidge, I wish it were you that we were to vote for in November. It would be the end of this horrible depression." A flicker of amusement passed over Calvin's face as he slowly replied: "It would be the beginning of mine."

The death of Dwight Morrow in 1931 was a blow to both of the Coolidges and they went to Englewood for the funeral. Like Mr. and Mrs. Stearns the Morrows had been an intimate part of their lives long before they went to the White House. Mr. Coolidge began to show fatigue at this time and his wife often caught him feeling his pulse surreptitiously. Some of his visitors thought that his color was poor and his step feeble, but others reported him in excellent trim. As the conventions of 1932 approached much pressure was brought to bear on him to campaign for Herbert Hoover. But neither Everett Sanders, who by this time was chairman of the Republican National

Committee, nor anyone else could get him to make speeches. He argued that he was ill prepared, since he was cut off from prime sources of information. On June 17, 1932, he wrote to Sanders: "You know I should be glad to do anything I can to help. My throat, you will remember, always bothers me and it is in such shape that I do not think I could do much of anything in the way of speaking. Just at present I am having some trouble about breathing again. I am going to Vermont tomorrow for an indefinite stay, where I can be out of doors, and think I shall be all right when I get a little exercise."

He made it quite clear to Sanders that he would never run for office again and he did not wish to have his name brought up in this connection. When Sanders visited him at Plymouth at the end of July and drove around the countryside with him, he was disturbed by his decline. "He was thinner and his face was paler than usual," he observed. "I had seen him daily and hourly at the White House for four years, and I knew the expression on his face and his movements almost as well as it was possible for anyone to know them." But he seemed to be greatly interested in the improvements he was making in his father's house. He added six rooms, taking particular care to make no changes in the essential structure. He puttered about quite happily, concerning himself with paints and woodwork and building plans. A spacious living room, a high porch to one side, and big windows from which he could take in the view he loved, were included in the plans. This was to be his summer home and his workshop for the years of his retirement. Sanders, watching the Coolidges in this quiet setting and remembering the hectic White House days, observed: "He was proud and happy with this mansion of ease without pillared posts or marble steps or official guard with golden braid."

Mrs. Coolidge added her own footnote to this in writing to the Robins: "As he grows older I think he will turn more and more to these peaceful hills. It is in the Coolidge blood and I think you will all agree that where he leads I follow . . ." And to Mrs. Hills she wrote: "Here we miss Calvin more than in any place other than at home but in spite of it we get comfort from being in the place he loved so much and near the little place where we tucked him up and bid him a last good-night."

Although Sanders on this visit begged his former chief to lend his immense influence to the campaign his arguments made no impression. However, he wrote an article for the *Saturday Evening Post* in which he spoke strongly for Herbert Hoover and characterized him as "safe and sound." He was optimistic about the Republican prospects at this time although Franklin D. Roosevelt loomed up as a formidable opponent. But Sanders had little hope of victory and pressed hard, not realizing how exhausted Coolidge was.

That same summer Stoddard visited him at Plymouth and found him reluctant to talk about politics, in spite of the pressure being put on him to help in the campaign. He asked him bluntly if he would speak at a Madison Square Garden rally in October. Finally he agreed to make just one speech, to last only half an hour. "Even one speech will be a strain," he said. "I am out of practice; it means big effort."

As he listened to him talk Stoddard wondered if he were actually enjoying the peace for which he had yearned. Two years earlier Coolidge had written to him: "You cannot realize how much I long for peace and privacy." He worried greatly as the date of the rally approached. He was dissatisfied with his prepared speech although Sanders thought well of it when he read it in New York before it was delivered. But Coolidge felt that it was ill-prepared and had been put together too hastily. He told Grace that he did not know how he would get through the ordeal. She and Mrs. Hills sat in the little room where he was born behind the store in Plymouth and listened apprehensively to the radio. His throat was sore and his wife knew that he was using his voice with care to enable him to finish. But it came through clearly and she thought there was much enthusiasm from the audience. He received an ovation and a shout came from the gallery: "That's Cal all right." But he was puzzled and rather upset by the burst of laughter that followed his remark: "When I was in Washington . . ." Later he told Grace that no audience had ever laughed at him before.

After he had finished speaking a woman rushed up to him and

exclaimed: "Oh, Mr. Coolidge, what a wonderful address! I stood up all through it!"

"So did I," said Calvin stolidly.

When he returned home he told Grace and Mrs. Hills that he thought it the worst speech he had ever made. They reassured him and the Republican leaders praised it highly and asked for more. He finally agreed to make a brief radio speech on the night before election. This was part of a three-way hook-up to the nation by President Hoover, on his way to California; Senator Capper in Shenandoah, Iowa; and Calvin Coolidge in Northampton. The aid of Mrs. Bailey, as an old Northampton friend and secretary of the Republican state committee, was sought in getting him to agree to this arrangement. She caught him after breakfast and he exploded with anger at the suggestion of another national speech. Later he apologized for the tirade he delivered that day as he marched up and down at The Beeches, explaining that he was suffering from a toothache at the time. In the end he agreed to speak from the library of his home, if no one were present.

Mrs. Coolidge was honorary president of the Republican Women's Club in Northampton but she did not take an active part in campaigning at any time. She and her husband learned soon enough that the Republican administration had run its course. Roosevelt was elected in the midst of tumult. Coolidge sat smoking on the porch of The Beeches, looking down into the valley, and pondering on the future. He seemed depressed. A month before his death he gave Stoddard, who had been the first publisher outside of New England to view him as a presidential possibility, some inkling of his feelings in an interview which appeared in the New York *Sun* the day after his death and later was published as a brochure: *I Do Not Fit in with These Times.*

Stoddard, who was ill at the time, had come from Stamford to meet the former President at the Vanderbilt Hotel in New York on December 14, 1932. He was struck by the fact that Coolidge seemed almost ruddy that day and walked with firm steps. When he had seen him in Plymouth some weeks earlier he had been feeble, walking like an old man, and his color had been poor. But his point of view on this occasion was firm and decisive. He reminded his interviewer that he had made up his mind at the start never to embarrass Herbert Hoover by comments on his policies, one way or the other, and he had stuck to his resolution. But he left no doubt in Stoddard's mind that he was turning his back forever on public life.

> I have been out of touch so long with political activities that I feel I no longer fit in with these times. We are in a new era to which I do not belong, and it would not be possible for me to adjust myself to it. When I read of the new-fangled things that are now so popular I realize that my time in public affairs is past. I wouldn't know how to handle them if I were called upon to do so. That is why I am through with public life forever. I shall never again hold public office . . .

These were his last published observations on public affairs. His associates thought that he seemed worried as he harped on the depressing business conditions and the downhill spin the country had taken. He greatly disliked a scoffing book about him that had just come out, and he had the air of an anxious man when he lunched with friends four days before his death.

"I am too old for my years," he told Charles A. Andrews, treasurer of Amherst. "I suppose the carrying of responsibilities as I have done takes its toll. I'm afraid I am all burned out."

He was in a pessimistic mood that day and remarked: "I now see nothing to give ground for hope—nothing of man. But there is still religion, which is the same yesterday, today and forever." Mrs. Coolidge knew that he was deeply depressed about the state of the nation. "I do not know what is going to become of us," he said to her toward the end. "I can find no place to rest my mind." And again, with the self-searching that plagues the sensitive man, he speculated: "If I had pursued other courses from those which I did follow results might have been different." Clearly he was a tired man, a sick man, and perhaps a disillusioned man as he watched the course events had taken.

His wife also knew how much physical misery he endured. She was aware that his health had been failing for some time, although a physical checkup shortly before his death had been reassuring. Later she disclosed that his asthma was unusually severe all that last summer in Plymouth. He was unable to lie down and scarcely a night passed that he did not have to use his nasal spray. She also felt that he was suffering from malnutrition as he dropped one item after another from his diet, hoping to improve his state.

"I was deeply concerned, but refrained from expressing anxiety, giving my attention to providing food which he could take without distress," she wrote. For many years she had coped with this ceaseless quest for digestive comfort but at the end his need had become acute. Knowing him as she did Mrs. Coolidge gave her own personal analysis of the factors that had worn him down: "His was not a rugged constitution, and the weight of responsibility which he had carried for many years took its toll. The death of our younger son was a severe shock and the zest for living never was the same for him afterward."

CHAPTER XII

A QUIET DEPARTURE

M RS. COOLIDGE returned from her morning's shopping shortly after noon on January 5, 1933. The Beeches was coated in ice. The trees were gaunt with winter hoar. She went upstairs to summon her husband for luncheon and found that he was dead. He lay on his back in his shirt sleeves in his dressing-room and his face had a peaceful expression. She knelt beside him and saw at once that he was gone. She ran down to the landing and called to Harry Ross, Mr. Coolidge's secretary: "My husband is dead."

The fact was as startling to the nation as it was to Mrs. Coolidge. John and Florence hastened to Northampton. Calvin Coolidge had drawn many headlines in his lifetime but none more dramatic or unexpected than the eight-column streamers that told the world he had succumbed to a coronary thrombosis. He was sixty years old when he died—with as little fuss as he had lived. Mrs. Coolidge thought the end had come as he walked to his combined dressing-room and bathroom to shave before luncheon. He had complained for several days of indigestion but this was more or less a chronic condition with him and she did not attach any special importance to it. He had risen as usual at seven that day. They had breakfasted together and at half past eight he had gone to his office. John Bukosky could remember nothing unusual afterward about his demeanor. He had merely commented on the state of the road as they drove along. He finished his letters soon after ten o'clock and told Harry Ross that he wished to go home. His secretary was under the impression then that he was not feeling well.

Grace was leaving to do her shopping when he returned. He asked her if she did not wish the car.

"No," she said. "It's such a nice day I'd rather walk than ride."

These were the last words they exchanged. He lingered in the library for a time, fitting a few pieces into the George Washington jigsaw puzzle that lay on a table. He spoke about Plymouth to Ross, mentioning the hay fever that had bothered him there in July and the partridge shooting that he had enjoyed later in the year. He went to the kitchen for a glass of water and he called downstairs to Bukosky, who was in the cellar. Then he went to his room while Harry Ross continued his work in the library, unaware of what was happening upstairs.

Mrs. Coolidge decided against an official funeral in Washington or Boston. She was sure her husband would have wished only the simplest of ceremonies. Arrangements were made for services in the Edwards Congregational Church in Northampton, and burial in Plymouth with his father, his son, and five generations of his ancestors. That night he lay in his own bed in a lighted room and Mrs. Coolidge was comforted by Mrs. Hills in an adjoining room. Few ever saw her weep or lose her self-control but for two nights her tears flowed without stint. In the daytime, with calm and fortitude she did everything that had to be done. She was quickly caught up in the web of ceremony that she and her husband had so disliked. She could not shut out the world as headlines, pictures, the panorama of their lives in the White House, her husband's rise to fame, his acts in office, his philosophy, his unique qualities as a man, were presented and discussed across the country.

President Hoover was with Henry L. Stimson, Secretary of State, when out of the blue he learned that Coolidge was dead. He was on his way out of office. Franklin D. Roosevelt was the President-elect.

Hoover immediately ordered thirty days of mourning for the nation. Senator Carter Glass of Virginia was addressing the Senate on a banking bill when he was informed of the news and a hush blanketed the chamber. Andrew Mellon was at sea on the *Majestic* when he sent off a message of sympathy to Mrs. Coolidge. Stearns was at his desk in Boston when he learned that his friend was dead. Nowhere was sorrow more intense and sincere than at Plymouth Notch. The news had come from Montpelier and had traveled through the valley so closely identified with Coolidge and his ancestors. Allen Brown, a farmer, tapped on Aurora's window pane at the family homestead. "Calvin's dead, Aurora," he shouted.

Newspapermen found Aurora weeping in the sitting room where he had taken the oath of office by the light of the lamp she had polished.

"Calvin was a great man, a good man and a kindly man," said Aurora, who had known him as well as anyone and had thought nothing of ordering him about, even after he became President. In the nearby post office Florence Cilley telegraphed to Mrs. Coolidge: "Accept sincere sympathies from Plymouth neighbors."

Flags fluttered at half-mast. Guns boomed at half hour intervals all day long across the country and in the evening there were slow salutes everywhere with forty-eight guns, symbolizing the states of the Union. The same front pages that carried news of Calvin Coolidge's death had headlines on his favorite Presidential topic—the budget. A rise in income tax and levies on gasoline were proposed as measures to balance the lopsided budget. The annual pilgrimage to the grave of another noted Republican President, Theodore Roosevelt, was carried through at Oyster Bay next day. More than 100,000 Chinese were fleeing from Japanese attacks. There was revolt in Spain and riots raged in Dublin. Christy Mathewson's widow had been killed in an airplane smash in China, an item that would have interested Mrs. Coolidge at any other time.

President Hoover and Mrs. Hoover arrived by special train on the day of the funeral. Charles Evans Hughes, Cabinet members, senators, diplomats, Mrs. Morrow, Bernard Baruch, Everett Sanders and many other distinguished citizens joined the official party. The

President-elect had sent Mrs. Coolidge a message of sympathy and regret, and had chosen Mrs. Roosevelt and James to represent him. Governors from adjoining states drove in to Northampton. Never had the plain oak pews of Edwards Congregational Church, named after Jonathan Edwards, held so notable a gathering. Calvin Coolidge had worshiped there the Sunday before his death.

The streets were lined with crowds well used by now to turning out for Coolidge events. There had been many triumphal occasions. But this was the end. There were no cheers now, only a deep hush. President and Mrs. Hoover rose to their feet as Grace Coolidge walked into the dimly lit church, white-faced, composed, her head held high. Her widow's veil did not screen her face and it was observed that she smiled wanly at the Hoovers. Outside the rain came down and it was so dark in the church that the lights were turned on during the brief service. Two hymns were sung. There was a Scripture reading. Chopin's *Funeral March* was played and then *Going Home*.

When President Hoover called at The Beeches Mrs. Coolidge urged him not to attempt the dangerous and icy ride to Plymouth. He stood looking at her, tears streaming down his cheeks, as he told her that he wished to go. In the end he conceded the point to Mrs. Coolidge and returned to Washington. Years later she recalled: "Once more I saw on the President's face the lines which are evidence of the heavy toll imposed by multifarious burdens. It was all so familiar to me. Fortunately Mr. Hoover was physically strong and had better recuperative powers than Mr. Coolidge had."

Light rain was falling as the motor cortege set off for Plymouth. Rolling slowly over rough roads it passed through villages where Boy Scouts and war veterans lined up at attention. Workmen in New England mills and factories dropped their tools and assembled in watchful groups. All farm work was suspended along the route for the time being, out of deference to a President who understood what farm work really was. Mist drifted down from the hills, but as they drove deeper into the Green Mountain region the scene turned stormy. Rain and hail enveloped them as they reached Plymouth over the narrow, rutted road leading to the cemetery. An icy wind blew down from the hills. The bronze coffin was borne up a steep path to the row where the name Coolidge appeared on many of the granite headstones.

Mrs. Coolidge, John, Florence and more than a score of relatives and close friends followed in single file. A temporary canvas shelter by the graveside protected the family as hail pelted down during the reading of the committal service. Mrs. Coolidge stood white-faced, with large sorrowful eyes, listening to the Reverend Albert J. Penner. When he had finished she lingered for a moment at the grave, then stretched out her hands to John who guided her down the steep path. After resting at the homestead for half an hour she returned to Northampton.

Snow came down that night and settled on the grave of Calvin Coolidge as old tales about him were revived in countless homes and restaurants across the country. It was Calvin Coolidge the man, not Calvin Coolidge, the statesman, who was remembered. It was his dry wit, not his acerbity; his steady purpose, not his political apathy, that were discussed as his widow set out on a new path, alone after twenty-eight years of marriage. She was now fifty-four years old. Her hair was graying. The lines of her strong face had deepened. Her life with Calvin Coolidge had had its share of drama. She knew that she could never sink into total obscurity again but she planned to remove herself as far as she could from the brass and cymbals of public life. However, she could not disentangle herself at once— messages reached her from around the world, testimony to the place her husband had held in public life. King George V cabled: "The Queen and I are deeply sorry to learn of your tragic and unexpected bereavement, and we hasten to assure you of our profound sympathy with you and your family in your irreparable loss."

Mussolini, President Paul von Hindenburg and Count Yasyua Uchida, among countless others, sent messages of sympathy. Memorial services were held at Smith College, Amherst and Plymouth. From coast to coast and abroad newspaper editorials gave Coolidge more generous appraisal than he had received in his lifetime. Inevitably they linked him to the era of prosperity, to the world that was gone. They noted the fact that he had remained an arresting personality to the end. His quips had been quoted; the homilies in his syndicated column had caused mild amusement. His dignified retirement and quiet ways had been honored. The public had not associated him directly with the travail through which they were passing. Herbert Hoover was bearing the brunt of the attack.

"In a very real sense the nation has lost the leader in whom it most completely trusted," the New York *Herald Tribune* commented. "Long before he left office the country had come to sense the warmth and sensibility that lay behind those tightly pressed lips and the deeply lined face." The Boston *Herald* pointed out that he came to the Presidency in the golden age of democracy and "left it as he found it, and probably his great predecessors would have been as reluctant as he was to disturb its tranquillity and prosperity."

The New York *Times* compared his death to the removal from the American scene of a well-rooted oak, "such was the deep impression made by his sturdy qualities, his homely virtues, the entire simplicity and propriety of his bearing since leaving the Presidency." Arthur Krock, who found him short of speech, dry in humor, unshakable in his convictions, typifying the traditions of the nation's founders, added his own special tribute to Mrs. Coolidge: "And no fortune which befell Calvin Coolidge was greater than that which gave him acquaintance with Grace Goodhue."

The Atlanta *Constitution* recalled that he "met with probably as little criticism as any Chief Executive in the history of the country . . . He was a unique figure in the annals of American public life, possessing public confidence in his sincerity and uprightness of character to a degree given to but few men." The Kansas City *Star* added: "Sneers by smart critics who thought him provincial had singularly little effect with the mass of the people. 'Cal,' they thought, 'always had his feet on the ground and was never swept away by hokum.' " His home-town paper, the *Daily Hampshire Gazette* cited his "dry, whimsical humor, his love of nature, his quiet generosity and his unwavering faith in divine providence." But his place in history had yet to be settled. "There was a very lovable side to Calvin Coolidge," said Bruce Barton in a radio broadcast on the night of his death. "He was unique. God broke the pattern when he was formed. There never has been any one like him in the White House. There never can be."

The President left his entire estate to his wife in a twenty-three-word will signed on December 20, 1926, while he was still in the White House. "Not unmindful of my son John, I give all my estate, both real and personal, to my wife, Grace Coolidge, in fee simple." He had set up a trust fund for John when his son married Florence Trumbull. His fortune at the time of his death was estimated at approximately $700,000. His father had left him a considerable sum of money and his writings had been profitable.

Mrs. Coolidge took up her daily round again, inwardly saddened, outwardly calm. There was much to settle and she was swamped at The Beeches with mail and demands of one sort and another. A President did not die without leaving countless echoes. Miss Mary Randolph arrived from Washington to aid her. Among the messages she most treasured was one from Pi Beta Phi. Replying to Miss Amy B. Onken, grand president, she wrote of her "two Calvins now reunited in life everlasting" and gave a revealing glimpse of her own feeling about her husband's death when she added: "My heart is so filled with joy for them who always understood one another to a remarkable degree that there is no room for sad thoughts of myself. I have John and Florence. No daughter could be more devoted and they are so near that they will come often for week-ends."

But Mrs. Keyes thought that Mrs. Coolidge's life lost both its purpose and its mainspring when her husband died. She felt that there had been strong interdependence between them and that while he "relied on her completely and comprehensively, in a different way she leaned on him." Even her dogs interested her less after this, and for a time she kept a white Angora cat, Omar Khayyam, "deaf as a post but beautiful," she noted.

The Beeches was dark and large and it oppressed her after Calvin's death. In February she went south to Mrs. Adams' home near Tryon in North Carolina. It was situated on the last mountain of the Blue Ridge chain, 3,000 feet above sea level. Karl S. Putnam, the architect who later designed a house for Mrs. Coolidge in Northampton, planned it and from its wide glass windows they could watch a magnificent panorama. To the north lay the Smokies; to the south the low country of South Carolina. Mrs. Coolidge, always sensitive to nature's beauties, delighted in the sunsets, and the constant variations of sky, cloud and light. She passed many weeks and months there during the next sixteen years until Mrs. Adams sold her place in 1949.

The echoes of the world seemed distant now as she read the news on her mountain top and recalled the days when Calvin Coolidge was a participant in world affairs. She found balm in the scene around her and wrote to Florence and John on a spring day:

> I see miles and miles of red fields prepared for the new seed. Here and there are patches of evergreen trees and green meadows with the Green River winding in and out. Beyond, the mountain ranges are tiered, purple and a little smoky today as a few forest fires are burning . . . I took my book and went out to the Easter rocks . . .

These trips to the mountains were deeply refreshing for Mrs. Coolidge. She had put in a good many years bowing and smiling to the public, and often doing things that were contrary to her natural instincts. She had coped with the nation's Executive Mansion, with many servants, with urgent social demands, with the spotlight she abhorred. Now she had solitude, a mountain retreat, time to recover her balance after the major events of a dazzling decade. She had always enjoyed association with people of all kinds but now she could pause for inner refreshment and self-development. She had time to read all she wished, to sit on the rocks with a book, to meditate, to catch her second wind. She slept out on the terrace. She walked in the woods with her shirt sleeves rolled up and soon she had her hair bobbed, although it looked exactly the same as before. She played cards—rummy and hilo jack and 500. She did jigsaw puzzles and double-crostics.

Mrs. Adams, a descendant of Sara Payson Willis Parton, better known as Fanny Fern, held strong political views and had a dynamic approach to life and community affairs. She was as violent a Democrat as Mrs. Coolidge was a Republican. She did her best to indoctrinate her with New Deal philosophy but Mrs. Coolidge listened and said nothing. She liked Mrs. Roosevelt and she did not share the prevailing Republican detestation of her husband. Mrs. Roosevelt was all the things she had not been and she watched and read of her doings with interest. She was not censorious of her fellow men or women. Mrs. Adams thought that she was inclined to be disinterested politically. "I am very vocal and there was regular propaganda on my side," she commented. "She'd always listen patiently, and sometimes she'd agree with me. If she had been trained politically, she would have been quite astute. I don't believe that anyone encouraged her, for Calvin felt that woman's place was at the sink."

But right back to her earliest knowledge of them on Massasoit Street Mrs. Adams had been struck by his devotion to Grace, although she had also observed that he never shared his political thoughts and opinions with her. She noticed that Grace rarely talked about the White House although she did make many allusions to her husband. She was particularly fond of her father and often quoted her mother on domestic matters. "She had a remarkably warm heart," Mrs. Adams said of Mrs. Coolidge, and the succession of scholarly women whom she brought to the house agreed with her. They had an amateur reading club of their own and took turns working their way through books, new and old. Mrs. Coolidge was always modest in presenting her views when in the company of intellectuals but although not of that mold herself she was uncommonly intelligent and well-informed. She enjoyed these discussions and was apt to knit and hold her peace when politics came to the fore.

New life soon followed in the wake of death and in October she was eagerly waiting the birth of her first grandchild. On October 1, 1933, she wrote to John that she was making a sweater and bonnet for his baby and had dug out young Calvin's crib. "I think about you much of the time and, always, my thoughts are happy ones," she wrote. "I know that these are precious days to you and I am praying that the heavenly Father may be very near to you as the day of days draws close. . . . My dearest love goes out to you continuingly."

Mrs. Coolidge had just been to a Wesleyan-Amherst game when the news of Cynthia's birth reached her late in October. She hastened to notify Mrs. Stearns and to make plans to see Florence and her new grandchild. At this time the young Coolidges were still living in their small apartment and Florence was doing all her own work. Coolidge pride forbade any more Trumbull assistance than gasoline to fill up their car tank when they visited Florence's parents on Sundays. Always delicately aware of family relationships Mrs. Coolidge suggested that the Trumbulls and Florence's sister Jean should have the first chance to see her and the baby. She felt that Florence must have quiet for a few days. She hoped that John would be there when she went to visit his wife and baby. Mrs. Coolidge had a horror of being an interfering or officious mother-in-law and she would hold back rather than impose herself in any way on John and Florence.

The child whom Calvin Coolidge had just missed seeing throve and grew into a tall girl with quiet Coolidge ways and deep reserve. Mrs. Coolidge always regretted that Calvin never saw Cynthia, for he was particularly fond of little girls. "The coming of a girl child into our family would have been the source of much gratification to him," she wrote. "He looked with a tinge of envy upon fathers of daughters and took an interest in their welfare."

John moved from the railroad to become head of the Connecticut Manifold Forms Company of Hartford, a post that he held until the late 1950s, when he retired and busied himself with a cheese factory at Plymouth, in the tradition of his ancestors, except that its size and modern equipment were far removed from the original.

In the spring of 1934, soon after Cynthia's birth, Mrs. Coolidge figured in the news in a fashion that she did not relish. "Where's Grandma, tonight?" she wrote humorously to John from Columbus, North Carolina. "Here she is, safe and sound and single, and in so far as she is aware, in her right mind. Somebody went crazy—but it was not she."

Irrepressible rumors were flying around that Mrs. Coolidge would marry Everett Sanders and live on his 500-acre estate in Maryland. They caught up with her in her mountain retreat in North Carolina, although she had had preliminary warning from Mrs. Hills, who had consistently denied the report. One day when she went on a hiking trip and picnic in the mountains with Mrs. Adams and three of her academic friends they were discovered sitting on some rocks, with a camping outfit and a pile of books. Mrs. Coolidge was knitting placidly when the car drove up. She quickly moved away from the group and turned her back on the woman reporter from a press association who had arrived to ask her point-blank if the marriage rumor were true. The reporter recognized Mrs. Adams but was not aware of Mrs. Coolidge, standing some distance away and partly hidden. One member of the group, who taught at Randolph-Macon College, quickly told her that there would be no comment on the report.

"We had a good laugh over the ridiculous episode and dismissed it from our minds to take up *Brazilian Adventure* again, the book we were reading," Mrs. Coolidge reported to John, whose wife had also been busy denying the rumor. But the story died hard and soon another reporter, who had been informed that Mrs. Adams and Mrs. Coolidge were hiking in the vicinity, caught up with them in a car and told Mrs. Adams that he had information that Mrs. Coolidge was on her honeymoon there. Again Mrs. Coolidge managed to elude the inquisition by ducking out of the car. "Florrie laughed and asked him if he took a third party on his honeymoon," she wrote to John. "She said she was sure he could not see me in the morning as I had consistently declined to be interviewed. The sum and substance of it was that she could positively state, of her own knowledge, that I was not married and here on my honeymoon. I cannot imagine what started up all this fuss."

There was substance, however, to the report that Sanders sought Mrs. Coolidge's hand in marriage. But Calvin's memory was green. She never forgot that she had shared a lifetime with him, and the better part of two terms in the White House. She shrank from further notice and carefully weighed the question. In the end she remained a widow. Sanders eventually married for the second time.

Mrs. Coolidge no longer had a grandstand seat in world events and was much relieved to be on the sidelines. Some of the prevailing stories wakened sharp echoes in her memory, however. All through the 1930s the country was struggling up from the depression. The Golden Years were referred to with cynical distrust. The Lean Years had tightened belts, choked off ambition, depressed all ages, and the rich and the poor had found a common talking point. Big plans were in the making. A social revolution, scarcely recognized at the time for what it was, seemed to be under way. The year 1934 was ripe with major change, at home and abroad. The Roosevelt administration was pounding along with drastic and novel measures. The industrial recovery program under NRA got under way, with West Virginia the first state to put all its employees under the blanket code of the emergency organization. The Blue Eagle appeared in store and factory windows across the country. The WPA soon started its spreading network of public works. Mrs. Coolidge jested gently over the multiplication of agencies identified by alphabet letters. In June, when the franking privilege came her way, she wrote to John: "I wonder if I come under XYZ of KLM or what—must be there are some letters which apply or that I come under one code or another."

The lawless era of prohibition had come to an end at last. There was ferment all over Europe. King Alexander of Yugoslavia was assassinated as he landed in Marseilles. Chancellor Engelbert Dollfuss came to the same end in Austria. Mussolini called on Gabriele d'Annunzio at Gardone Riviera and made peace with his antagonist. Hitler had risen to power as Chancellor of Germany, with a holocaust to follow. General Franco was making his early drive toward Madrid. There were strikes and revolt throughout Spain, and in Cuba Batista had risen to power through the revolt of the army. King Albert of Belgium died in a fall from a cliff near Namur. Diplomatic relations had been resumed between the United States and Russia.

But the event that interested Mrs. Coolidge most that year, from a human point of view, was the sequel to the kidnaping of the Lindbergh baby. She was bluefishing at Falmouth in October when her old friend, Charles A. Lindbergh, took the witness stand and identified Bruno Hauptmann by his voice as the man who had shouted to John F. Condon (Jafsie) in a Bronx cemetery about the ransom money for his child. Things moved briskly after that—to indictment, to conviction, to execution. She had many memories of Charles and Anne Lindbergh and deep feelings of sympathy for their suffering over their lost son.

Another great tussle involving a child was being fought out in the courts between Gloria Morgan Vanderbilt and her mother, Mrs. Laura Morgan, over the custody of little Gloria Vanderbilt. A happier echo of the times was the flourishing state of the Dionne quintuplets. The entire country talked about this twentieth-century miracle. In St. Louis a new municipal auditorium was dedicated, with the first grand opera heard in the Missouri city in seven years. In Minneapolis martial law was declared as the truckers went on strike. Dust storms and drought were destroying winter wheat in the Midwest at the rate of a million bushels a day. Three hundred million tons of topsoil were blown away and the atmosphere was darkened almost to the Atlantic seaboard.

John Dillinger, one of the more notorious gangsters of the era, was shot to death in Chicago. In the same city a large part of the stockyards was burned. The *Olympic* rammed and sank the Nantucket Shoals Lightship in a fog. The *Queen Mary* made her maiden trip across the Atlantic. The *Morro Castle* burned off Asbury Park with great loss of life. The United States open polo was played at Meadowbrook. At the same time the Civilian Conservation Corps operated work camps, representing another aspect of the national scene. Stock exchanges were brought under federal control. Banking laws were revised and bank deposits insured. Traditionalists cursed the President in their clubs as the New Deal challenged the established order. "The time has come," said Roosevelt in December 1934, "to take the profit out of war." On the same day his wife, already a peripatetic public figure, said over the radio that too much emphasis was put on the white collar worker. She advocated a year of training for manual work, and expressed the view that many parents who thought they were giving their children the best preparation for life by sending them to college "will really be giving them an opportunity to learn how easy it is to waste one's time."

In the same month—December, 1934—Mrs. Coolidge and Mrs. Adams passed quietly through Washington, with no one the wiser. Wild drums were beating there. New faces were on the front pages, in the public buildings. Dissonant voices rose in the clamor of the New Deal, with its rush of lettered agencies, its assorted officials, its professors, visionaries and men of varied political stripes. It was no longer the Washington that Mrs. Coolidge had known—moving at a more measured pace, with big business in high esteem, with the country prosperous, with good will enveloping the White House. Idolatry and hatred of Roosevelt and his wife were about equally balanced and grew deeper by the month.

It was strange to view the familiar scene and to drive to the entrance of the White House, which had been her home for seven years, without a flicker of recognition from the men on guard. This was how Mrs. Coolidge wished it. In twenty-eight years this was to be her only return visit to Washington. "I thought it was great larks to spend a night there undiscovered but I am glad that I did not have to stay," she wrote to John. She and Mrs. Adams visited the Freer Shakespearean Library, looked at the gowns of the Presidents' wives in the Smithsonian Institution, lunched unnoticed at the Allies Inn and drove around to look at the new departmental buildings. They called at Gunston Hall and explored the house and grounds. Mrs. Coolidge deliberately wore horn-rimmed glasses and no one in all Washington but a traffic officer close to the National Museum spotted her, in spite of her popularity while she was in the White House. He had been one of the Marines on duty on the *Mayflower*. She swore him to secrecy and "he was so pleased that I was almost glad he knew me," she wrote to John.

Traveling south they spent the first night at a small inn in Catonsville, outside Baltimore, the second at a hotel in Fredericksburg, and the third in Winston-Salem. A run of 165 miles through a downpour brought them to Columbus where their Chevrolet truck awaited them. Mrs. Coolidge and Mrs. Adams had many adventures along the highway. When driving north late one spring they left Tryon wearing heavy winter clothes. It was so steamy as they traveled along that Mrs. Coolidge decided to change. They stopped at a small store and she bought a thin dress off the rack, which she donned in the bushes. They were in the mountains at the time. They arrived in a disheveled state at a smart inn in Virginia where they had engaged rooms. After a close inspection they were told no rooms were available.

"Well, I engaged rooms," Mrs. Adams insisted.

"Yes, but they are all filled up," the major-domo replied. "There's a little hotel down in the town."

"Thank you," said Mrs. Adams. "I don't think we care to stay there."

Mrs. Coolidge was amused. They drove on until Mrs. Adams remembered that they had not picked up some important mail she expected. So she returned and said: "I wonder if there's any mail for Mrs. Adams and Mrs. Calvin Coolidge."

The man collapsed. "Oh, Mrs. Adams, I'm sure we could find some rooms."

"Thank you. I don't care to stay at this hotel."

He insisted on speaking to Mrs. Coolidge. Grace regarded him mildly: "Oh, no. You'll never persuade Mrs. Adams to stay. We can't stay. That's out of the question."

A well-known rabbi from New York appeared and offered Mrs. Coolidge his room. But the two women drove off, headed for White Sulphur Springs. The culprit had telephoned ahead and the bridal suite awaited them. Next morning reporters and cameramen descended on them. But this was the kind of thing that Mrs. Coolidge deplored. It made her reluctant to move from her own environment. She spent that Christmas, the second since her husband's death, in North Carolina with Mrs. Adams, Miss Florence Snow and other friends. They hung their stockings at the great fireplace. They had jokes and gadgets and a turkey dinner, music, cards and books. Mrs. Coolidge's favorite Christmas present that year was a picture of little Cynthia. "You are a wonderful group and I love you individually and collectively," she wrote to her family. "Your gift and her love make my Christmas complete. The air and the exercise seem to agree with us both and we are congenial companions."

In February she noted with interest in a letter to John that Herbert Hoover had joined the board of the New York Life Insurance Company. "Now he and Al Smith are both on it," she wrote. "Mr. Hoover seems to have been in fine fettle and he looked rested and well in the pictures. I was interested to read what he said at the Lincoln dinner that evening. I wonder if he has any idea that he can stage a comeback." At this time she was studying Mr. Hoover's appraisal of her husband, one of a number of articles done for *Good Housekeeping* by men and women who had known him. Mrs. Coolidge had been asked to edit and comment on each and she found some surprises in the material. It was unfamiliar work for her but her comments were frank and revealing. Mr. Hoover wrote of Calvin Coolidge that "his was a penetrating, analyzing mind which enjoyed stripping the tinsel from ideas; an acute wit and a large sense of humor over the passing event; a crisp capacity in narration of anecdote." He considered him the "incarnation of New England horse sense . . . endowed with certain Puritan rigidities that served the nation well."

Mrs. Coolidge was reluctant to interfere in any way with books about her husband. When Henry L. Stoddard was writing *It Costs to Be President* and asked for her help for his chapter "The Ten Years of Calvin Coolidge" she wrote to him on June 21, 1938: "You knew him better than I did and it seems to me that it is just as well that you should draw your picture without any suggestions from me." Dr. Fuess, his definitive biographer, had a number of interviews with her while he was writing *Calvin Coolidge*. She was of great help to him but when he had finished she told him that she would prefer not to read his book in manuscript, lest it should be thought that she had influenced him in any way, or controlled his work. "She was one of the most gracious, charming women I have ever known," Dr. Fuess said of her. "And she knew how to deal with people. Never has a First Lady been more discreet, more content to remain in the background, more removed from political intrigue."

They had their first meeting while Mr. Coolidge was still alive. They lunched together and, among other subjects, talked about Senator Lodge. Mrs. Fuess happened to be a Goodhue although she was no relation to Grace. The two wives walked about in the garden and discussed genealogy and flowers. At a subsequent meeting Mrs. Coolidge told Dr. Fuess that her husband was not by any means the silent man he was supposed to be but would talk at length about things that interested him. He was struck by her own reserve and realized that no one got too close to her.

There were times when he found her inscrutable in spite of a seemingly candid manner. She had much caution and she would study him with her extraordinary grayish-green eyes as if she were pondering whether or not to tell him something. "You could almost see her thinking 'I wonder if I dare tell him,' " Dr. Fuess recalled. Sometimes she did; at other times she held her peace, but on the whole he found her frank in discussing her husband. In his biographer's estimation Calvin Coolidge's special qualities were faithfulness to duty, reliability, discretion, tolerance, dignity and common sense, with a deep-seated regard for law, authority and tradition.

Self-confession books were just coming into vogue at this time and Mrs. Coolidge read with interest *The Story of My Life* by Queen Marie of Rumania. Cornelius Vanderbilt had put society and his mother on the griddle in *A Farewell to Fifth Avenue*. The curtain was rising on a new era of personal reminiscence. The revelations were mild compared with what followed, though they seemed *lèse-majesté* at the time. But one book that caused Mrs. Coolidge considerable grief was Ike Hoover's *Forty-two Years in the White House,* published posthumously. It was a best seller and was discussed across the country. The Chicago *Daily News* reported that "Walter Winchell and Samuel Pepys, hiding under White House davenports, could not have written a better extended gossip column than this masterpiece of subtly indiscreet revelation. Ike must have had his ear to every keyhole."

Calvin Coolidge and Herbert Hoover fared particularly badly in the line-up, and even the weathering Mrs. Coolidge had had when the book was serialized in advance did not wholly prepare her for the more extended revelations between hard covers. While the book was running in serial form she wrote to John:

Have you read the articles in the *Saturday Evening Post* written from Ike Hoover's notes? I had a long letter from Mrs. Hoover a day or two ago. She thoroughly disapproves of them and thinks that they are so foreign to anything that Mr. Hoover would have given out that she is quite stirred up over them. She feels that much has been put into them which have no relation to his brief notes as he jotted down the bare events of the day . . . Mrs. Stearns said that she read the first one and was so disgusted that she should not read any more.

Mrs. Coolidge at this time found more harmony in Gladys Hasty Carroll's *As the Earth Turns,* in *Mary Peters* by Mary Ellen Chase, a Northampton neighbor, and in Caroline Miller's prize novel of that year, *Lamb in His Bosom.* With her companions she read H. G. Wells and Charles Beard; *Mutiny on the Bounty* and *Men Against the Sea.* Sweeping the market at this time were John O'Hara's *Appointment in Samarra,* Bruce Lockhart's *Retreat from Glory,* Alexander Woollcott's *While Rome Burns,* Ruth Suckow's *The Folks,* Irving Stone's *Lust for Life* and Stark Young's *So Red the Rose.* The swashbuckling novel was about to have its liveliest revival since the days of Sir Walter Scott. The magazines were running the work of Edna Ferber, Willa Cather, Pearl Buck, F. Scott Fitzgerald, Sherwood Anderson and Katharine Brush, while such seasoned favorites as Ida Tarbell, Kathleen Norris, Temple Bailey and Margaret Deland were still to the fore.

But as the decade advanced a new school of writers was born out of the depression. The reckless, lost-world, supersophisticated touch of the 1920s faded into the stinging realism of such writers as James T. Farrell, creator of Studs Lonigan, and John Steinbeck whose book *The Grapes of Wrath,* published in 1939, mirrored the miseries of the migrant workers. From the depths of the economic collapse had sprung a new approach to the troubles of the submerged. The theater, the cinema, the world of books underwent convulsions and a new genre of writers battered their way to fame as the spokesmen of despair. The old favorites stood fast but their voices were lost in the proletarian clamor. Mrs. Coolidge read the new books as fast as they came out and was keenly alive to the changes going on around her.

In 1936, three years after her husband's death, she took her first airplane flight and her first trip to Europe—two things she had longed to do. She flew with Governor Trumbull, an enthusiastic aviator who went up in his plane every Sunday. "She enjoyed it," John recalled. "She was game to try anything and she loved something new, something different." In the preceding year Amelia Earhart had flown the Atlantic and Will Rogers had crashed with Wiley Post in Alaska.

When Jane Adams graduated from college and went abroad to study at the Royal Academy of Music in London, her mother decided to follow her to Europe and she urged Mrs. Coolidge to accompany her. Grace hesitated. She longed to go abroad but feared she could not travel without being recognized. The thought of running into publicity dismayed her. Mrs. Adams said they would drive everywhere in their own car and so pass unnoticed. But when Mrs. Coolidge's passport arrived it proved to be a diplomatic one and she was much upset.

However, they traveled from country to country unrecognized until they reached Switzerland. Mrs. Adams had written ahead to a Swiss town for reservations. An official of the hotel had gathered that the widow of a former President was arriving, so they were met with much bowing and scraping. Mrs. Coolidge went off to see their rooms while Mrs. Adams had the car garaged. When Mrs. Adams returned, the same official met her and said: "Mrs. Adams, would you sign for yourself and Mrs. Lincoln?"

Grace was heartily amused when the story was relayed to her.

"What did I tell you?" said Mrs. Adams. "They knew you were the widow of a President, but they moved you back to Mrs. Lincoln's period."

The diplomatic passport proved in the end to be useful, however. Writing from Majorca on April 14, 1936, to Miss Cole, Mrs. Coolidge said:

We stayed at Carcassonne until Good Friday as we could not get passage for Oliver until Saturday night. We drove from Carcassonne to Barcelona in one day—200 and some miles—crossed the border without a look at our luggage. The heretofore scorned diplomatic passport and the letters of foreign ambassadors to our country are now the objects of our deepest respect . . . The boat was crowded and our cabin de luxe smelly but we managed to put in a good night's sleep although short, for the boat docked at 7 a.m. Went to Palma in the bus to get Oliver Monday afternoon. We are so glad to have a car for drives about this lovely island. I shall not attempt a description as it is beyond my power and I should become too lyric.

Oliver was the name they gave their trusty car, an Auburn convertible phaeton that took the precipitous roads under Mrs. Adams' practiced hand. They traveled like two young college girls, picnicking at times, exploring out of the way places, taking things as they came, and always Mrs. Coolidge maintained the utmost good humor. They motored 12,000 miles through ten countries. It was the traditional tour—Florence, Venice and Rome; Paris and Avignon; Germany, Switzerland, Holland, Luxembourg, Spain, Sweden, Belgium and the British Isles. Edinburgh alone disappointed her. The weather was at its worst. She developed a severe cold and missed the beauties of the stately city. But she was full of zest again when they stopped at Abbotsford and were shown over the home of Sir Walter Scott. Mrs. Coolidge refused to look up dignitaries or use her position in any way and she passed through London like an unknown. George V had died in January and the young Prince whom she had entertained in the White House was unhappily seated on the throne, heading toward abdication in December and his memorable speech to the Empire on "the woman I love." London was already seething with talk about Mrs. Wallis Simpson.

Mrs. Coolidge wrote to her old friend, Charles Moore, of the National Commission on Fine Arts, about their tour and the buildings she had seen. "Pretty good for two old dames," she jested. "It was quite a surprise for me to find myself on foreign shores as I had assured myself that it was America first, last and forever for me. Now, like everybody else, I am all set to go again. In many ways Sweden was the high spot."

In this same letter she commented on Andrew Mellon's gift to the nation and hoped the work on the building to house his art would soon begin. She longed to go sightseeing with Mr. Moore to take stock of changes in Washington, she wrote. Mrs. Coolidge's interest in the world around her never flagged, and her trip abroad had only sharpened her taste for historical landmarks. After six months of touring she and Mrs. Adams returned with scrapbooks, pictures and memories. Full of enthusiasm for what she had seen Grace planned to return again but the second world war intervened. When she landed home on an August day in 1936 she was pressed for her political opinions. Franklin D. Roosevelt was on his way to reelection. She shook her head and smiled: "Well, we all are interested in politics—we should be. But I am not actively interested." At the moment the President was pushing cheap electric power and all the talk was of Grand Coulee Dam and the Tennessee Valley. These projects were held up by one faction as shocking examples of fiscal extravagance, but the President brushed aside the avalanche of counterstatistics while he talked of the more abundant life when electric energy would be plentiful and cheap.

In January 1937, Senator Carter Glass, a Democrat, introduced the bill that gave Mrs. Coolidge a pension of $5,000 a year, and it passed in record time. She had decided to sell The Beeches and for the time being she lived with Mrs. Adams and Miss Snow at 112 Washington Avenue in Northampton. "I think you have the mistaken idea that I didn't like The Beeches," she wrote to Mrs. Bailey, whose husband bought it. "But it was too much for one lone soul." Mrs. Coolidge planned to build a new house according to her own specifications.

While she was in Europe there was much talk about the fact that some of the Coolidge furniture had been sold at auction in Northampton. Her critics thought that no Calvin Coolidge item should end on the auction block. Actually she had merely disposed of some of the furniture they had had in their early days on Massasoit Street —an oak bedroom set, the couch built by her father for a wedding present, the Morris chair the President had used, and the oak bookcase he had had at Amherst. George H. Bean, an old friend, auctioned off the things. Later Mrs. Coolidge's critics learned that her intention was to give the proceeds to the Red Cross for the relief of sufferers from floods in New England. She had a passion for auctions. "My slogan is 'Never come home empty-handed,' " she wrote to the Robins. "My booty is sometimes amazing. My special interest is hands."

Of all the houses in which she lived Mrs. Coolidge perhaps was most attached to the old dwelling on Massasoit Street and to Road Forks, the brick and tile home that was built for her at this time across from Mrs. Adams' house. Karl S. Putnam and Frank S. Stuart drew up the plans for a most unusual type of building. The living rooms were all upstairs. She wished to be close to the treetops, she jested with friends, but they also knew that her horror of observation and prying eyes had caused her to plan a ground floor with only one small reception room. She built on land where she did not need the conventional cellar and she wished to avoid damp. A Dutch friend of Mrs. Adams, Dr. Alphonsus P. A. Varankamp, director of the Boymans Museum of Rotterdam, brought over from Holland part of a Hindeloopen interior, characteristic of the gaily painted houses of Friesland, around which Putnam developed a charming room that she used both for dining and as a sitting room. The house had a semicircular stairway, an unusual touch in Northampton, and the front porch was reminiscent of the Hopkins house on King Street, an excellent example of early American architecture. Mrs. Coolidge, who had always studied hands and thought them expressive of character, chose a doorknocker shaped in the form of the human hand.

There was some merriment—and also some publicity—over her attempt to have modern plumbing installed in her new house. A strict plumbing ordinance, enforced in Worcester and Northampton only, was at odds with the latest plumbing fixtures. The plumbing inspector was sure the penalties of the law would be exacted of him if he did not hold out for the ancient vent. Mrs. Coolidge was amused. "Go ahead," she jested. "I'll go to jail for it, if need be." The modern plumbing was installed. The inspector resigned and Mrs. Coolidge, to her dismay, found herself again in the headlines.

As the depressed and stormy 1930s came to a close people were flocking to the World's Fair in New York and the trylon and perisphere seemed the symbols of a new era. *Intermezzo*, with Leslie Howard and Ingrid Bergman, was thrilling crowds at Radio City Music Hall and *Goodbye, Mr. Chips* had dusted the classroom with romance. James Barton was playing his sixth year in *Tobacco Road*, and *Pins and Needles* was a blithe jab from the workers. *Abe Lincoln in Illinois* and *The Man Who Came to Dinner* were two Broadway favorites and Tallulah Bankhead was sizzling her audiences in *The Little Foxes*.

Abroad, the seeds of the second world war were being rapidly sown. Stalin's nonaggression pact and trade treaty with Germany in 1939 led directly to the seizure of eastern Poland, the attack on Finland and the further extension of Russian frontiers. The five-year plan was in operation in Russia and the party had been purged of Red Army generals and all members who questioned Stalin's authority. The Spanish Civil War was ending, a bloody contest that left lasting bitterness as a new dictatorship was set up in Madrid. Hitler was a growing menace and the headlines predicted that there would be war in earnest unless the United States took a firm stand.

An echo of the past for Mrs. Coolidge was the dedication in 1939 of the $1,250,000 Calvin Coolidge memorial bridge spanning the Connecticut River and linking Northampton and Hadley. A crowd of forty thousand turned out for the ceremony, with two thousand school children on parade. In christening the bridge Governor Leverett Saltonstall of Massachusetts quoted the man for whom it was named: "As Calvin Coolidge said, the forces of good are still superior to the forces of evil." There was nothing about the news of the day to bolster this belief.

To everyone's surprise Mrs. Coolidge was not present for the ceremonies. She was attending the wedding that day of Jane Adams, her friend's daughter. Three months later she celebrated her sixtieth birthday and replying to Miss Gertrude Heyman, who had sent her congratulations and commented on her red shoes in the Smithsonian Institution, she wrote:

> Surely sixty should be the "Age of Wisdom" but I often think that the older I grow the less wise I am. Dear, dear! The red slippers do seem quite frivolous but I do have to admit that I still have a pair in my shoe closet and, worse, I do sometimes wear them when I am feeling unsixtyish.

It was in the same spirit that Mrs. Coolidge urged the Robins to do something foolish once in a while. At sixty she had not lost her gay spirit or quick sense of repartee. Her hair by this time was steel gray. There were crinkles around her greenish eyes. But she moved about Northampton with the same old swinging stride and her smile spread warmth as she passed. Her grandchildren helped to keep her young. In 1941, when John and Florence were living for the time being in Orange, Connecticut, she nursed Cynthia through scarlet fever and wrote to the Robins: "I had the satisfaction of feeling that I was of some use to my children." She read *Little Women, Jo's Boys,* and *The Five Little Peppers* to the sick child—"which took me back a great many years to the days of my own childhood."

CHAPTER XIII

FRIEND OF THE DEAF

M RS. CALVIN COOLIDGE was a significant figure in the world of the deaf. From her early days as a teacher at the Clarke School for the Deaf in Northampton until her last years, when she served as trustee and president of the board, she gave lifelong support and dynamic impetus to the education of the deaf child. Her interest was personal and profound. She could spot a deaf child in any community and she knew precisely how to bring warmth and understanding into his lonely world. She had practical knowledge of the best techniques for his enlightenment and at the time of her death she was following with interest experiments in electronic aids being tried at the Clarke School.

It was not Mrs. Coolidge's custom to plead a cause or back a private interest while she was in the White House but her guests heard much about the deaf child, and she sparked a $2,000,000 endowment fund for the Clarke School before leaving Washington. Such men as Andrew W. Mellon, Edward S. Harkness, Cyrus H. K. Curtis, Jeremiah Milbank and many others responded generously. By the time the Coolidges left the White House the full sum had been subscribed. In the closing years of her life she touched off a centennial development program for the school, to reach fruition in 1967. With her handwriting wavering from ill health she sent letters to young Henry Cabot Lodge and to many of her friends of the past, urging them to serve on the national committee of sponsors, not just to raise funds but "to educate the general public about the enormous problems which face a deaf child." Helen Keller, Christian A. Herter, Leverett Saltonstall, Spencer Tracy, Gilbert Grosvenor, Herbert Hoover, Jr., and Claude M. Fuess were among those who agreed to serve on the committee, with Mrs. Coolidge acting as national chairman and treasurer, and Mrs. Russell William Magna as general chairman.

Her chief hope for the centennial fund was that it would hasten the time when deaf children might enjoy the same educational opportunities as those with hearing. She counted it a good day when joint degrees were given to graduates of the Clarke Teacher Education Department by Smith College, the University of Massachusetts and Syracuse University, to broaden the scope of their professional preparation. Her great concern for the deaf caused her husband to give special heed to all programs affecting the well-being of the handicapped. At the time of his death he was working with Helen Keller on a project for the blind. This work as a whole might be said to be Mrs. Coolidge's major humanitarian effort and it amounted to more than the public knew or dreamed. Her three years of training and teaching at the Clarke School had channeled the course of her life. There she met Calvin Coolidge. There she learned to understand the deaf child and to develop sympathy for his special needs. There she sat in counsel with such men as John F. Kennedy in the last years of her life and gave practical advice and enlightenment in a highly specialized field. It was all quietly done and after her death Senator Kennedy, who in 1961 would follow her husband to the White House from the state of Massachusetts, commented:

> As a fellow trustee of Clarke School for the Deaf in Northampton I have a strong personal recollection of her untiring devotion and labors throughout her life to this most worthy cause . . . Since her days in the White House she continued to epitomize the qualities of graciousness, charm and modesty which marked her as an ideal First Lady of the Land.

Mrs. Coolidge was a constant advocate of the oral method of teaching the deaf. She felt that the sign language limited them severely but that lip reading opened up wide channels of communication. Before her death she had the satisfaction of seeing Clarke School alumni scattered around the globe, with as many as 172 students enrolled in a year. She watched them move out into the professions, business, industry and the arts. She observed them as they learned to drive automobiles, share in team sports, take dancing lessons through vibrations transmitted from the floor, keep pace with their fellow students in academic subjects, go on to college, vocational school and full employment.

She visited the classrooms and stood beside their teachers while high-fidelity equipment was being tested. She followed the experiments with large hearing aids used on the group basis, and appraised the results of a five-year experiment which showed that the children who used them advanced much faster than their controls. She encouraged small children as they mastered sounds with their lips pressed against a balloon to catch vibrations, as a feather fluttered close to their mouths to encourage the correct use of consonants, as they blew out candle flames for breath control. She had watched the school grow, from the turn of the century until her death in 1957, when seventeen buildings stood on its twenty-acre campus on Round Hill and it conducted the most advanced work being done in electronics for the deaf.

Toward the end her interest was closely tied to the work of the Clarence W. Barron research department (named after her husband's old friend) in experimental phonetics, the heredity of deafness and the psychological difficulties of the deaf child. But above all she viewed the children always from the human point of view, as mortals needing special understanding. When she became too ill to go to Round Hill in person Dr. Archibald Galbraith, president of the Clarke School, and Dr. George T. Pratt, its principal, still went to Road Forks for advice on any problem large or small, certain that she would supply the practical touch. "She knew the mechanics by which the children hear and the gaps which leave them stranded," Dr. Galbraith recalled. "She was very much loved and respected. She followed each fresh development and was most alert to the advances made in electronics during the second world war and their potentialities for the deaf. But she never lost sight of the human side of the deaf child, the need for warm and sympathetic teaching."

Her wide smile, so well known to the country at large during the 1920s, was heartening to the deaf children at the Clarke School. "They loved her," commented Dr. Pratt, himself the father of a deaf daughter. "She understood them, and told me once that she felt the teaching of the deaf was a vocation to which one could give one's whole being. She had an instinctive understanding of their needs as well as a very practical knowledge of what was required. The fact that she was so interested made a good many people think our work must be worth while. Anyone she appealed to was apt to give his support but she would not lend her name to magazine stories or to any exploitation of her work for the deaf. She was quite firm about this. She was as fine a person as I ever knew, always gracious, charming and with enough time for the children."

When she died Dr. Pratt wrote to John that the world had lost its most famous teacher of the deaf but that her influence would be felt for years to come, "particularly in the general field of educating the public to the fact that deafness and its attendant difficulties are respectable." He had always found her counsel "wise and her decisions prompt, sharp and clear."

Mrs. Coolidge was instinctively responsive to the needs of children. In 1939 she raised funds to bring child refugees from Germany to the United States. That same year Lydia, her second granddaughter, was born to John and Florence. In 1940 she accepted the honorary chairmanship of the Northampton committee formed to raise money for the Queen Wilhelmina Fund for the Dutch victims of the Nazi invaders. In 1941 she joined the women's organization of the National Fight for Freedom Committee, sponsored by Mrs. Morrow. At this time the thunder of world events brought back to her many memories of the past. The days of insularity and fiscal economy had merged into an era of spending and world involvement. Massive national expansion had been crammed into a few cataclysmic years. The news each day was breath-taking, whether it came from Washington, London or Okinawa. Churchill, Roosevelt, Stalin were the world's Big Three as the sun went down with the rise of Hitler. London was blitzed, Leningrad was besieged. Pearl Harbor was struck and America threw its resources—men, money and supplies—into the struggle.

On December 12, 1941, Mrs. Coolidge wrote to the Robins: "How incredible it all seems . . . it will be a long hard conflict which will call for the utmost effort upon the part of every one of us but we cannot doubt that the forces which have truth and right and justice on their side will win. May God give us wisdom and leaders who will know how to establish the new peace upon foundations which will uphold it for long, long years to come."

After Pearl Harbor she devoted herself energetically to war work, helping the Red Cross, the civil defense authorities and wartime drives of all kinds. From 1942 to 1945 she became almost the symbol of the Waves in Northampton. During this period trim columns of girls in white and blue marched briskly across the college campus and overran the town. Smith College had been chosen by the United States Navy as the training ground for commissioned officers from all parts of the country. They made their headquarters in the Alumnae House. They lived on the campus and at the Hotel Northampton, but it was difficult to house them all, so Mrs. Coolidge rented Road Forks to the Waves for a nominal sum.

Soon they were using her Dutch parlor and getting to know her as a friendly neighbor. She had moved across the street to share the home of Mrs. Adams and Miss Snow, and she was conscious of the Navy recruits morning, noon and night. She attended their graduation exercises, reviewed parades, assisted in entertainments of all kinds, and was tea hostess to graduating classes of fifty. When Mrs. Eleanor Roosevelt arrived for one of the commencements, the erstwhile mistress of the White House was hostess to the current First Lady at a tea given at Road Forks.

Captain Herbert W. Underwood, who commanded the Waves, and his wife Frances were devoted to Mrs. Coolidge. They found her a "very charming, very interesting lady; only shy in the sense that she shunned publicity." When the captain drove her to New York to attend a review of the Waves at Hunter College he had trouble getting her to ride in a government car until she was persuaded that the mission was official and that it was her duty to go. She responded readily to the word "duty" but was scrupulous about government favors. In the same year she declined to serve as head of the Massachusetts Women's Defense Corps. That would have been too conspicuous for Mrs. Coolidge but she worked mightily on the home front and had a deep sense of responsibility for every phase of war work promoted in Northampton. "Every little inconvenience is a source of satisfaction to me for I feel it's a slight contribution to the business in hand," she wrote.

She might be found at any hour of the night or day at the warning center in the Court House, alert for trial alarms. She worked hard for the war bond sale sponsored by the city. She went to the station to see Northampton's sons go off to war. She joined in the Victory Book campaign of 1942 and campaigned for the salvage of fats, metal and waste paper. She set the pace in the days of gasoline rationing by pulling a little wheeled cart to the shopping section of town. In blustery snowstorms she might be seen bundled in a big leather jacket, with a waterproof hat, walking briskly to her destination. She carried her own parcels, waited her turn at the market, chatted with passersby, and continued to drop in at Rahar's Inn. She was served the first meal there after the murals with scenes from her husband's life were finished.

Her church work went on without interruption, whatever else she took on in the way of community effort. She still helped to run the church sales, to model aprons and foster drives. She applauded the energy of their young minister who was "stirring up the old bones and shooting plenty of grease into them." She wrote to the Robins: "He's doing a good job on me and I notice the old ones are not the only ones who are kicking up their heels." She organized the campaign for a new organ that resulted in $17,000 being raised. Mrs. Adams opened a Girl Scout thrift shop in Northampton and promoted a scout camp. Mrs. Coolidge gave her support enthusiastically to this work, although she was never as conspicuously identified with the organization as Mrs. Hoover. She was active in all Red Cross activities and on December 1, 1944, gave a good view of her varied activities in a letter addressed to Mrs. Adams, who was then at the Hotel Russell in New York:

> Am waiting at the British War Relief headquarters for the last report on organizations selling 6th War Loan Bonds. After they come in the Potter boy at the book shop will inscribe seven Treasury certificates, one for each organization to be awarded as prizes at the Grand Rally in John M. Greene this evening. They will then be put into frames and wrapped—my job. Over $400,-000 in bonds have been purchased. Orion and I are giving a dinner at the mess for the speakers and committee heads—fifteen in all . . . We finished the last surgical dressing yesterday and the rooms are being vacated today.

Orion was Miss Snow. Mrs. Coolidge had picked up her husband's habit of giving her friends jocular titles. This letter was from Mrs. Pot to Mrs. Kettle, the names used in badinage between Mrs. Coolidge and Mrs. Adams. After a long day's work at Red Cross headquarters Grace would take all her assistants to Beckmann's Restaurant to refresh them with a Dusty Miller sundae of coffee ice cream with butterscotch sauce, marshmallows and malted milk, a particular favorite of hers. Mrs. C. W. Hodges, of Beckmann's Restaurant, was the niece of Major Albert Beckmann, who accompanied Grace Coolidge and the class of high school students to Washington on the day she was snubbed for running her hands over the piano in the White House.

She was often seen in animated conversation under the low oak beams of Wiggins Tavern, dining with friends, entertaining her adopted soldiers, or fostering various community interests. She ran benefits and found time to raise money for the 75th anniversary fund of Smith College. From the start she failed to understand America Firsters and commented to the Robins on an encounter with a friend who felt strongly on this subject: "I told her a few things and asked her to let me know when she saw the light. And me, I'm usually so meek and mild. Shall we never grow up as individuals or as a nation?"

But in all of her activities Mrs. Coolidge shunned the spotlight and never permitted anyone to exploit the fact that she was President Coolidge's widow. The moment the shadow of her former fame fell on her she shrank back into silence. But by the spring of 1945 the end of the war was in sight. The lights of Paris blazed again for the first time since the beginning of the war. The Arc de Triomphe and the Cathedral of Notre Dame were lit by floodlights. The flame of the Unknown Soldier was rekindled and two million Parisians awoke from their dazed condition to respond to the glow of life again.

The Easter parade on Fifth Avenue was the gayest since the start of the war. Women laughed under tiny flowered hats and welcomed the return of hope and the near approach of peace. The Allies were sweeping on the Reich and the Russian armies were thirty-three miles from Vienna. Germany was pictured as a land of gloom. Hitler's defiant screams no longer spread terror. The charnel house he had created was now ready to consume him.

The Yalta Conference was still under discussion. The occupation of Germany was to follow a set plan, in three stages. The public was warned that the "American civilian heads toward a Spartan life with more shortages but no suffering or hardship." At the same time Bernard Baruch was predicting five years of prosperity. Suddenly the news came flashing across the world early in April that American troops had invaded Okinawa and had seized two airfields. "They walked in standing up" wired the first correspondent to record the fact that the troops had put through the most ambitious amphibious campaign ever attempted in the Pacific.

Preparations were under way at the time for the United Nations founding conference to be held in San Francisco late in April. Then lightning struck with the sudden death from a cerebral hemorrhage of President Roosevelt at Warm Springs, Georgia. The magnolia blossoms were falling, the dogwood was not yet out and the forsythia was in bloom in Northampton, Mrs. Coolidge noted in writing to tell Mrs. Adams how the news of Roosevelt's death reached her. She had been to a meeting of the People's Institute and had returned home just before six. Turning on her radio she caught the flash that the President was dead. Like the rest of the country she was stunned and wrote at once:

My mind turned back to 1923 when another President had died in office and all the events which followed the announcement. In many ways I am more sorry for Mrs. Truman than for anybody else. I wish that I knew more about the man who has succeeded, of his capabilities, his past record.

Roosevelt's memory would rest in the pages of history, most lauded and most vilified of Presidents since Abraham Lincoln, but at the moment all was praise. His funeral train rolled north from Georgia to Washington. April 14 was proclaimed a day of national mourning. The Trumans went to Blair House to give Mrs. Roosevelt time to move. They had been catapulted into the White House with the same suddenness as Calvin and Grace Coolidge when President Harding died in San Francisco. Bess Truman and her daughter Margaret, from complete obscurity, were suddenly on the front pages with every move under scrutiny. Mrs. Coolidge watched their course with sympathetic interest.

In churches, in streets, and in war plants men and women gathered to honor the memory of Franklin Roosevelt and around the globe the news of his death was received with a sense of shock. Mrs. Coolidge could picture the scene in the East Room as Mrs. Roosevelt stood by the bier with Elliott and Anna. The other Roosevelt sons, John and Franklin, were on naval duty, and James, on service in Manila, arrived only in time for the services at Hyde Park. With Mrs. Adams Grace attended the memorial service held in the John M. Greene auditorium in Northampton.

Roosevelt was dead but the war was not yet over. The charter of the United Nations had just been signed when President Truman told a startled nation: "An American airplane has dropped a bomb on Hiroshima . . . It is an atomic bomb. It is a harnessing of the basic power of the universe." Soon people could see for themselves on their television screens the mushrooming puff that initiated a fresh era of terror in man's affairs. Mrs. Coolidge reflected on the speed with which things had moved since the day in 1927 when Lindbergh made his electrifying dash across the Atlantic. These eighteen years had been packed with extraordinary events—a depression; social revolution at home and abroad; a changed map of Europe; barbaric cruelties in Germany; a ruthless war shared in by soldier and civilian alike; the landings of D-Day and the quick victory that followed; and the smoldering of unquenchable forces in the Orient.

Mrs. Adams and Mrs. Coolidge were in Goshen, near Northampton, when V-J Day arrived. They attended a service of thanksgiving in the local church. For the past three summers they had found rest and recreation at a cottage on the Goshen estate of Judge T. J. Hammond, Calvin Coolidge's former law partner. Here they swam and fished, and Grace cooked their catch over a wood stove. As usual, they sewed and read but could not take the long walks they had always enjoyed in the mountains. Mrs. Adams by this time had closed her Northampton house and Mrs. Coolidge had been staying at the home of Dr. Joseph D. Collins, who always escorted them to the baseball games. The Waves were now gone and Road Forks was being repainted and prepared again for occupancy.

The people of Northampton rejoiced with the rest of the country that peace had come at last. They turned out in an impromptu parade, danced the conga, shouted, whistled, blew horns and tossed torn paper along Main Street. The city had given 4,000 men and women to the armed forces out of a population of 25,000. There was deep relief but not quite the joyous abandon of the crowds that had celebrated the armistice after the first world war. The more thoughtful knew that strange new forces had been unleashed, that the future held fresh menace. A new age had dawned with the fall of the atom bomb. After reading John Hersey's piece on Hiroshima Mrs. Coolidge wrote to the Robins: "It gives one cold shivers and makes one question our justification for dropping the bomb on a thickly populated section."

But for the moment civilians relaxed. There was a rush for butter, cream, meat and sugar, for nylon stockings and gasoline, for all the necessities and luxuries of life that had been denied them in the strict days of rationing. War plants were dismantled and shiny new products flooded the hungry market. The GIs came home, to jobs, to welcoming families, to discontent, to readjustments, to postwar wounds and scars in their domestic affairs, as well as to unprecedented opportunities. They swarmed over college campuses, youths who had seen the world and suffered early. There were forty million automobiles across the country soon after the war ended and a whole new world of mechanical wonders. Even the sharecroppers had found a foothold. Housing developments dotted the cities and suburbs, and medical care was extended in scope. Science had opened up new worlds of discovery, from synthetic fabrics to nuclear fission.

For a time the mood was one of relief, but disenchantment followed. Reconversion led to inflation. Two coal miners' strikes in 1946 slowed down the nation's economy. Although a threatened railroad strike was headed off, labor trouble spread uneasiness. War contracts ended and up went prices, from newspapers and bus fares to food, clothing and housing. The Taft-Hartley Act was passed over President Truman's veto. General MacArthur was shaping a new Japan with a democratic constitution. The Atomic Energy Commission had taken over nuclear activities and a piloted plane had outdone the speed of sound. Mayor LaGuardia died and Babe Ruth gave a feeble valedictory at the Yankee Stadium as his own end approached.

Women were slow to return to their homes after the war. They liked the salaries they had earned, and missed the excitement of their war jobs. Some had had a novel taste of power. For the first time a President's wife was wielding international influence and flying around the world like a traveling ambassador. Juvenile delinquency was becoming a familiar topic and was thought at the time to spring in no small measure from neglected homes while women held down war jobs. Crime was on the rise, but had swung away from the gangsterism of the 1920s, when one thug murdered another, to the more terrifying spectacle of teen-agers murdering their elders or one another.

The jumpy nerves, frustrated ambitions and Freudian questionings that were stirring up womankind to a new unrest did not trouble Mrs. Coolidge. She seemed to move in a pool of peace and to foster repose in those around her. In 1946 she broke a lifelong habit and talked frankly to a reporter about herself. With a rare flash of insight she said: "I was born with peace of mind. It is a matter of inheritance, training and experience."

Her own granddaughters were growing up, going to school, and would be part of this new world. She watched them develop with the closest interest and in her last years wrote faithfully every week to John's family. She kept games and books on hand for the children and would arrive at their house with a carload of gifts for the girls. At this time John and Florence were establishing themselves in a new house in Farmington, not far from the Trumbull mansion. She wrote to them on February 10, 1946: "I do not much like your present quarters and want you to go ahead and build your house just as soon as you possibly can, even if you cannot get everything you want, and whatever it costs, even if it takes our last cent . . ."

But by the spring of 1947 John's business was flourishing and she was writing to him: "I feel proud to have a son who is in a business which can give a bonus to its workers and a dividend to the stockholders. You have certainly done well." John had sent her a dividend check which she said she would set aside to buy something for his new house. She watched the economic trends and had some of her husband's caution and concern for sound investments. She sometimes compared notes with John on business conditions. Coolidge had called the business of America business, but this was now an unpopular philosophy, much condemned. Big business was under heavy attack. The old League of Nations had been followed by the United Nations, and the network of international alliance that the United States had side-stepped was now tangled on its own doorstep. The San Francisco Conference had opened the windows on this new force in world affairs.

The larger historical canvas was now a constant factor in everyday living. The focus was shifting from Germany to Russia and the Red menace had taken form. Winston Churchill had coined the phrase Iron Curtain in a speech at Fulton, Missouri, and soon the term Cold War had slipped into the English language, helped along by Herbert Bayard Swope, Walter Lippmann and Bernard Baruch. People began to talk knowingly of the "containment of Communism" as the Marshall Plan took shape. For Communism was spreading noisily over the globe as Churchill in the spring of 1947 described Europe as a "rubble-heap, a charnel house, a breeding ground of pestilence and hate." Its crushing march throughout Europe was changing political alignments everywhere. Russia by this time had Hungary, Rumania, Poland, Bulgaria and Czechoslovakia under its yoke, and all closed off behind the Iron Curtain. But the Marshall Plan bore fruit, particularly in strife-torn Greece. And the airlift that had nullified the blockade of Berlin during 1947-1948 emerged as one of the more effective incidents of the Cold War. However, in 1948 Americans learned that Russia, too, had the atom bomb and the fact that the year was one of prosperity, inflation, high prices, high wages and peak employment did not blind people to this potential danger.

The issue was emphasized in 1949 when Whittaker Chambers and Alger Hiss faced each other dramatically in a courtroom with contradictory stories, and people across the nation discussed the "pumpkin papers," the typewritten notes, the history and personalities of two most unusual men. The extraordinary play of passion, the searing self-revelation of Chambers, the frenzied reactions the case aroused, made the two Hiss trials notable in jurisprudence. Each man had his defenders but all were sobered to see one of the architects of Roosevelt's policies marched off to jail handcuffed to a thief.

In that same year the atom bomb was exploded by the Russians; the Communists were defeated in Greece; Israel became a free nation; India and Pakistan tentatively made peace; and in the Orient the Communists proclaimed the People's Republic of China while Chiang Kai-shek set up government in Formosa. The New Deal had become the Fair Deal. The Point Four program was moving slowly through Congress—a plan for the distribution of knowledge and scientific aid around the world. General Eisenhower had resigned from the army and become President of Columbia University. Harry Truman had astounded everyone by winning an election that public opinion had virtually conceded to Thomas E. Dewey.

Like nearly everyone else Mrs. Coolidge had assumed that Governor Dewey would win. She wrote to John on November 7, 1948:

Connecticut and Massachusetts seem to have gone into the Democratic column together. Were you as surprised as most other people at the outcome of the elections? I do not think that anybody was more surprised than the two top candidates. We had a good joke on Florrie who had said that she was going to vote for President Truman because she believed in the two-party system and felt that the Democratic party should be kept alive. When she telephoned me next morning I told her how glad I was that she had breathed the breath of life into a collapsing lung.

In this same letter Mrs. Coolidge noted that she was reading Sol Bloom's autobiography, with the book propped up in front of her as she had her meals. She was finding it interesting. "He is an orthodox Jew and I think that Cynthia will be interested, as I was, in his definition of religion, 'True religion is no more and no less than the relationship between man and his God,' " she wrote.

Mrs. Coolidge often picked up thoughts from the books she read, to share with her family. That same year, while reading Ben Ames Williams' *House Divided* at the breakfast table she came on a paragraph which struck her as applying directly to contemporary conditions. Again she quoted it in a letter to her "Dearest Four:" "Time will hurt us. Had we been ready to use our time three months ago much might have been done; but we were not, and time is unforgiving. From now on, it will fight against us to avenge itself for our failure to appreciate its usefulness."

As the 1940s came to a close women affected the poodle hair-cut and the new Dior look. They glided around in long billowing skirts and ballet slippers. Storms raged at home—tornadoes in the South, a blizzard in California, an earthquake in the Far West. Yet there were great crops in 1949. The revolutionary farm machinery and new technology developed during the war were beginning to show results. Millions looked in on the second Truman inauguration through television. Harry Truman by this time was exhibiting some of the folksy characteristics that made a President a personality. Mrs. Truman pursued her way as quietly and discreetly as Mrs. Coolidge had done, although she did not spread such warmth. But Margaret had found a place for herself and the public showed affection for the tactful daughter of the White House, taking a sympathetic interest in her musical ambitions and romantic inclinations. No one knew too much of what Bess thought or felt but the President's reasoning was plain for all to see. His nippy temper, his sharp thrusts, his geniality were like summer and winter storms. He had made decisions of historic importance—such decisions as no President had ever been called on to face. Some thought that he had grown in stature.

Mrs. Roosevelt by this time was an active figure at the United Nations. On a February day in 1949 Mrs. Coolidge entertained a group of guests from the United Nations Secretariat visiting Northampton and Smith College. Mrs. Adams and she joined forces in entertaining them and transporting them from place to place. "No guests could be more fun to have and I have enjoyed them," she wrote to John and Florence. A Polish artist married to an Iranian delighted her in particular. She had written to John on this occasion thanking him for remembering her on young Calvin's birthday. "I do not feel that he is ever far away but on his birthday he seems especially near," she wrote, with the sadness that never left her.

Mrs. Coolidge's enthusiasm for baseball was at its peak at this time. Now that her war work was ended she no longer went about so much, but listened attentively to the broadcasts. Tuning in on Red Barber and Connie Desmond as they broadcast a Dodgers game in 1948 she learned that by sending the flap from a Post cereal box with a quarter she was eligible for a copy of the Red Barber edition of the 1948 baseball guide. With the enthusiasm of a teen-ager she wrote to John that not only had she received the booklet but also a letter from Red Barber that pleased her greatly.

"It means a great deal to us to know of your interest in baseball in general and the Brooklyn broadcast in particular," he wrote to her on May 4, 1948. "Bob Considine and the other Washington writers have told me of your very real interest in baseball and that when you went to the baseball park you went for nine innings or more, if necessary."

In writing to John about Red Barber's letter she must have reflected with amusement on her own frivolity, for she added a postscript: "Time is not wasted while I listen in on the ball game for I put it in on the chair seats." The needlepoint chairs that she made during this period became cherished possessions in John Coolidge's home in Farmington. On Easter Sunday, 1949, she wrote to John and Florence that she had not gone to the sunrise service for "the spirit was willing but the flesh was weak." She added: "You may have heard over the radio that I had picked the Rex Sox and the Braves to win the pennants this year. Bump Hadley had quite a spiel about it on his broadcast Friday night and mentioned the fact that he went to Mercersburg with you and Calvin . . . The game is now tied up so I shall have to stop and listen. The Underwoods sent me a corsage of two huge gardenias . . . I thought of you three girls with your gardenias."

When Joe Coleman, one-time star pitcher for the Philadelphia Athletics, was guest speaker at a men's club supper at Edwards Church the most astute questions tossed at him came from Mrs. Calvin Coolidge who had dropped in to listen to the baseball chatter. The press always looked to see if she was on hand for the big games in Boston and she usually was. Bob Considine, who admired her greatly, decided that her face broke into a smile "somewhere beyond the expression of Mona Lisa and short of an outright guffaw." He had often observed her as she sat intently in her box, following every move in the game, or leaning up against the railing of a hot-dog stand with her score card in one hand and a hot dog in the other.

In July, 1949, she and Mrs. Adams were sitting with Dr. Collins in a box next to the Red Sox dugout at Fenway Park when a spent ball hit Florrie on the side of her head. It was a glancing whack that raised a lump and left her with a sore head. Next morning she and Mrs. Coolidge shopped, then lunched at Huyler's. In the afternoon they went to see Fred Astaire and Ginger Rogers in a film, and the next day they took in a double feature, *Arrowsmith* and *Dodsworth*, with echoes of the era Mrs. Coolidge knew so well—the 1920s.

On their trips to Boston they now stayed at the Ritz, instead of at the old Adams House where Grace had gone as a young wife. She still liked to shop, to have ice cream at Howard Johnson's, to stock up on groceries at S. S. Pierce's, and to watch a good film. She moved about in Boston almost unrecognized and felt comfortably at home in the New England city. She could walk across the Common as unobserved as if she had never been the wife of the President of the United States. By the dawn of the 1950s the name Coolidge was all but lost in the din and clatter of New Deal and Fair Deal politics.

CHAPTER XIV

SUNSET IN NEW ENGLAND

WHILE THE WAR DRAGGED ON in Korea and the Red hunt became concentrated in the early 1950s Mrs. Coolidge pursued her way quietly in New England, trying to blot out at times the turmoil of the world through calm observation of the ways of nature. There was never a time in her life when she could not find refreshment in the outdoors. On a June day in 1950 she wrote to John:

A pair of sparrows have a nest in a hole in the maple tree by my back door. They are trying to coax their young to come out and learn to fly but the little birds seem to prefer to stay where they are and have their food brought to them. I have not seen any of them even stick out their heads. A pair of red-headed wood-peckers have a nest in another hole which they chipped out with their beaks. There were many chipping on the ground under the tree when they had completed the work and the edges of the hole look as smooth as though they had been sandpapered.

Something always needed to be done in the grounds, where dog-wood, rhododendrons, azaleas and roses bloomed in season and woodland scents poured in through the windows. The squirrels were

327

a problem and there were other invaders. On a bleak February day she wrote to John that "the evening grosbeaks have arrived in droves at my feeding bed and are eating me out of house and home in sunflower seeds." Indoors, she cultivated African violets in her last years and tended them as if they were children. She always said that they liked to be coddled, touched and arranged. But while she drew refreshment from nature she was not deaf to the pounding events of history. In February, 1952, she studied with interest the spectacle of three Queens, heavily veiled, weeping at the funeral of King George VI. She never lost her interest in the wives of rulers. "Oh, I wish I were going!" she exclaimed a year later when the coronation was held and Queen Elizabeth II, with traditional pomp, took her place as ruler of a much diminished empire.

Mrs. Coolidge was always stirred when a Presidential year came along. When both parties made bids for General Eisenhower she expressed the hope to John that he would run for the Republican party. She thought that he had all the qualifications necessary for a good President. The time of the Democrats was running out. They had been in power for five consecutive terms. The weather was increasingly stormy. The war in Korea was unpopular and was getting nowhere. Truman's recall of General Douglas MacArthur had not gone down well with the public and the warrior returned to great acclaim, voicing his classic curtain line: *Old soldiers never die; they just fade away.* But the attempted assassination of President Truman at Blair House injected a momentary note of sympathy and horror into the current scene.

Robert A. Taft and General Eisenhower led the field for the Republican party. The campaign issues were hot ones—war in Korea, international policies, high taxes, congressional investigations. Taft, soon to die of cancer, put up a stiff fight, but General Eisenhower, the popular hero, won the nomination and Adlai Stevenson moved into the field as his opponent. With sharp wit and polished phrases Mr. Stevenson drew the support of a group of zealous supporters who soon became known as the eggheads. Feeling ran high in the academic circles of New England but Vermont held tight to the Republican standard. General Eisenhower ran up a tremendous popular victory and Mrs. Coolidge rejoiced when the Republicans were returned to power for the first time since the days of Hoover. She watched with approval the discreet demeanor of the new First Lady as she moved into the White House in 1952 and noted with interest the President's Homburg hat on the day of inauguration. Calvin had always been zealous about top hats for state occasions. In fact, he had always been zealous about hats in general.

It soon was apparent that President Eisenhower, like her husband, would show concern for the budget. He made his promised trip to Korea. The war came to an end in the summer of 1953. By that time Stalin was dead at the age of seventy-three and his malign dictatorship was passing into other hands. Dr. Klaus Emil Julius Fuchs was serving a fourteen-year term in jail in Britain for feeding information to Russia from 1942 onward. Julius and Ethel Rosenberg were executed in June; suspects had been dropped from government rolls; and the arts were under intensive scrutiny. The tendrils of fear, suspicion and hatred that spread from this focus drew fire on many fronts. J. Robert Oppenheimer was suspended as consultant to the Atomic Energy Commission, clouds of suspicion surrounding him as a security risk. The eggheads argued over his fate as they did over that of Alger Hiss. He was one of their own and they clung tenaciously to his defense. In the nation's laboratories scientists moved quietly in a world of rockets, missiles and other weapons inimical to civilization and human life. The hydrogen bomb nullified much of their earlier work. Civil defense and air-raid shelters became matters of debate. The rapid spread of Communism gave urgency to many of the measures taken. China had fallen like a ripe plum into the Communist pattern. As Russia continued to have nuclear explosions "co-existence" took its place with "cold war" in the terminology of the day. Red China sentenced thirteen Americans as spies and President Eisenhower counseled patience.

At home the mood of the nation had changed. Investigations gripped the public imagination and stirred up conflicting passions at this time as Senator Joseph McCarthy niggled away at federal agencies for proof of Communist infiltration and Senator Estes Kefauver presided over a long parade of racketeers and master criminals. Frank Costello's restless hands became as familiar to the viewing public as Kefauver's drawl or McCarthy's spectacles and jolting drive in face of powerful opposition. The Fifth Amendment became the obbligato of the reluctant witness.

But Christmas, 1954, was one of unprecedented prosperity. The national income had reached a record-breaking point. The country was thriving economically, although uneasy to the core as Russia and China presented a solid wall of obstruction to the free world, and the unification of reviving Germany became a prime issue. There were strikes on the waterfront, scandals on federal and gubernatorial levels, and the public learned of a new hazard, the fall-out from nuclear explosions. Integration had by this time become a subject of hot debate, following the Supreme Court decision of 1953 that racial segregation in public schools was unconstitutional.

The soldiers came home from Korea to a world that was changing almost overnight, with nuclear developments and shifting alignments around the globe. There was much on the home front to dismay the observer, particularly the rise in crime. The aims and habits of the young had undergone a revolutionary change. No longer were they known as Flaming Youth, nor had the age of the beatnik arrived. The new generation studied the Kinsey findings, talked Existentialist and Freudian jargon and favored a realistic approach to life's problems. Many were thoughtful, studious and aware of world affairs. Mrs. Coolidge had seen young men come home from three wars and she viewed the new generation with optimistic spirit.

Everything was faster paced. More planes flew. Travel to Europe flourished. Students on Fulbright and other scholarships wandered amid the ruins of Rome and Athens, made love by the Arno, tramped through the Bavarian Alps again, explored the Scandinavian countries, and lived with foreign families. John Dewey and George Santayana were dead but a new generation of philosophers and economists fired the college campus. Science was pushed hard but the young were slow to switch their allegiance from the liberal arts to the uncharted field of nuclear discovery. However, some moved eagerly into this astral realm, and the school-boy dreams of a simpler age were surpassed by the realities of the 1950s. There were deeds of heroism in the air and on the sea. The conquest of Mount Everest seemed to belong to an earlier age. The trends of the times might be read into the names of the men who received the Nobel Prize at this time— Dr. Ralph Bunche, Winston Churchill, General Marshall, Dr. Albert Schweitzer, among others.

Public scandals were making people more ethics-conscious. Cheating at West Point shocked the nation into a realization that similar lapses might be found at other academic institutions. There was a recrudescence of religious feeling, too, as people turned to more church-going, to cults, to books on spiritual subjects, to the evangelism of Billy Graham. The popularity of *A Man Called Peter,* Dr. Norman Vincent Peale's *The Power of Positive Thinking* and Joshua L. Liebman's *Peace of Mind* suggested the quest for religious consolation, even while the market was flooded with the tough realism of Faulkner, Steinbeck, O'Hara, and others of the same school. Monsignor Fulton J. Sheen was giving dramatic emphasis to the teachings of the Catholic Church.

Mrs. Coolidge kept up with all the new books and commented on them in her letters to the Robins. She read Mary Ellen Chase's life of Abby Rockefeller in manuscript form. She had special interest in Mrs. Gutzon Borglum's biography of her husband because that "talented man" had always impressed her and she had met members of his family in the Black Hills. She had a stiff time reading F. Scott Fitzgerald and Sinclair Lewis. She could not understand why *From Here to Eternity* should top the best seller list. She found Van Wyck Brooks' *New England: Indian Summer* interesting but "very poorly put together." She enjoyed *Berlin Diary* and *The Raft.* She recommended Sumner Welles' *The Time for Decision.* She was touched by Ethel Waters' *His Eye is on the Sparrow."* She found the writings of Cornelia Otis Skinner and Emily Kimbrough ideal for reading aloud. She admired *How Green was My Valley* for the "lilt to the composition." She was drawn to the work of Honoré Willsie Morrow and Nelia Gardner White. She tried unsuccessfully to acquire a taste for detective stories "because our smartest people seem to revel in them and I am sure that I must prove myself sufficiently intelligent to hang on the fringes."

In the last two decades of her life Mrs. Coolidge did more reading than she had ever had time for as the wife of an active politician. The rush of postwar realism was taking hold of the book world and she did not shrink from the product of the hard-boiled school, although her own taste in fiction veered toward the novels of authors whom she knew, like Kenneth Roberts and Pearl Buck. She still liked the theater and when she slipped quietly in to New York with friends she usually went to a play or a concert. Broadway, as always, reflected the changing mood of the period, although there was still enough glitter and romance to offset the drama with political undertones, or the raw impact of Arthur Miller and Tennessee Williams plays. Ezio Pinza rocked the theater in a thrilling first-night performance with Mary Martin in *South Pacific,* reminding people that romance was not the sole prerogative of youth. At the other end of the scale Marlon Brando raised hackles with his dynamic posturings in *A Street Car Named Desire,* a Pulitzer prize-winning play.

Mrs. Coolidge liked to pick up a book or see a play or film that revived memories of the 1920s and she never failed to catch a Greta Garbo picture when it came her way. Both stage and television accented nostalgia, even while they projected an array of bright new stars. Grace Kelly's cool clear beauty had been recognized in *Rear Window.* Marilyn Monroe was showing up on the screen. Gary Cooper, whose beginnings she had watched, was still an idol. Mrs. Coolidge would never go to a play or picture in which characters representing Christ or Abraham Lincoln appeared. "Somehow that offends me," she wrote. Similarly, when reading *Love is Eternal,* she commented, "I suppose people called him Abe when he was President but I don't like the idea of calling the President by a nickname."

By 1954 there were 186 television stations across the nation and color sets had just gone on sale. The death of a King, a snub to a national hero, a riot in India, a fusillade in Korea, or the visage of a racketeer taking the Fifth Amendment before an investigating committee were transmitted in living essence to the American home. The average man could draw his own conclusions from what he saw, although a new breed of political columnist channeled his thinking more emphatically than in the age of Calvin Coolidge. The editorial note sounded ever more strongly in the press, on the air, on television, as conflicting opinions were flung at an attentive and, sometimes, a bored public. The names and faces of the commentators became as familiar as those of the cinema stars, and whipped up active response of one kind or another.

It was in 1954 that Mrs. Coolidge first took to watching television, although she still preferred her radio. She was sensitive to strident voices on the air and she felt that most of the good programs came after her early bedtime hour. But she never failed to react to good comedy. The industry was building up stars at a swifter pace than the cinema and theater. Jackie Gleason, Red Skelton, Bob Hope, Jack Benny, Fred Allen, Arthur Godfrey and Sid Caesar were more intimately known than the best that Broadway or Hollywood had produced. Hollywood felt the impact of this new diversion. Las Vegas lured the most glamorous stars, and the aging darlings of another era stepped back into view, from Marlene Dietrich in a glittering sheath that emphasized her famous shape, to unquenchable Gloria Swanson. Café society flourished, from such veterans as Barbara Hutton and Doris Duke to Zsa Zsa Gabor, Aly Khan and Porfirio Rubirosa.

The Boston Braves moved to Milwaukee and the St. Louis Browns to Baltimore. The Yankees won their fifth World Series in a row in 1953, matters of considerable interest to Mrs. Coolidge. By the following summer there were fifty-six million cars purring along the American highways. They were longer and glossier and came in rainbow tints. A constant struggle went on to find parking space for these sleek creations. By this time they had also accounted for a million deaths along the highways of America. Yet people on the whole were healthier. They lived so long that geriatrics had become a new subject to explore. The tuberculosis death rate had been cut 75 per cent in a decade. The Salk vaccine had dramatically reduced the score in infantile paralysis. Antibiotics of one kind and another were radically altering the medical picture. At the same time tranquillizers and barbiturates were in widespread use, and drug addiction was being publicized along with alcoholism. The psychiatric couch had become an expensive but prevailing fad, and mental health was getting a big push forward. The records of the trainees for Korea had made the public ask if the American youth was as physically fit as he needed to be.

But heart trouble made ever heavier inroads on a fast-paced generation, and Mrs. Coolidge was one of its victims. Her health began to fail in 1952. Her heart had troubled her for some time but an illness in the spring of that year had greatly weakened her and it was found that she could not take penicillin. After 1951 she never returned to Plymouth for her annual summer visit and John was conscious of a change in her. The first sign that she was failing was her disinclination to walk, which all who knew her recognized as an essential part of her daily life. She would fall asleep on a couch, an unfamiliar custom for energetic Grace Coolidge. But she was always reluctant to consult a doctor or to give in to invalidism.

In 1952 an elevator was installed at Road Forks so that she would not have to climb the stairs. She wrote to John that spring: "You will never know how much I appreciate your coming to see me every weekend while I was in the hospital. Your visits help me more than I can tell. You are a great comfort to me and I count myself a fortunate woman to be kin to you." She loved to have her granddaughters visit her. By 1954 Cynthia was twenty-one, a tall reposeful girl with the Coolidge features. Lydia was fifteen, a vivacious bronze-haired girl who had the knack of making her grandmother laugh.

Mrs. Coolidge prized every small attention from her family. There were visits back and forth between Northampton and Farmington. She exchanged notes with John and Florence about the girls' progress and education, about books, baseball and nature, about the meetings and functions she attended in Northampton, about money matters and investments. She sent recipes to Florence from time to time. She never intruded the personal element but wrote to her "Precious Four" with a light and humorous touch. However, after 1952 there were fewer meetings to record. She was forced to give up many of her activities and stay restfully at home. When John and Florence celebrated their twenty-fifth wedding anniversary with a party at the Country Club for their wedding guests and a few other friends she did not join them because "like a child, I get too much excited," she wrote, adding that she rejoiced with the Robins who drove their own cars and so were quite independent in their movements.

"Sitting out here on my porch with the sun shining through the autumn colored leaves on the trees I am in a mellow mood which I would like to pass on to you all," she wrote on September 28, 1954. The Robins had decided to dig into the past and recall their first love letters, and Mrs. Coolidge responded at once with the recollection of a boy named Roy Sturtevant who lived in Reading and "do I need to tell you that he had red hair?" She met him on her first trip away from home. She was staying with her Aunt Mary in Boston when Roy's mother invited her to visit them. She left her gloves behind her and when they were returned she found a wad of paper in one of the fingers. "My first love letter," she commented after a lapse of sixty-four years.

Dr. Collins, her unfailing companion at baseball games, died just before she did but for the last three years of their lives they made no attempt to attend the games but sat together following the World Series on the radio. But she was never forgotten by her baseball friends. When she could no longer attend the major games the president of the American League, who had always sent her tickets for the World Series, now sent her "amazing arrangements of flowers" on opening day. "I venture to say that not one of you cares a hoot about baseball but to me it is my very life," she wrote to the Robins exactly a year before her death. "I am not smart enough to follow the clues in 'who dun its' but have no trouble in following the play by play descriptions of the baseball games as the commentators bring them to us over the radio."

Mrs. Coolidge had always been so active that it was difficult for her to sit indoors and when the day dawned that she declined to go to Boston for an important baseball game Mrs. Adams knew that things were serious. At first Grace would not say why she refused. Then she confessed that she feared she might die in a public place and she shrank from the thought of the publicity that would ensue.

So for the last few years of her life she lived quietly at Road Forks with a household that included Ivah Gale, her girlhood friend; Lillian Carver, a bright young girl from Covington, Massachusetts, and John

Bukosky, the Polish chauffeur who had driven the Coolidges ever since they left the White House. Mrs. Coolidge was deeply devoted to Miss Gale, who by this time had become quite deaf. "She is more like a sister than any other friend I have," she wrote to the Robins on October 22, 1946. "She seems to like being here and I love to have her. She is the most unselfish person I know and has always lived for others." From the day she first welcomed her into the Goodhue home in Burlington, because she thought her lonely and friendless, Grace Coolidge was protective to gentle Ivah. Living her declining years in Northampton Miss Gale had many memories of a lifetime of kindness and loyalty from Mrs. Coolidge.

"I am not much of a housekeeper," she would say to Ivah and Lillian, leaving it to them to plan the menus, to prepare the food, to polish up the house. But she made their days merry with her laughter and her unfailing sense of humor about every trifle. The silver must shine and when she went down to the vault in the cellar and looked at some coffee urns she exclaimed: "Goodness, I haven't seen them since the White House days."

Mrs. Coolidge and Ivah were on different diets and Lillian tried to feed them all according to plan. But Mrs. Coolidge had whims of her own. At this stage in her life she liked Vermont cheese and soufflés, lobster, and light desserts. To the end she kept up a brisk exchange of recipes with Florence and the Robins. Her sweet potatoes, tomato marmalade, custard pie, chocolate pudding, spinach timbales and coffee soufflé were general favorites. She recommended to all her friends Mrs. Truman's Bing cherry molded salad. She passed along tips on surreptitious ways to use eggs in recipes, pointing out that she had had long practice in doing this for Calvin, who needed the nourishment but disliked eggs. She kept her larder well stocked with soups and other canned goods from S. S. Pierce's. She did her own shopping as long as she was able but toward the end she could not make the effort. She dreaded crowds and came home from the briefest of trips in a state of total exhaustion. She was always down for breakfast at nine o'clock but never made plans, because she said that as the day advanced she would lose all ambition to carry them through. Her knitting and her baseball, her books, her flowers, her radio, and her crossword puzzles kept her busy every minute, however. But she still went out from time to time to have her hair done. Friends begged her to consult a doctor as they saw the puffy state of her ankles, her swollen eyelids, the distended veins of her neck. But Mrs. Coolidge would laugh it off. Her letters still flowed out—to her family, to Washington friends like the Boones, to the Pi Phis, to old friends across the country, to men and women who had worked for her. On January 3, 1954, she wrote to John:

> As you know this is my 75th birthday. Your flowers sit here on a table nearby and I am enjoying them as well as delighting in the loving thoughts which they represent. They are arranged in a green vase, yellow roses, cream colored snapdragons, purple iris and acacia which scent up the whole room.

It was the same story on all the anniversaries. John never forgot and his mother was warmed by these remembrances. "I am blessed among mothers and beyond my deserving in having so devoted and thoughtful a son," she wrote on July 7, 1955, after he had sent her flowers on the anniversary of young Calvin's death. And again on her fiftieth wedding anniversary in the same year: "I cannot think of the words I need to tell you how deeply grateful I am for the gift of such a wonderful son. When you and Florence have been married fifty years I hope that you can celebrate together . . ."

As this was being written Ivah was listening to Dr. Ralph Sockman on the air. Mrs. Coolidge had just finished reading *Auntie Mame* by Patrick Dennis. She had found it mightily funny, she commented to John, and "by funny I mean provocative of laughter." One of the last books she read was *The Last Hurrah* and she noted with relish that James Curley thought it failed to do him justice. She took "a great shine to the sinner" when reading *Three Saints and a Sinner* and she found *The Nun's Story* interesting. Her handwriting was failing now. As she phrased it herself, it was "falling to rack and ruin from neglect and I do not feel at home with a pen." Her Buick had running boards, a foot rest and special handles to hold on to as she got in and out of her car, she wrote to Joseph McInerney on October 31, 1954. By this time he was working for the Ford family.

She recalled that Joe used to drive them in a Lincoln and that Mr. Coolidge had bought it from the Government when he left Washington. Now John Bukosky (known to the family as Johnny-Jump-Up) often ran her into town in his work clothes because he took care of the grounds and rarely had time to change if she was only going marketing.

In the spring of 1955 she was taken to the hospital in an ambulance and, in her own words, "was chucked into an oxygen tent." But on her return home, feeble though she was, she followed with close interest the Geneva Conference and wrote to the Robins on July 28: "I have faith to believe that more was accomplished at Geneva than we wot."

Dag Hammarskjold had succeeded Trygve Lie as Secretary General of the United Nations. Henry Cabot Lodge was emerging as a tough fighter at his post and John Foster Dulles was engaged in the diplomatic peregrinations that continued until his death from cancer in 1959. Three men notable in their fields had died—Cordell Hull, the statesman; Einstein, the scientist; and Robert E. Sherwood, the writer. But President Eisenhower had successfully weathered the severe heart attack he suffered in Denver.

Soon after this, in 1956, Mrs. Coolidge was deeply interested in a visit Florence paid to the White House. Mrs. Eisenhower had written to Grace when she became First Lady, urging her to visit her at any time and describing the White House as it looked at that time. But Mrs. Coolidge shrank from paying a return visit. However, she enjoyed a pleasant correspondence with the Eisenhowers and was particularly pleased when the President sent her a copy of the painting he did of George Washington, taken from Stuart's full-length portrait hanging in the White House. "As far as I can tell it looks every bit as good as the original," she commented.

But she regretted that Eisenhower did not feel more enthusiastic about the national sport. "I think that the President is making a mistake in not postponing his vacation for a day in order to throw out the traditional first ball," she wrote to the Robins on April 13, 1953.

Mrs. Eisenhower kept the coverlet Mrs. Coolidge made for the

Lincoln bed in a blue, satin-lined chest as a White House heirloom. When Florence was leaving for Washington Mrs. Coolidge told her to study the front doorway carefully, for she had always thought it particularly beautiful and usually paused to look at it when she entered. "I wonder who has the room that Margaret had," she speculated. "Perhaps Mother Doud has taken it over. I wonder how Mr. Daniel likes Papa Truman."

When Florence returned, full of enthusiasm over her visit, Mrs. Coolidge wrote to her: "I am pleased that Mrs. Eisenhower had the time to sit down and talk with you. How thoughtful of her to send the man after you with the lovely orchid." This was written within a year of her death, and her interest in the White House and Presidential doings remained undiminished. She was pleased when the great seal which used to be in the marble floor at the White House entrance was inserted in the molding over the door to the Blue Room, for many visitors had hesitated to walk on it. One of the last books she read was *The White House in Picture and Story* by Joseph Leeming and she commented on it to John in passing. That same summer President Eisenhower was operated on for ileitis and Mrs. Coolidge wrote to her son:

> I see from newspaper and radio reports the President's condition seems to be satisfactory to the doctors. His heart must be alright since he stood the general anesthetic with no trouble. I was much amused by his saying to the doctor "What a belly-ache!" It sounded so like a former President whom I knew.

Aurora Pierce had just died at Plymouth and in the same letter to John Mrs. Coolidge expressed deep concern over the end of their faithful friend and servant. "Aurora has been much on my mind since my telephone conversation with you, John," she wrote. "I wonder how long she had lain there on the floor before anybody got to her. It seems to me that she must have had a shock. I hope that she was not suffering." Actually, she had been taken to a hospital but she never recovered consciousness. Aurora had worked for the Coolidge family for forty-eight years. In her last days she sat primly behind a card table in front of a bay window, selling postcards and souvenirs. She liked to tell visitors the story of the swearing-in and to reminisce about Calvin Coolidge. The family honored her in this respect and made sure that no one disturbed Aurora in her operations. She was a privileged character. On winter days her tall, spare frame, bundled up in thick wrappings, might be seen as she knocked snow off the homestead roof. She bought one or two eggs at a time and saved every cent she made. She stuffed her money into a crock or a wastebasket, which was found to be remarkably well filled when she died.

Many of Mrs. Coolidge's friends had gone by this time. Both Ralph Hemenway and his son Kenneth were dead, leaving Mrs. Hemenway as lonely as she was herself. She was seventy-seven when she attended the dedication of the Calvin Coolidge Memorial Room at the Forbes Library in Northampton on September 16, 1956. She had shown great interest in the preparation of this magnificent room to hold books, papers, furniture, souvenirs and other memorabilia identified with Calvin Coolidge. Governor Christian A. Herter presided at the dedication ceremonies in the Helen Hills Hills Chapel of Smith College, Dr. Fuess was the speaker. Looking down at the shrunken figure seated beside John, Florence, Cynthia and Lydia, he said:

With Mr. Coolidge, to the great satisfaction of this community, came the lovely lady whom he had married in 1905 and who had lent to every office which he held, including the highest, the charm of her gracious, outgiving personality. We share with her today some of the rich memories which must come to her on this occasion.

She kissed Dr. Fuess when it was over and he thought how ill and emaciated she looked. Her large and still beautiful eyes shone dazzlingly from her sunken face. By the following February she was in the Cooley-Dickinson Hospital for treatment and when she returned to Road Forks it was clear that she would never be active again. She found a white violet plant awaiting her from Miss Cole. "I am writing to you from the Dutch room while I look at the beautiful white violet which you raised for me . . . I walk around the house and was out on the porch several days before the rains came. I need help in

getting up and down the two steps and the step on the porch." And
on May 12, 1957, she sent her last letter to Mrs. Hills: "Dear Lady
of the Rose Buds, The lovely rosebud which you brought me for
Mother's Day is in full bloom this morning. I sincerely appreciate
all the roses you have brought me. I am gaining strength day by day
but my legs are not very dependable yet . . ."

Early in July John was bringing his family back from Vermont
to Farmington when they stopped at Northampton to see his mother.
Cynthia at this time worked at Trinity College, Hartford, and Lydia
had just graduated from a private day school in Farmington. John
had only just got home when he was summoned back, but his mother
died twenty minutes before he arrived. The date was July 8, 1957.
She was seventy-eight years old and the specific cause of death was
kypho-scoliotic heart disease, a condition associated with curvature
of the spine. Mrs. Coolidge had become quite stooped, as many do
with age.

She had hoped to die as quietly as she had lived, but headlines
across the nation announced that a beloved national figure was gone.
Both President Eisenhower and Senator Kennedy, who was to follow
him in the White House, were among the first to send messages to
John and Florence. The President wired:

> Mrs. Eisenhower and I are deeply distressed to learn of the death
> of your distinguished mother. Although our contacts had been
> mainly limited to occasional correspondence, I, in common with
> a great majority of Americans, admired her tremendously. Mrs.
> Eisenhower had for her a particular fondness and joins me in
> profound sympathy to you and your family.

John asked that instead of flowers donations be given to the Heart
Fund. Federal and state officials gathered in the Edwards Congregational Church for a seventeen-minute service conducted by the Rev.
Richard Linde, who spoke of the virtues, the life, love, character
and service of Grace Coolidge. Doric Alvani, the church organist
who had often worked with her in parish affairs, played her favorite
hymn *Holy Spirit Truth Divine,* and one of her poems was read.

The four Coolidges sat in the family pew, along with Mrs. Robert

Lyman, of Atlanta, who had been Florence's classmate at Mount Holyoke. Admiral Boone had come up from Washington. Mrs. Coolidge's most intimate friends were there, as well as representatives of the Clarke School for the Deaf, Smith College, and two fraternity members, Mrs. George W. Westcott and Miss Sophie P. Woodman. Senator Saltonstall represented President Eisenhower and the cross of white gardenias and gladioli sent by the Eisenhowers dominated the flower-banked pulpit. The blanket of carnations on her coffin was from her family. Mrs. Coolidge had expressed a desire to be cremated, but her ashes were taken to the hilly cemetery in Plymouth where her husband and son were buried.

News of her death shared the front pages with headlines that a mysterious new jet bomber had been seen in Russian skies; that Khrushchev had left Moscow for a visit to Czechoslovakia; that two ex-aides of the United States had been indicted as spies; and that a mighty struggle was being waged in the Senate over the administration's civil rights bill. Mrs. Coolidge's public life had begun in the middle of a political storm and it ended with vast new issues at stake.

Editorial comment in the nation's press followed the news of her death. Partisan prejudice melted entirely before her unstudied charm and insatiable interest in human beings of all kinds, and she had no critics or enemies, the New York *Times* observed.

> Warm, outgoing, understanding and—in William Allen White's phrase—"above all amiable"—Grace Goodhue Coolidge was in many respects of personality the antithesis of her husband; but in one important respect they were alike. They were both unpretentious, unaffected children of the New England soil from which their forebears for generations had come . . . Mrs. Coolidge's death yesterday cannot help but recall a glittering era in American history, the "Golden Twenties"; but her qualities of mind and heart represented something far deeper and more lasting in American life.

Mrs. Coolidge left a will almost as brief as her husband's. It was a seventy-eight-word document to his twenty-three. In it she left everything to John and made him her executor. It was drawn up on January 29, 1936, three years after her husband's death. She had expressed a wish that her husband's birthplace should be turned over to the state of Vermont, and before the end of the year John and Florence had fulfilled her wishes. The homestead and all its contents were given to the state. John presented the deed to Governor Joseph B. Johnson at ceremonies which drew prominent figures from the political world, as well as a great gathering of native Vermonters. Joseph McInerey and Joseph Fountain, both of whom had witnessed the original ceremony, were there again to see it reenacted. The tiny hamlet relived its golden moment in American history, with the lamp, the Bible, and the sitting room just as they had been when the swearing-in took place.

President Eisenhower remembered Grace Coolidge in a touching way in his message on this occasion:

It is a matter of profound sorrow to all Americans that the beloved Mrs. Grace Coolidge could not have lived to participate in the dedication of this home which held so many happy memories for her. In setting aside this memorial Mrs. Coolidge might well have used her husband's own words: *Men build monuments above the graves of their heroes to mark the end of a great life; but women seek out the birthplace and build their shrines not where a great life had its ending but where it had its beginning; seeking with a truer instinct the common source of things, not in that which is gone forever but in that which they know will again be manifest. Life may depart, but the source of life is constant.*

The legislature approved an appropriation to restore the house to its original state. The Vermont Historic Sites Commission took over the development of Plymouth Notch as a Coolidge memorial center. Soon thousands of visitors each year were driving in to survey the homestead, the barn, the cheese factory, the little church where the Coolidges worshiped, the cemetery where they are buried, the Wilder House where the President's mother was born, and the vista of the Green Mountains that he loved. John moved the addition that his father had made to the house in 1931 up to a knoll overlooking the Coolidge farm to use as a summer home for his family. This left the homestead as it was. Close at hand is the Calvin Coolidge State

Forest with its 5,489 acres of woodland. And every mile of the roadway between the Notch and Woodstock Inn, where the Coolidges frequently lunched and dined, is identified with the family name. The shop and post office are separately run by Violet and Herman Pelkey. The Grace Coolidge garden, stocked with the simple flowers that Mrs. Coolidge loved, is a tribute to her memory created by the Ludlow Garden Club.

Mrs. Coolidge did not live to see all this come to pass but the plans were made before her death and she knew that Calvin would have approved them. While still in the White House she wrote to Mr. Hills: "Some day I hope to have the old farm house in Plymouth restored and furnished in the period with the quiet atmosphere of peace and contentment." She had lived through seven decades of storm and change and had moved unobtrusively from obscurity to national prominence. The world had changed as much between 1923, when her husband became President, and 1957, when she died, as in three previous centuries. But when friends deplored the prevailing trends she would exclaim with warmth: "Oh, but what a wonderful time to live in. I'm glad I'm alive." She savored life to the end, a fact about her that Admiral Boone observed. "She was philosophical and without any fear of death and I know she enjoyed life," he commented, with full appreciation of the qualities that had made her so sterling a figure.

In spite of her universal popularity and the absence of criticism to which Presidents' wives historically are subject, her immunity was by no means due to lack of character on Mrs. Coolidge's part. Time and again she exhibited the strain of quiet fortitude that flowed from her Puritan ancestors. In essence she was a practical woman with high ideals, a warm-hearted woman with common sense, a woman with rare charm and good will for her fellow men. Above all, she was a wife with perfect understanding of one of the most individualistic of American Presidents—Calvin Coolidge. To some, this in itself would give her a distinctive place in the gallery of Presidential wives.

NOTES

Chapter 1: *Springtime in Vermont*

Ralph Nading Hill, *The Story of the Ticonderoga;* New York *Times,* April 30-May 5, 1898; Robert Harrington Nylander, "The David Hubbard House, Hancock, New Hampshire," *Bulletin of the Society for the Preservation of New England Antiquities,* Vol. XLIX, 1959; A. Lawrence MacKenzie, "Schooldays of Mrs. Coolidge," Boston *Sunday Post,* September 24, 1936; personal recollections to author from Miss Ivah Gale, Mrs. Charles C. Guptil, George Marks, Mrs. D. Williams, Mrs. L. M. Valyeau, Rev. D. H. Sears, Mrs. R. Rea Reed, Mrs. Sophie Kerr Underwood, Dr. Archibald V. Galbraith, Dr. George T. Pratt, Mrs. Fred Ruble, Walter L. Stevens, Clarence Noyes, Miss Blanche Cole, Mrs. Florence B. Adams, Dr. Clarence S. Brigham, John and Florence Coolidge; Boston *Daily Globe,* July 10, 1959; *Daily Hampshire Gazette,* August 8, 1923, January 10, 1929, December 25, 1929, July 8, 1957; Claude M. Fuess, *Calvin Coolidge,* Calvin Coolidge to Colonel John Coolidge, January 28, 1901; Robert M. Washburn, *Calvin Coolidge; His First Biography* and *The Belle of Burlington;* Everett Sanders, "Last Letters of Calvin Coolidge," *Saturday Evening Post,* March 25, 1933; Calvin Coolidge on persistence, Everett Sanders papers, Lib. Cong.; Mrs. Coolidge to Edward Stern, January 7, 1939, Converse Library, Amherst; M. E. Hennessy, *Calvin Coolidge;* Agnes Wright Spring (Ed.), *The Arrow of Pi Beta Phi,* February 1936; *Good Housekeeping,* "The Real Calvin Coolidge, A First-Hand Story of His Life Told by Fifty People Who Knew Him Best," edited with comment by Grace Coolidge, February-June, 1935; New York *World,* October 5-10, 1905; Henry Wells Lawrence, *The Romance in Cal Coolidge's Life,* Coolidge papers, Forbes Library; Calvin Coolidge to his stepmother, May 13, 1894, Converse Library, Amherst; Walter Lord, *The Good Years;* New York *Times,* April 12, 1936, December 31, 1899, and Jan-

345

uary-December, 1905; Boston *Daily Globe,* July 9, 1957; F. W. Plummer, Boston *Daily Globe,* May 18-24, 1930; Lou Henry Hoover, "When Mrs. Coolidge Was a Girl," *The American Girl,* November, 1926; Calvin Coolidge, *The Autobiography of Calvin Coolidge.*

Chapter 2: *A Politician's Wife*

Calvin Coolidge, *The Autobiography of Calvin Coolidge;* Dr. Fuess, Mrs. Florence B. Adams, Mrs. Reuben B. Hills, Mrs. S. A. Bailey and Mrs. Francis Rugg to author; Governors' correspondence, Coolidge papers, Forbes Library; S. C. C. Watkins and Annie M. Hannay scrapbooks, Forbes Library; Agnes Macgregor Collis' personal scrapbook; New York *Times and* New York *Tribune,* 1905-12; Walter Lord, *The Good Years;* Grace Coolidge, "The Real Calvin Coolidge," *Good Housekeeping,* February-May, 1935; Grace Coolidge, *The American Magazine,* September, 1929; Cameron Rogers, *The Legend of Calvin Coolidge;* New York *Times,* May 1, 1959; John Coolidge, "The Real Calvin Coolidge," *Good Housekeeping,* April 1935; Edna Lawrence Spencer, "Lieutenant-Governor Calvin Coolidge's Life," *The Boston Review,* June 29, 1918; Ernestine Cady Perry, "The Real Calvin Coolidge," *Good Housekeeping,* March 1935; Lonnelle Aikman, "Inside the White House," *National Geographic Magazine,* January 1961; Mrs. Helen Woods, Lucius Beebe, Walter L. Stevens to author; Mrs. Coolidge to Ivah Gale, March 5, 1914 (courtesy Miss Gale); John Coolidge to author; New York *Times,* July 24, 1925; Dr. Fuess, *Calvin Coolidge,* Coolidge to Dr. George D. Olds, July 23, 1915, and Coolidge to Frank W. Stearns, November 1915; Calvin Coolidge to Frank W. Stearns, February 4, 1916, Stearns papers, Converse Library, Amherst; *The Arrow of Pi Beta Phi, History Number, 1867-36,* "The Twenty-third Biennial Convention," February 1936; Mrs. David D. Nickerson, Mrs. Francis Rugg and Mrs. Oliver Simmons to author; *Glendale Evening News,* June 1915; Calvin Coolidge, *Have Faith in Massachusetts,* address at Marshfield, July 4, 1916; Mrs. Coolidge to Mrs. Hills, January 2, 1917 (courtesy Mrs. Hills); Calvin Coolidge to Frank W. Stearns, August 15, 1918, Stearns papers, Converse Library, Amherst; *The Northampton Book;* Dr. Fuess, *Calvin Coolidge,* Frank W. Stearns to Dwight W. Morrow, January 8, 1919, and Henry Cabot Lodge to Theodore Roosevelt, October 7, 1918; Cameron Rogers, *The Legend of Calvin Coolidge;* Bruce Barton to author; Bruce Barton, "The Silent Man on Beacon Hill," *Woman's Home Companion,* March 1920; Alfred Pearce Dennis, "Calvin Coolidge After 20 Years," *Saturday Evening Post,* September 20, 1924; F. W. Plummer, Boston *Daily Globe,* May 18-24, 1930; William Allen White, *Calvin Coolidge* and *A Puritan in Babylon;* Boston *Herald,* September 12-14, 1919; New York *Times,* September 10-15, 1919; Mark Sullivan, *Our Times,* Vol. VI, Mrs. Coolidge to Mark Sullivan, June 8, 1935; Ralph W. Hemenway, "The Real Calvin Coolidge," *Good Housekeeping,* April 1935; Dr. Fuess, *Calvin Coolidge,* Frank W. Stearns to Coolidge, December 23, 1920.

Chapter 3: *Midnight at Plymouth Notch*

New York *Herald Tribune* and New York *Times,* March 5, 1921; Calvin Coolidge, *Autobiography;* *Daily Hampshire Gazette,* March 4, 1921; Edna M. Colman, *White House Gossip;* Mrs. Coolidge, "The Real Calvin Coolidge," *Good Housekeeping,* April 1935; Calvin Coolidge, *The Price of Freedom;*

Nicholas Murray Butler, *Across the Busy Years;* Alice Roosevelt Longworth, *Crowded Hours;* Dr. Fuess, *Calvin Coolidge;* William Allen White, *A Puritan in Babylon;* Mrs. Coolidge, *The American Magazine,* September 1929; Groucho Marx, *This Week,* February 19, 1961; Mrs. Coolidge to Frank W. Stearns, March 20, May 25, 1921, and July 7, 1921, Converse Library; Mrs. Coolidge to Foster Stearns, July 7, 1921, Converse Library; Mrs. Coolidge to Robins, December 2, 1921; Ethel J. Humphrey to Mrs. Coolidge, November 23, 1920, and Ruth M. Witherspoon, November 27, 1920, Coolidge papers, Forbes Library; Dr. Fuess, *Calvin Coolidge,* Coolidge to Colonel John Coolidge, May 10, 1921; Laurence Green, *The Era of Wonderful Nonsense;* Coolidge to Frank W. Stearns, Spring 1922, Converse Library; Dr. Fuess, *Calvin Coolidge,* Coolidge to Frank W. Stearns, March 16, 1922; Everett Sanders to White House gardener, September 15, 1928, Sanders papers, Lib. Cong.; Coolidge to Stearns, November 18, 1922, Converse Library; Edmund W. Starling, *Starling of the White House;* Mrs. Coolidge to Cyril Clymes, October 11, 1939, Forbes Library; New York *Times* and New York *Herald Tribune,* August 1-10, 1923; Joseph McInerney to author; "The Midnight Oath," *Ladies Home Journal,* April 1924; William H. Crawford, *Colliers Weekly,* May 25, 1923; Dr. Fuess, *Calvin Coolidge;* William Allen White, *A Puritan in Babylon;* Rutland *Herald,* September 4, 1959; Washington *Post,* August 6, 1923; scrapbooks in Forbes Library; William Howard Taft to Mrs. Taft, August 9 and 11, 1923, Taft papers, Lib. Cong.; Vrest Orton, *Guide Book and History of the President Calvin Coolidge Home at Plymouth Notch, Vermont.*

Chapter 4: *The White House*

Mrs. Coolidge, "The Real Calvin Coolidge," *Good Housekeeping,* April 1935; Mrs. Coolidge, "Making Ourselves at Home in the White House," *The American Magazine,* November 1929; Mrs. Coolidge to Mrs. Morrow, August 14, 1923, Smith College Archives; Coolidge to William Allen White, January 31, 1925, White papers, Lib. Cong.; New York *Herald Tribune,* July 9, 1957; William Allen White, *Calvin Cooldge;* Alice Roosevelt Longworth, *Crowded Hours;* Irwin H. Hoover, *Forty-two Years in the White House;* Edmund W. Starling, *Starling of the White House; Literary Digest,* August 18, 1923, and May 9, 1925; Alice Lockwood to Calvin Coolidge, October 28, 1923, Coolidge papers, Lib. Cong.; William Howard Taft to Mrs. Taft, November 9, 1923, and May 28, 1924; Mrs. Coolidge to Robins, November 26, 1923; Miss Ellen A. Riley to author; Dwight F. Davis and Mrs. Coolidge, "The Real Calvin Coolidge," *Good Housekeeping,* May 1935; James J. Davis, *Good Housekeeping,* May 1935; Mrs. Coolidge, *American Magazine,* September 1929; Washington *Post,* December 13, 1925; Mary Randolph, "Presidents and First Ladies," *Ladies Home Journal,* July 1936; French Strother, "A Week in the White House with President Coolidge," *The World's Work,* November 1923; Elizabeth Jaffray, *Secrets of the White House;* New York *World,* July 26, 1925; Mrs. Hills to author; White House bills, Forbes Library; Mrs. Coolidge, "How I Spent My Days in the White House," *The American Magazine,* October 1929; Harry Waters to author; Henry L. Stoddard, *It Costs to Be President;* Sallie V. H. Pickett, Washington *Star,* December 9, 1923; Springfield *Union,* July 13, 1957; Washington *Herald,* December 14, 1923; Washington *Times,* December 14, 1923; *Daily Hampshire Gazette,* May 13, 1925; Edna M. Colman, *White House Gossip;* Rev. Jason Noble Pierce to Calvin

Coolidge, December 11, 1924, Coolidge papers, Lib. Cong.; Mrs. Coolidge to
Mrs. Morrow, September 7, 1923, and December 23, 1923, Smith College
Archives; Washington *Star,* January 30, 1924; New York *World,* February 13,
1924; William Howard Taft to Mrs. Taft, April 19 and 21, 1924; Corinne
Rich, Universal Service, June 21, 1926; *Literary Digest,* April 5, 1924; Dr.
Fuess, *Calvin Coolidge;* William Allen White, *A Puritan in Babylon;* Morris
Werner, *Privileged Characters.*

Chapter 5: *Death of a Son*

Admiral Boone and Mrs. Hills to author; Elizabeth Jaffray, *Secrets of the
White House;* New York *Times* and New York *Herald Tribune,* July 4-10,
1924; Dr. Fuess, *Calvin Coolidge;* C. Bascom Slemp to Joseph McInerney,
July 7, 1924 (courtesy Joseph McInerney); Mary Randolph, *Presidents and
First Ladies;* Edmund W. Starling, *Starling of the White House;* William
Howard Taft to Mrs. Taft, July 10, 1924, Taft papers, Lib. Cong.; Alfred
Pearce Dennis, *Gods and Little Fishes;* Scrapbooks, Forbes Library; Funeral
Ceremonies for Calvin, Jr., Coolidge papers, Lib. Cong.; President Coolidge
to C. J. Hills, September 2, 1924, and Mrs. Coolidge to Mrs. Hills, July 7,
1924, April 2, 1924, August 7, 1923, August 3, 1924, December 9, 1924
(courtesy Mrs. Hills); Mercersburg Academy Year Book, 1934; Washington
Post, July 14, 1924; Washington *Times,* December 18, 1924; Washington
Herald, July 13, 1924; Washington *Star,* August 19, 1924; Calvin Coolidge,
Autobiography; Mary Randolph, "Presidents and First Ladies," *Ladies Home
Journal,* May 1936; John T. Lambert with comment by Mrs. Coolidge, "The
Real Calvin Coolidge," *Good Housekeeping,* March 1935; Mrs. Nickerson to
author; John Coolidge, "The Real Calvin Coolidge," *Good Housekeeping,*
April 1935; Admiral Boone, *Good Housekeeping,* February 1935; Mrs. Coo-
lidge to "Stewart," July 28, 1924 (courtesy Dr. Fuess); Mrs. Coolidge
to William F. Bigelow, July 1929, and Bigelow to Mrs. Coolidge, July
24, 1929; Grace Coolidge, "The Open Door," *Good Housekeeping,* October
1929; New York *Sun,* August 20, 1924; Chicago *Tribune,* August 26, 1924;
Irwin H. Hoover, *Forty-two Years in the White House;* Washington *Post,*
August 31, 1924; William Allen White, *A Puritan in Babylon;* William Howard
Taft to Mrs. Taft, April 26, 1924, Taft papers, Lib. Cong.; Mrs. Dwight W.
Morrow, "The Real Calvin Coolidge," *Good Housekeeping,* February 1935;
John and Florence Coolidge to author; Robert Considine, Springfield *Union,*
July 10, 1957; W. L. Chenery, New York *Times,* November 23, 1924; Mrs.
Adams to author; Mrs. Coolidge to Mrs. Morrow, November 7, 1924, Smith
College Archives; Dr. Fuess, *Calvin Coolidge;* William Allen White, *A Puri-
tan in Babylon.*

Chapter 6: *Red Dress, White Collie*

New York *Times,* March 5, 1925 and November 20, 1925; New York *Herald
Tribune,* March 5, 1925; Boston *Post,* March 28, 1925; Mrs. Coolidge to
Mrs. Hills, April 2, 1924, April 8, 1925, May 28, 1925 (courtesy Mrs. Hills);
Grace Coolidge, New York *American,* February 2, 1930; Irwin H. Hoover,
Forty-two Years in the White House; Edna Colman, *White House Gossip;*
Mary Randolph, *Presidents and First Ladies* and *Ladies Home Journal,* June,
1936; Mrs. Hills, Mrs. Rugg and Mrs. Nickerson to author; White House bills,
Forbes Library; Dr. Fuess, *Calvin Coolidge;* Calvin Coolidge to Mrs. John

Coolidge, Sr., January 7, 1920; John and Florence Coolidge to author; Mrs. Adams to author; Nellie Dalrymple to author; Vera Bloom, *There's No Place Like Washington;* Margaret W. Brown, *Dresses of the First Ladies of the White House;* Grace Coolidge and Ercole Cartotto, *Good Housekeeping,* March 1935; Frazier Hunt, "President Coolidge," *Cosmopolitan,* January 1926; Grace Coolidge and Howard Chandler Christy, *Good Housekeeping,* May 1935; Mrs. Coolidge to Robins, February 21, 1924, May 30, 1925, December 21, 1925; Grace Coolidge, "Home Again!" *The American Magazine,* January 1930; Mrs. Rugg, Mrs. Nickerson and Mrs. Simmons to author; "The Presentation of the Portrait of Grace Goodhue Coolidge," *The Arrow of Pi Beta Phi,* February 1936; Mrs. Mabel Scott Brown's ms. account of presentation, with Mrs. Coolidge's penciled corrections, July 18, 1942, and Mrs. Anna Nickerson's summation of preliminary arrangements (courtesy Mrs. Marion Simmons); New York *Times,* August 9, 1925; Washington *Star,* July 5, 1925; Washington *Times,* August 26, 1925; Charles Ray to Mrs. Coolidge, August, 1923, and Holbrook Blinn to Calvin Coolidge, February 4, 1925, Coolidge papers, Lib. Cong.; Grace Coolidge and General Dawes, "The Real Calvin Coolidge," *Good Housekeeping,* March 1935; William Allen White, *A Puritan in Babylon;* Cleveland Amory and Frederick Bradlee, *Vanity Fair;* Mrs. Coolidge to Mrs. Morrow, December 28, 1925, Smith College Archives.

Chapter 7: *A Year to Remember*

New York *Herald Tribune,* January 2, 1926; Dr. Fuess, *Calvin Coolidge,* Calvin Coolidge to his father, January 1, 1926; New York *World,* June 30, 1925; Washington *Post,* March 21, 1926; Frederick Lewis Allen, *Only Yesterday;* Edna Colman, *White House Gossip;* Grace Coolidge, "Home Again!", *The American Magazine,* January 1930; Grace Coolidge and Bruce Barton, *Good Housekeeping,* March 1935; Grace Coolidge and Alfred E. Smith, *Good Housekeeping,* February 1925; Calvin Coolidge, *The Price of Freedom;* Mrs. Nickerson to author; New York *Sun,* September 22, 1926; Edmund W. Starling, *Starling of the White House;* Mary Randolph, *Ladies Home Journal,* May and June 1936; Mrs. Nickerson, Mrs. Rena Ridenour, Mrs. Elizabeth A. Bonsteel, Miss Nellie Dalrymple, Miss Ellen A. Riley and Harry Waters to author; Grace Coolidge, "How I Spent My Days at the White House," and "Our Family Pets," *American Magazine,* October and December 1929; William Allen White, *A Puritan in Babylon;* Mrs. Coolidge to Robins, September 12, 1925 and April 3, 1926; John Coolidge and Mrs. Hills to author.

Chapter 8: *A Jester and a Queen*

Will Rogers to Everett Sanders, September 30, 1926, Sanders papers, Lib. Cong.; Will Rogers, "Letters of a Self-Made Diplomat to His President" and "A Letter from a Self-Made Diplomat to Constituents," *Saturday Evening Post,* October 2, 1926, and January 8, 1927; Mary Randolph, *Ladies Home Journal,* June 1936; Irwin H. Hoover, *Forty-two Years in the White House;* New York *Times, Herald Tribune* and Washington *Herald,* October 19 and 20, 1926; Grace Coolidge, *Good Housekeeping,* February and March 1935; Henry Morton Robinson, *Fantastic Interim;* Frederick Lewis Allen, *Only Yesterday;* Lloyd Morris, *Postscript to Yesterday;* Eric F. Goldman, *The Crucial Decade;* Isabel Leighton (Ed.), *The Aspirin Age;* John Gunther and

Bernard Quint, *Days to Remember;* Mrs. Coolidge and Bernard Baruch, *Good Housekeeping,* February 1935; Mrs. Coolidge, "Making Ourselves at Home in the White House," *The American Magazine,* November 1929; John Coolidge to author; official papers on Lindbergh reception, Coolidge papers, Lib. Cong.; New York *Times, Herald Tribune* and Washington *Star,* June 1-30, 1927; Harold Nicholson, *Dwight Morrow;* Mrs. Coolidge to Mrs. Hills, March 10, 1927 (courtesy Mrs. Hills).

Chapter 9: *"I Do Not Choose to Run"*

Everett Sanders statement on Calvin Coolidge's declination, November 22, 1938, and text of Coolidge announcement, Sanders papers, Lib. Cong.; Mrs. Coolidge, *The American Magazine,* September 1929; John Coolidge to author; Dr. Fuess, *Calvin Coolidge;* William Allen White, *A Puritan in Babylon;* New York *Times, Herald Tribune,* Washington *Post,* August 1-31, 1927; Boston *Herald,* September 27, 1928; *Daily Hampshire Gazette,* August 19, 1929; Arthur Capper, Boston *Globe,* August 18, 1927; Boston *Transcript,* August 3, 1927; Mrs. Coolidge and Mrs. Morrow, *Good Housekeeping,* February 1935; Mrs. Coolidge and Edward T. Clark, *Good Housekeeping,* March 1935; Mrs. Coolidge and Curtis D. Wilbur, *Good Housekeeping,* April 1935; Edmund W. Starling, *Starling of the White House;* William Howard Taft to Robert Taft, August 16, 1927, and June 5, 1927, Taft papers, Lib. Cong.; Philadelphia *Public Ledger,* July 17, 1927; Washington *Star,* June 23, 1927; Washington *Post,* June 28, 1927; Miss Dalrymple to author; Calvin Coolidge, *Autobiography;* Coolidge Christmas message, 1927, Coolidge papers, Lib. Cong.

Chapter 10: *A Trip to Cuba*

Official documents on trip to Cuba, January 1928, Coolidge papers, Lib. Cong.; *Literary Digest,* October 22, 1927; William Howard Taft to Mrs. Taft, May 26, 1928, Taft papers, Lib. Cong.; Mrs. Hills to author; John and Florence Coolidge to author; Mrs. Coolidge to John, June 10, 1956 (courtesy John and Florence Coolidge); *Congregationalist and Herald of Gospel Liberty,* January 1953; Mrs. Coolidge to Frank W. Stearns, May 25, 1921, Converse Library; Irwin Hoover, *Forty-two Years in the White House;* Burlington *Daily News,* September 20, 1928; Boston *Herald,* June 16 and 19, 1928; Boston *Globe,* August 3, 1928; Boston *Transcript,* August 8, 1928; Mrs. Coolidge, *The American Magazine,* September 1929; Mrs. Nickerson to author; Coolidge to Park Pollard, September 1928, Lib. Cong.; Tribute to Vermont, Coolidge speech at Bennington, September 21, 1928, Forbes Library; Mrs. Coolidge and Roy West, *Good Housekeeping,* February 1935; Edmund W. Starling, *Starling of the White House;* Dr. Fuess, *Calvin Coolidge;* H. L. Mencken, *The American Mercury,* April 1933; William Allen White, *Calvin Coolidge;* Dr. Fuess, *Calvin Coolidge;* Mrs. S. A. Bailey to author; Anne Hard, *Pictorial Review,* September 1926; Princess Cantacuzene, "The First Lady of the Land at Home," *Ladies Home Journal,* June 1924; Alice Booth, "America's Twelve Greatest Women," *Good Housekeeping,* July 1931; Mrs. Coolidge to Mrs. Hills, June 20, 1927, June 16 and 19, 1928, August 6, 1928, September 28 and 31, 1928, January 7, 1929 (courtesy Mrs. Hills); Mrs. Coolidge to Robins, January 19, 1928, and September 1, 1928.

Chapter 11: *Farewell to Washington*

Grace Coolidge, "Home Again!" *The American Magazine,* January 1930; New York *Times,* New York *Herald Tribune* and Washington *Star,* March 4, 5 and 6, 1929; Mary Randolph, *Presidents and First Ladies;* Irwin H. Hoover, *Forty-two Years in the White House;* Mrs. Coolidge to John, August 25, 1929, December 11, 1934 and April 20, 1935; Mrs. Coolidge to Florence Coolidge, March 18, 1956 (courtesy John and Florence Coolidge); John and Florence Coolidge to author; Edmund W. Starling, *Starling of the White House;* New York *Times* and *Herald Tribune,* September 23-30, 1929; *Daily Hampshire Gazette,* September 29, 1926; C. H. Lyman notes, Forbes Library; Dr. Clarence S. Brigham to author; Bruce Barton, *The American Magazine,* March 1931; Mrs. Adams to author; David C. Mearns to author; J. L. Harrison to Mrs. Coolidge, November 21, 1935, and April 21, 1936; Mrs. Coolidge to Harrison, May 21, 1936; Forbes Library; Mrs. Coolidge, *Good Housekeeping,* February and June 1935; Frederick Lewis Allen, *Only Yesterday;* John Gunther and Bernard Quint, *Days to Remember;* Laurence Greene, *The Era of Wonderful Nonsense;* Calvin Coolidge, "Reflections from Private Life," *Cosmopolitan,* May 1930; Henry L. Stoddard interview with Calvin Coolidge, New York *Sun,* January 6, 1933; Stoddard, "As I Knew Them"; Bruce Barton and Mrs. S. A. Bailey to author; Mrs. Coolidge to Mrs. Helen Woods, August 29, 1929 and Christmas, 1930; *The New Yorker,* April 19, 1930; Coolidge to Sanders, June 17 and 22, 1932, Lib. Cong.; Herman Beaty, "The Calvin Coolidge Nobody Knew," *Hearst's International-Cosmopolitan,* April 1933; Mrs. Coolidge to Robins, March 27, 1929, October 4, 1929, November 8, 1930, September 26, 1931; Mrs. Coolidge to Mrs. Hills, September 29, 1931 (courtesy Mrs. Hills); Mrs. Coolidge to Mrs. Sol Bloom, April 21, 1930; Vera Bloom, *There's No Place Like Washington.*

Chapter 12: *A Quiet Departure*

New York *Times, Herald Tribune,* Boston *Herald,* Atlanta *Constitution* and *Daily Hampshire Gazette,* January 6-14, 1933; Arthur Krock, New York *Times,* January 8, 1933; funeral ceremonies, Coolidge papers, Lib. Cong.; scrapbooks, Forbes Library; Bruce Barton broadcast, N.B.C., January 5, 1933; Mrs. Coolidge, *Good Housekeeping,* April 1935; Clarence Day, *In the Green Mountain Country;* Mrs. Hills, Mrs. Hemenway, Mrs. Flibotte to author; Mrs. Coolidge to John and Florence, October 1 and 27, 1933, February 25, 1934, April 9 and 22, 1934, June 25, 1934, December 11, 1934, February, 1935 (courtesy John and Florence Coolidge); New York *Herald Tribune,* October 1-31, 1934; Mrs. Coolidge and Herbert Hoover, *Good Housekeeping,* April 1935; Dr. Fuess to author; Irwin H. Hoover, *Forty-two Years in the White House;* authors' letters, Gertrude Lane papers, Lib. Cong.; John and Florence Coolidge to author; Mrs. Adams to author; Mrs. Coolidge to Blanche Cole, April 14, 1936 (courtesy Miss Cole); Mrs. Coolidge to Charles Moore, January 20, 1937, Moore papers, Lib. Cong.; Mrs. S. A. Bailey, Karl S. Putnam and Walter L. Stevens to author; Delos W. Lovelace, New York *Evening Sun,* March 3, 1945; Mrs. Coolidge to Mrs. Gertrude Heyman (undated), Presidential papers, New York Public Library.

Chapter 13: *Friend of the Deaf*

Dr. Archibald V. Galbraith and Dr. George T. Pratt to author; letters, pamphlets, documents, pictures from Clarke School for the Deaf files (courtesy Dr. Pratt); John F. Kennedy's tribute to Mrs. Coolidge, *Daily Hampshire Gazette,* July 8, 1957; Dr. Pratt to John Coolidge, July 19, 1957 (courtesy Dr. Pratt); Mrs. Adams, and John and Florence Coolidge to author; Captain Herbert W. Underwood and Mrs. F. Whitwell Underwood letters to author, July 28, 1960; Mrs. Coolidge to Mrs. Adams, April 16, 1945, and December 1, 1944 (courtesy Mrs. Adams); recollections of Mrs. Coolidge to author from Mrs. C. W. Hodges, Mrs. Merrill Torrey, Mrs. Harold P. Kingsbury, Mrs. Ralph W. Hemenway, Mrs. Robert Huxley, Mrs. S. A. Bailey, Miss Ivah Gale, Miss Lillian Garver and John Bukosky; New York *Times,* April 2-30, 1945; Eric F. Goldman, *The Crucial Decade;* John Gunther and Bernard Quint, *Days to Remember;* Lloyd Morris, *Postscript to Yesterday;* Mrs. Coolidge to John, "Dearest Children" or "Dearest Four," February 10, 1946, March 3, 1947, April 4, 11 and 19, 1948, May 4, 1948, November 7, 1948, April 7, 1949 (courtesy John and Florence Coolidge); Robert Considine to Mrs. Coolidge, May 4, 1949 (courtesy John Coolidge).

Chapter 14: *Sunset in New England*

Mrs. Coolidge to John, Florence or her "Dearest Four," June 11, 1950, May 4, 1952, January 3, 1954, July 7, 1955, October 4, 1955, June 10, 1954, July 5, 1954, March 18, 1956 (courtesy John and Florence Coolidge); Mrs. Coolidge to Mrs. Anna Nickerson, September 28, 1954 and January 26, 1957 (courtesy Mrs. Nickerson); recollections of Mrs. Hemenway, Mrs. Adams, Mrs. Hills, Mrs. Bailey, Mr. and Mrs. Karl S. Putnam, Walter L. Stevens, Lawrence Wikander, Dr. Fuess, Miss Ivah Gale, Miss Lillian Garver, Joseph McInerney, John Bukosky, Mrs. Flibotte, Miss Blanche Cole, Miss Edith Hill, Mrs. Helen Woods; Dedication of Coolidge Memorial Room, Forbes Library, September 16, 1956, papers in Forbes Library; Mrs. Coolidge to Joseph McInerney, October 10 and 31, 1954 (courtesy Mr. McInerney); Mrs. Coolidge to Miss Blanche Cole, February, 1957 (courtesy Miss Cole); Mrs. Coolidge to Mrs. Hills, May 12, 1957 (courtesy Mrs. Hills); Boston Daily *Globe,* September 17, 1956; New York *Times* and *Herald Tribune,* July 9-15, 1957; Boston *Traveler,* July 8, 1957; Springfield *Daily News,* July 15, 1957; *Daily Hampshire Gazette,* July 13, August 3 and 5, 1957; Rutland *Daily Herald,* August 5, 1957; *White River Valley Herald,* July 18, 1957; John Coolidge and Admiral Boone to author.

BIBLIOGRAPHY

Adams, Samuel Hopkins. *The Incredible Era.* Boston: Houghton Mifflin Company, 1929.

Allen, Frederick Lewis. *Only Yesterday.* New York: Harper & Brothers, 1931.

Amory, Cleveland and Bradlee, Frederic. *Vanity Fair.* New York: The Viking Press, 1960.

Bloom, Vera. *There's No Place Like Washington.* New York: G. P. Putnam's Sons, 1944.

Bradford, Gamaliel. *The Quick and the Dead.* Boston: Houghton Mifflin Company, 1931.

Butler, Nicholas Murray. *Across the Busy Years.* Charles Scribner's Sons, 1939.

Colman, Edna M. *White House Gossip: From Andrew Jackson to Calvin Coolidge.* Garden City: Doubleday, Page & Company, 1927.

Coolidge, Calvin. *Have Faith in Massachusetts.* Boston: Houghton Mifflin Company, 1919.

———. *The Autobiography of Calvin Coolidge.* New York: Cosmopolitan Book Corporation, 1929.

———. *The Price of Freedom.* New York: Charles Scribner's Sons, 1924.

Day, Clarence. *In the Green Mountain Country.* New Haven: Yale University Press, 1934.

Dennis, Alfred Pearce. *Gods and Little Fishes.* Indianapolis: The Bobbs-Merrill Company, 1924.

Faulkner, Harold U. *From Versailles to the New Deal.* New Haven: Yale University Press, 1950.

Fisher, Dorothy Canfield. *Vermont Tradition.* Boston: Little, Brown & Company, 1953.

Fisher, Irving. *The Stock Market Crash and After.* New York: The Macmillan Company, 1930.

Franklin, Joe. *A Pictorial Treasury.* New York: The Citadel Press, 1959.

Fuess, Claude M. *Calvin Coolidge.* Boston: Little, Brown & Company, 1940.

Galbraith, John Kenneth. *The Great Crash.* Boston: Houghton Mifflin Company, 1955.

Gilfond, Duff. *The Rise of Saint Calvin.* New York: The Vanguard Press, 1932.

Goldman, Eric F. *The Crucial Decade.* New York: Alfred A. Knopf, 1959.

Green, Horace. *The Life of Calvin Coolidge.* New York: Duffield & Company, 1924.

Greene, Laurence. *The Era of Wonderful Nonsense.* Indianapolis: The Bobbs-Merrill Company, 1939.

Gunther, John and Quint, Bernard. *Days to Remember.* New York: Harper & Brothers, 1956.

Helburn, Theresa. *A Wayward Guest.* Boston: Little, Brown & Company, 1960.

Hennessy, M. E. *Calvin Coolidge.* New York: G. P. Putnam's Sons, 1924.

Hill, Ralph Nading. *The Story of the Ticonderoga.* Burlington, Vermont: The Lane Press, 1957.

Hoover, Irwin H. (Ike). *Forty-two Years in the White House.* Boston: Houghton Mifflin Company, 1934.

Hornblow, Arthur. *A History of the Theater in America.* Vol. 2. Philadelphia: J. B. Lippincott Company, 1919.

Jaffray, Elizabeth. *Secrets of the White House.* New York: Cosmopolitan Book Corporation, 1927.

Keyes, Frances Parkinson. *Capital Kaleidoscope.* New York: Harper & Brothers, 1937.

———. *Letters from a Senator's Wife.* New York: D. Appleton & Company, 1924.

Lathem, Edward Connery. (ed.) *Meet Calvin Coolidge.* Brattleboro, Vermont: The Stephen Greene Press, 1960.

Leighton, Isabel. (ed.) *The Aspirin Age.* New York: Simon & Schuster, 1949.

Leonard, Jonathan Norton. *Three Years Down.* New York: Carrick & Evans, 1939.

Lippmann, Walter. *Men of Destiny.* New York: The Macmillan Company, 1927.

Longworth, Alice Roosevelt. *Crowded Hours.* New York: Charles Scribner's Sons, 1933.

Lord, Walter. *The Good Years.* New York: Harper & Brothers, 1960.

McBride, Mary Margaret. *The Story of Dwight W. Morrow.* New York: Farrar & Rinehart, 1930.

McKee, John Hiram. *Coolidge Wit and Wisdom.* New York: Frederick A. Stokes Company, 1933.

Morris, Lloyd. *Postscript to Yesterday.* New York: Random House, 1947.

Nicolson, Harold. *Dwight Morrow.* New York: Harcourt, Brace & Company, 1935.

Northampton: The Tercentenary Committee. *The Northampton Book.* The Tercentenary Committee, 1954.

Orton, Vrest. *Guide Book and History of the President Calvin Coolidge*

Home at Plymouth Notch, Vermont. Montpelier, Vermont: Vermont Historic Sites Commission, 1957.

Pringle, Henry F. *The Life and Times of William Howard Taft.* New York: Farrar & Rinehart, 1939.

Randolph, Mary. *Presidents and First Ladies.* New York: D. Appleton-Century Company, 1936.

Rinehart, Mary Roberts. *My Story.* New York: Farrar & Rinehart, 1931.

Robinson, Henry Morton. *Fantastic Interim.* New York: Harcourt, Brace & Company, 1943.

Rogers, Cameron. *The Legend of Calvin Coolidge.* Garden City: Doubleday, Doran & Company, 1928.

Slemp, C. Bascom. (ed.) *The Mind of the President.* Garden City: Doubleday, Doran & Company, 1926.

Spring, Agnes Wright. (ed.) *The Arrow of Pi Beta Phi.* History Number 1867-1936. Marshall, Illinois: George Banta Publishing Company, 1936.

Starling, Colonel Edmund W., as told to Thomas Sugrue. *Starling of the White House.* New York: Simon & Schuster, 1946.

Stoddard, Henry L. *As I Knew Them: President and Politics from Grant to Coolidge.* New York: Harper & Brothers, 1927.

——. *It Costs to Be President.* New York: Harper & Brothers, 1938.

Sullivan, Mark. *Our Times.* Vol. 6. New York: Charles Scribner's Sons, 1935.

Taylor, Dwight. *Joy Ride.* New York: G. P. Putnam's Sons, 1959.

Washburn, Robert M. *Calvin Coolidge: His First Biography.* Boston: Small, Maynard & Company, 1923.

——. *The Belle of Burlington.* Cambridge: Cambridge University Press, 1939.

Werner, Morris. *Privileged Characters.* New York: Robert M. McBride & Company, 1935.

White, William Allen. *A Puritan in Babylon.* New York: The Macmillan Company, 1938.

——. *Calvin Coolidge. The Man Who Is President.* New York: The Macmillan Company, 1925.

Yale, Caroline A. *Years of Building.* New York: The Dial Press, 1931.

INDEX

357